SAVING CAPITALISM

FROM THE CAPITALISTS

SAVING CAPITALISM
FROM THE
CAPITALISTS

Unleashing the Power of Financial Markets
to Create Wealth and Spread Opportunity

RAGHURAM G. RAJAN
&
LUIGI ZINGALES

CROWN
BUSINESS
NEW YORK

Published in the United States, Canada, and the Philippine Islands by
Princeton University Press, 41 William Street, Princeton, New Jersey 08540

Published by arrangement with Crown Business, an imprint of Random House, Inc.

First Princeton edition, with a new preface, 2004

Library of Congress Cataloging-in-Publication Data

Rajan, Raghuram.
Saving capitalism from the capitalists : unleashing the power of financial markets to
create wealth and spread opportunity / Raghuram G. Rajan & Luigi Zingales ; with a new
preface by the authors.
p.   cm.
Originally published: 1st ed. New York : Crown Business, c2003.
Includes bibliographical references and index.
ISBN 0-691-12128-1 (pbk. : alk. paper)
1. Capital market.   2. Capital market—State supervision.   3. Capitalism—Moral and
ethical aspects.   4. Common good—Economic aspects.   I. Zingales, Luigi.   II. Title.
HG4523.R345 2004
332'.041—dc22   2004040095

Printed on acid-free paper. ∞

pup.princeton.edu

Printed in the United States of America

5   7   9   10   8   6   4

To our families

CONTENTS

Contents

PREFACE TO THE PAPERBACK EDITION

WHEN WE WROTE the preface to the hardcover edition in 2003, we were worried at the then turn of events in the United States such as the unraveling corporate scandals and the loss of jobs and wealth from the bursting of the Internet bubble. We feared that while these events suggested a need to rethink some market regulation, they unduly strengthened the hands of those who were viscerally opposed to markets.

Unfortunately, subsequent events have made the case for our book even more compelling. Distrust of markets and competition is growing. The small but very visible number of white-collar jobs outsourced to India and other developing countries has turned a significant number of influential people employed in high-paying service jobs against free trade. Since we wrote our book, nearly eighty bills aimed at limiting international outsourcing have been introduced in about thirty states. While public anxiety with free trade invariably increases in economic downturns, the continuing revelations of corporate wrongdoing further reinforce the perception that the whole system is rigged to benefit the few at the expense of the many.

If even the citizens of the country that has benefited most from free markets can become disillusioned with them, what of people from other countries that have never enjoyed the access and the choice that truly free markets offer, but always suffered the risks? What of people in Latin America, who have seen their countries swing from euphoric growth to wrenching crisis time after time? What of the Russians, who identify capitalism not with greater choice or opportunities but with the "oligarchs" who have cornered much of the wealth in their country?

Why should we be concerned about the public mood? The reason is that capitalism needs a basic framework of rules and regulations to make the system accessible to all and thus competitive. Usually, this infrastructure has to be provided by the government. Consider an example. If you wanted to fly and there was no supervisory authority in the airline industry and no regulations enforcing safety standards, you would be very reluctant to fly fledgling airlines. You would prefer the established ones that had the track record and the reputation. So a complete lack of safety regulations in the airline industry would favor established firms, making the entry of new ones impossible and killing competition and consumer choice. The absence of government can be anticompetitive and retard free markets. Of course, too much government—for example, one that allows entry only to its favorites and not to others—can be detrimental to markets also.

The behavior of government is determined, in part, by public mood. But to a greater extent, it is also determined by the special interests being regulated. This is why the free market system is fragile. Not economically (as Marx theorized), but *politically*. While everyone benefits from competitive markets, no one in particular makes huge profits from keeping the system competitive and the playing field level. Thus, nobody has a strong vested interest in promoting and defending free markets.

On the contrary, many people have a special interest in restraining them. Not only do the ranks of the opponents of markets include distressed workers who lose their jobs because of competitive pressures, but also large industrialists themselves: truly free markets create competition, which undermines the position of established firms, forcing them to prove their competence again and again. Unfortunately, the latter group is very politically influential and often hides behind the former to promote policies aimed at restricting competition and stifling entry. This is the real danger resulting from the atmosphere of uneasiness and disillusionment with the market.

At least, this is only a danger in the United States, for markets by and large do work here and have significant public support. Unfortunately, it is a reality in much of the developing world, where markets have never been allowed to work well. As a consequence, people do not know what markets are capable of, the demand for markets to work is not widespread, and they remain underdeveloped. True capitalism never has a chance.

That the market system gets distorted by politically powerful elites is actually a point on which the Right and the Left agree—one of the few places where the Nobel Prize–winning Chicago economist George Stigler echoes Karl Marx. But the solution proposed by both wings is wrong.

The Left is wrong in saying that markets need to be replaced by the government, for that will just perpetuate the capture by the elite. And the Right is wrong in saying we can dispense with the government. What we need therefore is a "Goldilocks" government—not too interventionist and not too laissez-faire, a government that is "just right." The difficulty with this Goldilocks position is, of course, in how to get the correct mix.

Somehow this has been happening around the world for the last three decades. However, our rationale for why free markets became more popular at the end of the twentieth century raises worries about their staying power. The reason why politicians in countries as diverse as France and Germany, Korea and India embraced the market and attempted to provide the governance markets need is not that they suddenly became more public spirited or that the influence of moneyed interests diminished. Rather, it is that the interests of the elites changed with the opening of borders to goods and capital. Once competition comes from a foreign jurisdiction that local elites cannot influence, they have no benefit in distorting the domestic infrastructure. Instead, incumbent firms want domestic markets to work well, to allow them to compete in the worldwide market. Open borders to goods and capital are the most important way to get at least some domestic capitalists to turn from opposing to supporting better and more competitive markets: Competition between countries is what makes markets within countries work well for the majority of the people.

This is an especially important message to remember now as the tide of protectionism is rising again. In fact, the antiglobalization movement has got it completely upside down here. Rather than making us slaves of multinationals, globalization liberates us from serfdom to local elites, who control the domestic political agenda.

This is not to say there are no downsides to globalization. Nor is it to say that countries that have hitherto not been well integrated into the global economy should simply drop their controls on the flow of goods and capital all at once. But we do strongly believe that far too many ills in the world today and far too few of the successes are ascribed to globalization.

All this implies a special responsibility for developed countries, who already enjoy well-functioning markets, to open their own borders to imports from developing countries so that the latter can become more market oriented. While this may hurt certain groups in the developed countries in the short run (and as we argue in the book, they have to be identified and helped), it will be beneficial in general. In the long run, it will be immensely beneficial to the world as the open borders of the now-developing countries serve to lock developed countries into the free market system. For the world's sake, the breakdown of trade talks at Cancun in 2003 should be only a hiccup on the way to greater international trade.

Stronger economic times will return, and the public's faith in the system will hopefully endure and strengthen again. Our aim in writing *Saving Capitalism from the Capitalists* was not only to emphasize the benefits of free markets but also to create awareness of the threats they face. If our book helps in even a small way to build support for them and ensure their longevity, then we will have been amply rewarded for writing it.

PREFACE

IF OUR PUBLISHER had the power to influence current events to promote this book and he did not give a fig for human misery, he could not have done better. Newspapers are full of corporate scandals. The implosion of the Internet bubble has produced the greatest peacetime destruction of paper wealth the world has ever seen. Antimarket protesters have gained strength in country after country. Questions about the viability or the political fragility of the capitalist system, which appeared preposterous when we started this book three years ago, seem reasonable now.

Is unbridled capitalism still the best, or the least bad, economic system? Are reforms needed? And should these reforms go in the direction of fixing the system or of changing it completely? Will the current public disillusionment with free markets outlast the dip in the stock market? Even if the disillusionment is a passing wave, in what form will capitalism survive in the twenty-first century?

Even though our book was conceived and largely written before most of the recent scandals surfaced, it attempts to place them in perspective. Every market boom produces new crooks. And every market bust sets off its witch-hunts. This book aims to see beyond the immediate consequences of market fluctuations to their deeper and more long-lasting effects on the system of free enterprise. Through our focus on financial markets, we seek to identify the fundamental strengths and weaknesses of the capitalist system, not only in its ideal form, but also in its historical realizations.

We base our arguments on a vast academic literature, much of it produced in the last twenty years. But this is not a book aimed at a specialized audience, because we think our message is relevant to the wider public. We eschew the presentation of detailed econometric analysis, not because we do not think it important, but because the flavor of the results can be conveyed equally well through words for the general reader, while the interested can be directed to more detailed sources. This book is also more than simply a survey of a literature—it weaves a broad argument. While we will marshal historical facts, and draw on our own studies, as well as the studies of others, history gives us few natural experiments with which to test all aspects of broad argument. Therefore, at certain junctures, we will try and persuade the reader as much by logic as by the historical authorities and evidence we cite.

The purist may not approve of this approach. Unfortunately, any attempt at integration of different fields, and evidence across time and studies, is usually unsatisfactory to purists, partly because the weights one places on different aspects are pregnant with biases. We would apologize for these were it not for our firm belief that bias is inevitable in all work, and it is competition between biases that generally drives thought ahead.

This has been a shared voyage of discovery in which we have learned much together along the way. We have to acknowledge those who have taught us either directly or indirectly. The modern field of finance has been created during our lifetimes, and we certainly owe an immense intellectual debt to the pioneers, many of whom are still active in research. But we owe a special debt to those who advised us in our early years. In particular, we would like to thank Oliver Hart, Don Lessard, Stewart Myers, John Parsons, Jim Poterba, David Scharfstein, Andrei Shleifer, and Jeremy Stein. We have also benefited tremendously from our colleagues at the University of Chicago's Graduate School of Business, some of whom have been partners in our voyages of intellectual discovery, while others have provided immensely useful friendly criticism. Douglas Diamond, Eugene Fama, Steven Kaplan, Randall Kroszner, Canice Prendergast, Richard Thaler, and Rob Vishny are a few we would like to name, without diminishing the debt we owe the others. Our book also reflects the joint work we have done with others. We owe thanks especially to Abhijit Banerjee, Alexander Dyck, Luigi Guiso, Mitchell Petersen, Paola Sapienza, and Henri Servaes, whose efforts have helped mold our thinking.

Many people read early drafts of the chapters in this book. Heitor Almeida, Oliver Hart, Peter Hogfeldt, Steven Kaplan, Ross Levine,

Rajnish Mehra, Canice Prendergast, Radhika Puri, Roberta Romano, Gianni Toniolo, Andrei Shleifer, and Richard Thaler provided very useful comments. Joyce Van Grondelle did an excellent job (as always) of vetting the references and the bibliography, while Adam Cartabiano, Laura Pisani, and Talha Muhammad helped us check figures and track references down.

Barbara Rifkind helped us put together a coherent proposal, and most important, find John Mahaney, our editor. He has been invaluable in getting us to focus our work so that we can address our various intended audiences in an intelligible way. We owe him thanks for many useful suggestions that have vastly improved the book. Shana Wingert, his assistant, patiently helped us manage the logistics of the book-writing process. Sam Peltzman and the Center for Study of the State and the Economy provided encouragement and crucial financial support during the course of this project.

And finally, personal notes:

Raghu:

I hope my parents will finally have a glimpse in this book of what I do for a living. This book reflects in many ways what they taught me, from the history my father used to read aloud when I was a boy to the love of reading my mother tried to inculcate in me. This book would not have been finished were it not for my daughter, Tara, asking repeatedly, Daddy, have you finished your book yet? Tara, I am sorry this book does not need an illustrator, else I would certainly have used you. I owe you and Akhil many weekends that could have been spent in the park or on the beach. And most of all, I thank my wife, Radhika, for all the love and advice she has given over the course of this project.

Luigi:

This book was written during a difficult period of my life. I want to acknowledge all the people who provided moral support throughout: Elizabeth Paparo, Maria Coller, Francesca Cornelli, Mary Doheny, Leonardo Felli, Enrico Piccinin, Carol Rubin, Paola Sapienza, Abbie Smith, Stefano Visentin, Maria Zingales, and Raghu himself, whose patience and understanding went beyond what could be expected from a friend. I am indebted to my parents for the wonderful education they gave me. I dedicate this book to my children, Giuseppe and Gloria, purpose and joy of my life.

SAVING CAPITALISM
FROM THE CAPITALISTS

Introduction

CAPITALISM, or more precisely, the free market system, is the most effective way to organize production and distribution that human beings have found. While free markets, particularly free financial markets, fatten people's wallets, they have made surprisingly few inroads into their hearts and minds. Financial markets are among the most highly criticized and least understood parts of the capitalist system. The behavior of those involved in recent scandals like the collapse of Enron only solidifies the public conviction that these markets are simply tools for the rich to get richer at the expense of the general public. Yet, as we argue, healthy and competitive financial markets are an extraordinarily effective tool in spreading opportunity and fighting poverty. Because of their role in financing new ideas, financial markets keep alive the process of "creative destruction"—whereby old ideas and organizations are constantly challenged and replaced by new, better ones. Without vibrant, innovative financial markets, economies would invariably ossify and decline.

In the United States, constant financial innovation creates devices to channel risk capital to people with daring ideas. While commonplace here, such financing vehicles are still treated as radical, even in developed countries like Germany. And the situation in third-world countries borders on the hopeless: people find it difficult to get access to even a few dollars of financing, which would give them the freedom to earn an independent, fulfilling living. If financial markets bring prosperity, why are they so underdeveloped around the world, and why were they repressed, until recently, even in the United States?

Throughout its history, the free market system has been held back, not so much by its own economic deficiencies, as Marxists would have it, but because of its reliance on political goodwill for its infrastructure. The threat primarily comes from two groups of opponents. The first are incumbents, those who already have an established position in the marketplace and would prefer to see it remain exclusive. The identity of the most dangerous incumbents depends on the country and the time period, but the part has been played at various times by the landed aristocracy, the owners and managers of large corporations, their financiers, and organized labor.

The second group of opponents, the distressed, tends to surface in times of economic downturn. Those who have lost out in the process of creative destruction unleashed by markets—unemployed workers, penniless investors, and bankrupt firms—see no legitimacy in a system in which they have been proved losers. They want relief, and since the markets offer them none, they will try the route of politics.

The unlikely alliance of the incumbent industrialist—the capitalist in the title—and the distressed unemployed worker is especially powerful amid the debris of corporate bankruptcies and layoffs. In an economic downturn, the capitalist is more likely to focus on costs of the competition emanating from free markets than on the opportunities they create. And the unemployed worker will find many others in a similar condition and with anxieties similar to his, which will make it easy for them to organize together. Using the cover and the political organization provided by the distressed, the capitalist captures the political agenda.

For at such times, it requires an extremely courageous (or foolhardy) politician to extol the virtues of free markets. Instead of viewing destruction as the inevitable counterpart of creation, it is far easier for the politician to give in to the capitalist, who ostensibly champions the distressed by demanding that competition be shackled and markets suppressed. Under the guise of making improvements to markets so as to prevent future downturns, political intervention at such times is aimed at impeding their working. The capitalist can turn against the most effective organ of capitalism and the public, whose future is directly harmed by these actions, stands on the sidelines, seldom protesting, often uncomprehending, and occasionally applauding.

This book starts with the reminder that much of the prosperity, innovation, and increased opportunity we have experienced in recent decades should be attributed to the reemergence of free markets, especially free financial markets. We then move on to our central thesis:

because free markets depend on political goodwill for their existence and because they have powerful political enemies among the establishment, their continued survival cannot be taken for granted, even in developed countries. Based on our reading of the reasons for the fall and rise of markets in recent history, we propose policies that can help make free markets more viable politically.

After the longest peacetime economic expansion in recent history, an expansion that has seen the implosion of socialist economies, it may seem overly alarmist to worry about the future of free markets. Perhaps! But success tends to breed complacency. Recent corporate scandals, the booms and busts engendered by financial markets, and economic hardship have led to growing distrust of markets. Other worrying signs abound, ranging from the virulent anti-immigration rhetoric of the extreme right to the antiglobalization protests of the rejuvenated left. And imminent demographic and technological change will create new tensions. It is important to understand that the ascendancy of free markets is not necessarily the culmination of an inevitable process of economic development—the end of economic history, so to speak—but may well be an interlude, as it has been in the past. For free markets to become politically more viable, we have to repeat to ourselves and to others, often and loudly, why they are so beneficial. We have to recognize and address their deficiencies. And we have to act to shore up their defenses. This book is a contribution toward these goals.

We start the book by explaining why competitive free markets are so useful. Perhaps the least understood of markets, the most unfairly criticized, and the one most critical to making a country competitive is the financial market. It is also the market that is most sensitive to political winds. Many of the most important changes in our economic environment in the last three decades are due to changes in the financial market. For all these reasons, and because it is a fitting representative of its genus, we will pay particular attention to the financial market.

We start with two examples, the first from a country where financial markets do not exist, and the second from a country where they are vibrant. All too often, finance is criticized as merely a tool of the rich. Yet, as our first example suggests, the poor may be totally incapacitated when they do not have access to finance. For the poor to have better access, financial markets have to develop and become more competitive. And when they do so, as our second example suggests, all that holds back individuals is their talent and their capacity to dream.

The Stool Maker of Jobra Village

There is perhaps no greater authority on how to make credit available to the poor than Muhammad Yunus, the founder of the Grameen Bank. In his autobiography, Yunus described how he came to understand the importance of finance when he was a professor of economics in a Bangladeshi university. Appalled by the consequences of a recent famine on the poor, he wandered out of the sheltered walls of the university to the neighboring village, Jobra, to find out how the poor made a living. He started up a conversation with a young mother, Sufiya Begum, who was making bamboo stools.[1]

He learned that Sufiya Begum needed 22 cents to buy the raw material for the stools. Because she did not have any money, she borrowed it from middlemen and was forced to sell the stools back to them as repayment for the loan. That left her with a profit of only 2 cents. Yunus was appalled:

> I watched as she set to work again, her small brown hands plaiting the strands of bamboo as they had every day for months and years on end. . . . How would her children break the cycle of poverty she had started? How could they go to school when the income Sufiya earned was barely enough to feed her, let alone shelter her family and clothe them properly?[2]

Because Sufiya did not have 22 cents, she was forced into the clutches of the middlemen. The middlemen made her accept a measly pittance of 2 cents for a hard day's labor. Finance would liberate her from the middlemen and enable her to sell directly to customers. But the middlemen would not let her have finance, for then they would lose their hold over her. For want of 22 cents, Sufiya Begum's labor was captive.

The paucity of finance, which is all too often the normal state of affairs in much of the world, is rendered even more stark when one contrasts it with the alternative: the extraordinary impact of the financial revolution in some parts of the world. To see this, we move to California for our second example.

The Search Fund

Kevin Taweel, who was about to graduate from Stanford Business School, was not excited by the idea of going to work for a large, traditional corporation. His goal was to start running his own business.

Job offers were plentiful, but no one gave him the opportunity to be his own boss. After all, who would trust someone with so little experience to run their firm? The choice was clear. If he wanted to run a company, he had to buy one. But how? Not only did he not have the money, he did not even have enough to pay for his expenses while he searched for an attractive target.

Kevin's situation is common. For millions around the world, the lack of resources to fund their ideas is the main roadblock to riches. All too often, you have to have money to make money. But Kevin overcame this barrier by making use of a little-known financing device called a search fund. Slightly over two years after leaving Stanford, he was running his own firm.

A search fund is a pool of money to finance a search for companies that might be willing to be bought out.[3] Typically, a recent graduate from a business or law school, with no money of his own, puts the fund together. The fund pays for the expenses of the search and some living expenses for the principal (the searching graduate). After identifying an appropriate target, the principal has to negotiate the purchase as well as arrange financing. In return for their initial investment in the pool, investors in the search fund get the right to invest in the acquisition at favorable terms. Once the target is acquired, the principal runs the firm for a few years and eventually sells it, pays off investors, and hopefully, keeps a sizable fortune for himself.

In December 1993, Kevin raised $250,000 to fund his search. A year and a half later, with the help of a fellow graduate, Jim Ellis, Kevin identified a suitable target, an emergency road services company. The owner asked for $8.5 million to sell out, a sum that Kevin and Jim were able to raise from banks and individual investors (most of them the original investors in the search fund). In fact, the prospects they offered the individual investors were so attractive, they were able to raise the money they sought in just twenty-four hours!

Under Kevin and Jim's management, the acquired company grew at an extremely rapid pace, both through internal expansion and through acquisitions. While sales in 1995 were only $6 million, in 2001 they reached $200 million. The company delivered a fantastic return to investors: shares bought by investors at $3 in 1995 were bought back by the company at the end of 1999 for $115.

Not all search funds have such a happy ending. Some principals run out of money before they find an attractive target. Others do succeed in finding a target but are not as successful in running it. In general, however, search funds are very profitable, yielding an average 36 percent annual return to investors and much more to the principals.[4]

But more remarkable than their average return is the concept behind search funds. What is being financed in a search fund is not a hard asset that offers good collateral to the financiers. It is not even a solid business proposition. What is being financed is a search for a business proposition—in effect, a search for an idea. The search fund hints at a world that did not exist in the past, a world where a person's ability to create wealth and attain economic freedom is determined by the quality of her ideas rather than the size of her bank balance.

The search fund reflects a revolutionary improvement in the ability of a broad sector of people to obtain access to finance. This has had profound implications for their lives, often in ways to which they are oblivious. For example, throughout much of history, labor was plentiful, while only a privileged few had access to capital. As a result, employees were weak relative to capital—in the prototypical large corporation of yesteryear, the owners of capital (the shareholders) or their nominees (top management) made decisions, while those lower in the hierarchy had no alternative but to obey. With the widespread availability of capital from developed financial markets, the human being has gained in strength in many industries relative to the owners of capital. Increasingly, the term *capitalism* as a description of free market enterprise is becoming an anachronism in many industries.

While this may seem hard to believe in the midst of a recession, the average educated worker or manager in developed countries does indeed have far more choice than before. Phenomena ranging from worker empowerment to the flattening of corporate hierarchies, from the growth of employee ownership to the breakup of large firms, are all, in some significant measure, consequences of the development of financial markets.

The Puzzle

There are many obvious differences between Kevin or Jim and Sufiya Begum. A Stanford M.B.A., whether in his Hickey Freeman suit or in Birkenstock sandals, is indeed far removed from a barefoot villager in Bangladesh with callused hands and nails black with grime. But there are important similarities: both have valuable skills that only need to be supplemented with resources. As a multiple of the value of the income each one expects to generate, the amount of financing they seek is not very different. Neither has hard assets or prior wealth to offer as collateral. Yet Kevin and Jim obtained the funding they needed, while Sufiya Begum continued to be trapped in poverty.

Why could Sufiya Begum not get 22 cents at a reasonable interest rate while Kevin and Jim could raise hundreds of thousands of dollars easily in setting up their search fund? Why are financial markets developed in some countries only and not in others? Will even the countries where they are developed continue to enjoy the fruits of finance, or is the surge in financial markets that we have experienced in the last two decades a temporary lull in millennia of financial oppression?

The "Conventional" Answer

The search fund works because it gives the searching M.B.A. the right incentives. For this, it relies on a variety of *institutions.* The rights of the principal and those of the investors are clearly demarcated by contract, not just when the fund is set up but going forward. The legal system works so contracts can be enforced at low cost. Secure in their shares, the parties do not have incentives to deceive or manipulate each other. An effective accounting and disclosure system and a reliable system of public recordkeeping contribute to mutual trust. This also helps make everyone's stakes liquid. The principal knows that he is not locked in to the firm for life but can make improvements to the target firm and then exit by selling his stake in a liquid stock market. Since the market will capitalize the entire future stream of profits, the principal will get a tremendous compensation for his effort in locating underperforming firms. Thus, the best talent is attracted to this business, further improving the level of trust . . .

The main reason why Sufiya Begum cannot get finance at a reasonable rate is that countries like Bangladesh are deficient in institutions: ownership rights are neither well demarcated nor well enforced; there are no agencies collecting, storing, and disseminating information on the creditworthiness of potential borrowers; there is little competition between moneylenders; the laws governing credit are outdated; contracts are not enforced because the judiciary is all too often either asleep or corrupt . . .

To remedy the deficiency in Bangladesh, however, one has to go beyond the conventional answer, "Fix the institutions!" One has to understand first why the necessary institutions do not exist. Perhaps the existing institutions cannot be changed because they run too deep in a country's history or a people's psyche. If this were the case, countries like Bangladesh would be condemned to remain underdeveloped for many years to come. Fortunately, as we argue in this book, the historic evidence does not suggest that the legacy of history necessarily dooms a people. Thanks to human ingenuity, whenever allowed to do so, people create substitute institutions if the existing ones cannot be fixed cheaply. In doing so, they demonstrate that institutional change is possible no matter how damned a country is by its history.

Perhaps poor countries lack the necessary endowments, such as trained manpower, wealth, and sophisticated technologies to create new institutions. The difficulty with this explanation is that the logic is somewhat circular: countries are poor because they do not have institutions, and they do not have institutions because they are poor. This sheds little light on how some countries managed to break out of this vicious cycle. It does not explain why some countries that are rich—in 1790, the richest country in the world on a per capita basis was Haiti—never develop the necessary institutions and fall behind.[5] And it does not explain why countries do not develop the specific institutions that facilitate access to finance, even though they have other basic market institutions. Ten years ago, something like the search fund would have been virtually impossible to contemplate in France or Germany. These countries did not lack the capacity to create the institutions necessary for a vibrant, competitive financial sector: their laws are detailed and well enforced; their people are no less educated than Americans; their industries no less reliant on high technology . . . We have to seek elsewhere to explain why the institutions necessary for competitive financial markets in particular, and markets in general, are so underdeveloped or nonexistent in many countries.

The Politics of Markets

Our explanation is simple. Small, informal markets are no doubt possible without much institutional infrastructure. But the large, arm's-length markets required in a modern capitalist economy need a substantial amount of infrastructure to support them. These market institutions are underdeveloped when the powerful see them as undermining their power. The economically powerful are concerned about the institutions underpinning free markets because they treat people equally, making power redundant. The markets themselves add insult to injury. They are a source of competition, forcing the powerful to prove their competence again and again. Since a person may be powerful because of his past accomplishments or inheritance rather than his current abilities, the powerful have a reason to fear markets.

Of course, the powerful also benefit from some markets. What use is it being the monopoly producer of bananas in a republic if there is no market in which to sell them? But when these markets exist, the powerful like to control them, as the father of economics, Adam Smith, recognized long ago:

> To widen the market and to narrow the competition is always the interest of the dealers. . . . The proposal of any new law or regulation of commerce which comes from this order, ought always to be listened to with great precaution, and ought never to be adopted, till after having been long and carefully examined, not only with the most scrupulous, but with the most suspicious attention. It comes from an order of men, whose interest is never exactly the same with that of the public, who generally have an interest to deceive and even oppress the public, and who accordingly have, upon many occasions, both deceived and oppressed it.[6]

The powerful particularly oppose the setting up of infrastructure that would broaden access to the market and level the playing field. The middlemen who have Sufiya Begum in their grasp have the power and the local knowledge to get around the otherwise byzantine system for recovering from defaulting borrowers. Better laws, better demarcation of property, and the creation of public credit-rating agencies would create a vibrant competitive financial market, bring in outside lenders, and make these middlemen's skills redundant, thus jeopardizing the fat profits they make. Anticipating this, the middlemen would rather not see the market develop at all. What better way than opposing the creation of the necessary institutions?

It is not just incumbents in poor countries who have to fear the increase in competition as financial markets develop. In the United States, which has a vibrant financial market, fully half the top twenty firms by sales in 1999 were not in the top twenty in 1985. By contrast, in Germany, where the financial markets till recently were dormant, 80 percent of the firms in the top twenty in 1999 were also in the top twenty in 1985. While other factors are partially responsible for these differences, financial markets do seem to affect corporate mobility even in rich countries, threatening the establishment.[7]

Our point thus far is a simple one. Those in power—the incumbents—prefer to stay in power. They feel threatened by free markets. Free financial markets are especially problematic because they provide resources to newcomers, who then can make other markets competitive. Hence, financial markets are especially worthy of opposition.

For this to be more than a conspiracy theory, it has to be useful in predicting when and where markets will develop. If incumbents have a stranglehold on power, markets will develop either when the incumbents benefit directly from them or when the incumbents have no other choice. There are at least three phases in the historical development of financial markets that can be easily identified: the initial phase, when a country obtains more representative government and begins to respect property rights; a second phase, when it opens its borders to tame the incumbent groups that would otherwise capture democratic government; and a third reactionary phase, when incumbent groups ride the coattails of the distressed back into power. The phases do not inevitably follow one another, nor do they occur in all countries. But they are general enough to merit greater attention.

The Initial Phase: Respect for Property Rights

For free competitive markets to develop, the first step is that the government has to respect and guarantee the property rights of even the weakest and most defenseless citizen. The greatest threat, historically, has often been the government itself: under the guise of protecting citizens from foreign or ideological enemies, governments used their powerful armies or police forces to prey on their own citizens. In some societies, governments changed character quite early on and became representative of the people, policing their interactions with a firm but light hand and inspiring trust rather than fear. In others, rulers still treat their countries as personal fiefdoms, to be looted as they please. Why were some countries fortunate while others are still damned?

While one-dimensional answers to such questions rarely satisfy, the historical evidence suggests an intriguing pattern: in many of the fortunate countries, the distribution of property, especially land, was typically much more egalitarian. For example, among the countries of the New World, land in Canada and the northern United States was widely distributed, with a sizable number of "yeoman" farmers managing moderate plots of land. In the countries of the Caribbean and in Latin America, the norm was large estates, often run by owners exploiting slave labor or reliant on feudal relationships with the docile local population.[8]

The link between land distribution and responsive government may not be a coincidence. In North America, most farmers were individually too small to create their own police force. It made collective sense to create transparent, representative government in which each citizen was treated similarly according to the rule of law. Moreover, because the yeoman farmer in North America owned his land, he had strong incentives to farm it well and to try to improve his production techniques. Over time, he grew to understand his land—the right crops and the right times to plant and harvest as well as the right scientific techniques to use. Even if ownership was initially distributed almost by accident as immigrants enclosed their plots and started farming them, over time the yeoman farmer grew to be a productive owner of his land. Even the most rapacious government would think twice about disturbing his ownership. It was far better to tax the farmer steadily than kill the goose, so to speak, by seizing his property.

In short, because property was held widely, the propertied in North America pressed for a government that would be open, fair, and respect the rule of law. The small but prosperous farmers had the collective economic might to press for such a government. And because the farmers were close to their property and managed it well, it made economic sense to respect their property rights. All this created a fertile ground for the emergence of a strong free market economy.

Let us now turn to South America. The European colonists set up large plantations and haciendas operated with the help of imported slave labor or docile indigenous populations.9 But the estate owners had quite different incentives from the yeomanry in North America. These powerful incumbents had no use for an impartial, representative government. Instead, they had sufficient size to maintain their own police forces and sufficient money to influence whatever government existed.

With the passage of time, civilization forced the emancipation of slaves, and the docile domestic population became aware of their rights. This changed the economics of producing in large estates for the worse. The only way for these estates to remain profitable was for the owners to ensure that the working population had few other economic opportunities—for example, by ensuring that they were starved of education and finance.10 Far from creating free market institutions, therefore, the powerful incumbents had an incentive to actively suppress them.

Of course, history is too colorful for each country to precisely follow our sketch. But the broad pattern is clear: countries, or even areas such as southern Italy or northeast India, that were dominated by large feudal estates had a difficult time establishing the rule of law and respect for property.

The stranglehold of the incumbent magnates was not unbreakable. But typically, dramatic internal political upheaval or challenge from forces outside a country was necessary for change to take place. In England, the Tudors destroyed the great lords and the church in order to shore up their power, and this led to the rise of Parliament and constitutional government. In Brazil, economic reforms followed the revolution in the late nineteenth century. In the countries of continental Europe, land reform and political reform followed on the seismic waves generated by the French Revolution and the subsequent Napoleonic conquests. Many of these countries joined the ranks of the fortunate. The unfortunate ones, shielded from reforming internal or external disturbances, continued to be slowly strangulated.

The Second Phase: Taming Incumbents in Democracies

The emergence of a constitutionally bound democracy is a big step toward free financial markets because citizens obtain greater assurance that their property will be respected. But it is not sufficient. For even in an industrialized democracy, there are powerful incumbents—established industrial firms and established financiers. They can be opposed to free access to finance simply because they already have enough financing of their own, and the financial markets fund unwanted new competitors.

Incumbents have the power to block the institutions necessary for finance because they are an organized group, focused on their goal, and endowed with plentiful resources. They have a far greater ability to sway legislators and bureaucrats to their view than the larger mass of unorganized citizens. Consider whom the U.S. Congress first sought to help after the terrible tragedy of September 11, 2001. The terrorist attacks affected the entire tourism industry. But the first legislation was not relief for the hundreds of thousands of taxi drivers or restaurant and hotel workers, but for the airlines, which conducted an organized lobbying effort for taxpayer subsidies.

Analogously, if industrial and financial incumbents are opposed to financial development, they have the organization and the political clout to prevent institution building from becoming an important part of a government's agenda. Finance can languish even if the people want it, simply because they do not have the organization to push for it.

To see how political expediency can overcome the public interest, one only has to turn to the rural South in the United States not so long ago.

> For the farmer who needed credit in the rural South in the early years of the 20th century, the alternatives were dismal. Few banks would even consider making agricultural loans, and those who did charged extremely high interest rates. Rural credit was fertile ground for the loan sharks, and year after year, farmers turned over their crops to help pay exorbitant interest charges on loans made to keep their farms operating. Should a crop fail, the chances of a farmer extricating himself and his family from a loan shark's clutches were virtually non-existent.[11]

The root of the problem was that state banking laws in the United States were not designed with the public in mind. Some states did not allow banks to open more than one branch. Many states also debarred out-of-state banks from opening branches. The reason, quite simply, was to ensure that competition among banks was limited so that existing in-state banks could remain profitable. It did not matter that without competition, in-state banks became fat and lazy, and that with limits on branching, banks were too small and risky and thus may not have wanted to make agricultural loans that would tie them even more closely to the vicissitudes of local weather. The people of the state were served badly. But the in-state banks contributed large sums to political campaigns, and their will prevailed for a long time against the needs of the people. It was only in the 1990s that these archaic banking regulations in the United States were finally repealed.

If the most powerful economic players in a state or a country decide to oppose the creation of free market institutions, then there is only one hope for the emergence of markets: competition from outside. This is because the political restraints imposed on domestic competition and markets tend to make domestic players, no matter how powerful internally, inefficient and uncompetitive relative to outside players who have cut their teeth in a more competitive environment. As a result, if competition seeps through from outside across political borders, domestic incumbents have only two choices: remove the regulations that stand in the way of free domestic markets or perish. Typically, they make the rational choice.

This is, in fact, what happened with regulations limiting bank branching in the United States. As technology improved the ability of banks to lend and borrow from customers at a distance, competition from out-of-state banks increased, even though they had no in-state branches. Local politicians could not stamp this competition out since they had no jurisdiction over it. Rather than seeing their small, inefficient local champions being overwhelmed by outsiders, they withdrew the regulations limiting branching. With the exception of a few inefficient banks, studies show that everyone benefited. The withdrawal of these regulations typically led to a significant increase in the growth rate of per capita income in the state and a reduction in bank riskiness.[12]

Similarly, cross-border trade and cross-border capital flows subject incumbents in a country to vigorous competition from outside. Countries are forced to do what is necessary to make their economies competitive, not what is best for their incumbents. Typically, this means strengthening the institutions necessary for domestic markets.

For example, in Japan in the early 1980s, corporate bond markets were tiny. This was because commercial banks controlled the so-called Bond Committee, an official body to which each firm desiring to issue unsecured bonds (bonds that are not backed by collateral) had to apply. Ostensibly, the reason for this arrangement was to ensure that companies marketed only safe issues to the public. The *real* reason was that banks used the Bond Committee to protect their commercial lending business. Hitachi—then a blue-chip AA-rated firm (AAA being the highest rating)—couldn't obtain permission to issue bonds and thus had to borrow from the banks at high rates.

The growth of the Euromarket (an offshore market in London) and the opening of Japan's borders to capital flows in 1980 finally loosened the banks' longtime stranglehold on companies. Large Japanese firms now bypassed domestic banks to borrow in the Euromarket. There, they faced no collateral requirements, and they could freely issue a wide range of instruments in different maturities and currencies. Whereas Euromarket issues accounted for only 1.7 percent of Japanese corporate financing in the early 1970s, they accounted for 36.2 percent of it by 1984. The Bond Committee was forced to disband—not because the government or the banks saw how inefficient it was but because cross-border competition dictated it.

More generally, during the twentieth century, periods of high international mobility of goods and capital (1900–1930 and 1990–2000) have paralleled periods of maximum development of financial markets. More telling, countries that proved most open to international trade during these eras boasted more mature financial markets. As one example, small countries like Hong Kong, Luxembourg, and Switzerland have to be open by necessity and, not coincidentally, tend to be important financial centers. Open borders limit the ability of domestic politics to close down competition and retard financial and economic growth. They help save capitalism from the capitalists!

The hope, then, for countries like Bangladesh is that as they become integrated into the world economy, the archaic institutions that literally and figuratively imprison their people will be forced to change for the better. People will have free access to finance and, with that, a hope of economic freedom.

In sum, our argument thus far is that each stage in a country's development brings its own set of incumbents who have an interest in allowing only those institutions that sustain their power. If economic power in the country is concentrated in the hands of those who do not have economic ability—the feudal lords or the inefficient plantation owners—promarket institutions have a chance of emerging only after political change democratizes power. But democratization may not be sufficient. Even in a democracy, incumbents can have their way, relying on the tendency of the general public to be apathetic toward political action. A free press, active political participation, and competitive political parties help mitigate this, but what ultimately keeps a new set of incumbents from capturing a country's economic policies is competitive pressure from outside a country's political borders. This pressure forces domestic politicians to adopt more efficient, market-friendly policies, if only to help domestic incumbents survive. Competition among political systems gives free markets a chance.

The Third Phase: The Reaction

But if all that stands between the tyranny of incumbents and competitive free markets is open borders, how stable are markets? Is the opening of a country's borders to foreign goods and services not itself a political decision, dependent on the mood of a country's people? If so, do free markets rest on shifting and fragile foundations?

The foundations can shift, but not with every political whim and fancy. A country's borders are porous. When the rest of the world is open, it is difficult for any single country to put up barriers to the flow of goods, capital, and people. There will always be ways through, around, or under the barriers a country puts up. So when the world is open, a country's borders will perforce be open unless it is a police state. Incumbent interests will be subdued. This is perhaps why the Asian crisis in 1998, which occurred when much of the world was steaming ahead healthily, did not change the stance of most East Asian governments toward open borders.

Matters can change if a number of large countries close their borders. Not only will such actions weaken the champions of openness in each open country, they will also make it easier for a country to control flows across its own borders. So a reversal in globalization can be contagious. Such concerted action is not unthinkable. Not only can a global downturn reverberate in many countries, it also can turn significant vocal segments of the public against competitive markets and, by association, open borders.

To understand why economic downturns spawn opposition to markets, consider the natural consequences of a competitive and transparent market: it creates new risks and destroys traditional sources of insurance. The dark side of risks is invariably experienced in downturns, and the lack of insurance keenly felt then. No wonder opposition mounts.

Let us explain in more detail. Competition naturally distinguishes the competent from the incompetent, the hardworking from the lazy, the lucky from the unlucky. It thus adds to the risk that firms and individuals face. It also increases risk by expanding opportunities in good times and reducing them in bad ones, thus subjecting people to a roller coaster of a ride. Ultimately, most people are better off, but the ride is not always pleasant, and some do fall off.

Also, when competition is limited, individuals and firms enjoy various forms of implicit insurance. This can dry up as markets develop. An example should make the point clear. When competition among firms for workers is limited, firms know that their workers will have little mobility in the future. Knowing that their workers will be loyal, firms would rather retrain than fire their workers in times of trouble, providing them some insurance against bad times. By contrast, in a competitive economy, workers have greater mobility in good times. This makes it hard for a firm to justify retraining or holding on to excess employees in bad times because the firm knows full well that the employees need not be loyal when the economy turns around. Similarly, traditional forms of implicit insurance between firms and lenders, suppliers and customers, citizens and communities can all become more strained as markets develop and provide participants more choice. Often, explicit forms of insurance do not, or cannot, fully replace traditional sources.

In short, a competitive market not only creates clearly identified losers, it also deprives them of traditional safety nets. These people become the distressed—the workers whose industries have no future as a result of competition, the investors who lose their entire life savings, the small-business owners and farmers who are overburdened with debt taken to finance investment in rosier times . . . The distressed, staring at destitution, will have a strong incentive to organize and obtain protection through the political system. If they do manage to organize, though, they will demand far more than subsidies. Indeed, their demands are likely to turn against the economic system that led to their plight, especially because these demands coincide with the desires of incumbent capitalists. This is not just a theoretical possibility; it has happened before.

The Great Reversal

The world experienced a period of increasing globalization and a great expansion of markets at least once before. Reflecting on his times, the president of the International Congress of Historical Studies said in 1913:

> The world is becoming one in an altogether new sense. . . . As the earth has been narrowed through the new forces science has placed at our disposal . . . the movements of politics, of economics, and of thought, in each of its regions, become more closely interwoven. . . . Whatever happens in any part of the globe has now a significance for every other part. World History is tending to become One History.[13]

Markets were indeed vibrant at the time he spoke those words. But soon after, the First World War and the Great Depression created great dislocation and unemployment. These events occurred at a time when the level of formal insurance available to ordinary people ranged from minimal to nonexistent (only 20 percent of the labor force in Western Europe had some form of pension insurance in 1910, only 22 percent had health insurance, and unemployment insurance was almost unheard of). Workers, many of whom had become politically aware in the trenches of World War I, organized to demand some form of protection against economic adversity. But the reaction really set in during the Great Depression, when they were joined in country after country by others who had lost out—farmers, investors, war veterans, the elderly . . .

Politicians had to respond, but such a large demand for protection could not be satisfied within the tight constraints on government budgets imposed by the gold standard. Hence, the world abandoned the straitjacket of the gold standard, which at that time was the prime guarantor of free trade and free capital flows. Borders closed.

Governments obtained control over access to financial markets, and many countries also nationalized significant portions of their banking systems. With their ability to turn on or turn off finance, governments obtained extraordinary power over private business. In addition, they intervened more directly by nationalizing industrial firms or by setting up government-sponsored cartels. In part, these actions reflected a distrust of the market; in part, they reflected the inadequacies of past government policies. Since the government could not set up a reasonable safety net quickly, it tried to directly limit the size of market fluctuations by limiting competition.

With no external competition, and with the government willing to intervene to protect jobs and firms, incumbents had a field day. They used this period when domestic policies were no longer disciplined by international competition not just to gain temporary advantage but to mold legislation in their own favor so that their advantage would continue into rosier times, when they would not be able to direct the anger of the distressed against markets. The reversal in openness provided the conditions under which markets could be, and indeed were, repressed. And this repression lasted for a long time.

As competition dried up, a few large firms dominated most industries. New entrants did not get a chance. Worse, economies could no longer renew themselves through creative destruction, whereby old and jaded institutions give way to the young and innovative. While all this may not have mattered in the immediate post–World War II years, when the emphasis through much of the world was on reconstruction, eventually the world economy began to slow.

It is only through the progressive opening up of the world economy in the last three decades, driven in no small part by the realization that closed borders produce economic stagnation, that finance, and economies, have become free again.

In sum, history suggests that the political consensus in favor of free markets cannot be taken for granted, even in the developed countries of the world. The political battle has to be fought again and again to preserve economic freedom. Sufiya Begum's plight, although extreme, is not that distant from us!

The Dangers of the Antiglobalization Movement

Open borders have improved the well-being of a broad swath of people—many of whom are equally oblivious to the role that finance has played in their lives *and* to the risk that closing borders would pose for them personally. Unfortunately, too few people understand this, which is why antiglobalization protests grow unchecked around the world. With a serious economic downturn, open borders will look less and less attractive, even though they are politically most beneficial at such times.

Markets will always create losers if they are to do their job. There is no denying that the costs of competition and technological change fall disproportionately on some. Unfortunately, it is largely their voice, rather than the desires of the silent majority or the interests of future generations, that will influence politicians. The danger, stemming from conservative politics, is to ignore the concerns of the losers or the threat they pose to general prosperity. Liberal politics is equally misguided when it attacks the system that created losers instead of seeing that it is an inevitable aspect of the market.

Recent developments do not augur well. The increase in militarism across the globe may hopefully be only a minor footnote in history. Regardless of whether it is or not, war fervor tends to increase faith in action by governments, even in the economic arena, while reducing the public's faith in the logic of open markets. An economic downturn with many cheated of prosperity that seemed to be within their grasp, corporate scandals that undermine the public's perception that markets are fair, a chance of a prolonged war, and a backlash against open borders—we have seen such conditions before. Markets did not come out well from the encounter.

That is not to say that we have learned nothing from the 1930s. History is not so boring as to repeat itself exactly. Developed countries have built safety nets for their people, though there are holes in even the best of them. But newly developed and developing countries are still reliant on informal safety nets that have frayed long ago under the onslaught of markets. It is not inconceivable that the antimarket movement may gather strength there and then spread to developed countries.

And developed countries have to face new problems. Technological change and the economic growth of countries like India and China are forcing entire industries to shrink and restructure. The aging of populations in developed countries and the consequent need for immigration from developing countries may fuel great political tension in the future, when working immigrants will be asked to pay benefits to the retired old indigenous population. Furthermore, as the retired in the rich West merely own but do not create value, conflicts over property rights can increase.

None of these looming problems is without resolution. But they require policies that are pragmatic rather than ideological, and we will suggest some. Broadly speaking, borders have to be kept open so that countries can enjoy competitive free markets and keep the playing field level. But open borders and free markets also have to be made politically palatable. There is little common ground between free markets and incumbents, but what little there is can be expanded. More common ground can be found between free markets and the distressed. To prevent politics from working at cross-purposes to the market, those who lose out in competition should be helped, not to continue the lost fight but to ease their pain and to prepare them for a better future.

To sum up, the central point of this book is the fundamental tension between markets and politics. Large arm's-length markets require substantial infrastructure. The difficulty of organizing collective action makes it hard to develop this infrastructure without the assistance of the government. But such assistance suffers from a similar problem: the very same difficulties of organizing collective action make it hard for the public to ensure that the government acts in the public interest. The traditional Left and the Right each emphasize only one side of this tension: the Left the need for government intervention, the Right the corruption of the government. If both are correct, as they undoubtedly are, the political stability of free markets cannot rest on one-sided ideological prescriptions. Instead, it needs a sophisticated web of checks and balances. To see what these might be, we need to understand better why free markets are beneficial, how they emerge, who opposes them, and when this opposition gains strength. These are the issues examined in this book.

PART ONE

THE
BENEFITS
OF FREE
FINANCIAL
MARKETS

CHAPTER ONE

Does Finance Benefit Only the Rich?

FOR THE POLITICAL foundations of free markets to become stronger, society has to become more cognizant of how much it owes them. The first step in mounting a defense of markets is to create awareness about both their true benefits and their limitations. Because the free market system is so weak politically, the forms of capitalism that are experienced in many countries are very far from the ideal. They are a corrupted version, in which powerful interests prevent competition from playing its natural, healthy role. To defend free markets against their critics, therefore, we have to show not only how much of our plentiful lives we owe to them but also why the grim parodies of capitalism through much of even recent history are not truly representative of free market enterprise. And further, we will try to convince the reader that we are not faced today with the Hobson's choice between a corrupt socialism and a corrupt capitalism, as has been the case through much of history. There is a better way, and it is largely within our reach.

One group of markets, the financial markets, attract even more opprobrium than others. Few trained economists in the developed world today would be against free markets in goods and services, but a sizable number can still be found who would oppose free financial markets. Not only are financial markets more misunderstood than other markets, they are also more important because, as we will argue later, free financial markets are the elixir that fuels the process of creative destruction, continuously rejuvenating the capitalist system. As such, they are also the primary target of the powerful interests that fear change. Through much of the book, therefore, we focus on the financial markets as our representative example.

To mount a defense, however, we have to know what we must defend against. So let us now examine what the public believes financial markets and financiers do. One belief that is widely held is that Wall Street is a parasite living off of Main Street. At best, the financier takes from Peter and gives to Paul, while keeping back a significant commission to furnish a luxury apartment overlooking Central Park. Tom Wolfe's *The Bonfire of the Vanities* perfectly captures this view of financiers. Here is a passage from it in which Judy McCoy explains to her daughter Campbell what exactly her father, a bond salesman, does:

> "*Daddy doesn't build roads or hospitals, and he doesn't help build them, but he does handle the bonds for the people who raise the money.*"
> "*Bonds?*"
> "*Yes. Just imagine that a bond is a slice of cake, and you didn't bake the cake, but every time you hand somebody a slice of the cake a tiny little bit comes off, like a little crumb, and you can keep that.*"
> *Judy was smiling, and so was Campbell who seemed to realize that this was a joke, a kind of fairy tale based on what her daddy did.*
> "*Little crumbs?*" *she said encouragingly.*
> "*Yes,*" *said Judy.* "*Or you have to imagine little crumbs, but a lot of little crumbs. If you pass around enough slices of cake, then pretty soon you have enough crumbs to make a gigantic cake.*"[1]

Wolfe is not in a minority in deprecating financiers. Works ranging from Shakespeare's *Merchant of Venice* to Émile Zola's *Money* have financiers occupying a moral space considerably below that of prostitutes.

Even while many view them as leeches, others see them as too powerful. Consider these words of Woodrow Wilson during the United States presidential campaign of 1912:

The great monopoly in this country is the money monopoly. So long as it exists, our old variety and freedom and individual energy of development are out of question. A great industrial nation is controlled by its system of credit. Our system of credit is concentrated. The growth of the nation, therefore, and all our activities are in the hands of few men, who, even if their actions be honest and intended for the public interest, are necessarily concentrated upon the great undertakings in which their own money is involved and who, necessarily, by every reason of their own limitations, chill and check and destroy genuine economic freedom.[2]

Wilson recognized the importance of finance ("a great industrial nation is controlled by . . . credit") but lamented that its power was used to "chill and check and destroy genuine economic freedom." Are these two seemingly opposite perceptions—financiers' being useless while at the same time being too powerful—compatible?

They are, and they characterize financiers well, but only in an underdeveloped financial system—a system lacking in basic financial infrastructure such as good and speedily enforced laws, clear accounting standards, and effective regulatory and supervisory authorities. The reason why these beliefs are valid is simple. Talent and business acumen are worth nothing without the funds to put them to work. A good financial system broadens access to funds. By contrast, in an underdeveloped financial system, access is limited. Because funds are so important, the financier who controls access is powerful, but because access is so limited, the financier can make money doing very little. His role is simply that of a gatekeeper, keeping the rich within the gates safe while keeping out those who would compete for resources. He thus validates both Judy McCoy's view that he scrounges crumbs from the cake that others create and Woodrow Wilson's view that financiers "chill and check and destroy genuine economic freedom."

Why is finance so limited in an economy without financial infrastructure? Financing is the exchange of a sum of money today for a promise to return more money in the future. Not surprisingly, such an exchange can be problematic. First, even the most honest borrower may be unable to live up to her promise, due to the uncertainty intrinsic in any investment. Thus, financiers have to bear some risk. When the risk involved is substantial and concentrated, it becomes difficult to find people willing to bear it. Second, promises are hard to value. People who do not intend to keep them are more willing to promise a lot. Hence, the very nature of the exchange tends to favor the dishonest. Finally, even individuals with the best intentions may be tempted to behave in an opportunistic way when they owe money. In an economy without the infrastructure to mitigate these problems, financing becomes restricted to the few who have the necessary connections or wealth to reassure financiers. The financier can prosper simply by acting as a gatekeeper. As we explain in this chapter, the limited access to finance severely reduces the choices citizens have in determining the way they work and live.

In the next chapter, we explain why this does not *need* to happen. With the appropriate infrastructure in place, the intrinsic problems we describe can be overcome, so that the financier can broaden access to funds and enhance economic freedom. And this is not just utopian thinking. As we describe in Chapter 3, the revolution that has taken place in the U.S. financial markets in the last twenty years has already enhanced economic freedom greatly, placing the human being rather than capital at the center of economic activity. All this suggests that those who want to oppose free access to finance and the attendant freedoms it brings need focus merely on holding back the institutional infrastructure needed for a modern financial market. The problems intrinsic to finance will do the rest by restricting access. Once we understand this, we will be ready to embark on the rest of the book.

The Problems Intrinsic to Financing

Chance, ignorance, or knavery—in the jargon, uncertainty, adverse selection, or moral hazard—can intervene to prevent financing from being repaid. Let us quickly explain why.

Few investments are perfectly safe—there is typically some *uncertainty* about whether they will succeed. To attract funds to risky ventures, individuals or firms undertaking them have to promise their investors a *risk premium* over what they would earn on safe investments. In a developed financial system, financiers reduce the premium required of a borrower by spreading risk widely over a variety of investors or allocating it to those investors who can best bear it. Because financiers in an underdeveloped financial system do not have the ability to distribute risk appropriately, the risk premium their investors demand is high, and finance becomes extremely costly.

The problems caused by uncertainty are exacerbated because not all people are intrinsically honest. Without extensive information on a borrower's past credit history, it is hard for a financier to tell the honest from the dishonest. Even if there is a default, it is not easy to separate bad luck from crookery. Since the dishonest are hard to identify and punish, financiers with limited information again have to resort to charging high rates.

There is a limit, however, to the rates a financier can charge. One problem the financier faces is termed *adverse selection.*[3] Honest borrowers who intend to repay are very sensitive to the interest rate. They expect to bear the full burden of repaying the high rate. The higher the rate is, the more honest borrowers will drop out of the pool of applicants, realizing that the credit is not worth the high repayments. By contrast, borrowers who have no intention of repaying will apply for credit and remain in the pool of applicants, no matter how high the rate. In short, the higher the rate is raised, the more the pool of applicants will be "adversely selected" to be primarily bad borrowers. But the higher the concentration of bad borrowers, the higher the interest rate a financier should charge to break even, in light of the higher expected rate of default. This is a vicious circle. The more he raises the rate, the more the financier needs to raise it, till the point at which all good customers are discouraged from borrowing. At that point, the financier certainly does not want to lend because he knows that the only customers willing to borrow are the ones who will not repay!

In short, there may be no interest rate that allows lending to be profitable, so the financier simply denies credit to applicants who do not have a solid credit history. In an underdeveloped system, this leaves a large fraction of the population without any access to credit.

Uncertainty and dishonesty are not the only problems a financier faces. Even an intrinsically honest borrower may take actions contrary to the financier's interests—a phenomenon known as *moral hazard*—when the terms of repayment are poorly structured. For example, if repayments become too onerous, the borrower may see that the only way he can even hope to repay the loan is by taking on greater risk. Such "gambling for resurrection" may be against the financier's interests because the projects the borrower takes on may be disasters most of the time. In a developed financial system, the financier has the information to know when the borrower's financing terms start creating perverse incentives for the borrower. He has the skills to write the right kind of new contracts and can rely on an efficient legal system to help restructure the old contracts (a nontrivial task when a borrower has many financiers) and enforce the new ones. In a system in which the techniques of contract design, contract renegotiation, and contract enforcement are underdeveloped, it is hard to provide borrowers with the right incentives throughout the term of the project, so financiers are again reluctant to lend.

The Tyranny of Collateral

Because the financier risks losing his money to uncertainty, adverse selection, or moral hazard, he hesitates to lend when the financial infrastructure is not adequate to resolve these problems. But he can still protect himself by requiring collateral—valuable assets that the financier can keep in case the borrower defaults. This is the principle behind pawnbroking, which is prevalent even in the most underdeveloped economies.

Collateral reduces the problem of uncertainty, since the lender can recover some, or all, of his loan even if the venture fails. It also reduces information asymmetries—it is often easier to value physical assets than to value character. Moreover, the borrower will find it costly to put up valuable collateral if she intends to decamp with the proceeds of the loan, because she will lose the collateral. Thus, a collateral requirement can force rogues to self-select themselves out of the pool of applicants for loans, leaving only those bona fide applicants who fully intend to pay back the loan.

The potential loss of her collateral also makes the borrower think twice before adopting a riskier course of action. Collateral's twin effects, of keeping rogues from applying for loans and reducing the borrowers' incentive to take undue risks, make it a valuable device in encouraging lending. The potential financier sees lower risk in a collateralized loan, while the borrower benefits from the consequent lower interest rate the financier charges.[4] In most underdeveloped economies, and in the ghettos of even the developed ones, collateralized borrowing may, in fact, be the only way to obtain finance from outside the circle of family and friends.

The romantics among us cannot, or do not want to, recognize the logic of this economic transaction. They castigate Shylock when he comes for his pound of flesh but do not see that this is the collateral that enabled the merchant of Venice to borrow. Furthermore, a dispassionate economic transaction is marred by the vile nature of (who else?) the financier and his hatred for the borrower. The logic, however, is impeccable. The borrower in need is prepared to sacrifice something valuable in order to obtain finance. In fact, were it not for the gruesome nature of the collateral and the prior strained relationship between the contracting parties, the collateral would be perfect. The lender has better use for money than for the pound of the borrower's flesh and would not collect unless the borrower defaulted. The borrower values his flesh immensely and would not default lightly.[5] We cannot merely look at the unfortunate eventuality when the financier comes to collect on the collateral to portray the transaction as inequitable.

Study after study has shown that the easier it is for a financier to seize collateral, the more lending takes place. The ease with which a creditor can collect on pledged collateral differs among countries. In England, for instance, it takes a lender on average a year and a sum of approximately 4.75 percent of the cost of the house to repossess a house from an insolvent borrower. Mortgage loans amount to 52 percent of gross domestic product (GDP) in England. In Italy, a country with roughly the same GDP per capita as England, it takes between three and five years at a cost of between 18 and 20 percent of the value of a house to foreclose on it. Mortgage loans amount to a far lower 5.5 percent of GDP.[6]

Politicians in the United States give us yet more evidence that the ability to pledge collateral is important. In an attempt to protect households from the consumer credit industry that "forced" them to take on too much debt, the Commission on the Bankruptcy Laws argued in 1973 that it would be beneficial for less-well-off households if they could retain some assets after filing for bankruptcy. The commission advocated that a substantial portion of household assets be exempted from seizure by creditors (these assets are called "bankruptcy exemptions") so that poor households would have the wherewithal to make a fresh start.

Following these recommendations, a number of states adopted exemptions. Some of these were extremely generous. For instance, in Texas, a bankrupt can retain his house no matter how expensive it is, in addition to $30,000 of other property. A bankruptcy exemption is a form of insurance: it prevents the borrower from losing everything in case of a personal calamity. This can make borrowers more willing to tolerate high debt levels. But it also prevents the exempt assets from serving as collateral, making lenders less willing to offer loans.

Higher state bankruptcy exemptions led to a significantly higher probability that households would be turned down for credit or discouraged from borrowing.[7] Poor households were disproportionately adversely affected. Since their house is often their only form of collateral, the exemption laws effectively deprived them of their only means of obtaining finance. They had much less access to borrowing in the high-exemption states, and paid higher interest rates, than in the low-exemption states. By contrast, rich households typically have enough unprotected assets to borrow. The diminished willingness of financiers to lend after the passage of the exemptions did not affect them much. In fact, their debt went up in high-exemption states: rich households became more willing to borrow because more of their assets could be protected from seizure. Thus, financial legislation that was intended to help the poor households ended up hurting them and benefiting the well-to-do. We will see example after example of this in the book—more perhaps than one could ascribe purely to legislative ignorance of economics.

The inequity in collateral requirements is therefore not that the lender will seize assets if the borrower defaults—the borrower can avoid this in the first place by refraining from borrowing. The problem is that only those with assets can borrow. In many ways, the world of underdeveloped finance is as in Matthew (25:29):

> Unto everyone that hath shall be given, and he shall have abundance: but from him that hath not shall be taken away even that which he hath.

In such a world, wealth, not productive ideas, begets finance.

Some argue that matters are not so bleak for the poor. In an insightful recent book, *The Mystery of Capital,* Peruvian economist Hernando de Soto notes that the poor in much of the developing world have property that could be pledged as collateral if its legal status were not murky.[8] For example, houses built in the Dharavi slum in Bombay are solidly constructed and sit on prime land. But since they are encroachments on government or private land, they have no legal status. Because their property cannot serve as collateral, de Soto argues, the poor have no access to finance. The solution to this problem, he suggests, is to offer the poor clear title to their land.

While there is substantial merit to his idea, it is no panacea. If the poor are squatting on someone else's private property or, as is typically the case in the developing world, government land, legalizing encroachment could lead to a free-for-all to occupy the remaining land, leading to widespread insecurity of property, the opposite effect of that intended.

If, on the other hand, the poor have had a long history of occupying the land and have the sanction of the community in doing so (paren-thetically, it is astonishing how easily age and custom sanctify the murky origins of property), the incentives created by legalizing may not be altogether perverse. But if it is the local community that enforces prop-erty rights, then it is unclear that a title from a remote government would be enough to make the property good collateral. It would take a really brave bank officer to attempt to repossess a house in the Dharavi slum against the wishes of the local mafia, and an even braver individual to move in, displacing the original occupant. In other words, some of the poor may have collateral, but unless there is a ready liquid market in it—and legalization is only one step in creating that market—it is unclear that they will still be able to borrow. A better approach to improving the access of the poor, especially those among them who have no assets, would be to develop the financial infrastructure more broadly. We return to this later in the book.

. . . and Connections

A financier in an underdeveloped financial system may be willing to lend even without collateral if he knows the borrower and has other levers of control over him. Repayment of amounts borrowed from within the circle of family, friends, and neighbors, for instance, can be enforced through the threat of social ostracism, as in the Grameen Bank example presented in the introduction (apart from maternal overconfi-dence in one's progeny's capabilities, this probably explains why the sin-gle largest source of external funding for start-up businesses is from family and friends).[9] But the poor tend not to have rich friends or rela-tives. So, again, it is typically the rich who have the right connections to obtain financing.

The paucity of public, reliable, timely information about borrowers can only reinforce the narrowness of the group that has access to finance. When mechanisms for reliable transmission of information are not in place, a financier's primary source of information is from per-sonal relationships in the surrounding community or from business transactions. Since information about the creditworthiness of the bor-rower is key, friends, relatives, and business associates are the most likely recipients of his loans. In the absence of reliable real-time information, a financier will also rely more heavily on reputation. Established busi-nesses, which have been around for a longer time, stand a better chance of having developed that reputation. Once again, financing tends to gravitate toward a small clique of incumbents and those closely tied to them.

As one example of the importance of connections, membership in social clubs seems to affect the lending policies of banks in Italy, a country where disclosure is still very deficient and there are few mechanisms for the reliable transmission of information.[10] A bank is two and a half times more likely to extend a line of credit to a firm if its loan officer belongs to the same club as the owner of the firm than if he does not. It is also seven times more likely to be the firm's main bank (that is, the bank with the largest share of loans to the firm). Not only does belonging to the same club enhance the likelihood that credit will be available, it also increases the magnitude of credit available. The loans made by banks to firms whose owner shares the same club are 20 percent larger than the loans made by banks whose officers are not as close socially.

Recently, this type of finance has been derided as crony capitalism, something peculiar to Eastern or Latin cultures that are overly tolerant of corruption, at least by Western standards. But historical studies indicate that lending to related parties reflects financial underdevelopment in an economy rather than some cultural propensity toward being devious. New England banks in the early nineteenth century lent a large proportion of their funds to members of their own boards of directors or to others with close personal connections to the board.[11] What prevented this practice from being overly oppressive was that free entry was allowed into banking. Nevertheless, because only the rich or reputable could set up banks, finance was effectively restricted to incumbents. "Insider-lending" practices were a solution to the primitive informational and contractual infrastructure at that time and did not persist once infrastructure developed.

Should We Be Concerned?

That finance ends up benefiting the rich is often attributed to active discrimination against the poor. We hope we have convinced the reader that when financial infrastructure is underdeveloped, financing is not easy. The financier will naturally gravitate toward financing the haves simply because they have the collateral or connections to assuage his concerns. Any rational lender would behave the same way. In fact, economists call such behavior rational discrimination, to differentiate it from the more traditional form of discrimination, which is based on individual distaste for specific groups.

Nevertheless, should we be concerned? We believe yes, both because the economy cannot produce as much as its potential and because what it does produce is not distributed fairly.

Clearly, the wealthy and the well connected are not the only ones with talents. If not all the talented can obtain the resources necessary to carry out their ideas, society is the poorer for it. Furthermore, without access to external finance, one avenue of opportunity—self-employment—is shut off. As a result, the poor are doubly damned, not only because they lose an option but also because their bargaining power when they work for those who have resources is weakened.

Equally invidious, as we will see, is that when the few control all resources, they find it easier to collude to make profits off the rest of the economy. For instance, if reliable information is not publicly available about borrowers, it is easier for bankers to get together in the proverbial smoke-filled room and agree to divide up the market. After all, in an environment in which information is inadequate, it is costly for an "outside" banker to compete a firm away from an established relationship with its traditional banker: since the "inside" banker knows much more about his client firms than outside bankers, the only firms that the outsider is likely to come away with are probably ones that the inside banker did not find profitable.[12] With limited outside competition, banks will find it easy to form cartels. It is no wonder that the Pujo Committee, created in 1911 by the United States Congress to investigate the prevailing practices in the financial sector, found that

> the possibility of competition between these banking houses . . . is further removed from the understanding between them and others, that one will not seek, by offering better terms, to take away from another, a customer which it has theretofore served. . . . This is described as a principle of banking ethics.[13]

The Pujo Committee labeled the financial sector "the money trust," reminiscent of the trusts or cartels in railroads, steel, and oil that were attracting opprobrium around that time.

When financiers collude, they see little reason to upset the status quo. This has other effects—for example, that they do not want to take on risk by encouraging innovation. Justice Louis Brandeis, appointed to the Supreme Court by President Wilson, wrote a searing indictment of finance in his book *Other People's Money*. He decried the reluctance of banks to support innovation, listing a series of innovations during the nineteenth and early twentieth centuries that had changed the world. These ranged from the steamship to the telegraph. None, he claimed, was funded by banks.

In sum, finance in an underdeveloped system tends to be clubby, uncompetitive, and conservative, an apt description of finance in the United States in the beginning of the twentieth century. What effect did it have on individual choice and economic freedom? This is what we now turn to.

The Second Industrial Revolution and the Importance of Finance

Until around the middle of the nineteenth century, the U.S. (and world) economy had few firms with more than a hundred employees. Most were managed by their owners. The historian Eric Hobsbawm contrasted the 150 top families in Bordeaux (France) in 1848 with the 450 top families in the same region in 1960 and found that the largest group in the latter period, the salaried business executive, was completely absent in the earlier time.[14]

The reason for the emergence of salaried managers was that a new organizational form emerged in the latter half of the nineteenth century: large, vertically integrated firms that Harvard business historian Alfred Chandler calls the *modern business enterprise*. Many of these firms were founded in the late nineteenth century or the early twentieth century but dominated their respective economies until recently. Their durability is remarkable. Of those firms on the U.S. *Fortune* 500 in 1994, 247, or nearly half, were founded between 1880 and 1930. The early firms include Kodak, Johnson and Johnson, Coca-Cola, and Sears, founded in the 1880s, and General Electric, PepsiCo, and Goodyear, in the 1890s.[15] Firms have been even more durable in Germany. Of the thirty largest German firms ranked by sales in 1994, 19 were founded between 1860 and 1930, and 4, even earlier. The 19 firms include household names like Daimler Benz, BMW, Hoechst, Bayer, and BASF.[16]

Why did these giants emerge? Chandler argues that advances in transportation (in particular, the advent of the railways) and in communications (the telegraph) made possible larger markets for goods. The large volumes of goods that were required allowed manufacturers to amortize setup costs and capital investment quickly. As a result, large, capital-intensive manufacturing units sprang up to exploit technologies that could realize lower per-unit costs than smaller outfits. For example, before the introduction of the Bessemer process, which makes steel from molten pig iron, there were hundreds of blast furnaces in the United States. None produced more than 1 or 2 percent of national output. With the diffusion of the Bessemer process, manufacturers were forced to increase scale. As a result, by 1880, the entire production of Bessemer steel came from just thirteen plants.[17]

The scale of transformation can be gauged by the fact that between 1869 and 1899, capital invested per worker in the United States nearly tripled in constant dollars. To measure productivity increases due to technological improvements, economists use a concept called *total factor productivity* growth. It is the component of growth in the value of goods and services produced by an economy that is left over after accounting for the increased use of capital and labor. Total annual factor productivity growth, which had held steady at about 0.3 percent in the United States throughout much of the nineteenth century, rose to 1.7 percent between 1889 and 1919. These unprecedented increases in industrial growth have led economists to call this period the second industrial revolution.[18]

According to Chandler, these firms had three distinctive characteristics.[19] The first was, of course, the enormous investment in production facilities so as to exploit potential economies of scale and scope in production. But the inherent scale economies also gave the early entrants first-mover advantages: once they set up on a large enough scale and learned how to produce at low cost, it made little sense for other firms to enter. The initial entrants had already gone down the learning curve without the irritation of competition and were thus better prepared to compete. With the knowledge that the alternative to driving out new entrants was to be driven out themselves, the early entrants also had an incentive to compete fiercely to protect their investments. Moreover, as they became profitable, their earnings from operations could give them the resources to fight price wars. By contrast, new entrants not only had to make large initial investments but also had to suffer huge losses while going down the learning curve before they were in a position to compete effectively. Few potential entrants had the necessary internal fin?
resources or the confidence of financiers to support such entr·
result, capital-intensive industries soon became oligopolistic, w·

firms dominating the market and very little entry occurring. It is no wonder these firms have proved so durable!

A classic example of such a firm was John D. Rockefeller's Standard Oil trust, formed in 1882 out of a previously loose alliance of the major kerosene producers and refiners. The purpose of forming the trust was not primarily to establish a monopoly, though it later came to be seen as that. The alliance already held a monopoly and controlled over 90 percent of American refineries and pipelines.[20] Instead, it was a way of centralizing control through ownership so that economies of scale could be realized. Refineries were shut, others reorganized, and new ones opened so that all the oil could be forced to pass through a few large refineries. While the average refinery in 1880 had a daily capacity of 1,500 to 2,000 barrels of kerosene, Rockefeller plants had a capacity of 5,000 to 6,500 barrels of kerosene.[21] And in 1886, the trust chose to build a plant in Lima, Ohio, that could process 36,000 barrels a day![22] So while the cost of production for plants of average size in 1885 was 1.5 cents per gallon, Standard Oil's cost was only 0.45 cent per gallon.[23]

The second characteristic Chandler ascribed to these titanic firms was that they integrated both forward and backward. They built a nationwide (or even international) sales and distribution network that could sell goods in the large new markets. The reason the firms had to create their own networks rather than rely on others to retail their products was simple. They were too big and the products too specialized for an independent distributor to handle. If the independent distributor specialized its sales force to handle a large manufacturer's products well, it would soon find that it was overly dependent on the manufacturer and would face the inevitable erosion in margins as the manufacturer took advantage of this situation. On the other hand, if its sales force remained unspecialized so as to handle the products of all the existing manufacturers, no manufacturer would feel adequately served. Since market share was so important in keeping production costs low, few large manufacturers were willing to rely on the uncertain motives of an independent sales and distribution network, and many developed their own. For similar reasons, they also integrated backward to secure their supply networks.

Again, Standard Oil epitomizes these developments. It owned pipelines and railcars. It had tremendous power over the railroads because it was a large-volume user, so much so that it not only commanded low freight charges but also set the charges for smaller independent rivals. For example, in 1885, a Standard Oil employee struck a deal with a railroad such that the railroad charged Standard Oil 10 cents for each barrel of oil shipped while a pesky rival was charged 35 cents. In addition, Standard Oil was to be paid 25 cents for every barrel of oil the rival shipped! If the railroad did not comply, Standard Oil threatened to build a competing pipeline and drive it out of business.[24] Clearly, even if Standard Oil did not own its entire distribution network, its power was such that it effectively owned it.

As a result of these two investments, in manufacturing scale and in integration, each industry came to be dominated by a few vertically integrated giants, with few independent suppliers in intermediate markets. Interestingly, once the pattern of limited competition in intermediate markets was established, it probably became self-reinforcing. The vertically integrated firm had distinctive products and standards. Any supplier of intermediate products would have to produce a very specialized product with only one likely buyer—not a prospect that would elicit much interest from prospective suppliers! With fewer opportunities for niche players, it is not surprising that in the United States, the period of emergence of these large, integrated corporations in the last quarter of the nineteenth century coincided with the beginning of a century-long decline in the fraction of the self-employed as a proportion of the total population of nonagricultural workers. It is only in the 1970s that the steady decline has been reversed, not just in the United States but in other developed countries as well.[25]

The third characteristic of the large firms that dominated industry toward the end of the nineteenth century was the emergence of a hierarchy of professional managers. This was a natural consequence of the first two characteristics. In earlier times when firms were small and capital investment minuscule, the owner and his kith and kin were enough to manage the firm. This was the natural order, even if there were others who could perhaps manage the firm more ably. Why entrust the management of the firm to a possibly untrustworthy outsider and risk the chance of his stealing the firm or its profits from you? Even if he did not literally make away with the firm, there was little to prevent him from learning the firm's secrets and using his savings to set up as competition. After all, the capital investment required was insignificant. And if he was more able than the owners to start with, he could indeed prove fierce competition. Why tempt fate for the sake of a few dollars more?

While the owners of the small firms of the first industrial revolution chose not to rely on professional managers (as evidenced by the complete absence of the latter class in Hobsbawm's picture of Bordeaux in 1848), the owners of the large firms of the second industrial revolution had no such alternative. It was impossible for these behemoths to be managed by a single family. Professional managers were needed to coordinate and control the vast operations of these firms. What kept them from setting up their own rival enterprises? Or even if they did not break away, what kept them loyal to their owners, steadily returning them a dividend year after year instead of feathering their own nest?[26]

The greater ability of owners of the firms of the second industrial revolution to control their managers was precisely because these firms were capital-intensive and finance was underdeveloped. Managers, even very senior ones, could not contemplate life outside the firm. They could not set up as suppliers of intermediate goods (producing, for example, brake linings for an automobile assembly line), since the market for intermediate products was thin. A new entrant could hope to survive profitably in the long term only as a vertically integrated enterprise. But such an enterprise required vast amounts of financing and even then faced the uncertain prospect of a bloody, unprofitable battle against the incumbent. Financiers were not so foolhardy, even if the prospective entrant could furnish the collateral, or had the connections, to get a start! So the firms' vertical integration, and their first-mover advantage, protected them against competition, not just from outsiders but also from their own management.

The modern business enterprise required very specific functional and product-related skills of its managers.[27] Given that there was little market for intermediate products, there was no need to standardize processes (to a common industry standard) within the firm at each stage. Each firm had its own idiosyncratic processes. There was far less benchmarking or adoption of industrywide "best practices." In combination with the limited competition, the consequence was that jobs across integrated firms were not strictly comparable. And even if a manager saw a comparable position in a rival, he would find it difficult to move because of "gentlemen's agreements" among players in the industry not to poach one another's employees. Because the manager's skills were highly specific, he had little hope of being employed in a commensurate position outside the industry. Managerial jobs were jobs for life. If a manager were to find his owner oppressive, or a poor paymaster, he had little redress.

Because work practices were specialized, the firm could also not easily hire trained managers from the outside. But by overstaffing the ranks, the firm could create internal competition for management that would keep wages in check.[28] With few outside options and some internal competition, the manager had no alternative but to be loyal.

Fear cannot, however, be the only source of motivation. Given the enormous concentration of power in the hands of the owners of the modern business enterprise, they had to find some way of providing positive reinforcement to managers who performed well. In large part, firms achieved this, perhaps unknowingly, by creating steep organizational hierarchies, in which the owner communicated with lower management only through intermediate managers in the hierarchy. This organizational pyramid was no doubt necessary—given natural limitations on a manager's span of control—to coordinate the enormous organizations. But also intermediate positions in the hierarchy accumulated some power because they were the channels through which the owner communicated with, and controlled, the mass of lower-level employees. In other words, the steep hierarchy was a way for the owner to cede some power to intermediate management by giving it control over still lower-level employees. Higher levels in the hierarchy carried with them higher pay (and less overstaffing) and were a reward for employees who dedicated themselves to the firm.[29] No wonder these firms spawned strong cultures and the stereotypical organization man.

At the bottom of this organizational pyramid were the common workers. If unspecialized and unskilled, they were paid low wages. But since these workers were not particularly tied to the firm in any way, the firm had little power over them. If dissatisfied, these workers could pack up and leave, securing an equivalent job elsewhere. The truly disadvantaged were the skilled workers, who, because they were specialized to the processes of their firm, could not leave without abandoning a substantial portion of their human capital. The firm had power over these workers in the same way as it had power over the managers. But unlike managers, skilled workers did not occupy critical positions in the hierarchy and obtained little countervailing positional power inside the firm. It was the wages of the skilled workers and, to a lesser extent, management, but not the wages of the unskilled workers, that were repressed in these large organizations.

Interestingly, between 1890 and 1950, the period of the rise of Chandler's large industrial enterprise, there was a tremendous compression of the wages of educated, white-collar workers relative to blue-collar workers.[30] The ratio of wages of clerical employees to those of production workers fell from approximately 1.7 to 1.1 between 1890 and 1950. Since, typically, the educated are also relatively more skilled, these facts are consistent with the consolidation of industry into large, monolithic organizations shackling the skilled and compressing the wage differential. Of course, other factors also partly account for this compression—as with all economic resources, ultimately demand and supply determine the relative prices of skilled labor. Our point is simply that organizational change may have had a profound additional influence.

All this is not to say that skilled workers were powerless. It has been shown that, on average, wages in democracies are higher, perhaps because workers in a democracy can form organizations such as unions or they can support worker parties that try to secure them rights outside the economic process.[31] It is perhaps no coincidence that strong labor movements soon followed the emergence of the modern business enterprise. But political intervention in a fundamentally economic matter is no panacea, an issue we examine later. Moreover, worker rights secured through political intervention are, perforce, general in nature and not tailored to specific situations. They are often riddled with loopholes, so that they can easily be circumvented by astute owners, or too rigid, diminishing the viability of the firms being regulated. There had to be a better way to achieve a balance of power. That is what we examine in the next chapter.

Summary

Financiers are accused of being useless parasites yet feared because they have too much power. In this chapter, we have tried to explain that there is no contradiction in these beliefs. In the modern economy, access to finance is vital. When the financial system is underdeveloped, a small group of financiers can control whatever limited access there is to credit. Ironically, the less financiers do to broaden access, the greater is their individual power. They therefore do little more than guard the gates of the temple, keeping all but the wealthy and the well connected from obtaining access. They are indeed powerful, but the power they have is the power to deny, not create, and they "chill and check and destroy genuine economic freedom." Many of the evils of capitalism—the tyranny of capital over labor, the excessive concentration of industry, the unequal distribution of income in favor of the owners of capital, the relative lack of opportunity for the poor—can be attributed, in some if not substantial measure, to the underdevelopment of finance.

That said, individual financiers in such a system are not particularly unpleasant people; they only do what comes naturally to them given the constraints the system imposes. Even the distasteful Shylock, in his pursuit of collateral, is only taking the contract to its natural end. Were the courts to place impediments in his way, credit would become even scarcer.

Given the right infrastructure, however, financiers can overcome the tyranny of collateral and connections and make credit available even to the poor. They become a power for the good rather than the guardians of the status quo. In the next chapter, we explain in greater detail how this is possible.

CHAPTER TWO

Shylock Transformed

SOCIALISTS like Marx and Engels argued that the way to reduce the power of the owners of capital was for the state to hold power itself by expropriating all private property that was used as a means of production. But this solution only worsens the problem. In a socialist state, the power associated with ownership passes on to the state. While, in theory, the state could be benevolent and act in the best interests of the workers, in practice, the state acts in the best interests of those in power. And the power of a state bureaucrat over workers in a socialist state is considerably more than that of the greediest entrepreneur in a capitalist economy because the government in the socialist state also determines the level of competition it faces.

Competition, as all company owners know, is inconvenient because it disciplines their most rapacious tendencies. So radical socialist governments typically abolish both economic and political competition. As a result, while company owners in a capitalist economy cannot set wages completely arbitrarily, partly because they have to compete to some extent with other owners for workers and partly because they are restrained by the political process, the government in a socialist economy can pretty much decide what it wants to pay. While, theoretically, it could set wages (and other prices) in the most efficient fashion, in practice, it will set them so as to benefit favored groups. Moreover, the lack of restraints on the government implies that the favored groups (other than itself) can change arbitrarily over time with the government's whims and fancies. No one will have the incentive to undertake long-term investment—whether in acquiring specialized skills or in building physical capital—when there is no clarity about what the rules of the game are. Thus, the societal pie shrinks, and more and more of what remains goes to the ruling clique because they have the arbitrary power to determine shares. The socialist economy eventually fails to increase the size of the societal pie or even to redistribute the shrunken remains equitably.

The socialists had the wrong answer to the right question. The right answer is not to concentrate economic power even more but to disperse it more widely. And one way to do this is to expand access to finance. In this chapter, we examine how a developed financial system overcomes the frictions to which we have alluded and improves access to finance.

Reducing the Risk Premium

One obstacle in the way of broadening access to finance is the degree to which risk is concentrated in an underdeveloped system. A developed system distributes risk widely and allocates it to those who can best hold it. We now describe some ways in which a developed system spreads risk and reduces the risk premium demanded by investors to part with their money.

During the 1950s, Nobel Prize–winning work by Harry Markowitz and James Tobin showed that the risk of an investment should be considered not in isolation but in the context of the overall portfolio of investments an individual or a firm makes. The price of gold, for instance, is very volatile. Thus, in isolation, gold is a very risky investment. If added to a stock portfolio, however, it can reduce the overall volatility of the portfolio because gold prices tend to rise during recessions, when stock prices generally fall (technically, the price of gold is *negatively correlated* with equity prices). A well-diversified investor can tolerate a risky investment that he would not be willing to hold if that were his only investment.

Portfolio investment and diversification were made possible by one of the more ingenious economic institutions created by mankind, the limited-liability joint stock company. Prior to the enactment of legislation in the mid–nineteenth century allowing free incorporation with limited liability, owners were jointly and severally liable for the debts of a company (except for the few rare cases in which owners had obtained special government assent to limitations on their liability). This meant that if an owner's partners were paupers, the owner's fortune bore the brunt of the repayment to debtors. Moreover, the owner had to know the management intimately before investing since his loss from trusting an unscrupulous operator was unlimited. Therefore, an investor could not own stocks in more than a few companies, else he would not be able to give each company the close attention it demanded.

Limited liability limits an individual investor's responsibility to the amount of capital he invests. This enables him to diversify his risk across many investments, because his exposure to any single investment is limited. To the extent that he is well diversified, he is reliant on the average scruples of society, which are easily discernible, rather than on those of any individual management. Thus, the institution of limited liability draws in passive investors who expand the pool of capital willing to absorb risk, and it also allows investors to hold well-diversified portfolios, reducing the risk any one investor has to bear. The larger pool of capital willing to finance risk and the greater tolerance for risk means that larger, riskier projects can be financed and access to finance expands.

While diversification cannot eliminate all risk in a portfolio of stocks (for example, all stocks tank when a large economy like that of the United States enters a recession, so U.S. economic risk is hard to diversify away regardless of where the investor is located), it can substantially reduce it. The broader the spectrum of investors who can bear a risk, the more easily it is borne. For example, citizens of Vietnam are likely to have enormous exposure to that country's economy—their jobs depend on the economy's doing well, as does the value of their financial assets and real estate. By contrast, American investors typically have little exposure to Vietnamese risk. Any Vietnamese shares they hold constitute only a small portion of their overall portfolio of stocks. For the Vietnamese investor who has little access to international financial markets, a downturn in the local economy is a major disaster. For the American investor, it is a fleabite. If, therefore, the Vietnamese government allows American investors to buy shares, not only will the economy's risks be placed on the broader shoulders of American investors, but also the return premium investors require of Vietnamese companies will fall. This will reduce the companies' cost of financing, allowing them to undertake more investment.

There is evidence that firms' cost of equity financing falls, and corporate investment increases, when a country opens up its markets to foreign investors.[1] This seems to occur, in part, because the incoming investors have a greater tolerance for domestic risk: stocks of firms exposed to risks that are hardest for domestic investors to diversify away but that are easy for foreign investors to bear have the highest run-up in price when a country opens up its stock market to foreign investors. The greater the amount foreigners are allowed to invest in such stock (even countries with open markets have rules preventing foreigners from investing in some firms or holding more than a certain fraction of a firm's outstanding stock), the greater the run-up in price. Since an increase in stock price reflects a fall in the required return, the evidence suggests that open financial markets can reduce how much is demanded of business ventures by spreading the risk and placing it well. As a result, valuable but risky ventures get financed.

This is what Judy McCoy from *The Bonfire of the Vanities* does not appreciate: it is in large part because financial markets keep the cost of capital low that in the year 2000 alone, $26 billion was spent by the major drug manufacturers in the United States on the development of lifesaving drugs. Financiers do help build roads and hospitals, and even invent drugs, but in a way that is invisible to most people.

While stocks are crude instruments for allocating risk, financial derivatives can slice and dice risk precisely, placing it on those who can best bear it and making risky ventures even easier to finance.[2] Since the 1970s, major developments in financial economics have greatly expanded the potential uses of derivatives. The critical breakthrough was made in the early 1970s when three professors at M.I.T. came up with the eponymous Black Scholes Merton options-pricing formula. The formula helped put a precise price on these complex instruments. Equally important, theoretical studies also showed how banks could sell these instruments to their clients and then offset their risky positions by undertaking a set of trades in more liquid markets.

Consider an example of how useful derivatives can be in encouraging investment in stocks by those who are traditionally unwilling to invest. In 1993, the French government wanted to privatize Rhone-Poulenc, a chemical company.[3] One of the stated objectives of the government was to enhance employee ownership of the company, in part to make privatization more politically palatable. In France, however, stock ownership was not very popular. Employees were reluctant to buy shares in their own company, even at a large discount, for fear of losing some of the money invested. Rhone-Poulenc did not want to provide a guarantee of a minimum share price to its own employees, and the French treasury did not want to offer it either, possibly for fear of the political backlash in the event of a significant drop in the stock price.

A U.S. bank, Bankers Trust, proposed the following deal, which met everyone's requirements: if employees were to buy the stock, they would be guaranteed a minimum return of 25 percent over four and a half years plus two-thirds of the appreciation of the stock over its initial level. Bankers Trust agreed to be responsible for the risk that the stock price would fall—in which case, the stock would not provide the minimum return of 25 percent to investors, and Bankers Trust would have to make up the difference. In return for offering the guaranteed minimum return, Bankers Trust obtained the one-third of the stock price appreciation that employees were willing to forgo.

Bankers Trust did not bear any risk itself. Using a technique called dynamic hedging, it traded liquid Rhone-Poulenc shares and bonds in the financial markets to transform the one-third of share price appreciation it was to get into a guarantee for the employees plus a tidy profit margin for itself. The bank was able to honor the commitment to employees and, at the same time, protect itself fully. In the process, it allowed the government to meet its political objectives and employees to get a security that met their risk appetite.

More generally, through risk management using derivatives and dynamic hedges, financial firms like banks and investment banks reduce the risk of their financing activities to acceptable levels. This allows them to raise money from investors and fund firms with risky but worthwhile projects, thus expanding access and spreading wealth.

RISK MANAGEMENT is valuable but not easy. A tremendous amount of innovation goes on in the modern financial sector so as to allocate risk properly and expand access to finance. Take, for example, a bank financing a home in an earthquake-prone area in California. The banker has the house as collateral, but he will worry that an earthquake might destroy it. So he will demand that the owner of the house purchase earthquake insurance. A Californian insurance company, however, is not very well diversified against earthquake risk. An earthquake could trigger a spate of claims that could force the firm to default. This is, of course, a source of concern to policyholders. After all, who wants to buy insurance if the company will default when you file your claim?

Such large-scale risks are known in the industry as "catastrophic risks," or cat risks. They can be substantial. Hurricane Andrew in 1992 resulted in a loss of nearly $20 billion for the U.S. insurance industry, while the Northridge earthquake in 1994 resulted in a loss of $13 billion.[4] By some estimates, an earthquake along the New Madrid fault (running through the midwestern states of the United States) could result in a loss of over $100 billion. Such losses can bring many an insurance company to its knees. The insurance company will find cat insurance very valuable because it helps avoid such a meltdown while at the same time inspiring confidence in its customers and giving them access to home financing.

How can the insurance company insure itself? One way for the insurance company to lay off catastrophic risk is to buy insurance from reinsurers that are well diversified across geographic areas. Since catastrophes rarely occur simultaneously across the world, the hit sustained by the reinsurer when an earthquake hits California is small relative to the size of the premiums it collects from all over the world. So the individual buys insurance from an insurance company, which, in turn, buys insurance from a reinsurer, and so on . . . Ultimately, the risk of loss from a California earthquake is borne by investors in the reinsurance company that lies at the end of this chain. However, since the risk has been spread so widely, no individual investor has to be overly concerned about it.

Reinsurance can be very expensive if a few companies monopolize the business. Fortunately, there is an alternative: sharing the risk directly with individual investors. Recently, insurance companies have started issuing cat bonds. When such a bond is issued, the proceeds are invested in safe securities such as government bonds. In the event that a specific catastrophe hits (say, the California earthquake), the government bonds become the property of the insurance company, and it uses them to pay the claims filed by its policyholders. The cat bondholders get nothing. If, however, no catastrophe hits, the cat bondholders not only get paid the interest on the government bonds (and the principal on maturity) but also get an additional premium to compensate them for the risk they bear. Everyone wins through this innovative instrument. The homeowner gets the insurance he needs for the loan, the insurance company gets much-needed funds in the event of the earthquake, while bondholders get high interest rates at all other times. As long as the bondholder is not from California, and as long as she holds only a small fraction of her wealth in the bonds, she need not become too concerned about losing the entire value of the bonds in the remote eventuality that a sizable earthquake hits California.

Despite their seeming simplicity, it is not easy to create securities such as the cat bond. Myriad issues have to be settled before ordinary investors are willing to buy them. For example, how does one know when a catastrophe has occurred? Since so much money turns on this definition in a cat bond, it is important to be precise. One could base the definition on the total amount of damage caused, but how does one estimate this? Who will do the estimation? Even if an unbiased party can be trusted to collect damage reports and put them together, it may take weeks or even months for a precise estimate to come out. The insurance company needs the money long before then to pay claimants. The definition could be based on the total amount of damage done in a particular square mile. But that square mile may have escaped relatively undamaged . . . Any ambiguity in how the security will work is an additional source of risk, for which the investor will demand additional compensation. Therefore, before an innovative financial instrument such as a cat bond can be issued, all these questions have to be answered clearly so that the investor can price the security in full knowledge of what is her due. The investment bankers and lawyers who create such instruments do earn their pay!

Another interesting example of how financial innovation can improve our access to funds comes from a recently introduced security called viatical. The name *viatical* comes from the Latin *viaticum,* meaning a "purse given to a traveler in preparation for a journey." Here is what it does. AIDS patients often have little money to pay for their expensive treatment. Even if they bought life insurance before contracting the disease, they cannot benefit from it personally. The idea behind the viatical is to allow infected people to trade what is sometimes their only valuable possession—their insurance policy—to help enhance the quality of their life before they die.

The viatical is essentially a claim on the life insurance that will be paid on the death of a person infected with AIDS. The security may seem macabre, and financiers may appear to be trafficking in death, but it fulfills a very real need: by *securitizing* the life insurance policy, the financial market transforms an illiquid asset into funds that the patient can use and enjoy in the last days of his life. Financial innovation again broadens access.

Of course, there is a fair amount of risk involved for the buyer of the viatical. The timing of the patient's death is not certain, and the disease is recent enough that reliable statistics are not available. In addition, medical advances can prolong the life of patients to the detriment of investors in these securities. Given these risks for investors, it is best for a number of insurance policies to be packaged together and securities sold against the income they produce. Not only are the risks of investing more widely dispersed and thus better borne, it also makes the securities more palatable. Investors do not have to be on a deathwatch for a particular individual, with all the moral recrimination that that can bring.

This example is particularly useful in illustrating the ease with which finance can attract moral opprobrium. On the one hand, this security could be portrayed as yet another example of heartless financiers willing to profit from sick people. On the other hand, the security serves a very useful, even morally laudable, function: to provide dying AIDS patients (and more recently, other kinds of terminally ill patients) with the money that will ease their pain and suffering in their final days. Interestingly, it is the very existence of profit-minded investors (a.k.a. "greedy" speculators) who are willing to shut their minds to the implications of the security they are buying that makes this market possible. It is because *pecunia non olet*—money has no odor—that the AIDS patient can get succor. This apparent contradiction is not surprising to economists. As Adam Smith, the father of modern economics, wrote, it is not because of the benevolence of the baker that we eat fresh bread every morning but because of his desire to make money.

Reducing Information Problems

In addition to uncertainty or risk, we described two other obstacles that stand in the way of broadening access to finance: the limited information financiers or investors have about borrowers and their prospects and the possibility that borrowers may not act in the best interest of the financier. As financial infrastructure develops, financiers can overcome both obstacles. First, consider the problem of limited information.

In the small, self-contained communities of the past, the local banker generally obtained information about the creditworthiness of borrowers through the grapevine. Today, enormous corporations maintain data on the credit history of borrowers. For example, Dun and Bradstreet (D&B) collects information about a firm from millions of on-site and telephone contacts with business owners and managers as well as from government filings, the firm's banking and trade partners, and public news sources. In the last three decades, the number of firms on which D&B has records has grown 6.3 percent per year, a rate over two and a half times the real growth of the economy![5]

The wider availability of information has greatly expanded the availability of credit. It is fairly easy for credit histories to be verified anywhere in the United States, so potential borrowers are no longer tied to their local banker. Moreover, the availability of information about a borrower in real time through these credit agencies allows a lender to intervene quickly when he sees the borrower getting into difficulty. This helps limit the lender's losses.

One indication that the extraordinary expansion of information availability has increased borrower choices and credit availability is that small firms in the United States have been able to borrow from increasingly distant lenders over time. While a small firm's banker was, on average, no more than sixteen miles away in 1976, in 1992, she was sixty-eight miles away on average, more than four times farther away.[6]

THE STOCK MARKET

The financial sector does more than evaluate our fitness to receive finance, based on what we have done in the past; it also serves as a beacon to us on our future prospects, relative to the prospects of others. In particular, the stock market in a developed economy generates information, which helps guide investment. In doing so, it plays a critical role in economic activity.

Why does such a need exist? Wouldn't it be better to leave resource allocation to the wisdom of a competent, trained bureaucracy than to leave it to an unorganized and chaotic market? How can the ability of an extremely intelligent French bureaucrat trained at the elite École Nationale de l'Administration be matched by high school dropouts shouting in the trading pit in Chicago's Mercantile Exchange? The conventional wisdom in the 1930s and the 1940s was that a market economy could not do a better job of allocating resources than a centrally planned economy.

The Austrian economist Friederich von Hayek challenged this notion. Hayek recognized that planning requires information and information is diffused in society. In the automobile market, for example, each car dealer has a rich variety of experiences that give him some idea of which models are most popular. As a result, all car dealers together have a very good sense of consumer trends. The problem is how to aggregate this information and make it travel to the places where investment decisions are made.

The usual way is through the corporate bureaucracy. Each car dealer reports his views to a regional sales representative, who reports to a national sales manager, who reports to the central budget office. Unfortunately, much of the information is lost on the way. This is because a lot of information is tacit. For example, gut feel, the basis for much business decision making, is qualitative, hard to explain, and even harder to communicate in a standardized report. Without some form of standardization, the higher levels in the hierarchy would find it impossible to process information from many sources. But with standardization, many important pieces get lost.

A second problem has to do with the incentives that different levels of the bureaucracy have to transmit the information accurately. Imagine for a moment that the information held by the car dealer is really detrimental to him—that consumers like the cars but hate the after-sales service he provides. What incentives does he have to report this information to his superiors? If he does not, how can top management become aware of the problem?

Organizations can also be unconsciously biased in where they get information. Firms may pay too much attention to the needs of existing clients, who typically demand refinements of existing technologies. In the process, they tend to ignore emergent technologies that may not immediately meet their clients' needs. For example, in the 1980s, the leading company in each new wave of innovation in the disk drive industry was different from the leading company in the previous one. This suggests that firms did not pay enough attention to emerging technologies because they were too focused on listening to existing clients—thus the ease with which leaders lost their positions.[7]

Selective hearing may be compounded, as earlier, by selective interest. The firm's managers, having become successful with the old technology, may be reluctant to espouse new ones if it means sharing power with upstart managers who understand these technologies better. Mature organizations like firms or bureaucracies can completely close down certain channels of information acquisition, to their own detriment. Entrants, by contrast, do not have the baggage of existing clientele or entrenched interests and may thus develop these "disruptive" technologies in niche markets until they become capable of taking over the entire market.

Hayek's fundamental contribution was to recognize that market prices can play a role in aggregating information in a way that is not biased by organizational disabilities. The market price of oil, for instance, is established every day on the commodity exchange by the forces of demand and supply for this product. Producers and consumers do not write a report but simply express their interest—which reflects their unbiased and informed expectations of the future—through the price at which they are willing to sell or buy oil. Most important, they do so not to fulfill a bureaucratic requirement but because they have the purest of motives—self-interest. No matter how qualitative each one's information is, no matter how detrimental to some people, as long as there is a functioning market, its prices aggregate each individual's information.

Hayek's story is theoretically appealing. But what is the evidence that the stock market provides any information? Every day, seemingly frantic confusion reigns on the floor of any stock exchange (at least those that still have a floor, and a human presence on it). Some traders acknowledge that they buy and sell on the basis of their gut feelings, or on the basis of arcane patterns they see in prices, rather than from any knowledge of fundamentals. How can this process distill any useful information?

One advantage we have in studying stock exchanges today is that there are so many more of them than in the recent past, many of them newly set up. In newer markets, the extensive apparatus to gather information that exists in developed markets—the accounting standards, the hordes of analysts, the financial press, the audit watchdogs, and so forth—has not yet been fully established. One way to gauge the effect of having a more developed stock market is to see what happens when a firm from an underdeveloped market cross-lists in the United States, which despite the aberrations toward the end of the recent boom has, arguably, the most sophisticated financial market in the world.[8] When a firm cross-lists in the United States, the number of analysts following its stock increases, and most important, the accuracy of their forecasts about the firm's earnings improves.[9] This enhanced accuracy translates into a higher valuation of the stock itself. Thus, more developed financial markets provide better incentives to collect information and eventually generate more information.

If the information generated in underdeveloped markets is less useful, more based on aggregate economywide indicators or the moods of the stock market than on hard, company-specific information, we would see that stock prices of individual firms would tend to move together in such markets. By contrast, if more developed markets produce more varied, firm-specific information, stock prices of individual firms would reflect this variety by diverging a lot from one another. This is in fact the case.[10] While in the United States, marketwide comovements explain only 3 percent of the daily variation of individual stocks, in Taiwan, they explain approximately 40 percent and, in Poland, almost 60 percent. Thus, markets do produce company-specific information that is incorporated into stock prices, and more developed markets produce more of it.

The greater quantities of information produced in developed markets do seem to influence investment decisions. Countries where more firm-specific information is produced by the stock market see much more extensive reallocation of investment away from industries with declining prospects to industries with bright prospects. The differences in the extent to which reallocations take place are big: for the same positive signal about the prospects of an industry, investment would increase by more than 7 percent on average if the industry were in the United States but only by 1 percent if the industry were in India.[11]

Managers do not pay attention to stock prices only because they care about maximizing the wealth of their shareholders. The stock market is also a billboard reflecting their performance to all who care to look, and too low a stock price invites a disciplinary hostile takeover bid. Managers therefore tend to reverse actions the stock market does not like. For example, in September 2001, UniCredito, the second-largest Italian bank, engaged in talks to acquire Commerzbank, one of the largest German banks. Unexpectedly, the news of their talks leaked to the market before the final agreement was signed. The market received the news very poorly. UniCredito stock dropped 6.7 percent the day the news leaked to the press and 17 percent over the month.[12] The market reaction, as suggested by these numbers, was so negative that the two companies chose to abandon further talks. The market price of UniCredito surged 6 percent on the announcement that merger talks had been abandoned.[13]

Market prices are thus able to influence managers' decisions. And those who do not listen suffer the consequences. When a corporate acquisition in the United States is poorly received by the market (that is, when the acquirer's stock return is significantly negative on announcement), the acquiring company is much more likely to subsequently become the target of a takeover. Eventually, many such companies divest the assets they acquire.[14] The negative return alerts market participants to the fact that the acquirer is run by managers who are incompetent or unconcerned about shareholder value. In turn, this suggests an opportunity for some other firm to take over the acquirer, replace its management, and utilize its resources better—for example, by divesting the poorly fitting target—thus improving value for shareholders.

So market prices do reveal useful information that contributes to a better allocation of the economy's resources and thus expanded access to finance. This is not to say the process is perfect. It cannot be, because the process relies on there being compensation for human greed: It requires myriad traders' searching out information no one else has— whether they obtain it by searching through the garbage disposed from corporate offices or by skimming through trade publications no one else reads. It relies on the traders' analyzing this information using their own complex models. It demands that they trade on the basis of their analysis, thus embedding their information in a small way into the market price. The price then reflects the collective information of the traders and all their analysis. It cannot, however, be too accurate because if prices did fully and instantaneously reveal all available information, the process could not work.[15] If an investor went to all the trouble of finding undervalued companies but could not buy shares without pushing the price up to true value, she would simply stop wasting her time. In practice, therefore, stock prices have to be moderately inaccurate—inaccurate enough for expert traders to make some profit. Nevertheless, in the long run, and on average, they are accurate enough from the perspective of most investors (and corporate managers). Those who think they can make extraordinary returns playing the market quickly discover this timeless truth.

Reducing Misappropriation

All the risk spreading effected by markets and the resources spent in improving the market's knowledge about the firm and its prospects are for naught if managers appropriate or waste all these earnings, leaving nothing for investors. So a third and important step in expanding access to finance is to ensure that the recipient of the financing uses the money well in creating value for investors.

OUTRIGHT DEFALCATION

In many countries, managers have no qualms about lining their pockets at the expense of the public shareholder. In Russia, for instance, oil companies trade at one-hundredth of what they would trade in the United States.[16] Such an enormous difference cannot be explained simply by differences in market liquidity or risk preferences of participants in the two markets. The only plausible explanation is that the market expects that Russian oil companies will be systematically looted by insiders. This is consistent with repeated accounts of oil being sold by these firms to middlemen controlled by insiders at a below-market price and then resold at market price.[17]

Unfortunately, this is not just a Russian phenomenon. Consider the sale of blocks of publicly traded shares large enough to transfer management control to the buying party.[18] The day after the transaction is announced, the market price of the company shares reflects what ordinary shareholders who do not have control over management expect to receive in the long run in dividends and capital appreciation. Any additional amount paid by the acquirers for the controlling block should then reflect some special benefits they expect to receive, which other shareholders will not. In the jargon, these are euphemistically termed "private benefits of control." They range from the psychic value the acquirer enjoys by being in power to the value they plan to appropriate for themselves at the expense of noncontrolling shareholders through actions like self-dealing (for example, selling oil at rock-bottom prices to a company they wholly own so that they can then resell the oil at market prices and obtain the full profit for themselves). In most developed countries, the estimated value of these private benefits in the period 1990–2000 is small (around 2 percent of their market value), but in a sizable number of countries, it exceeds 25 percent. For example, in Brazil, private benefits may be as large as 65 percent and in the Czech Republic, 58 percent.

The possibility of misappropriation can seriously jeopardize a firm's ability to obtain finance. In countries where private benefits are larger, equity markets are smaller, fewer companies go public, and ownership tends to be more concentrated.[19] With such concentrated holdings, risk cannot be spread widely, further reducing access.

How can a country escape this underdevelopment trap? One answer is better laws. Private benefits tend to be larger in countries where shareholders have fewer legal protections.[20] Of course, it is not just the laws on the books that matter: the quality of legal enforcement matters as well. Even if the courts are fair and efficient, it is costly for individual shareholders to move courts. The possibility of class-action lawsuits and contingency fees can give lawyers the incentive to seek out instances of corporate malfeasance and sue on behalf of shareholders, thus imposing some discipline on managers.

An important role is also played by tax enforcement agencies. The corporate income tax effectively gives the government a large, noncontrolling stake in all companies. Its incentives are perfectly aligned with those of minority shareholders: both want the company to disclose and distribute profits. But the government has a big advantage: it has better enforcement tools and has a large enough stake in each firm to care. For example, the Internal Revenue Service closely scrutinizes the prices at which goods are transferred between related firms to make sure that income is not being transferred to a low-tax entity. Such scrutiny can also help prevent self-dealing, whereby management transfers goods from the public company it runs to a private company it fully owns. The tax authority therefore helps keep management malfeasance in check. The estimated private benefits in a country are indeed lower when it has better tax enforcement.[21]

Of course, corporations themselves have an incentive to put in place strong controls on their management so that their access to finance will improve. A corporation can bind its management with a corporate charter or code of conduct that prohibits share issuances below market price or restricts asset transfers to other firms. Such internally imposed rules go a long way in addressing the undervaluation of Russian companies. The Russian company with the best corporate governance practices (including being cross-listed in the United States) has a ratio of actual market value to potential market value (its value if it were a U.S. company) 450 times higher than one with the worst practices.[22]

WASTE

Better laws and judicial enforcement make outright theft harder but do not prevent waste or incompetence. These cannot be stopped by legal means without risking corporate paralysis. Since investments are intrinsically risky, a system that allows a manager to be sued every time she makes a mistake will ensure that no manager will ever make a risky decision. U.S. jurisprudence recognizes this problem and has adopted what it terms the "business judgment rule." This rule keeps a court from second-guessing any managerial decision provided it follows the processes set down by law and is not tainted by possible conflicts of interest. Thus, as far as the law is concerned, managers cannot steal, but they can waste resources at will provided they do so following due process.

The problem is particularly acute for mature firms. Because of their size and past successes, mature firms face limited competition. They also generate tremendous amounts of cash and, with limited legitimate investment prospects in their existing businesses, have no need for new financing. They have what Michael Jensen, professor emeritus of Harvard Business School, calls the "free cash flow problem": too much cash on their hands.[23] Instead of paying it back to investors, management may waste it on pet projects, plush offices, executive jets, or charitable donations that enhance their status more than the company's image. When waste is unchecked, tremendous value can be destroyed since mature firms typically have sizable resources to run down.

For example, alarm bells should start ringing in investors' minds when a firm spends immense sums making an architectural statement with a new building. This often reflects the fact that the firm has little better to do with its money than waste it and that the chief executive officer has little better to do with his time than build a mausoleum to himself. Examples of this kind of phenomenon are legion. Phillipe Kahn of Borland International started building a $100 million headquarters—complete with a full-size basketball court, pool, and two tennis courts—in 1992.[24] Almost to the year, the building of the new headquarters marked the beginning of Borland's eclipse from the front ranks of software makers.

It is useful to see a more detailed example of how a mature company can suddenly find itself destroying value as the changing environment makes its strategy obsolete. Consider the case of Beatrice, a U.S. conglomerate.[25] Started in 1891 as a food distributor, by 1940 it became one of the largest dairy product firms in the country. Between 1940 and 1976, Beatrice grew through the purchase of other food businesses. During this period, Beatrice's skill was to pick targets—typically family-run businesses—that could benefit from Beatrice's ability to raise financing and its professional management techniques. Until the late 1970s, this approach seemed to work well: Beatrice's shareholders obtained a healthy 14 percent annual return over a twenty-five-year period.

In the first half of the 1980s, however, Beatrice became the classic example of a company whose core strategy had become obsolete. Finance was increasingly widely available to the family-owned firms that had been Beatrice's traditional target. These kinds of firms did not need Beatrice's deep financial pockets as much as in the past. Moreover, once Beatrice's financial control over its divisions started slipping because of the wide availability of finance, it had to reassert control by introducing more layers of supervisory management and giving up its old decentralized approach. Finally, in order to help headquarters add some value to the divisions, marketing was centralized and marketing budgets increased.

Beatrice management did everything but recognize the handwriting on the wall. It undertook new, expensive acquisitions—in particular, that of the Coca-Cola Bottling Division of Northwest Industries for over twenty-two times earnings. Beatrice's stock price fell by 7.1 percent on the announcement of this acquisition. The drop infuriated stockholders, who had been expecting money to be returned to them via a stock repurchase. The response of the then CEO James Dutt was, "You buy back your stock when you don't have better use for your money."[26] He was right, except he did not recognize that Beatrice had no better use for its money!

Instead, the firm wasted money on all the things management does when it runs out of investment ideas. Management moved to larger and more luxurious buildings and increased the size of central staff, from 161 in 1976 to 750 by 1985. It "reengineered" the organization every year. It changed its name and embarked on a corporate awareness campaign that seemed primarily targeted at glorifying CEO Dutt. Particularly egregious was the sponsorship of two auto-racing teams, which led to the expenditure of more than $70 million over a number of years. Apart from Dutt's enthusiasm for the sport and his hobby of collecting

automobiles, there seemed little connection between Beatrice and racing. The only subsidiary remotely related to automobile racing was
worth just $97 million and slated to be sold.

Between 1976 and 1985, an estimated $2 billion in Beatrice's value
was destroyed. Responding to the abysmal stock price performance and
a revolt from middle management, the board finally fired Dutt in 1985.
He had one of the saddest epitaphs a CEO can have: Beatrice's stock
price rose 6 percent on the news of his firing!

Beatrice is not an exception. Consider what managements do when
they receive the corporate equivalent of manna from heaven—when
they win a lawsuit where the judgment mandates a cash payment to the
winner and has no other effect on the firm's business opportunities.[27]
An example of such a windfall is the one Pennzoil obtained from Texaco
in 1988. Pennzoil had an agreement to merge with Getty. Texaco inter-
fered with this process, got sued, and when the dust settled after all the
litigation and appeals, Pennzoil obtained $2.3 billion in compensation.

What did Pennzoil do with the money? Pennzoil paid about 5 percent
of the award as an increased dividend to shareholders over the next
three years after receiving the award. But it also reduced share repur-
chases (a way for the firm to pay shareholders that, except for tax con-
siderations, is equivalent to dividends) by about 32 percent of the award
amount over this period. Perhaps Pennzoil had been repurchasing
shares earlier in anticipation of the award. Be that as it may, the net payout to shareholders fell by 27 percent of the award amount! Far from
paying more to shareholders, Pennzoil actually reduced what they got!

But Pennzoil managers did not seem to suffer with their shareholders. They started on an acquisition spree, only to divest the major new
line of business they had acquired just two years later, and at high cost.
According to an estimate, "Pennzoil . . . destroyed 2 to 4 billion dollars
of value relative to a more passive investment strategy in the three years
after the award."[28] Interestingly, as the payment from Texaco to Pennzoil
became more and more certain as a result of the litigation, the combined market value of the two firms declined. The market correctly
anticipated that Pennzoil managers would be like children who chance
on a hundred-dollar bill near a candy shop: shareholders (and the children's anxious parents) would have been better off if their managers had
never got the money.

Despite this terrible performance, managers also paid themselves more. Pennzoil's president had retired a year before the award, but the company brought him back and delayed the retirement of two other senior executives. These three retired soon after the award, collecting over $20 million!

The conclusion from an exhaustive study of such cases is that "an evaluation of the investment and diversification strategies of these firms suggested that the median firm does not use the award to create value."[29] Too much cash is a real problem!

Anticipating that cash will be wasted when a company matures, investors will be reluctant to fund young firms. Therefore, a developed financial market has to find ways of mitigating the free cash flow problem. The most controversial (at least in the public perception) is a corporate takeover.

A free market for corporate takeovers is one way that the inefficient parts of a diseased corporation can be destroyed and the profitable parts given a new lease on life. In theory, it works as follows. As the stock market becomes aware that a firm is not being managed well, its share price declines. The more it declines, the more profitable it is for someone to buy shares, obtain control of the company, and restructure it. Restructuring usually begins with a change of management and its policies and eventually leads to the closing of some loss-making units and the selling of others to those who can manage them better. By the end of it all, a bloated, overweight firm becomes a nimble competitor. This is, in fact, what happened to Beatrice.

Within two months of Dutt's departure, the firm was sold to a management group allied with the leveraged-buyout partnership of Kohlberg, Kravis, and Roberts (KKR). The offer made by the buyout group to shareholders just about compensated for the value that had been destroyed by previous management. Much of the offer was financed through a mixture of bank and low-rated debt, so that Beatrice emerged with 85 percent of its capital structure as debt. There was no way this debt could be paid off without Beatrice's cutting unnecessary expenditures, selling assets, and breaking itself up. But this was precisely the objective. The unwieldy mix of assets that had been assembled under Beatrice's roof was now to be broken up and returned to more capable owners. In the process, the nearly hundred-year-old firm would disappear.

While it may seem sad that a firm with such a tradition vanished, this was almost inevitable given the changed environment. The buyout only speeded up the inevitable. If Beatrice had held together, the dysfunctional conglomerate would have slowly bled to death, taking all its parts with it to the grave. With the breakup, at least most parts of the firm survived, albeit under different owners.

Some employees, certainly those at headquarters, did lose jobs. But other workers benefited because they had the opportunity to create more value and earn more, unfettered by inept management. And yet others benefited because they got the opportunity to run a business well. Reginald Lewis became the first African-American CEO of a *Fortune* 500 company when he obtained financing to buy a piece of Beatrice.

Changes in corporate control effected through takeovers or management buyouts are yet another example of the gap between public perception and the reality of finance. Few arouse as much indignation as corporate raiders such as T. Boone Pickens, who made hostile bids for a number of oil companies in the 1980s. Their creed, immortalized by Gordon Gekko in the movie *Wall Street,* is supposedly "Greed is good." They are often portrayed as vultures, profiting by destroying stable managements, laying off employees who have given their lives to the firm, and exploiting those who stay by paying them miserable salaries. In truth, as Jerry Sterner says in the popular play and movie *Other People's Money,* their role is similar to that of undertakers, a loathsome profession to some but absolutely crucial to a well-functioning society. An economy cannot be vibrant unless resources are taken from dying sectors and redeployed in sunrise ones. It is this process that corporate raiders speed up. To see why this is important, one only has to look at Japan, where sick firms and banks have sapped, and continue to sap, the strength of healthy ones as the economy attempts to share pain collectively.

Corporate takeovers are only one, and not necessarily the most effective, way to address corporate waste. Institutional investors who own large stakes in companies can also pressure the management. Higher institutional ownership does seem to be associated with higher company value.[30] On average, a 1 percent increase in institutional ownership in the United States translates to a 0.6 percent higher market value (as a percentage of book value) or $125 million more in value for an average-sized firm. Of course, it may be that institutional investors simply choose to invest in more valuable companies and have no direct effect on firm value. There are ways of ruling this explanation out. When a company is included in the S&P 500 index, many mutual funds simply replicate the index and invest in the company. The higher institutional ownership in these "index" companies does not reflect the value judgment of institutional investors but simply the application of a mechanical rule. Even institutional ownership driven by such mechanical considerations has a positive effect on firm value.

More evidence that institutional ownership is beneficial comes from examining the consequences of regulatory change.[31] Before 1992, if ten or more investors in the United States wanted to discuss the performance of a particular company, they had to file a report with the Securities and Exchange Commission, detailing the purpose of, and participants in, the discussion. These requirements made it onerous for institutional investors to coordinate their actions. In 1992, this rule was done away with. The relationship between institutional shareholdings and firm value is twice as large after 1992 as before, consistent with the idea that institutional investors force companies to be better managed. That institutional investors help reduce waste in companies flush with cash is bolstered by the finding that the relationship between institutional shareholding and firm value is especially strong in firms that generate more free cash flow.

For mature firms, therefore, financiers play the role of policemen and undertakers, preventing the theft of resources and burying the dead. In other instances, however, they play the more creative role of midwife. Young firms need a very different kind of assistance than established, mature firms. Young firms have tremendous growth opportunities, and in an economy with good laws and decent accounting, most managers of young firms have the incentive to succeed (rather than steal or waste investors' money). Top management runs the company in trust, not just for shareholders but also for junior management, which expects to succeed top management. The rewards for a growing firm come not from misappropriating current free cash, which is meager, but from the prospect of running a larger, more profitable firm. So managers can be relied upon to keep obvious wrongdoing by other members of the management team in check.[32] The reason management needs close monitoring is that management may be inexperienced and headstrong and may unwittingly do the wrong thing.

Consider how venture capitalists (VCs) help inexperienced management, as gleaned from venture capitalists' internal memos, written at the time an investment is decided. After investing, U.S. venture capitalists typically expect to play an active advisory role in about 50 percent of their clients. For approximately 14 percent of their clients, they intervene even before investing.[33]

It would hurt the management's sense of initiative if a venture capitalist shadowed its every move. Consequently, venture capitalists, in general, monitor lightly. However, the intensity of VC monitoring increases when performance deteriorates, leading to more direct involvement in the company's management. In biotech start-ups, venture capitalists replace a start-up's chief executive officer in 18 percent of the cases and increase the presence of VC-backed directors after the officer leaves.[34] VC monitoring is so intense that being physically too distant is a problem. So the decision to finance a deal is influenced by whether the VC is geographically close. Over half of the VC-backed firms have on their board a venture capitalist with an office within sixty miles of their headquarters, and 25 percent have a VC within seven miles.[35]

The benefits of monitoring are augmented if the monitor has the power to intervene when she identifies a problem. For this reason, the right contract should provide investors not only with the right incentives to monitor but also with the power to intervene whenever needed. Venture capitalists insert many contingencies in their financing contract. For example, the contract may have a clause requiring the firm to accomplish a certain goal, such as generating positive cash flows, by a certain date. These are meant to be financial trip wires. Their purpose is not to trigger default but to provide the financier with a warning that some intervention may need to take place at that particular moment. The contract may also give the financier greater rights in decision making or a greater share in the firm's cash flows if the goal is not met on time. If appropriately designed, these contracts give entrepreneurs powerful incentives to perform and give the venture capitalist some ability to intervene when matters deteriorate.[36]

Given the great uncertainty surrounding start-ups, however, contingencies may be insufficient to provide the VC with the ability to intervene whenever needed. This is why most VC firms also use another instrument to control their investments: the staging of funds. Rather than providing a start-up with all the funds needed to develop its product, the typical VC funds a project for just a year. After that, the entrepreneur has to go back and ask for new money. Staging therefore assigns to the original VC a de facto right to terminate a company once a year. Between financing rounds, the lead venture capitalist visits the entrepreneur once a month on average and spends four to five hours at the facility during each visit.[37]

All these forms of direct monitoring, however, are very expensive. The minimum return venture capitalists need from a successful project for it to be worth investing in is around 50 percent. While this required return reflects, in part, the high probability of failure of start-ups (out of four companies, one fails, two do moderately well, and only one is successful enough to go public), it cannot be justified on that basis alone. A large part of the justification for such a high return is compensation for the time and effort spent monitoring and advising a company. Financiers in developed systems do earn their pay.

Summary

In the first chapter, we illustrated the obstacles in the way of expanding access to finance and the consequences on everyday life when access is limited to those with collateral and connections. In this chapter, we have shown how these obstacles can be overcome. What is especially noteworthy is the extensive infrastructure that makes expanded access possible, ranging from academics who resolve knotty financial problems to investment bankers who find creative ways of allocating risk, from credit-reporting agencies that make credit histories widely available to experienced courts that know how to enforce complex financial contracts.

With this infrastructure in place, financiers can move away from lending only against collateral or on the basis of prior contacts to financing on a truly arm's-length basis. This is not to say that there will be no role for collateral or contacts, but there will be substantial quantities of financing available even without them. Financing will rely much more on spreading risk widely, making use of publicly available credit histories and real-time information on borrower performance, and on designing financial contracts to provide the right incentives.

In the last thirty years, dramatic changes in financial systems around the world amounting, de facto, to a revolution have brought many of the advances described in this chapter to us. We have come closer to the utopia of finance for all. In the next chapter, we describe the magnitude of the changes, which will explain why we think of this as a revolution. We then examine some of the steps that made this financial revolution possible and explore how expanded access has changed our lives, giving us more economic freedom than ever before.

CHAPTER THREE

The Financial Revolution and Individual Economic Freedom

A VERITABLE REVOLUTION has taken place in finance throughout much of the developed world in the last three decades. In 1970, the ratio of the value of all listed U.S. stocks to GDP was 0.66; by the year 2000, it had climbed to 1.5.[1] The increase in other countries is even more dramatic. In France, stock market capitalization rose from just 0.16 of GDP in 1970 to 1.1 times GDP in the year 2000.[2] Despite the recent fall in stock prices, markets today are many times larger relative to the economy than they were a few decades ago. The explosion in the size of stock markets is just one indication of what has happened. Entire new markets such as NASDAQ have emerged catering specifically to young firms. Institutions such as money market funds did not exist in the early 1970s. Now they hold over $2 trillion in assets in the United States. A large number of financial derivatives that are commonplace today, such as index options or interest rate swaps, had not yet been invented three decades ago. The turnover in the trading of such derivative instruments was $163 *trillion* in the fourth quarter of 2001, about 16 times the annual gross domestic product of the United States.[3]

In the same way as corporations have obtained new instruments with which to raise finance and allocate risks, individuals also now have expanded choices. Revolving consumer credit such as credit card debt has exploded from near nothing in the United States in the late 1960s to nearly $700 billion in late 2001.[4] Firms and individuals can borrow not just from domestic institutions but also from foreign markets and institutions. Gross cross-border capital flows as a fraction of GDP have increased nearly tenfold in developed countries since 1970 and more than fivefold for developing countries. In the decade of the

1990s alone, these flows more than quadrupled for developed countries.[5]

We explain later in the book why the financial revolution took place when it did. For now, let us focus on the process by which it came about. There was no single magic action that led to this explosion. Instead, there were many interconnected processes at work. Let us examine some of these, then see what the consequences of expanding access to finance have been on daily life.

Financial Development

The foundations for today's vibrant financial system in the United States were laid in the 1930s. That was a time when many countries decided to curtail financial markets and replace them with government control. There was such an undercurrent even in the United States— and we dwell on these issues later in the book—but it came up against a tradition in American political thought that has always retained a healthy skepticism about the possibility of fixing problems by legislative fiat. In a letter in 1922, Justice Brandeis wrote:

> Do not believe that you can find a universal remedy for evil conditions or immoral practices in effecting a fundamental change in society (as by State Socialism). And do not pin too much faith in legislation. Remedial institutions are apt to fall under control of the enemy and to become instruments of oppression.[6]

Instead, his proposed alternative was what we would now call transparency, which he referred to as publicity.

> Publicity is justly commended as a remedy for social and industrial diseases. Sunlight is said to be the best of disinfectants; electric light the most efficient policemen.[7]

This philosophy permeated the "New Deal" financial legislation that was rushed through Congress in 1933 and 1934, soon after Franklin Roosevelt became president. In fact, Roosevelt's speeches often paraphrased the above quote from Brandeis.[8] Some of the New Deal legislation was politically, rather than economically, motivated, and not all of it, especially not the banking legislation, promoted competition.[9] But the legislation gave the U.S. financial system the accounting, regulatory, and legal foundation on which to build. When the shackles were finally taken off finance in the early 1970s, a truly vibrant financial sector emerged.

In this process of financial development, deregulation, competition, and innovation—both in academia and outside—fed on one another in a way that is impossible to disentangle. Consider first a case in which academia influenced the process of deregulation, which then led to financial innovation.

DIVERSIFICATION AND THE EMERGENCE OF THE PRIVATE EQUITY MARKET

Harry Markowitz's work, described in the previous chapter, showed that a well-diversified investor may be able to tolerate a risky investment when it is held in a portfolio even if he would not be willing to hold it if that were his only investment. This idea seems obvious today, in part because Markowitz's message has so completely permeated the investment industry. (Markowitz also provided the less-obvious mathematics to calculate diversified portfolios that would offer the lowest risk for a given return.) Eventually, these advances changed the way the investment industry was regulated.

Consider the so-called prudent man rule. This rule describes what are considered reasonable investments for pension fund managers. Over time, it has become the standard of behavior to which fund managers adhere. Until 1979, the prudent man rule was interpreted as preventing any significant investment in assets considered risky. Even stocks of companies that did not pay dividends, typical of most stocks today, were considered too risky then! In 1979, the U.S. Department of Labor finally clarified the concept of prudence: risky investments were deemed legitimate if they were part of a well-diversified portfolio strategy.

As a result of this decision, pension funds and large endowments were able to start investing in riskier intermediaries such as venture capital funds (which finance start-up companies), buyout funds (which finance the acquisition of existing companies), and "vulture" funds (which buy debt of financially distressed firms while hoping to profit from their restructuring). This new market, called the private equity market, emerged and grew with breathtaking speed. While in 1980 the U.S. private equity market accounted for only $5 billion in investment, in 1999, it was over $175 billion. This is roughly equal to the total amount of investment made annually by a country like Italy, the fifth-biggest economy in the world.[10]

The financial intermediaries that the private equity market funded broadened access in all kinds of ways. Unlike relatively passive institutional investors like mutual funds, we have seen that venture capitalists are more hands-on and are more nurturing toward the young companies they fund. In 2000, venture capitalists channeled more than $100 billion into 5,608 new companies.[11] In 2001, even after the collapse of euphoria about the Internet, 3,244 companies obtained more than $38 billion in venture capital finance. Only ten years earlier, the total amount financed was just $3 billion spread over 1,143 companies.

The private equity market also funded buyout funds, which, through breakup takeovers of companies like Beatrice, have been key to the changes in corporate governance that have taken place in the last two decades. Buyout funds also buy small private companies, making it easier for entrepreneurs to exit their investment at a reasonable price, thus facilitating a better match between these companies and new entrepreneurial talent (recall the search fund, discussed in the introduction).

Finally, the private equity market gave rise to vulture funds. Their name, though curious, is apt. In the same way as vultures dispose of corpses and keep the environment clean, vulture funds search for corporate carrion—buying companies on the verge of bankruptcy—and help to clean them up by divesting what is redundant and straightening out what is worth keeping. In doing so, they prevent these firms from wasting their investors' money. This then improves the access these firms have to funds early on in their lives, as investors lend, confident that the company, if troubled, will not be able to destroy their investment completely. In sum, the explosive growth of the private equity market broadened access to funds not only directly but also indirectly, enhancing the overall efficiency of the financial system.

Not only did the clarification of the prudent man rule make more risk capital available, but the ways in which the capital could be deployed were also multiplied by innovations that stemmed from the better understanding of risk. Consider one example: junk bonds. Having studied finance at the University of Pennsylvania's Wharton School, Michael Milken, an upstart investment banker working for a third-tier investment house, was convinced that the rating agencies were overly cautious in handing out ratings to companies. They focused on a firm's track record and the cushion of physical assets it had, ignoring the talent its management possessed and its likely future prospects.[12] He felt that low-rated bonds, unflatteringly labeled "junk" bonds, were much less risky than people thought, especially if held in a diversified portfolio (he did study Markowitz!). According to Milken, their high yield more than compensated for any additional riskiness. He then started selling this message to institutional investors.

While there is some controversy about whether Milken was actually right about the profitability and riskiness of these bonds, what cannot be disputed is his success in creating a liquid market for these instruments. In a matter of a few years, issues of junk bonds went from $1 billion to more than $30 billion.[13]

Some financial instruments may appear very risky a priori, and apprehensions about their risk may indeed be justified. But if sufficient investors become interested in them, liquidity in the instrument increases, and more resources are devoted to understanding and laying off its risks. As a result, the instrument may eventually turn out to be quite attractive and safe. This is what happened with junk bonds. After an initial setback, the junk bond market survived both the incarceration of Michael Milken and the demise of the investment bank for which he worked. By early 2002, outstanding junk bonds exceeded $650 billion.[14]

Junk bonds play a major role in financing young, medium-sized firms. These firms are too small or have too few hard assets to be able to issue highly rated public debt and are too large or too risky to borrow from their local banks. Moreover, they typically have not established connections with large banks. Junk bond financing tides them over till such time as they become more acceptable to large financial institutions or to the equity market. Junk bonds are an example of how an improvement in the financial sector's understanding of risk and return can allow individuals and firms to escape the tyranny of collateral and connections.

Junk bonds also help improve corporate governance. A market for corporate control, as we saw in the last chapter, helps reallocate corporate assets to their best use and helps discipline lazy or incompetent management by taking away its control. But bad management is unlikely to depart willingly. And first-tier commercial and investment banks are usually reluctant to upset their blue-chip clients by financing raids on them. This is where junk bonds come in. Because investors in junk bonds have no relationships to protect, they are willing to finance anyone who looks reasonably creditworthy. During the takeover boom of the late 1980s, less-established challengers obtained financing in the junk bond market to undertake "hostile" takeovers (takeovers opposed by incumbent management) of large blue-chip corporations like Beatrice, Revlon, Singer, and RJR Nabisco. Once they realized that size did not buy protection from takeovers, established managements started paying more attention to improving efficiency and creating shareholder value. In turn, this drew more investors to the stock markets. Finance became more available.

THE COST OF TRADING AND THE GROWTH OF THE MARKETS FOR DERIVATIVES

We have just seen a situation in which academia laid the groundwork for deregulation and financial innovation. Consider now the elimination of fixed commissions on the New York Stock Exchange, where deregulation created an atmosphere in which the ideas of academia could be implemented and financial innovation could flourish. Before Congress mandated that the practice of fixed commissions end by May 1, 1975, exchange members were not allowed to offer quantity discounts to their clients. If a brokerage firm received an order to buy 100 shares at $40 per share, it received a commission mandated by the exchange of $39. If the order was for 100,000 shares, the commission rate remained proportionately the same—that is, $39,000. Since buying 100,000 shares was only slightly more labor-intensive than buying 100 shares, there were huge profit margins for the brokerage houses built into large orders.

Before fixed commissions were eliminated, large financial institutions such as mutual funds and pension funds were doubly disadvantaged relative to individual investors. Not only did they not pay lower commissions, but since they had to trade large amounts, they also obtained unfavorable prices.[15] Once fixed commissions were eliminated, large financial institutions had a very low cost of trading. This had a number of knock-on effects.

The first was the growth of the market for derivatives. We have seen how financial derivatives like the guarantee Bankers Trust wrote for the employees of Rhone-Poulenc help investors obtain fixed minimum returns. They also help firms and farmers reduce risk by enabling them to lock in the prices of essential inputs or key outputs. Key to a financial institution's selling such an instrument is its ability to hedge away the risk in the instrument. While academia in the early 1970s had explained how derivatives could be hedged exactly with a series of trades in financial markets, fixed commissions made such trades prohibitively expensive. With the elimination of fixed commissions, however, financial institutions like commercial banks could offer derivatives fairly cheaply, and the use of derivatives to lay off risk grew exponentially, as did entirely new areas of financial activity, such as risk management and financial engineering.[16]

The second effect was the institutionalization of stock ownership. As we saw in the last chapter, large institutional investors have a large enough stake in each company to find it worthwhile to analyze the companies they hold very carefully and to call up management if anything troubles them. They also can organize together more easily to force management's hand. With the elimination of fixed commissions, it made much more sense for individuals to invest their money passively in large funds and allow the funds to manage it on their behalf. From 1980 to 2000, the fraction of public equity owned by institutional investors in the United States went from below 30 percent to over 60 percent, while the fraction owned by individuals declined in tandem.[17] The number of mutual funds increased from 564 in 1980 to 8,171 in 2000.[18] There are now more mutual funds in existence in the United States than there are domestic companies listed on U.S. stock exchanges!

As institutional investors with larger stakes took over from individual investors, and as raiders obtained easier financing, the power of investors vis-à-vis company management has grown. The official statements of the Business Roundtable, an association of chief executive officers of leading U.S. corporations aimed at promoting the CEOs' policy perspective, provide a good indicator of the radical shift in the balance of power. Until the mid-1990s, the Business Roundtable consistently opposed any substantial change in corporate governance practices, defending the right of CEOs to resist takeovers, even those that greatly increased value for shareholders. In 1997, it changed its position and declared, "the paramount duty of management and the board is to the shareholder and not . . . to other stakeholders."[19]

Because governance has improved, firms have been paying more attention to the utilization of the funds they generate from operations. These so-called internal funds were traditionally thought to be free by corporations. Corporations only factored in the cost of money actually raised from outside in evaluating investment decisions, placing a very low cost on internally generated funds. But internal funds can be paid back to shareholders, so they should not be thought of as "free cash flow." The pressure from hostile takeovers during the 1980s and from institutional investors during the 1990s changed practice. Now most companies do factor in the cost of internal capital in evaluating managers, as evidenced by the popularity of measures of managerial performance like economic value added (which subtracts a cost for the capital a manager uses from the profits she generates, thus forcing her to face up to the cost of even investments made out of internal cash flow). The consequence of this newfound awareness has been a substantial increase in the average rate of return on corporate assets. While in 1980 it had dropped as low as 5.7 percent, by 1996, it was a healthy 9.9 percent.[20]

As governance improves, and managers begin to work in their investors' interests, everyone benefits. Resources are not wasted. Investors become more confident that they will get a return and become more willing to entrust managers, even those they know less well, with funds. Access to finance expands.

We have described only some of the ways that the revolution in finance has expanded access. There is much that this sketch has left out—for example, how individuals now have much greater choice in managing their finances than ever before. We do not have the space to describe how this came about. Suffice it to say that forces similar to those we described above have played a part: they include advances in academia, the increasing ability of financial institutions to price a variety of exotic instruments and to assess and spread their risks, the greater availability of timely and accurate data on potential customers, greater competition leading to better prices in financial markets, a variety of more appropriate new institutions as a result of deregulation, courts that are more conversant with finance and enforce contracts speedily and predictably, regulators who are more skilled and informed (but who nevertheless still lag behind the complexity of the market) . . .

We could go on and on about the changes in finance. But at the same time as the revolution in finance was taking place, there were other major changes in developed economies. We think two are particularly important: the increases in competition and the spread of new technologies. The greater availability of finance has been critical to these developments, and in turn, competition and technological progress prompted a change in the political mind-set leading to other changes such as deregulation. All this has fundamentally altered the nature of the interaction between the capitalist and her employee. That is what we turn to now.

The Breakup of Vertically Integrated Firms

Vertically integrated firms dominated capital-intensive industries in the second industrial revolution. They commanded profits because their assets, brand names, or even government charters gave them a strong position in domestic industry, a position made impregnable because access to finance was limited. Despite antitrust legislation passed to combat these behemoths, industry became increasingly concentrated right up to the 1970s, for reasons we examine later in the book.[21] Some countries nationalized these firms, but this merely changed the identity of the monopolist owner without changing the behavior of these firms.

The cozy cocoon that enveloped these firms was shredded by a number of forces starting in the 1970s. It is hard to be precise about what came first and how the increased access to finance strengthened and interacted with these forces, but here is a quick interpretation of what happened.

INCREASE IN COMPETITION

Cross-border trade expanded market size tremendously. The volume of trade (exports plus imports) to gross domestic product in the United States went up from just 8 percent of GDP in 1950 to 11 percent in 1970 to over 26 percent in 2000.[22] The expansion in foreign trade was not confined to the United States but took place in most developed countries. Firms that were once oligopolists with a first-mover advantage in their own small domestic markets now had to fight it out in a larger, competitive world market.

As markets became more open, vertically integrated firms faced competition from foreign firms that were often differently organized. This created niches where small intermediate-goods manufacturers could enter. For example, in the late 1980s, General Motors employed 750,000 workers to make 8 million cars, while Toyota employed only 65,000 workers to produce more than 4.5 million cars. While Toyota was certainly more efficient, the extraordinary difference in workers per car is because General Motors was much more vertically integrated. Toyota, by contrast, had a tradition of outsourcing at the intermediate level. When firms like Toyota started manufacturing in the United States, they developed a few independent local (U.S.) suppliers for their U.S. factories. The suppliers were willing to make large investments because the Japanese firms had a reputation for fair treatment of suppliers in Japan. The production of intermediate goods became a viable proposition.

Competition also highlighted the inefficient parts of the integrated firm's value chain and created internal pressure for change. When only vertically integrated firms competed, it was hard for any single unit of a firm to know how it was doing. As intermediate-goods producers started flourishing, internal units in the vertically integrated firm could now benchmark their performance against the outside. Profitable units in the vertically integrated firm became aware of the bottlenecks created by poorly performing units. The vertically integrated firm that did not produce at the optimum level at each stage faced much stiffer competition from less-integrated competitors, which could buy from the best. The need for efficiency throughout the firm gave good performers the incentive to push for outsourcing products that were previously made by inefficient internal units. Some managers of profitable units sought complete independence, proposing management buyouts whereby they would pay their parent firm to be set free. They would no longer have to be charitable corporate citizens, moving at the pace of the worst-performing unit and providing it constantly with subsidies. The vertically integrated firm was being deconstructed from the inside.

Finally, competition eroded some of the advantages the vertically integrated corporation had. The routines the large corporation had acquired were very effective in stable environments in which the emphasis was on reducing the cost of large-scale production (as Henry Ford is famously reported to have said, "People can have the Model T in any color they want so long as it is black"). But as competition forced companies to constantly find new consumer needs and ways of exploiting them, adaptability and flexibility became important. Large, typically bureaucratic organizations were at a disadvantage in handling rapid change.[23]

TECHNOLOGY AND SCALE

Technological change also contributed to the pressures on the vertically integrated corporation. In the 1960s and 1970s, new technologies of manufacturing—such as the use of computer numerically controlled machines, robots, and flexible manufacturing systems—were developed.[24] Because these technologies were flexible, intermediate-goods manufacturers did not have to be locked in to large production runs for a single customer. Independence became less hazardous. Moreover, flexible production systems require fewer machines to accomplish a given set of tasks. Studies show that the average size of plants in industries adopting flexible manufacturing technologies fell faster than in other industries.[25] The reduced scale of even intermediate-goods production further reduced the barriers to creating and financing such ventures.

Improvements in information technology reduced the costs of exchanging information with entities outside the firm. With product specifications becoming easier to transmit, and bids becoming easier to collect and adjudicate, the costs of transacting with outsiders fell. While the cost of communicating within firms fell at the same time, allowing the efficient size of the firm to expand, studies show that the use of information technology in the manufacturing sector has tended, on net, to be associated with smaller average firm size.[26]

Technology is also making redundant certain assets that hitherto had given incumbent firms a comparative advantage. Consider the recent history of the record companies.[27] In early 2000, there were four major firms in the record industry. Among them, they accounted for 80 percent of sales. This is down from six large firms as recently as 1998. The increasing concentration of the industry is, paradoxically, not a result of growing scale economies. In responding to a question about whether the merger of Time Warner and EMI's record business was tightening the merged firm's control over the industry, the president of Time Warner said, "The ability to control is gradually being eroded by the diminishing barriers to getting into this business."[28] Of course, given the concerns of antitrust authorities, it would have been hard for him to agree with the premise of the question, but there may well be truth in the statement.

To see why, consider the primary functions of a record company. They are to find music artists, make tapes or CDs, distribute them, and market them. Historically, small firms found the artists but then passed them on to the majors when the artists became successful, since the majors enjoyed scale economies in the other three functions. The Internet, however, has changed matters. The record company no longer has to manufacture tapes and CDs and then distribute them through thousands of retail outlets. Instead, it only has to store the music on its Web site and allow it to be downloaded on payment of a fee. This completely changes the functions of production and distribution and makes scale economies irrelevant. As for the last function, that of marketing, the Internet label can target people interested in its brand of music through E-mail and the Internet much more cost-effectively than can a major through bricks-and-mortar retail stores. As the chairman of Warner Music put it, "The role of traditional distribution is clearly going to decline. And if there was anything the record companies had, it was a distribution network."[29]

Of course, as with every fear or hope associated with the Internet, there may be an element of hyperbole in the last statement. The general point, however, is the following: Large firms hitherto had the advantage that they serviced a large market and therefore could use very specialized resources profitably. As flexible modern technology allows small firms to replicate the specialized resources of incumbent large firms (for example, the distribution system) at low cost, a key source of comparative advantage for the large firms evaporates. Technology thus contributes to leveling the playing field between the entrenched large and the upstart small.

INCREASED WORKER MOBILITY

The rise in cross-border and domestic competition, the emergence of technologies favoring small firms, and the increased access to finance have completely changed employment dynamics in firms. The skilled manager or worker of yesteryear was trapped in his firm. He had few outside opportunities. The closest alternative was another integrated firm, which typically had a different culture, different standards, and a different, specialized technology. Now, as more suppliers of intermediate goods flourish, firms that continue to be integrated have had to restructure their processes so as to be able to use outside suppliers whenever advantageous. As processes have become more similar across firms, the opportunities for managers to move have increased. At the same time, as production technologies have become more flexible, skills have become more portable because the same technology is used in very diverse firms.

In the United States today, the average worker has had nine jobs between the ages of eighteen and thirty-four.[30] While some of these jobs are meant to be temporary and reflect the transience of youth, even between the ages of thirty and thirty-four, the average worker holds 2.4 jobs. To be able to attribute this mobility to the changes we have described, however, we want to know whether workers had lower mobility in the past (leaving aside our impression that our fathers had only one job). In fact, there is little evidence of an overall increase in the fraction of employees with tenure of less than one year, at least over the period 1973 to 1996. But there does seem to be an increase in the fraction of workers with less than ten years' tenure, especially among workers over age forty, and especially in the 1990s.[31] In other words, job mobility has increased for those whom one might think are most specialized and who used to be most locked in to their employer in the past.

Access to finance has also increased the opportunities of managers and skilled workers by enabling them to start their own business. The ideas, experience, and coworkers they carry from their old firms can be invaluable seed resources.[32] Not having to start from scratch is indeed a benefit: Intel—one of the most innovative and profitable firms of our time—was started in 1968 by Gordon Moore and Robert Noyce and a number of subordinates because they felt their employer, Fairchild Semiconductors, was ignoring important new technologies.[33] It took Noyce just one phone call to raise the money, and by 1971, the company went public, well on its way to the nearly $200 billion in market capitalization it has as of the time of this writing. Intel is not an exception. Approximately 71 percent of the firms included in the U.S. Inc 500 (a list of young, fast-growing firms) were founded by people who replicated or modified an idea encountered in their previous job.[34]

These trends toward entrepreneurship are also seen in the wider population. Between 1974 and 1996, the number of business owners as a fraction of total nonagricultural employment in the United States reversed a century-long decline. It went up from 8.2 percent to 11.4 percent, a striking increase of almost 38 percent![35] The increase can be seen for both men and women and in a number of other developed countries also.

THE SHRINKING FIRM

Increased competition, changes in technology, and widespread access to finance have reduced the advantages of the large, vertically integrated firm. We should therefore expect the largest firms to have shrunk. This is indeed the case. The share of the *Fortune* 500 firms (the largest firms in the United States) in total workers employed in manufacturing fell from 79 percent in 1975 to 58 percent in 1996. Their share in total manufacturing shipments fell from 83 percent to 75 percent.[36]

The relatively slower decline in shipments relative to employment is probably because these firms outsourced more. In the 1990s, General Motors moved toward Toyota's model of buying rather than making intermediate products. Even though it entered a variety of other businesses since the late 1980s, in 2001, General Motors had only 362,000 employees (compared to 750,000 in 1989), and it made 8.5 million cars (compared to 8 million in 1989).[37]

Perhaps the largest decline in GM's workforce came when it spun off its Delphi auto-parts unit in 1999. The unit had about 200,000 workers and had revenues of over $30 billion. Interestingly, the breakup was welcomed by the heads of both GM and Delphi. GM Chairman John Smith said on announcing the spin-off:

We have a rich and proud history of self-sufficiency in General Motors. This is a major step to limit that vertical integration. It is not an advantage today to be vertically integrated. We are going to be a much faster company and focus on our core business of building cars and trucks.

Delphi President J. T. Battenberg remarked that independence would enable the new Delphi to be nimbler and better able to attract business from rival automakers, which currently worried about its connection with GM. The company could also use its own stock to provide incentives to employees and help finance its global expansion, making Delphi "a very, very tough competitor."[38]

The trend toward smaller organizations is observable more widely. The fraction of employees who work in large establishments in the United States dropped significantly between 1967 and 1985.[39] The fraction of private-sector employees who work in establishments with over 1,000 employees declined by 13 percent from 1967 to 1973 and by a further 18 percent from 1974 to 1985. Similarly, the fraction employed in establishments with 250 to 999 employees also declined. Interestingly, this trend toward employment in small organizations is largely seen in goods-producing industries. In the service sector, by contrast, more than two-thirds of industries analyzed over this period showed an increase in employment by large establishments.

The shrinkage in average firm size does seem hard to reconcile with the news of the megamergers that are announced every day in the papers. And some studies do show that, by some measures, average firm size in the United States increased as a result of the mergers in the 1990s.[40] Nevertheless, the increase in size in the 1990s did not offset the steady decrease that had taken place from the mid-1970s. Much as we like to believe that ours is the age of the megacorporation, we are off by at least a few decades.

Let us now try to draw lessons from the breakup of the large, vertically integrated corporation about how the nature of the workplace might change in the future. To do that, it helps to have a framework to understand the past. Recent work on the economics of the firm provides just such a framework. This is what we turn to now.

Critical Resource Theory and the New Corporation

Academics often get fixated by a single question that, innocuous as it may seem, reflects the central puzzle in their area of study. To economists studying firms, the central question has been "Why is a firm owner's employee different from her grocer?" Let us explain.[41] The owner pays her employee to work for her. She also pays her grocer for the goods he provides. We believe, however, that she has more power of command over her employee than she has over her grocer. From where does this additional power arise, since it would seem that the only power she has is the power of money—the wage she pays the employee and the price she pays the grocer for goods?

The answer seems to lie in the nature of the relationship between the owner and the employee and the resources the former possesses. If the employee is a temporary worker who has been hired for the day, and if there are plenty of jobs around, then he is in much the same situation as the owner's grocer. If the owner does not pay his wage or asks him to do more than strictly contracted for, the employee will not deliver his services, much as the grocer will refuse to serve the owner if the latter is overly demanding.

But if the employee has been working for the same firm owner for some time, he becomes specialized to the firm's assets—the machines it uses, the patents it has, the databases and software on which its processes run, the bureaucratic routines it follows—as well as attached to the people who work for the firm and surround the employee. Thus, the owner has additional power because she controls access to *critical resources* on which the employee has come to rely and that make the employee more productive.[42] When the owner fires the employee, she does more than separate the employee from his wages, she separates him from some of the human capital he has built. The grocer, however, has little human capital vested in a relationship with a customer (typically) and is less concerned about being "fired."

Clearly, the power relationship is not all one-way. When the employee is fired, he leaves a hole in the firm's processes that has to be filled. To the extent that a replacement may not have the same skills, or will take time to learn the ropes and build relationships with other employees, the employee has countervailing power. This then means that the distribution of power in the relationship between the employer and the employee turns on two questions: how easy is it for the employer to replace the specific employee, and how easy is it for the employee to replace his firm? The harder the employee is to replace and the easier it is for the employee to replicate his work situation, the more the distribution of power shifts to the employee.

This, then, is the simple framework we have implicitly been using thus far. Like all frameworks, it abstracts from the complexity in the real world, but in doing so, it allows us to focus on the underlying source of power in the large, vertically integrated corporation. Because the corporation was vertically integrated, its production processes could be structured and operated in a unique way. Most employees could be trained quickly to operate on only one portion of the production process. Because there was little standardization in production, the skills these employees acquired were not easily transferred to another corporation. So they had little bargaining power, especially because the firm ensured that they had internal competition for their positions. Some employees did indeed oversee far more of the firm's operations. But again, their skills were not easily carried to competitors. Moreover, because few firms were not integrated, a new enterprise producing intermediate goods did not have a large market. Therefore, managers leaving an existing firm to start up a new venture in the same industry did not have obvious niches they could enter. Instead, if they were serious, they had to raise enough finance to build a fully integrated enterprise. Since these employees, sheltered within the corporation, had little wealth or reputation and few connections, financiers had little incentive to oblige.

In short, employees had few opportunities outside the firm. Because there was little product market competition, firms did not have to harness the innovative energies of their employees and could design workflow so that most jobs were routine: not only did employees have few outside opportunities, but they also were replaceable.

Thus, the critical resource in the large, vertically integrated firm was not the human capital of its employees but its alienable assets—its property, plant, equipment, brand names, and patents—which, having already been paid for, gave it an unassailable position in the market. Owners and top management could exercise power over the employee simply because the law gave them control over access to these assets, and they could separate the employee from them almost at will (perhaps explaining why labor laws were needed then to constrain them). And since ownership of inanimate assets was the primary source of power, there were few limits to the size of the vertically integrated corporation. Simply by owning his plants, Henry Ford could rule comfortably over a vast corporate hierarchy and have tremendous authority over workers he had never seen. He did not have to work to establish authority.

As finance has become more easily available, and as competition has reduced the necessary scale for entry, the "outside option" employees have has improved dramatically. They have a greater chance of starting out on their own by "replicating" the assets of their former employer. The breakup of the vertically integrated corporation has also led to more standardization and greater transportability of employee skills across firms. Increasing competition has meant that jobs can no longer be routine. Instead, the innovative energy of employees has to be harnessed in making the firm more creative and productive. Employees are no longer placeholders performing routine tasks but important assets who significantly enrich their workplace. Power is shifting to the employee.

One way the growing importance of employee skills manifests itself is in the increasing number of positions that are deemed to be of managerial level. In 1983, 10.6 percent of employed civilians in the United States were classified as managers. In 2000, 14.6 percent were classified as managers. By contrast, 16 percent of employed civilians were classified as "operators, fabricators, or laborers" in 1983, and such workers fell to 13.5 percent by 2000.[43] We are all becoming managers now!

These economywide statistics do not simply represent jobs moving from low-skill industries to high-skill industries. Even within industries—for example, in banking—the share of jobs going to college graduates has increased considerably in the last two decades. The share of work accounted for by tellers—the most routine position—in the banking industry has been steadily falling.[44]

One possible explanation is simply the increased automation in banking (or, in the jargon, "skill-biased technological change"). But automation could equally well reduce the need for skills—exemplified by the cash register at McDonald's, which has pictures of the various goods on offer, eliminating the need for the server to be able to read or add.

There is another explanation: bank strategy has had to change to deal with competition. To a large extent, the banks' primary asset in the past used to be their ability to raise money from captive depositors at low cost and channel credit at a healthy margin to borrowers who, typically, had little choice. Outsiders could own this asset by virtue of their ownership of the bank's charter. And top management's control of this asset gave it authority over the bank's employees. Take, for example, loan officers. While the credit-evaluation skills of the loan officer mattered, they were of secondary importance to the funds that the bank placed in her hands to lend. Without the funds, the officer had little value. And regulatory restrictions on competition meant there were not many banks competing in the same region to which the loan officer could transfer her skills if the bank let her go.

Deregulation allowed banks to open more branches and eliminated ceilings on interest rates. Technological change permitted depositors to interact with distant banks via ATMs or the phone. New institutions like credit-reporting agencies eliminated the bank's monopoly of knowledge about the creditworthiness of its customers. Taken together, these changes have severely weakened the link between depositors or borrowers and the local bank. With competition, the bank's owners' critical asset, their monopoly over customers, has been devalued. Banks have had to scramble for ways of improving their profitability, and employees have become key.

On the retail side, this has meant automating routine work such as check deposits or account balance inquiries and guiding customers who want these services toward machines rather than people. But it also means paying closer attention to which customers are profitable and selling them a variety of high-margin services—such as home equity loans—in addition to the basic checking account for which they come to the bank. Since all banks offer similar products, the employee who is in direct contact with the customer is critical, for she has to evaluate the customer and make the appropriate sales, effectively customizing the bank's services. The employees who do such cross-selling cannot be the tellers of old who barely had a high school education. Not only do these new employees have to have the educational level to understand a variety of products, but they also have to be able to fashion customized packages for their clients and have the deportment and savoir faire to market those packages in a pleasant way.[45] Customer relationship officers or account officers, as these positions are called, are management jobs (even though the officer may have no subordinates) and are typically occupied by college graduates. Thus, the routine aspects of a teller's job have been given over largely to machines, while the nonroutine aspects have been augmented and an entirely new position created.

Similarly, on the wholesale side, rather than simply keeping her hand on the spigot controlling the flow of funds, the loan officer has to create new ideas for structured financing for her client firms to attract their attention in an increasingly competitive and crowded market. Innovative and customized deals are the source of profits now rather than the old plain-vanilla loan, which has become a commodity. In fact, machines again, in the form of credit-scoring models, have replaced a lot of routine lending.

In short, the human capital of bank employees, both in terms of their product or industry knowledge and in terms of their client relationships, has become an important source of value to the commercial bank. This has substantially raised the power of those who have not yet been replaced by automation. The frontline employee, who has the personal relationship with the client, has an important bargaining chip in her negotiations with the bank over pay. Banks that have attempted to force their officers to share their relationships with other parts of the bank so that more products can be "cross-sold" have often faced subtle sabotage or seen officers leave, taking their clients with them. The more savvy banks have first sat down with their officers to negotiate sharing of the client relationship and safeguards for the officers' "property rights."[46] These negotiations would never have been necessary in the past.

The deskilling or automation of some jobs and the upgrading of many others is reflected in the growing "returns to skills." The wage differential between those with a university education and those with a high school education in the United States has increased steadily since the 1980s.[47] In trying to explain this pattern, some empiricists have departed from simple demand-supply rationales to argue, as we do, that the most likely explanation is that firms are becoming more dependent on human capital.[48]

RESTRUCTURING THE RELATIONSHIP BETWEEN OWNERS AND WORKERS

Competition and access to finance have increased the worker's importance and widened her options, thus changing the balance of power within firms. The single biggest challenge for the owners or top management today is to manage in an atmosphere of diminished authority. Authority has to be gained by persuading lower managers and workers that the workplace is an attractive one and one that they would hate to lose. To do this, top management has to ensure that work is enriching, that responsibilities are handed down, and that rich bonds develop among workers and between themselves and workers. The emphasis on a kinder, gentler firm in most recent management tomes is not without foundation.

In the vertically integrated firm of the past, steep, overstaffed hierarchies were necessary to control as well as provide incentives for subordinate managers. As firms have shrunk and as managers have more outside options, the steep hierarchies are no longer necessary. In fact, they may now be detrimental. Consider again the loan officer in today's bank. Every loan officer across the country has access to the same databases containing hard information about clients, such as their profitability, their assets, and their payment history. The loan officer can get ahead only by going the extra step, meeting the client and gathering soft information that is unlikely to be captured on the databases—the strength of the client firm CEO's handshake, the regard in which she is held by employees, the confidence she exudes . . . But ultimately, the loan officer has to get approval for the loan, which means sending a report up. In part, because soft information does not transmit well up steep corporate hierarchies (how do you report the strength of the CEO's handshake?), some banks have eliminated entire layers of middle management even while delegating more authority to the front lines. Organizations have become flatter and more decentralized.[49]

There is another reason for the flattening organization. As the centralized command-and-control system that resulted from the ownership of inanimate assets has been weakened, top management can no longer exercise control at a distance. It has to be in the thick of the action or see others take the power it once had.

Consider, for instance, Salomon Brothers' bond-trading group in the late 1980s and early 1990s. It consisted of extremely talented traders and "rocket scientists" (Ph.D.'s who use mathematical models to uncover financial market anomalies from which the firm could profit) who made enormous sums of money for Salomon. But there was not much that Salomon gave them other than its capital and name. As we have argued above, capital became easily available elsewhere, so Salomon became less and less able to control the group and had to fork out enormous salaries and bonuses just to keep it happy.

In 1991, a misguided attempt to corner the Treasury bond auction by a member of the group led Salomon to lose an enormous amount of capital and besmirched its reputation. Even though John Meriwether, the head of the group, was fired, this had little long-run punitive effect. Over time, a number of talented traders, responsible for 87 percent of Salomon's profits between 1990 and 1993, left to join him in a new venture, Long Term Capital Management.[50] Located in Greenwich, Connecticut, it became known as Salomon North for good reason. The bonds of human capital proved much stronger than the bonds of ownership, a fact that even Salomon's then CEO did not realize.[51]

In truth, the bond-trading group had been a part of Salomon in name only. It merely rented space, Salomon's name, and capital and turned over some share of its profits as rent. Its effective leader was not the top management of the investment bank but Meriwether, who was respected by the group, had become central to its working over time, and was thus crucial to its creation of value. Once his human capital was key to its smooth functioning, whether in making decisions about investments or in resolving interpersonal conflicts, he had power over the group.

Power therefore resides more and more in the charismatic and talented individuals who hold groups of human beings together rather than in the anonymous owners who may have no resource other than their capital or anonymous top managers who reside on the top floor and rarely mingle.[52] CEOs who realize this understand that they have to become much more involved in activities like job design, the structuring of incentives, and the management of interpersonal relationships so that they knit their workers to the firm. All this requires an intimate knowledge of the situation at ground level: top managers have had to descend from heaven or risk becoming impotent.

Ownership of Knowledge Assets—Is It Déjà Vu All Over Again?

As finance has made many traditional inanimate corporate assets easily replicable, corporations have looked to create new assets that can be ring-fenced, which can then serve as a source of control. In particular, as knowledge, networks, and new ways of transacting with customers have become important, attempts are being made to create legal assets out of these.

Dell Computers has been enormously successful in recent years, not because its personal computers are so much better than those of other manufacturers (the personal computer is essentially a commodity) but because its build-to-order system has given it a much more efficient method of production. Dell now protects its method of doing business with a large number of patents.[53] The increasing willingness of courts to grant patents for broad ideas and business methods suggests that we will have a whole new conflict emerging in the future—that between the owners of intellectual property and labor.

Intellectual property like proprietary databases or software is often much harder to replicate than physical assets and, when protected by patents, cannot be replicated legally even by those who have access to finance. Similarly, the value of proprietary networks depends on the number of people linked to them (and offering services through them). When a network attracts enough use, it becomes virtually a monopoly since no other network has enough "liquidity" to compete. Microsoft Windows has become so popular as an operating system in part because so many other people use it and make content for it. What is to prevent these hard-to-replace assets from becoming the critical resource around which a new hierarchical corporation reemerges?

This is not an unthinkable proposition. There is a vital difference, though. In an era of incremental innovation, the plant and machinery of the vertically integrated corporation of yesteryear retained value for a long time, eroding only through normal depreciation. The power of owners therefore eroded slowly. Innovation, however, is needed to create intellectual property, and it can also destroy it quickly (how many of us remember Visicalc, the industry-standard spreadsheet in the 1980s?). If a network does not continue to meet its customers' needs, it can lose liquidity, and its fall can be as precipitous as its rise. Unlike physical assets, these new age assets have to be continuously renewed by the creativity and toil of the firm's employees. For one, this means that employees have to be provided with incentives to exert themselves. This naturally limits the power owners have. Second, as long as finance is available to fund innovation, there is always the possibility that an upstart can innovate enough to render completely redundant the knowledge or network assets of incumbent firms. Even in the rare eventuality that these forces are not sufficient, the reader should take comfort that developed societies have rarely respected property rights that hold them completely in thrall. But this is a subject to which we come back later in the book.

Summary

In *The Coming of Post-Industrial Society,* written in 1973, sociologist Daniel Bell offered a prescient look at the future of developed economies. He argued that the then incipient trend in developed economies of jobs moving from manufacturing to services would continue and that sectors like health care, education, and government, with skilled professional and technical workers, would displace sectors like manufacturing, with largely unskilled workers. All this has come to pass. In this chapter, we have described an analogous phenomenon occurring within traditional corporations, as they have struggled to adapt to greater competition, technological change, and the greater availability of finance. Human capital is replacing inanimate assets as the most important source of corporate capabilities and value. In both their organizational structure and their promotion and compensation policies, large firms are becoming more like professional partnerships.

The popular belief that large corporations are taking over the world is simply not true. While there has been a jump in mergers in recent years, in part because new geographic markets have opened up, the steady trend is toward smallness. Firms are becoming smaller because large corporations have become unwieldy and less easy to control, even while the greater availability of finance has destroyed one competitive advantage they had of being able to finance new investment through internally generated funds.

In fact, the internal capital market within large firms is seen as more of a liability than an asset. The funds large firms pour ineffectively into poorly performing units are now there for everyone to see. Competition, as well as internal pressure, has forced firms to outsource what they cannot do well. Not only has this created more opportunity for entrepreneurship in society, it has also made society more productive.

Firms are now less authoritarian places in which to work. Layers of middle management, whose only role was to supervise, have been removed. Even though politicians have castigated this kind of "downsizing" as firms' putting profits over people, and even though some downsizing exercises have been carried out without much thought, the end result in our view has been to make the firms correspond better with economic realities. In these leaner firms, there are fewer redundant workers, and the ones that remain have more power and more responsibility. Corporate downsizing, in our view, is not a naked exercise of power by owners of corporations but, ultimately, a reflection of their loss of power and control.

Not only are workers treated much better by employers, but the competent skilled worker has far more options today. The other side of greater worker mobility is, of course, the loss of a guaranteed job for life that used to characterize private-sector employment in most developed countries a generation or two ago. Some, especially the unskilled or the incompetent, might be willing to give up the greater opportunity today for the greater security of yesterday. But for the majority, greater security came at the cost of a more authoritarian workplace and less freedom. The greater equality in wages across job categories was, in part, because the skilled had less bargaining power. As opportunities have grown again, the trend toward wage compression has reversed, and wages better reflect skills. It is a philosophical issue whether this is fair. But from an economic perspective, it is much better to allow wages to reflect the true value of resources so that the right allocation decisions can be made, and to provide social security through other means, than to try to do too much through wages.

Finally, when discussing pay, it is hard to ignore the enormous increase in pay for top executives of large corporations, which has been portrayed in the press as naked greed run amok. The high pay is often justified to shareholders as necessary for enhancing the incentives of the top managers to increase shareholder value. Yet there is precious little evidence that higher pay improves incentives to perform at senior levels.[54] Instead, the enormous wages seem to reflect the increased importance of human capital. Firms pay their managers more, not so much to provide incentives—though couching it in those terms keeps shareholders more docile—but because the labor market for top managers gives them no alternative. As management faces pressure from newly empowered shareholders to perform while at the same time coming to terms with the diminished authority it has within firms, it is all the more important to have the right managers in place. While we cannot say whether the spectacular levels of CEO pay in recent years are excessive or not (hindsight would certainly indicate that some managers were grossly overpaid), and while the occasional "pet" board still rewards its CEO for spectacular underperformance, the trend in higher pay for CEOs the world over cannot be dismissed as simply greed or the sudden discovery that incentives matter.

One statistic best sums up the changes that have taken place: in 1929, 70 percent of the income of the top 0.01 percent of income earners in the United States came from holdings of capital—income such as dividends, interest, and rents. The rich were truly the idle rich. In 1998, wages and entrepreneurial income made up 80 percent of the income of the top 0.01 percent of income earners in the United States, and only 20 percent came from capital.[55] Seen another way, in the 1890s the richest 10 percent of the population worked fewer hours than the poorest 10 percent.[56] Today, the reverse is true. The idle rich have become the working rich!

Instead of an aristocracy of the merely rich, we are moving to an aristocracy of the capable *and* the rich. The financial revolution is opening the gates of the aristocratic clubs to everyone. In this respect, the financial revolution is thoroughly liberal in spirit. Instead of capital, it puts the human being at the center of economic activity because, when capital is freely available, it is skills, ideas, hard work, and inescapably, luck that create wealth.

CHAPTER FOUR

The Dark Side of Finance

THUS FAR WE HAVE chanted the virtues of free financial markets. Is there no downside to the development of financial markets? What about scandals like Enron, in which billions of dollars of financial contracts collapse in a worthless virtual heap? Can stock prices be reliable measures of value if the NASDAQ market in the United States first gains, then loses, over $3 trillion in value between 1998 and 2001? Is financial liberalization a good thing for a developing country if it results in a banking crisis that lops 30 percent off the country's GDP and subjects the country to years of economic turmoil? In other words, should we not also pay heed to the dark side of finance? That is what we turn to in this chapter.

Let us first address the issue of financial scandals. Every so often, a financial institution collapses with a rapidity that leads the astonished public to ask, "Are the magnificent downtown headquarters of financial institutions simply fronts for houses of cards built by cardsharps?"

Even though the business of managing, and dealing with, money is likely to attract more than its fair share of rogues, financial markets know this and protect themselves by placing a greater emphasis on reputations and risk controls than other businesses. The proportion of the unscrupulous in the financial business is not very different from the norm. For every Enron, there is a "real" business like Global Crossing whose managers have managed to wipe out their own investors through actions that are, at best, of questionable legality.

Nevertheless, when in trouble, financial firms tend to collapse much more quickly than industrial firms. There is a reason for this. The modern financial firm can create or destroy value much more rapidly than industrial firms. Take, for example, derivatives. They are much like dynamite. Used properly, they can be extremely beneficial, as we have seen. In incompetent or unscrupulous hands, however, they can in a few moments blow a hole in balance sheets the size of which cannot be matched by even years of incompetent management at an industrial firm. When Barings, one of the most prestigious of English investment banks, went into receivership on February 27, 1995, it had outstanding futures positions of a notional amount of $27 billion, while its capital was only about $615 million.[1] A single trader, Nick Leeson, took the bank down. In the first two months of 1995, Leeson succeeded in accumulating a loss of $890 million, on top of the $270 million that he had lost (and hidden) the previous year. Such large bets would simply be impossible in an industrial firm—or even in an underdeveloped financial market.

Further compounding the problem is that financial markets are aware of the possibilities for misbehavior and take action to protect themselves. Debt markets are loath to lend very long term to financial firms because they know that a financial firm's creditworthiness can change overnight.[2] They would prefer to lend very short term so that they can reassess the financial firm's risk periodically. And if there is even a hint of trouble, the financial firm finds that its sources of financing evaporate overnight, which makes the firm's collapse even more rapid. Salomon Brothers suffered a near-death experience after the government started investigating its attempt to manipulate the Treasury bond auction. The investment bank had to sell over $50 billion worth of assets within a month in 1991 to pay off creditors. If Salomon had indeed gone under, many would no doubt have wondered about the solidity of a business that evaporated at the hint of sleaze.

In short, the liquidity available in modern financial markets, and the leveraged positions possible with new instruments, does expand the scope for ruinous managerial misbehavior.[3] But players in financial markets are aware of this and do put in place strong controls to limit such behavior. The rapid collapse of an Enron or a Barings after misbehavior comes to light is, in some ways, a reflection of the value financial markets place on probity and self-control rather than the opposite.

Of course, the collapse of firms like Enron suggests that some deficiencies need to be corrected, but it is not an indictment of the entire financial system. More worrisome are problems that envelop the entire system: for instance, when stock prices take off as if there were nothing anchoring them and then plummet as if there were no bottom; or when the entire banking system is enveloped in a lending frenzy so that anyone who walks in with a half-witted plan gets financing, only to be followed by a bust in which even the most creditworthy get the cold shoulder. The bust suggests that the boom was a search for a chimera. If the financial sector creates or exacerbates these fluctuations, it should be indicted on two counts: first, of misallocating resources and, second, of creating unnecessary risk for ordinary citizens. Can the financial sector get it spectacularly wrong? And does the chance of its being wrong fall as it gets more developed? That is what we ask in this chapter.

Deviations from Fundamental Value

To establish whether the financial sector gets it wrong, we need to know what getting it right means. A firm's stock price should reflect today's value of the stream of payments (dividends) the firm will pay into the future—what, in the jargon, is called the "fundamental value" of a stock. Unfortunately, we usually do not have a very precise estimate of the fundamental value because we do not know what the firm's future earnings, and thus dividends, will be. Hence, in general, we find it very difficult to determine whether the stock market gets it right.

However, there are special instances when two different financial assets are claims on the same underlying stream of dividends. While these are somewhat unique situations, they do allow us to test the law of one price—that is, that two financial assets representing claims on identical underlying real assets should be priced the same.[4] If the law does not hold, we have to question our faith in the market's getting it right.

Consider this example. As a result of the 1907 alliance between Royal Dutch and Shell, the oil giant Royal Dutch/Shell has two types of shares that represent claims on the very same stream of cash flows, the earnings generated by Royal Dutch/Shell. As stated in the corporate charter, 60 percent of all dividends and future distributions will go to Royal Dutch shareholders, while 40 percent will go to Shell shareholders. If the companies have the same number of shareholders, 1 Royal Dutch share then has a claim on the same amount of dividends as 1.5 Shell shares (where 1.5 = 60/40). Thus, 1 Royal Dutch share should trade at the same price as 1.5 Shell shares. In practice, however, between 1980 and 1995, the relative prices of those two shares deviated from the theoretical parity by as much as 35 percent below and 10 percent above.[5]

An example of even greater seeming deviation from the law of one price occurred when Palm Computing, the manufacturer of the personal digital assistant Palm Pilot, was floated on the stock exchange. On March 2, 2000, 3Com sold 5 percent of its stake in Palm to the general public, retaining the remaining 95 percent.[6] It also announced that it would eventually distribute its remaining shares of Palm to 3Com shareholders before the end of the year. Thus, 3Com shareholders would receive 1.5 shares of Palm for every share of 3Com that they owned. Even valuing all the remaining assets of 3Com at zero (implausible because 3Com held more than $10 per share in cash in addition to other profitable businesses), the price of 3Com should not have been less than 1.5 times the price of Palm. In fact, after the first day of trading, the market valued 1 share of 3Com at $63 *less* than 1.5 shares of Palm. In other words, the stock market was saying that the value of 3Com's non-Palm business was a negative $22 billion—impossible given limited liability! A negative valuation persisted for more than two months.

Such evidence has started to undermine academics' belief in the efficiency of markets. The belief was based on a simple, but strong, theoretical argument. If the mistakes made by the market are predictable, then one can easily profit from these mistakes by buying assets that are systematically undervalued and selling those that are overpriced. Furthermore, since transactions in financial markets can be easily scaled up, if these systematic mistakes persist, a trader can replicate this strategy manyfold and become extremely rich. "If you are so smart, why aren't you rich?" is the daunting question that faces anyone who claims to have found evidence that the market is wrong in pricing some securities.[7] As long as thousands of smart financial managers are looking for ways to improve the performance of the funds they manage, systematic mispricing as in the case of Shell or Palm should not last more than a split second, the time needed for someone to notice it and start trading on it. As such trades take place—a process called *arbitrage*—the price of the undervalued security is driven up and the price of the overvalued security is driven down. Thus, arbitrage eliminates the profit opportunity and reestablishes the equality in prices between the two securities.

The widespread belief in market efficiency did not rest on theoretical arguments alone. During the 1970s, an ample body of evidence emerged showing that there were few systematic patterns in stock prices that could be exploited, so much so that in 1978, a distinguished scholar stated, "There is no other proposition in economics which has more solid empirical evidence supporting it than the Efficient Market Hypothesis."[8]

While much of the work showing that markets are efficient has since been criticized as being inconclusive, the theoretical argument about arbitrage still makes sense.[9] How can we then explain anomalies like Royal Dutch/Shell and Palm?

One emerging answer is that the simple "riskless" arbitrage to which the theory refers cannot always be conducted in practice.[10] Consider Royal Dutch/Shell. There is no risk of a trader's losing money by buying the undervalued stock and selling the overvalued stock if she plans to hold the two stocks forever. However, if a trader has to close out her positions before eternity (sell what she owns and buy what she is short) or even has to be evaluated on the market value of her portfolio sometime in the not-too-distant future, then at that time, she faces the risk that the prices of Royal Dutch and Shell might have moved even further apart. Facing the risk of a loss at that time, arbitrageurs will be very cautious in taking large positions in the two stocks, even when there is considerable evidence of mispricing.

This is not just a theoretical concern. Long Term Capital Management (LTCM) was set up by John Meriwether precisely to undertake arbitrage trades. The firm looked for situations in which it believed the relative price of two financial securities had diverged from what fundamentals suggested it should be. It bought the theoretically underpriced security, sold the overpriced security, and held the position till prices converged, making a small margin on each such trade—according to one report, just 0.67 cents per dollar invested.[11] Of course, such small profits do not pay for all the financial skills that were brought to bear in that talented firm, so LTCM multiplied the size of the bets by taking on debt. With $30 of debt for every dollar of equity, profits per dollar of equity were now a much more respectable 20 cents a year. In fact, the actual amount of leverage was higher, so LTCM reported a return on equity of 47 percent in 1995, 45 percent in 1996, and 17 percent in 1997. These are very healthy returns considering that LTCM purported to take little risk in its trades—so healthy, in fact, that LTCM returned equity to a number of its investors in 1997, hoping to keep more of the profits for the inner circle of partners.

But the risk LTCM was taking was about to reveal itself. Many of LTCM's trades in 1998 involved selling low-risk Treasury securities and buying high-risk bonds, on the notion that the market had become overly frightened of credit risk. Unfortunately, before the prices came together, they widened—especially after Russia defaulted in August 1998. Even the spread between Royal Dutch and Shell, a position LTCM was taking, widened at that time.

As a result, in the first nine months of 1998, LTCM lost almost 90 percent of its shrunken equity capital, losing 40 percent in August alone. As signs of trouble emerged, the financial markets squeezed the firm further, refusing it credit and making it costlier for it to unwind its positions. LTCM was rescued by a group of banks through the good offices of the Federal Reserve (literally; the New York Federal Reserve provided a conference room where financial institutions decided the terms of the rescue). The positions that LTCM was holding eventually converged and made money, but LTCM as an institution did not survive to see that happen.

The point is that even if there is a tiny amount of risk in an arbitrage trade, it can prove extremely costly for an institution undertaking it, unless it has an unlimited amount of equity to sustain the position. There are limits to arbitrage, so mispricing may not draw forth the quantum of trade needed to make it disappear, and prices may deviate from fundamentals.

With minor modifications, what we have laid out above can explain why the seemingly flagrant mispricing of Palm shares was not quickly rectified. Even though 3Com set a date when it would distribute the remaining shares of Palm to its shareholders (so that each holder of a 3Com share would get 1.5 shares of Palm on that date), and arbitrageurs knew that they could close their arbitrage at a profit on this date, prices did not converge because the arbitrage was not completely risk-free. Because 3Com made the distribution contingent on the Internal Revenue Service's ruling that the distribution would not attract taxes, 3Com shareholders did not have a guarantee that they would have 1.5 shares of Palm on that date. Even the slightest chance of a negative ruling imposed a huge amount of risk on any potential arbitrageur, since the price of Palm shares oscillated widely. During the first day of trading, Palm, which was sold in the initial public offering at $38 per share, opened at $145 and went as high as $165, before closing at $95.[12] It was too dangerous to lean against the wind! On May 8, 2000, however, when the Internal Revenue Service announced a favorable tax treatment for the distribution and 3Com set a precise date for the distribution, smart money could close the gap without taking risks since the distribution would be made for sure.[13] With smart investors willing to do the arbitrage, the arbitrage opportunity disappeared.[14]

The theoretical argument in favor of market efficiency, thus, is more fragile than it looks at first sight. If arbitrage cannot be easily implemented, prices can deviate from fundamentals without necessarily creating a risk-free opportunity to make money.[15] But this suggests that stock price deviations from fundamental values can persist for long periods of time.

That prices can be away from fundamentals does not explain why they indeed are away from them. Why were some investors willing to pay such a large premium for owning Palm directly instead of buying it through 3Com? As suggested by two of our colleagues, "the answer must involve either irrationality, ignorance, institutional constraints, or insane preferences."[16] The more traditional economists who believed in market efficiency did not rule out the possibility that some investors might be irrational, but they thought that rational arbitrageurs would prevent such investors from affecting prices.[17] This can no longer be taken for granted.

The possibility that there may be little check on prices' straying away from fundamentals if enough "naive" investors push prices away strikes at the foundation of the belief that markets are efficient all the time. This is not to suggest that prices will stay forever away from fundamentals. But the mechanism by which convergence takes place will be different. Instead of nipping discrepancies in the bud by arbitraging away mispricing, the smart money may feed the appetites of the naive investors until they can absorb no more, at which point it becomes easier to nudge prices back to fundamentals. But this can imply a long period over which market prices, at least for some sectors, may depart from fundamentals. It can also imply substantial value destruction as resources follow the prices. Consider what many are now terming the Internet "bubble."

The Internet Bubble

Toward the end of the twentieth century, convinced by the seemingly limitless opportunities opened up by the Internet, millions of individual investors poured their money into Internet and telecommunication stocks. The effect was a sharp surge in prices. Between the end of 1998 and February 2000, the price of Internet stocks rose to over five times their initial value.[18] The crash was equally precipitous. In early 2002, many shares, if they traded at all, were only a percent or two of what they were valued at their peak. To many, this episode was reminiscent of the "Tulip mania" that gripped Holland in the seventeenth century.

In these episodes, the dynamics go roughly as follows. The initial success of a new investment (opportunity or instrument) attracts the attention of unsophisticated investors. Since these investments are new, unsophisticated investors find it difficult to get any guidance on what constitutes a reasonable price. There is always a plausible story that can be concocted to justify the price that is demanded. Hence, they keep buying these instruments, even when hindsight establishes that prices far exceeded any measure of their intrinsic value. Some sophisticated investors may well become aware that prices are out of kilter with fundamentals, but they fear leaning against the wind, because they know that a rapid influx of more unsophisticated investors can drive prices even higher.

In fact, in the initial phases of a bubble, there may be few enough examples of the investment that is sought after (say, Internet stock) that there is not enough to meet the growing demand from investors who hear from their friends, and from financial analysts, how wonderful their own initial returns have been.[19] Thus, already inflated prices might continue rising, reinforcing the interest of investors. But while smart money might not want to stand in the way of the rampaging herd, it certainly soon attempts to profit by it by creating more of the overpriced instrument that is so sought after and selling it to the ever-eager investor. For example, between June 1998 and August 1999, 147 firms changed their name to give the appearance that their business was related to the Internet.[20]

Perhaps taking the cake for audacity was Zapata, a meat-casing and fish-oil company founded in 1953 by former president George H. W. Bush. On April 27, 1998, Zapata annouced that it would form a new company to acquire and consolidate (not to create) Internet and E-commerce businesses. A few weeks later, it bid for Excite, the second-largest Internet search directory, but the bid was rejected because Excite saw a "complete lack of synergies." During the early fall of the same year, as the market for Internet stocks deteriorated, Zapata announced it was reevaluating its Internet business strategy. By December 1998, however, Internet stocks were back in favor, and Zapata promptly announced it was getting back to the Internet business, forming the subsidiary Zap.com. On this news, its stock price surged 98 percent! Hope springs eternal in the human breast!

Eventually, of course, the naive public money feeding the bubble starts drying up, and smart money switches from feeding the public what it wants to betting against what it has bought so as to bring prices in line with reality. The bubble bursts, and many investors are left sadder, poorer, and no doubt wiser. For the silver lining is that the implosion of the bubble teaches investors a useful lesson. They learn to evaluate the new investments and understand much better what they are buying. The consequences of the boom and bust eventually disappear. Until, of course, the next generation of investors gets taken in by the next new new thing . . .

Does Financial Development Do Away with Bubbles?

Is mispricing or a bubble a disease of underdeveloped financial markets that is likely to disappear as the financial sector becomes more sophisticated? Clearly, even if there is such a level of sophistication, we are not there yet since investors in the most financially sophisticated market in the world seem to have been infected only recently.

There is reason, however, to believe that something very similar to the Internet boom will not repeat itself quickly. Bubbles are often pumped up by a whole new set of investors who do not have the experience or knowledge to invest carefully. The stock market boom in the 1920s in the United States was fueled in part by individual investors who had no prior experience of stock investing but became comfortable (perhaps overly so) with risk because of their successful investment in Liberty bonds during World War I. Similarly, a significant portion of the trading in Internet stocks was done by the so-called day traders, a whole new set of investors drawn to the markets by the ease of trading on the Internet. As these investors become more acquainted with the many facets of risk, and as the markets transfer money away from the most naive, these phenomena tend to subside.

Nevertheless, there is no guarantee that even in a developed financial market the next new sector with limitless possibilities will not attract its own set of gullible investors. So whether developed markets can resist these booms and busts depends on whether they have enough investors willing to lean against the wind. And here it is not at all clear that a developed market does a better job than an underdeveloped market.

On the positive side, in a developed market, an arbitrageur has many more ways of using his money to correct prices. For example, if an entire market seems overvalued, he can buy puts on the market index (an option to sell at a predetermined price if the price of the index falls) at a fraction of the cost it would take to trade the underlying stocks. Derivatives such as puts allow arbitrageurs to assume very large positions with only limited capital. There is some evidence that the introduction of these derivatives calms down prices. In January 1990, Japanese stock prices started to come off their unrealistic peak when put options on the Nikkei index were introduced.[21]

While new instruments allow arbitrageurs to be a greater force for eradicating mispricing in developed markets (provided naive investors do not use these very instruments to multiply their bets), there is a countervailing force that could reduce the capital employed in arbitrage: the predominance of institutional investors in developed markets.

We have seen that institutions have a cost advantage over individuals in managing a portfolio of investments, so as a financial market develops, individuals buy shares in a mutual fund, delegating the task of picking stocks to a professional manager. Delegation, however, creates a new problem: how does one measure performance? The true measure of performance is the additional return produced over a perfectly safe investment like Treasury bills, per unit of risk taken. In many situations, either return (in the case of investments that are infrequently traded) or risk, or sometimes both, are hard to measure. Moreover, it is unclear over what interval investors should evaluate managers.

What usually happens then is that the financial manager's performance is measured in terms of "excess returns"—the returns he produces over and above an appropriate *benchmark* portfolio with a similar level of risk. Since performance measures are updated frequently, investors can decide what interval they want to use to judge their managers. The combination of these two factors, however, distorts the managers' behavior. Knowing that they are evaluated frequently against a benchmark, financial managers are wary of leaning against the wind.

Jeffrey Vinik, the manager of the legendary Fidelity Magellan fund, is often cited as a cautionary example of the consequences of bucking the trend. In the March 31, 1996, report of the fund, he wrote, "I believe it is critical not to be part of the herd when investing in financial markets. Just because investors are moving in a particular direction doesn't make it the best direction; in fact, often it means the opposite."[22] This was written to justify the Magellan fund's reducing its holding of technology stock from nearly 40 percent to less than 4 percent and, correspondingly, increasing its investments in bonds and short-term instruments. Unfortunately, following the shift, the Magellan fund underperformed all its competitors. Vinik was probably too far ahead of the herd: his decision was right in 2000 but not in 1996. Needless to say, he and the Magellan fund parted company.

Fund managers who are evaluated against a common benchmark like the S&P 500 index have an incentive to buy the stocks included in the index as a form of insurance, since only severe underperformance triggers dismissal.[23] Even if they suspect the stocks are overvalued, they know they will be excused if they perform very poorly when their benchmark also performs poorly. Hence, they have an incentive to follow the herd, even when they know the right strategy would be to buck the trend. Thus, delegation could reduce the amount of capital that is willing to lean against the wind. Since there is more delegation in developed financial systems, it is possible that developed financial markets might be more, rather than less, prone to mispricing.

The Effects of Mispricing on Investments

Since financial development may not rid us of booms and busts, we should evaluate their real cost. Bubbles clearly have redistributive effects: wealth is transferred from the buyers of overpriced securities to their sellers. If the buyers typically are less than financially sophisticated middle-class individuals and the sellers are rich speculators, this might create some serious political problems in itself. But even if we are willing to ignore this redistribution (and it is not clear we should), there is another important concern: bubbles may affect the real allocation of resources if mispricing affects firms' real investment decisions (their investment in plant, machinery, and knowledge creation, for example). What is the evidence on this?

The current consensus seems to be that investments do respond to stock prices after we account for fundamentals, but their additional explanatory power is limited.[24] Mispricing, thus, can have some effect on investments but not a lot. The ambiguous nature of this evidence is also confirmed by a detailed analysis of significant past stock booms and busts—the leading situations for mispricing: the 1929 boom, the 1987 stock market crash, and the recent Internet episode.

In the second half of the 1920s, stock prices boomed. Between 1925 and 1929, they rose on average 22 percent per year. This did not trigger a corresponding boom in investments. Only in 1929 did real investments surge, growing by 34 percent over the previous year.[25] Following the crash, investment plummeted, but much more than predicted by the drop in stock prices.[26] While the boom-time stock prices did not seem to trigger excessive investment, the crash seemed to lead to an excessive curtailment of investment. So the evidence is quite unclear on whether mispricing had an impact on investments.

Around the 1987 stock market crash, it is clear that stock returns had no impact on investments. The rapid surge in prices during 1986 and 1987 (on average, a growth rate of 24 percent per year) was not accompanied by a corresponding surge in investments, which remained rather flat (a growth rate of −0.1 percent). By contrast, investments rose in 1988, despite the 8 percent decline in stock prices. The absence of an impact of stock prices on investment around the 1987 crash is also confirmed by a study commissioned by the Conference Board in January 1988. The survey asked top executives whether the stock market crash had affected their investment plans. More than two-thirds answered no.[27] In this case, we can conclude that mispricing had no real effects.

The evidence emerging from the latest episode is less reassuring. Between 1996 and 1999, the S&P 500 index had an average return of 27 percent.[28] During this period, total nonresidential investments grew on average at 9 percent per year.[29] This growth rate reached 10 percent in 2000, perhaps driven by the sustained rise in market prices during the first quarter of the year. In 2001, however, following the stock market decline, total investments dropped by 2 percent. In this instance, thus, the extreme movements in stock prices seem to have had an impact on real investments. The stock market euphoria seemed to have infected corporate managers, especially in the telecommunication sector. The astronomical prices paid for the so-called 3G mobile phone licenses (a technology not fully tested yet) is an illustrative example. The high price at which existing licenses were trading on the market clearly affected participants' bidding strategies. Now, many of these companies, such as Sonera, the Finnish telecom operator, are giving up for free licenses for which they paid billions only a few months before.[30]

Fortunately, the money paid in those auctions did not get wasted, at least no more than all the money we pay in taxes, because it went to fill the coffers of various national governments that were running the auctions. We cannot be so sanguine about the real investments that took place during the same time period. While it is too early to make a systematic assessment, the initial reports are alarming. According to one estimate, there is such overcapacity in "bandwidth" that if all the 6 billion people in the world talked continously for a year, their words could be transmitted in a few hours.[31] No doubt, we will find new kinds of information to send along these wires, and eventually much of this investment will be utilized. But at present, it seems that these investments were too much and too early from the perspective of the shareholders of these firms.

Between 1996 and 2001, telecommunication companies raised $1.8 trillion in the capital markets.[32] This represents a lower bound of the amount invested in the sector, since it does not include all the internal cash flow that large operators invested in the business. The market value of the telecommunication companies that did not go bankrupt dropped by an average of 60 percent. The recovery rate for the assets of the companies that did go bankrupt is about 10 percent. It is not unreasonable, thus, to estimate that at least a quarter of the money invested has been wasted. By this measure, the telecommunication boom and bust may have cost nearly half a trillion dollars! The conclusion is inescapable: resources can be grossly misallocated even in countries with developed financial markets.

The Risks in Development

Thus far, we have examined only the desirability of having a developed financial sector. We have not asked if, once a country decides to go for development, the process will be a smooth one. This is not a trivial issue. Many countries have underdeveloped financial sectors that have been severely constrained by limitations on competition: interest rates have been fixed, entry into the financial sector has been restricted, and foreign competition has been disallowed. The sudden liberalization of the financial sector can have much the same effect as forcing a sedentary man who has never exercised in his life to go on an exhausting regimen. The man will either drop dead or emerge invigorated and with a greater zest for life.

In other words, the transition to a competitive free market system is risky. Even if a liberal, market-oriented economy is more productive and fair—and we have just questioned this premise—we also have to ask if the costs for an economy that has spent decades protected from competition to transition to a functioning market economy are worth it. Subjecting these economies at short order to the full gale-force winds of international competition is, according to some, a recipe for disaster.

These cautious reformers may have the weight of evidence on their side. According to a recent study, in eighteen of twenty-six banking crises in the last two decades, the financial sector was liberalized in the preceding five years.[33] In other words, there seems to be a positive correlation between liberalization—government actions such as the freeing of interest rates, the opening of the economy, the deregulation of entry—and financial crisis. One should not immediately conclude that correlation means causation. Often, economies liberalize when they are in a dire way and have no alternative: India's liberalization took off in 1991 when it was a few weeks away from running out of foreign currency reserves.

But there is probably a more direct connection. When an economy liberalizes, new competition squeezes profits. New skills are needed to lend in a world where business acumen rather than collateral or connections matter. Moreover, new infrastructure—better accounting, more information gathering and reporting, better contract writing, and better debt-collection mechanisms—is needed. When new skills are acquired and the new infrastructure is created, lenders will be able to make better loans than they did in the past. But in the transition phase from the old uncompetitive system to the new one, lenders may have to make decisions without the benefit of the necessary skills or infrastructure. And they do not have the profits to cushion their mistakes or keep their incentives from going awry. No wonder that when an economy liberalizes, so many bankers act like deer frozen in headlights and end up as roadkill.

Summary

In this chapter, we have raised some natural questions about financial development. For every fan who extols the invigorating virtues of competitive financial markets, there are critics who do not believe that these markets can be used as a reliable guide for investment and who point to the resources wasted in mistaken periods of euphoria. Yet others see a competitive, developed financial sector as a desirable end but point to the pitfalls in treating a moribund system with shock therapy. The patient may not survive the cure.

At this point, the reader might recollect the old saw that policy makers would like economists to be one-handed because economists always list on the one hand a series of arguments in favor of a proposition but on the other hand an equally compelling series of arguments against it. We seem to have spoken on both sides of the case for financial development. On the one hand, a free financial sector can play an important role in allocating resources and managing risk, both of which can be immensely valuable for many sectors of the economy. On the other hand, the financial sector can itself be a source of risk, so that it will occasionally waste resources in a spectacular way. With free financial markets having the power to do great good and great evil, should the world really want more financial liberalization?

Fortunately, there is a way out that does not require us to lose a limb each: we can turn to the empirical evidence to see whether the benefits, on average, to a country from financial development outweigh the costs. While anecdotes are useful to illustrate points, they can be carefully selected to support a preexisting bias. To really pass judgment about whether free finance is, on balance, a good thing, we have to move from an analysis of particular episodes and cases to systematic studies of countries over time. Paraphrasing Winston Churchill, is a developed financial sector with competitive, vibrant, arm's-length financial markets the worst of all financial systems except those that have been tried? This is the question we address in the next chapter.

CHAPTER FIVE

The Bottom Line on
Financial Development

N O   O N E   W O U L D   question that resources are necessary for human endeavor, and few would dispute the fact that risk is costly. But the financial markets are only one way to marry resources with ideas while spreading the associated risk. There are others. For example, existing firms could use their internally generated cash flows, or their wealth, to buy ideas from innovators. Alternatively, they could employ the innovators directly. They could thereby do away with some of the functions of a financial system. How can we tell whether financial development is good on net, promoting the matching between resources and ideas, spreading risk, and reducing the cost of funds? The question is especially pertinent given that financial markets can misallocate resources and financial development can increase risks.

We cannot simply look at a country's level of prosperity. Countries can be prosperous because they are rich in natural resources or because of the fortuitous circumstances of history. Two hundred years ago, the inhabitants of Haiti and Barbados were richer than those of the United States, and until the early eighteenth century, North America was not more developed than South America.[1] In the long run, however, initial conditions tend to be swamped by the effects of growth. So we should have greater confidence in the ability of finance to ameliorate the human condition if we can show that the development of a country's financial sector increases the rate of growth of its economy.

Equally important is finance's ability to create competition for the establishment. Competition is always good for citizens in an economy. But to the extent that this happens because newcomers are financed, finance also spreads opportunity and infuses fresh ideas. Further, it promotes economic mobility, much as a democracy promotes political and social mobility.

Of course, it is easy to find anecdotes "proving" something as well as anecdotes supporting its opposite. To attempt to settle the questions we have raised about the consequences of financial development, in this chapter we examine evidence from systematic studies conducted across or within countries. We begin with the link between finance and economic growth.

Finance and Growth

There is strong evidence that a developed financial sector and a strong economy go together.[2] But this is not enough to conclude that financial development contributes to making the economy strong. Economists care deeply about the difference between a simple correlation (two events happen together) and causality (one event causes the other). The reason is that it can make a world of difference to economic policy.

An example should make this clear. Birds fly away from a railway track as a train approaches. The birds flying and the train approaching are correlated events, but the former does not cause the latter. If we did not determine the direction of causality, our observation of a correlation would suggest strange policies. In order to speed up the arrival of a tardy train, irate passengers should resort to scaring away the birds sitting on the tracks! Correlation is the basis for superstition, while causality is the basis for science.

In the past, many economists, while convinced that a sound financial sector goes hand in hand with a healthy economy, were downright skeptical that it was a prerequisite for economic development. They believed that the time and investment required to build a well-functioning financial sector were relatively minor. So if there were an economic need for financial markets and institutions, then these would emerge to fulfill the need. They felt that even if the financial sector were underdeveloped when the economic need arose, this would not impede economic growth.[3] To convince these skeptics that finance was independently important, one had to show that it caused economic growth.

In the natural sciences, causality is investigated with controlled experiments. In economics, this is generally not possible. Instead, one has to try to identify situations that simulate a controlled experiment.

One way to make a beginning at a causal link is to show that financial development precedes, rather than follows, economic growth. And it does. In a sample of eighty countries over the period 1960–1989, different measures of beginning-of-period financial development are associated with higher subsequent rates of growth in the country's gross domestic product, its capital stock, and its productivity over the subsequent decade.[4] Countries where much of the credit is allocated by the central bank rather than by commercial banks are typically considered to have underdeveloped financial systems. If, in 1970, Zaire had had a share of domestic credit allocated by commercial banks equal to the average for developing countries (about 57 percent) instead of a mere 26 percent, it would have grown about 0.9 percent faster each year in the 1970s, and by 1980, per capita GDP would have been 9 percent above its actual level.[5]

This is a first step, but not enough to show causality. After all, the birds departed the tracks before the train without causing its arrival. Do the financial markets simply sense impending economic growth and swell in anticipation? We need more evidence to rule this possibility out.

There are two kinds of evidence that might be convincing. To consider the first kind, let us go back to the analogy. If we wanted to argue that the approaching train caused the birds to fly away rather than vice versa, our position would be strengthened if we could find evidence of the mechanism by which this happened. Specifically, suppose we conjectured that vibrations through the rail track alerted the birds. And further suppose that we had two kinds of rail tracks, one that did not vibrate at all and one that vibrated. We also had two kinds of birds, ones that sensed vibrations and ones that did not. If we found that the sensitive birds flew away much earlier than the insensitive birds when both were on the vibrating tracks than when both were on the nonvibrating tracks, we would be much more convinced that vibrations, and thus the approach of the train, caused the birds to fly rather than vice versa.

Applied to our context, this idea suggests that if financial development really causes growth, it should have a very different effect on the growth of firms in some industries relative to firms in others. To see why, start with the fact that in almost every country, a significant portion of a firm's investment is financed through cash it generates from operations. This is why, for example, high-growth firms do not pay dividends—they plow whatever cash they generate back into the business. Firms prefer to first use their own cash flow, also termed internal finance, for making investments because they feel they have to pay a substantial premium for money raised from outside (termed external finance). As we argued earlier, outsiders demand this premium because they do not know as much as the firm's managers about the firm and its prospects and do not fully trust the managers to act in the interest of outside investors.

The process of financial development reduces the cost of external finance by improving disclosure and information dissemination and aligning the incentives of a firm's management with the interests of investors through clever contracts and speedy enforcement. Therefore, the industries that should benefit most from financial development should be those that, in the normal course, need a lot of external finance. For example, a typical project in the therapeutic drug industry requires a long period of research and development, and substantial investment, before a commercially viable drug emerges. During the process of research, the project is an enormous cash sink, and even the largest drug firm will require external financing. By contrast, the amount of necessary investment, as well as the lag between investment and the generation of cash flows, is likely to be small for a firm in an industry like tobacco. Since they need little long-term outside funding, tobacco firms are less likely to benefit from financial development than drug firms. Therefore, if financial development really causes growth, drug firms (the sensitive birds) should grow relatively faster than tobacco firms (the insensitive birds) in countries with better financial markets (the vibrating track).

They do.[6] Consider, for instance, Malaysia, Korea, and Chile, which were all moderate-income, fast-growing countries in the 1980s but differed considerably in the standards of their accounting. Accounting standards are a commonly used measure of how much firms disclose and thus of how good a country's financial development is. In Malaysia, which had the most highly developed financial sector by this metric, the value added by the drug industry grew at a 4 percent higher annual real rate over the 1980s than did tobacco (adjusting the growth rate for each industry by the worldwide growth rate of that industry). In Korea, which was moderately financially developed, drugs grew at a 3 percent higher rate than tobacco. In Chile, which was in the lowest quartile of financial development among the countries in our sample, drugs grew at a 2.5 percent *lower* rate than tobacco. So financial development seems to affect relative growth rates of industries (the relative speed with which sensitive birds depart the tracks) in the way predicted.

Apart from finding evidence of the mechanism through which

finance affects growth, and thus putting a causal connection on firmer footing, we can rule out another explanation for the finance-growth correlation: that financial infrastructure is set up as needed to meet the demands of high-growth industries. It turns out that industries that are small to begin with but depend on external sources for funding seem to benefit as much from financial development as large industries. Since it is unlikely that the financial sector would have cared enough about the needs of these small industries to develop itself in anticipation, it is safe to conclude that the observed correlation between financial development and growth is not because the financial sector is set up in anticipation of demand.

Let us now move to the second kind of evidence that might be persuasive. For this, we go back to the birds. Suppose we had only one type of bird, and these birds were on the track that vibrated relatively little. However, we had the ability to replace the track on which the birds were sitting with the track that vibrated much more. If we repeated this experiment a number of times (and at random times) and found that, after the track was replaced, birds invariably flew off much earlier on the approach of a train than before it was replaced, we could conclude with greater confidence that it was the vibrations that caused the birds to fly away.

The patterns of banking deregulation in the United States created the ideal conditions for such an experiment. As described in the introduction, for a long period, the United States had state laws preventing out-of-state banks from opening branches in the state and in-state banks from expanding their branch network. Some states—called unit-banking states—even had laws restricting banks to just one branch in the state. Competition among banks was muted in states with strict antibranching laws, resulting in bloated and inefficient banks, passing on their costs and indifference to their clients.

Between 1972 and 1991, many states did away with regulations preventing banks from opening multiple branches within the state. The subsequent changes in bank performance were significant. On average, loan losses (the amount banks lose because of poor credit decisions) decreased after deregulation—in the short run, by about 29 cents per hundred dollars of loans made and, in the long run, by about 48 cents per hundred dollars of loans. These are large numbers relative to the total size of loan losses, which rarely amount to more than a few dollars per hundred in a healthy banking system. Also, operating costs decreased by about 4.2 percent initially and by about 8 percent in the long run.[7] Average compensation for bank employees fell as the industry became more competitive, with wages declining by about 12 percent for males and 3 percent for females (in other words, wages fell but became less discriminatory—a natural effect of competition).[8]

What did all this mean for bank customers? States that deregulated saw a reduction in loan rates to borrowers and a milder increase in rates paid to depositors. So deregulation made bank customers, both borrowers and lenders, better off. Deregulation was tantamount to a quantum jump in the development of the financial sector within a state, because it allowed more efficient banks to provide services at lower prices. If financial development does cause growth, deregulation (the change of tracks) should have had a positive effect on growth rates of per capita income and output in the state (the length of time by which the birds anticipated the train).

It did! The annual growth rate in a state increased by 0.51 to 1.19 percentage points a year after deregulation.[9] Given that average growth rates over this period were about 1.5 percent per year, this is a huge increase. By contrast, states that did not deregulate over this period experienced an average *decline* in growth of about 0.6 percent![10]

More recently, a spate of new studies has bolstered these findings. For example, when countries open up to foreign capital inflows (which typically causes indicators of financial development in that country to skyrocket), the country's growth rates increase significantly. Countries that open up their equity market to foreign inflows experience an average increase in GDP growth rate of about 1.1 percent per year.[11]

Because of all this evidence, few would now doubt that there exists a causal link between the development of the financial sector and the growth of the economy. This is not to say that a country can be bereft of ideas or talented people and still grow its economy simply on the strength of a streamlined financial sector. Nor does it say that a country cannot grow if the financial sector is underdeveloped: the success of China in the last two decades certainly shows this. Finance cannot create opportunities. It only makes it easier to exploit them: what it can do is identify the areas of opportunity and decline, and achieve a better match by giving to sectors with a future while taking away from those with only a past. Finance can find and mold the clay of opportunity, but it cannot create the clay itself.

Finance and Competition

Growth is not the only metric by which to measure the effects of finance. In Chapter 3, we argued that finance, by reducing barriers to entry, enhances competition and opens the gates to opportunity for firms and for individuals. What evidence is there for this claim?

Financial development seems to facilitate new entry. The deregulation of U.S. banking, to which we alluded earlier in this book, led to a substantial increase in the degree of development and competition in the financial sector in states that deregulated. These states experienced a significant increase in the rate of creation of new enterprises after deregulation.[12] Similarly, more new establishments are created in countries with more advanced financial systems, and this effect is more pronounced in industries that depend more on external finance, suggesting that availability of finance is indeed the cause of this increase.[13]

That financial development facilitates new entry, however, does not mean it necessarily reduces economic concentration: established firms could benefit even more from financial development than entrants, acquiring a greater share of production and squeezing out competition. We therefore have to look at the effects of financial development on competition more directly.

One measure of the degree of competition is the profit margin. All other things being equal, a firm in a more competitive market should have a lower profit margin. If firms in areas that have better access to finance have lower profit margins, this would suggest that access to finance makes competition more intense. To check this, let us go to Italy, where there are tremendous variations across regions in the quality of the infrastructure necessary for good finance—such as an efficient judicial system. This affects access to finance: an individual with similar personal characteristics has twice the probability of being rejected for a loan in certain Italian regions than in others, even after adjusting for economic factors that should matter.

These regional differences in access to finance seem to affect competition at the local level. Firms in the most financially developed regions have a profit margin 1.6 percentage points lower—about a third below the average profit margin of 5.9 percent—than in the least financially developed region. Reassuringly, this effect is present only for small and medium firms: large firms can raise funds nationwide, and competition in industries with large firms should not be affected by local financial development.[14]

Perhaps the most persuasive evidence of the effects of finance on competition would come if we found an industry in which access to capital is the primary barrier to entry and then compared competition in this industry across a number of countries over time.

Such an industry indeed exists—the cotton textile industry—and it has been studied by Stanford University economic historian Stephen Haber.[15] The minimum economic scale of production in this industry has historically not been large; therefore, incumbent firms could not build tremendous barriers to entry by setting up massive plants. Moreover, over the period it was studied—approximately the second half of the nineteenth century and the first half of the twentieth century—there were few important patents in the industry, and advertising did not play a major role. As a result, the main barrier to entry was the financing required to acquire the small but not insignificant amount of plant, machinery, and working capital needed for production. Haber compared the industry in two countries that took very different paths toward financial development, Mexico and Brazil.

Financial Markets in Mexico and Brazil around 1900

Over much of the nineteenth century, the Mexican government had only a few sources of revenue, such as customs duties, and these were very volatile because of large and abrupt fluctuations in foreign trade.[16] Governments were also unstable, and finance ministers changed frequently. As ministers had only a short horizon, they found it expedient to default on the government's obligations, especially in times of crisis or war. As a result, the rates of interest on government loans were high and volatile, touching 200 percent at times.[17]

As with other predatory governments, the Mexican government found that only a few rich financiers were willing to lend to it. This was not only because these financiers were the main possessors of surplus capital but also because only these financiers had the muscle to ensure that the government would try to repay. Thus, there was a symbiotic relationship between the government and its principal lenders, which translated into the latter's obtaining a variety of concessions, including the state mints, the state tobacco monopoly, the salt mining administration, toll routes, and so forth.[18]

These financiers had little incentive to see competition develop. The beginnings of even a basic banking system had to wait till 1864, with the establishment of the Banco de Londres y México. There were only eight banks in 1884 and just forty-seven in 1911, of which only ten could legally lend for terms of more than one year.[19] Moreover, even the small banking system was very concentrated. In 1895, the three largest banks accounted for two-thirds of the capital invested in the system.[20] Of course, the clique of old financiers also had control over much of the banking system.

The concentration of the banking system was in the interest of the government. The government wanted to retain a stable market for its debt, and this could not be achieved if banks competed away profits while serving the larger public. So the largest bank, Banamex, the prime government financier, had many privileges, including reserve requirements that were half that required of other banks, an exemption from taxes, and the sole right to open branches. Entry requirements for other banks were onerous, including high capital and reserve requirements and the necessity of obtaining permission for entry from both the secretary of the Treasury and Congress. It does not take much to guess how often authorization for entry would be granted to someone outside the circles of power.[21]

The public markets were also underdeveloped for much of the century, mainly consisting of various vintages of government debt differing primarily in when they were likely to default. Eventually, however, under Porfirio Díaz (effectively the dictator of Mexico from 1877 to 1911), some stability was brought to the government and its finances. Foreign loans were raised, and the proceeds were used, in part, to restructure old government debt. Nevertheless, the government was still dependent on a fairly narrow set of domestic financiers—in particular, the large banks such as Banamex.

The government did undertake some reforms. Laws governing mortgaging lending were passed in 1884, and a law allowing free incorporation with limited liability was established in 1889.[22] But the reforms facilitating the financing of corporations were, at best, halfhearted. For instance, financial reporting requirements were loosely enforced. Manufacturing firms often failed to publish balance sheets for years, even though required to do so by law.[23] Of course, the paucity of public information made the public reliant on the few large financiers for certifying and monitoring the companies in which it was safe to invest. It should be no surprise that only the few promoters who had connections to prominent financiers could raise equity.

Brazil, before the collapse of the empire in 1889, had very similar policies toward financial markets and institutions as did Mexico. There was an organized stock exchange in Rio de Janeiro since the beginning of the nineteenth century, but it was not used to finance firms. Between 1850 and 1885, only one manufacturing firm was listed on the exchange, and its shares traded in only three of those thirty-six years![24] The banking system was small and concentrated, again primarily because the government wanted a stable source of finance. Finally, there were many barriers placed in the way of the limited-liability corporation. Promoters had to obtain the permission of the imperial government to incorporate and even then did not enjoy limited liability: an investor was held responsible for a firm's debts even after he had sold his stock. Banks were prohibited from investing in stock, and investors could not buy stock on margin.[25]

However, Brazil, unlike Mexico, had the kind of bourgeois revolution that swept through continental Europe in the latter half of the nineteenth century. The urban middle class and powerful coffee planters led the movement that overthrew Emperor Pedro II. They viewed the emperor as too closely tied to the old landed aristocracy and felt that a republic would better suit the interests of industrialization.

After the setting up of the republic, policies toward the financial sector changed significantly. The government was now interested in transforming an agrarian, slave-based economy into a modern industrial economy. Slavery had been abolished and new entry permitted into banking in the last year of the empire. The new government opened the banking system up further to entry, removed restrictions on what banks could invest in, allowed margin loans, and made limited liability easy for corporations. It also continued the policy of requiring corporations to publish their financial statements regularly and list the names of their shareholders as well as the shares each controlled. Thus, the investing public had fairly good information on the firms and who controlled them.[26]

The result was a huge expansion of the financial sector. The number of banks exploded from twenty-six in 1888 to sixty-eight in 1891. In the first year of the boom, stock-trading volume in the hitherto sleepy Rio de Janeiro stock exchange was almost as much as in the past sixty years combined! A market for public corporate debt also started up. New debt issues financed 32 percent of investment in the period 1905 to 1915.

With such rapid and largely uncontrolled liberalization, it would have been surprising if there were no accidents on the way. It takes time for supervisory authorities to learn how to regulate in a liberal environment, and it takes experience for a businessman to learn how to make money when all restrictions are removed. The clever are ever present to take advantage of situations of euphoria. Almost inevitably, the boom turned into a speculative bubble and then a bust. The banking system nearly collapsed, and in 1906, there were only ten banks in operation.[27] But the reforming genie had been let out of the bottle. Even though the banking system became moribund, the equity and public debt markets continued to serve as a source of finance for firms. In 1915, there were as many as thirty-two initial public offerings on the Rio Bolsa (the Rio stock exchange). In that year, twenty-four firms raised debt from the public market, and bonds accounted for 21 percent of long-term corporate capital.[28] To put this in perspective, today even in countries with highly developed debt markets like the United States, only about 20 percent of total investment is financed through corporate debt issues.

To summarize, Brazil's arm's-length markets and, for a period, banks were ready to finance firms, while Mexico had a concentrated banking system that doled out money only to its favorites. The differences this made in the ways the textile industry was financed were significant. In 1912, only 4 of the 100 operating firms in the Mexican textile industry had publicly traded equity. By contrast, 32 of the 180 firms (18 percent) in the Brazilian textile industry were publicly traded in 1915. The publicly traded Brazilian firms were also among the larger ones, accounting for 34 percent of total output.[29]

There was very little debt financing available to the Mexican firms, and when available, it was those that had connections that obtained it, and much of it was short-term. The debt-equity ratio of the largest cotton producers in Mexico, which presumably had the greatest access to finance, was only 0.09 between 1907 and 1913. By contrast, the debt-equity ratio of large textile firms in Brazil in 1914 was seven times larger, at 0.64, consisting mostly of long-term debt raised from the public market.

Most interesting is how the different extent to which the financial sector in each country developed affected the textile industry. In 1883, Brazil had forty-four firms with approximately sixty-six thousand spindles. The fraction of sales accounted for by the four largest firms was as high as 37 percent. In 1878, Mexico had almost twice as many firms, four times as many spindles, and its four largest firms accounted for only 16 percent of sales. Thus, the Mexican textile industry started out much bigger and less concentrated.[30]

A few decades into the Brazilian republic and the Mexican Díaz dictatorship, the figures reversed. In 1915, Brazil had 180 firms, nearly 1.5 million spindles, and the 4 largest firms accounted for only 16 percent of sales. By contrast, in Mexico in 1912, there were only 100 firms, approximately .75 million spindles, and the 4 largest firms now accounted for 27 percent of sales.[31] Not only did Brazilian industry grow faster, but it also became less concentrated! A natural explanation is that the more tightly controlled Mexican financial sector dribbled out finance to its favorites, resulting in both the slower growth and the increasing concentration. Interestingly, the poor enforcement of disclosure rules made it difficult even for foreigners to subvert the status quo. As a result, they financed only the largest and best-known firms that already had access to financing, exacerbating the concentration. This is a pattern that persists even today in countries that open up cosmetically to foreign financing without deep-rooted reform.

It is important, of course, to check whether other factors could be responsible for the outcomes in the textile industry. In the textile industry, the differences in outcomes cannot be attributed to differences in the growth rates of the two countries or differences in demand for textiles. Mexico's national income grew between 1877 and 1910 from 55 percent of Brazilian income to 93 percent. Its per capita income grew ten times faster than Brazil's (Brazil had much greater population growth due to immigration; otherwise, Mexico would have had a larger national income). Since the demand for textiles grows disproportionately with per capita income, all the evidence suggests that the Mexican textile industry should have grown faster. It did not, suggesting that financial underdevelopment inhibited competition and growth in textiles.

For those who might think that the textile industry in developing countries is a special case, it is instructive to look at competition in the U.S. cotton textile industry over a similar period of time. Much of the cotton textile industry was in New England, and finance in New England through much of the nineteenth century was "relationship-based." Industrialists started banks so that they could lend to their own enterprises. What prevented a small clique from getting a complete stranglehold over access to finance was that there was free entry into banking. And there was an increasingly large number of banks. From 17 banks in 1800, New England went up to 505 banks in 1860.[32] Also, over time, as accounting became more trustworthy and laws were better enforced, finance became less insider-based, expanding the availability of finance even further.

The evidence strongly supports the role of finance in enhancing industrial competition. Not only was the concentration of the textile industry in the more financially developed United States always less than it was in Brazil or Mexico, it also decreased steadily over this period of time as the availability of finance expanded. So while the top four firms controlled 12.6 percent of the market in 1860, their share had fallen by 1920 to only 6.6 percent.[33]

Finance in Declining Industries

The discussion so far illustrates the importance of a developed financial system in a growing industry. The role played by finance, however, is even more important in declining sectors. By permitting new entry, arm's-length finance can help an industry adapt to change. Let us stay with the textile industry and examine what happened to it in the United States in recent years.

In the last few decades, the U.S. textile industry has been declining under the intense pressure of foreign competition.[34] While in 1976, there were 275,000 shuttle looms in the industry, by 1997, there were only 10,000. There were only two-thirds as many textile plants in the United States in 1992 as there were in 1972. Jobs in textiles declined about 35 percent over this period. These numbers suggest an industry in severe decline, with very limited need for external finance. The reality, however, is more complex.

Plants have indeed shut down. But there has also been significant new entry. For example, between 1987 and 1992, 31 percent of the existing plants shut down. But in 1992, new entrants controlled 28 percent of plants. It might seem paradoxical that new firms opened shop at the same time old, established firms shut down and left the industry. But this turnover greatly facilitated the transformation of the industry.

Firms have become more capital-intensive—for example, they now use more robotics—and employ fewer workers. As a result, the U.S. textile industry has become more productive—partly because surviving firms have become more productive, partly because those firms that have been forced to exit have been unproductive ones, and partly because new entrants have been more productive.

U.S. textile firms have also started producing new products such as Gore-Tex and Polartec that did not exist before. As a result, the industry has managed to increase exports even while imports into the United States have surged. In this dramatic restructuring, new entry has played a crucial role, overcoming incumbents' resistance to change. And new entry is greatly affected by the ability to access external resources. Thus, even in declining industries, the role of finance is key.

Individual Mobility

What we have just seen is that finance helps upstart corporations enter and challenge the establishment, thus keeping competition keen and refreshing. Let us now see if it also helps expand opportunity for individuals.

One obvious way to measure how finance expands opportunities is to assess its impact on the probability that individuals will start out on their own. Self-employment, whether as a plumber or a storekeeper, typically requires initial funds. For all but the lucky few who were born wealthy, the financial system is the only source for these funds. Thus, a more developed financial system should make it easier for individuals to become self-employed. What is the evidence?

Across Italian regions, differences in availability of finance translate into differences in individual mobility. Even after controlling for other regional differences, an individual living in the most financially developed region is 33 percent more likely to start out on her own than an individual with the same characteristics living in the least financially developed regions.[35] By reducing the importance of the initial wealth, financial development also allows people to start out younger on their own (as in the search fund example in the introduction). In the most financially developed regions, entrepreneurs are on average 5.5 years younger. Thus, financial development has a significant impact on economic mobility.

Another way to measure mobility is to look at the very rich and see how they came by their wealth. Since 1987, *Forbes* has put out a list of the world's richest people, indicating whether they inherited the bulk of their wealth or whether they are self-made. The last year for which *Forbes* reported all the people whose wealth exceeded $1 billion was 1996 (after that, the number of billionaires became too large). We start by looking at the number of billionaires present in each country in 1996. This is largely before the Internet boom created a whole new generation of instant (and ephemeral) billionaires. To compare countries with very different sizes, we divide the number of billionaires by how many million people live in that country.

The country with the highest frequency of billionaires per million inhabitants is Hong Kong (2.6), followed by Bahrain and Switzerland (1.7), and Singapore (1.4). At the bottom of the distribution, we find poorer countries like Peru (0.04) but also rich countries like Norway (0) and South Africa (0.05).

More revealing than the frequency of billionaries is the frequency of *self-made* billionaires per million inhabitants. Not surprisingly, countries that have grown fast recently, such as Japan or the Asian Tigers—Hong Kong, Singapore, South Korea, and Taiwan—tend to have a high frequency of self-made billionaires. What is interesting is that the frequency of self-made billionaries per million inhabitants in the United States (0.26 per million) is much higher than that in the large European countries: the United Kingdom, Germany, and France have on average 0.08 self-made billionaire per million inhabitants.

There is a very strong positive correlation between the frequency of self-made billionaires in a country and the size of its equity market. This correlation is not just due to Hong Kong, which stands out on both measures. If we eliminate the former British colony, the positive correlation persists. An increase in the size of the equity market from the level in France (50 percent of GDP in 1996) to the level in the United States (140 percent of GDP) would be associated with an increase in the frequency of self-made billionaires in France from 0.07 per million to approximately 0.30. All the difference between the United States and France in the frequency of self-made billionaires per million inhabitants can be explained by the better-developed financial markets in the United States![36]

All we have is a correlation, which, as we have previously emphasized, is not evidence of causation. A lot of other factors, such as the extent to which a country favors free enterprise, may affect the ability of an individual to accumulate a fortune during her lifetime. As long as these other factors are relatively constant, however, we can eliminate their influence by looking at changes in the frequency of billionaires per million people over a certain period of time. Since the earliest survey conducted by *Forbes* is in 1987, we look at the changes in the frequency of self-made billionaires between 1987 and 1996. During this decade, the frequency of self-made billionaires tends to increase most in countries that started the decade with a more developed financial system. The effect on the frequency of inheriting billionaires is much smaller.

FINALLY, does it really matter if the rich are composed of those who inherit their wealth rather than those who are self-made? It does! Countries in which those who inherit their billions account for a large fraction of the GDP grow more slowly and spend less on innovation than other countries at similar levels of economic development.[37] Firms controlled by heirs tend to have lower performance within their industries and lower spending on research and development.[38] Perhaps the strongest evidence that inheritance has adverse effects on the creation of wealth comes from the stock market. When a publicly traded firm appoints an offspring of the founder as a CEO, the stock price drops by 1 percent, while when it appoints an outsider, the stock price goes up by 2 percent.[39] These differences in market reaction do indeed reflect its anticipation of differences in performance. Firms run by an offspring of the founder experience an 18 percent decline in return on assets in the two years following the appointment.

The problem is not just inheritance but the absence of financial development. More financial development would allow the would-be rich to compete with inheritors, forcing the latter to show that they deserve to keep control of their inherited firms. It would also allow good entrepreneurs to buy out incompetent inheritors, thus preventing valuable resources from being run into the ground. While some inheritors might refuse to part with control at any price, developed financial markets mitigate the size of the problem. It is excessive inherited wealth in a financially underdeveloped society that is particularly harmful to national prosperity.

Summary

Every revolution that sends bankers to the guillotine soon finds the need to resurrect them as the wheels of commerce grind to a halt. Finance lubricates the process of economic growth. It also expands economic opportunities for those without resources. The Austrian economist Joseph Schumpeter wrote in 1911:

> That the structure of modern industry could not have been erected without it [finance], that it makes the individual to a certain extent independent of inherited possessions, that talent in economic life "rides to success on its debts," even the most conservative orthodoxy of the theorists cannot well deny.[40]

Since he wrote those words, many theorists have indeed disputed whether finance does play such a role. Recent evidence suggests that Schumpeter was right.

Critics have then moved from questioning whether finance has any effect to complaining about the risks associated with the process of liberalizing the financial sector. Financial crises are indeed more likely when a country liberalizes. This should not be surprising. In the same way as a man who never stirs out of bed cannot be hit by a speeding car, an economy that does not liberalize will not suffer a crisis but will slowly die from a sedentary lifestyle.

In fact, the process of liberalization is harmful primarily for countries with a weak institutional environment—characterized by widespread corruption, inefficient government bureaucracies, and inadequate contractual enforcement.[41] Instead of embracing competition, established firms in such countries try to fight it. They get enmeshed in a web of defensive cartels and connected lending that renders the whole system opaque, inflexible, and especially prone to adverse economic shocks.

It might be tempting to suggest that countries with a weak institutional environment should postpone financial sector liberalization till they strengthen their institutions. We disagree with such a prescription. The institutional environment, as we will argue, is not independent of the degree of competition and openness in the economy. A powerful few acquire positions of power in an underdeveloped environment and are loath to see institutions improve. Their grip on political power will weaken only if competition reduces their economic power. So the institutional environment will be unlikely to improve without competition.

This means that even countries with weak institutions will be better off embracing liberalization even though they will face heightened risks of crises. There is evidence to support this view.[42] Policy makers should take measures to reduce the costs of a potential crisis on the most vulnerable as well as the risks of a political backlash. But ultimately, the citizens have to be satisfied by the knowledge that with the heightened risk from liberalization comes the prospect of a very real return.

We started this book claiming that capitalism—or more precisely, the free market system—is the most effective way to organize economic activity and that free financial markets are at the core of such a system. The first part of this book was devoted to substantiating this claim. We have seen that despite all their imperfections, free financial markets create opportunity, breed competition, foster innovation, and ultimately promote growth. Furthermore, while capitalist systems seem full of problems, many of these problems are a result of the underdevelopment of finance and are likely to diminish as finance develops.

Now that we have seen that, on balance, free financial markets contribute greatly to spreading prosperity and opportunity, we immediately face the question "Why do some countries have flourishing financial markets and others not?" This question is what we turn to in the second part of the book.

PART TWO

WHEN DO FINANCIAL MARKETS EMERGE?

CHAPTER SIX

The Taming of the Government[1]

IF FINANCE is so beneficial, why don't we see more of it? Why, by and large, did robust financial systems start to emerge only in the nineteenth century, and why did they take off in many developed countries only at the end of the twentieth century? Why is a functioning financial system still a chimera in most countries?

Our answer will be both simple and detailed. Simple, because we will argue that finance does not develop primarily because those who control or influence the levers of power do not want it. Detailed, because we need to explain why this opposition to finance arises, what forms it takes, and when and why it can be overcome. In fact, addressing all these questions will take up the second part of this book.

A sine qua non for almost any institution of capitalism to work is that the property of each citizen be respected. This means more than simply allowing and enforcing each individual's right to own private property: it also means respecting the rule of law more broadly by facilitating and enforcing private contracts, preventing arbitrary coercion, and preventing arbitrary taxation. All this is especially important in the case of finance—for savers will not be willing to reveal, let alone lend, their wealth when they don't have the confidence that it will not be stolen or, equivalently, taxed away.

The critical element in ensuring security of property in most countries today is not how covetous other citizens are—a strong government can always beat down the greedy. It is not even how rapacious foreign invaders are—warfare in recent times has not typically been conducted for the express purpose of pillaging the property of enemy citizens. The critical element in ensuring security of property has been the commitment of a country's government to respect the property rights of its own citizens.

Some countries have come a long way. The United States or the United Kingdom, models of rectitude in their respect for property today, routinely expropriated wealthy creditors in the past. Others are less respectful today than in the past, suggesting that governments do not have permanent sinecures on their ability to commit to respect their citizens' property. Despite Rome's being the cradle of law and Venice's being the source of much innovation historically in business contracting, Italy today lags considerably behind some of its northern neighbors in measures of respect for the rule of law and respect for property. So if it is not something immutable in a people's culture or psyche that causes them collectively to agree to respect property, what is it? Should citizens in developed countries be worried about whether their governments will continue to respect property? We seek an answer in this chapter.

Respect for basic property rights is only the first step for finance to develop. If, in addition, the government does not build the necessary infrastructure for finance, or if it shackles finance with regulations, the financial sector may again remain moribund. The primary reason why, even in constitutional democracies, the government might not take the necessary steps for finance to develop or, worse, move in the opposite direction is that governance is captured by small, powerful interest groups that prefer that others have little access to finance. In other words, the rapacious government is just the first hurdle. The next is the "democratic" government of the few, by the few, and for the few. Who the few might be is the subject of Chapter 7.

When can the power of these interest groups be overcome? In Chapter 8, we discuss the conditions under which finance becomes liberated from the shackles of these special interests. We argue that the recent explosion in financial development across the world has, in no small part, been due to the emergence of these favorable conditions. This then sets the stage for the third part of the book, which asks if financial development is an irreversible process. The answer, unfortunately, is "Not necessarily!" But we're getting ahead of ourselves. Let us first ask why the government needs to be tamed and how this might happen.

The Main Argument

A property right is a form of monopoly. It gives the owner of an asset the exclusive right to use the asset and exclude others from its use. But what gives the owner this right? We might be tempted to answer, "the law." While it is true that in modern developed societies, property rights are enforced by the legal system, this answer begs the question of what gives the law force. Why, in certain countries, is the law respected and enforced, even against the might of the government, while, in others, it is not?

One possible explanation is the nature of the government. Some have argued that by constitutionally enhancing the "countervailing" power of parliament and the judiciary, a government can offer a credible commitment not to expropriate its citizens.[2] There is, however, something incomplete in the argument that the government can show its commitment to respect property by setting up a more democratic political process, which keeps the arbitrary powers of the government in check. At the national level, most rules can be changed. The government can dispense with the democratic political process. Political power is therefore not easily conferred by legislative fiat or a change in the constitution. It is more fruitful to think of the devolution of political power and the security of property not as a political or legal phenomenon alone but partly as an economic phenomenon. This is the approach we take.

To do so, we need to go back in time, to when legal enforcement was doubtful even in countries where property is now well respected, and understand, step by step, how basic respect for property emerged. To root ourselves firmly in facts, we will examine how England moved in little over a hundred years from being a state under an arbitrary despot to being ruled by a constitutional monarchy. Before we do so, however, it is useful to preview the logic of our argument.

A property right is much more defensible when the owner manages the property much better than anyone else. There is a substantial cost to taking the property away, for the owner's skills would no longer be available—certainly not to the extent that they were earlier—for generating value with the property. Thus, property that is owned by those who can manage it best is property that not only has the law to support it but also has economic value backing it. To the extent that the government respects economic value, because of either the power it can purchase or the taxes it can pay, an economically efficient distribution of ownership is much more secure than a distribution based on the accident of history or on the whims of the king.[3]

A political institution like parliament is not irrelevant here. To the extent that owners are dispersed, parliament can help them gather and coordinate their actions. But democratic institutions are an instrument, not the source, of their power. This is not just a matter of semantics. With the "wrong" distribution of property, a country will find it very hard to achieve the right balance between the power of the government and the power of the people, no matter how many democratic institutions it has.

At this point, all this may seem just conjecture, but we will now substantiate it. We will examine why respect for property rights emerged when it did in England and why it took so long for other countries to follow in England's footsteps. While mainly historical, our analysis is relevant today, not just for countries like Russia that are attempting to establish secure property rights for their citizens but also for countries where property is secure today, so that its continued security can be assured.

The Rapacious Government

Security of property started with protection from foreign invaders. The generalized improvement in standards of living, which occurred in western Europe from the beginning of the second millennium, is attributable, at least in part, to the security of its eastern borders, which led to the end of the barbarian invasions. Thus, military security is an important element of economic and financial development. But it is not sufficient. Nor is it true that more military security is always better for finance. In fact, within western Europe, the cities that emerged as the most important financial centers (first Florence, Genoa, and Venice, then Hamburg and the cities of the Hanseatic League) were not the political capitals of the then military superpowers but independent political entities, very much exposed, with the possible exception of Venice, to the risk of foreign invasions. Why did they succeed where Paris, Vienna, and Madrid did not?

A nation's military might does not necessarily translate into a sense of economic security for its citizens. In fact, through much of history it has been quite the opposite. The stronger a government's military power, the greater is its need for funds to feed and pay its soldiers and the stronger is its temptation to simply take from its own citizens (especially if even-more-tempting alien citizens are not at hand). History is rife with examples of how the rich attracted the unwanted attentions of their own powerful monarch. The fate of the Templars in the early fourteenth century offers a salutary warning of what happened when a needy king went up against his citizens, no matter how morally and physically powerful they might be.

Members of the Military Order of the Knights of the Temple of Solomon, better known as the Knights Templar, were the first significant international bankers. They were recruited largely from the younger sons of nobility who stood no chance of inheriting titles or wealth. They devoted themselves to the church and initially lived near the ruins of the Temple of Solomon in Jerusalem, from which they took their name. They took upon themselves the duty of policing the highways used by pilgrims going to Jerusalem. Their lives were chaste and austere, and they reserved their passion for warfare. Because they apparently did not fear death, they were among the most feared warriors on earth.[4]

As a result of gifts from the grateful and the faithful, they grew in wealth. They came to own some of the strongest castles in the world. Given their military prowess, these served as ideal repositories for valuables in those troubled times. King John of England used the London temple as a repository for the crown jewels, and in 1261, his son Henry III, who was in trouble with his nobles, felt that the jewels would be safer if transferred to the Templar fortress in Paris.[5]

These castles formed a network of "branch offices," which meant they could make cash available at both ends of the Mediterranean as well as in Paris or London, when needed and in the form that was locally accepted.[6] A knight could deposit money in Paris and receive it in the appropriate currency in Jerusalem. Crusading knights used this network, the American Express of the Crusades, to keep themselves in funds as they traveled. Of course, the Templars charged a fee for both the exchange and the transfer. Local banking functions were also performed. A number of surviving parchments suggest that the temple in Paris operated what looks like a modern bank's cash desk, open at prespecified times and allowing clients to deposit and withdraw money. Clients appeared to be a who's who of the time and included the royal family, important church officials, nobles, and rich merchants.[7]

The Templars' financial functions soon rivaled or exceeded their military functions. They were trustees for crusaders and administered their wills, they acted as revenue agents for various monarchs and popes, and they served as financial advisers for the rich and powerful.

Substantial amounts of money were in Templar vaults at any point in time. Unfortunately, while their castles were strong, they were no match for a determined sovereign. In 1263, during the conflict with Simon of Montfort, Prince Edward of England overcame Templar opposition to enter its treasury. He broke into strongboxes and seized money belonging to a number of barons and merchants. His son, Edward II, did a similar thing on his father's death. Peter III of Aragon broke into the Templar treasury in Perpignan. In fact, the surprising fact is not that monarchs violated the Templar strongholds but that the violations were so few in number given the temptations and the impecunious state of royal treasuries. The restraint exercised by monarchs over the century and a half of Templar ascendancy must be attributed to the moral force exerted by the Templars as well as the concern that a raid demonstrating naked greed would undermine the monarchs' own standing with the church.

In 1307, Philip IV of France, motivated by the terrible financial state of his economy and having already raised all the money he could through the traditional medieval sources of debasing the currency and seizing the property of the Lombards or the Jews, turned on the Templars. Philip began a propaganda campaign that aimed to strip the Templars of their moral standing. Templar leaders were arrested in a surprise raid and were accused of heresy, apostasy, devil worship, sexual perversion, and a number of other sins against the medieval code of morality.[8] The Templar leaders confessed under torture, and even though they later recanted, they were found guilty and many were burned at the stake.

The properties of the Templars were carefully inventoried, lands rented out, and the treasury taken over by royal officials. The church, with no hope of expressing moral outrage, decided to join the predators. Pope Clement V abolished the order in 1312 and devoted his energies to securing some of its properties for other orders in the church. Thus, Philip succeeded in his aim of reducing the moral standing of the Templars and seizing its assets. But despite his protestations otherwise, the act in more commercially minded countries such as Italy was seen as one of pure avarice.[9]

The lesson from the demise of the Templars, which was repeated time and again, was that no agent, however powerful or sacrosanct, could protect wealth against a determined government. Interestingly, an important outcome of Philip IV's depredations was that the church realized the threat monarchs represented to its own property. For this reason, it turned from accepting property as a necessary evil (after all, Jesus inveighed against riches) to stoutly defending it as an inalienable right. Clerical scholars started to argue that the state did not have rights over the property of its subjects, and secular scholars soon took this theme up, finding support for it in Roman law.[10] Perhaps as a result, outright expropriation became more rare in western Europe and was generally targeted at infidels, such as Arabs or Jews.

Greed was not the only, nor even the most important, reason why governments coveted the wealth of their citizens. They were led to expropriate their own citizens by their desperate needs for funds to finance their military efforts. In the long run, states could fund expenditure through taxes. But war brooked no delay. The alternative to confiscating citizens' wealth was to borrow—an alternative a modern government knows all too well. But this led to a paradox. It is both costly and unpopular to levy taxes on the wider population so as to pay a few creditors. One reason a government would repay its debt even in the face of these costs is to keep the spigot of future financing open. But if it had the ability to persuade a few citizens to put up more when it was in need (what in medieval times was euphemistically called a forced loan), then it had little incentive to repay old loans. Since creditors, as a result, had no punitive power over the government, they had no reason to trust the government to repay. This then made it all the more certain that the government would renege on any debt contracted in good faith and resort periodically to expropriation, disguised as forced loans or defaults.

The easy targets (after the usual suspects like the Jews had been shaken down) were, of course, the rich, especially financiers. The manifest usurer was anathema to the church and hence accepted prey. Financiers were also likely to keep their wealth in a liquid, and conveniently removable, form. This is an aspect that makes, even in modern days, financiers the likely target of government taxation or expropriation. In this, the governments' logic essentially parallels that of the bank robber Willie Sutton, who, when asked why he robbed banks, answered, "Because that is where the money is." In an atmosphere of forced loans and repeated defaults, finance, not surprisingly, did not flourish.

The resolution to this paradox was simple. The government had to find a way to make it more credible that it would repay. This would then make the route of borrowing and repayment via steady taxation more credible. The conventional wisdom is that the Venetian republic, the Netherlands, and in the late seventeenth century, England managed to devolve power to investors: government in these countries was more representative of the rich investor than were the absolute monarchies that prevailed elsewhere.[11] This then made it hard for the government to default. The process by which the devolution of power took place is much more controversial. To understand why, consider England.

The Transformation of the English Monarchy

The early Tudors, Henry VII and Henry VIII, were among the most rapacious and arbitrary monarchs. They had their way with all the institutions of governance that were meant to check their power—the aristocracy, the church, the parliament, and even the judiciary. Henry VII steadily expropriated the great lords whom he feared as threats to the throne. Henry VIII not only continued along his father's path, but in one of the greatest land grabs in history, he dissolved the monasteries in England and took over their land, amounting by some estimates to over 30 percent of the landholdings in England at that time. This, however, was not enough. In addition, the Tudors resorted to repeated "voluntary" loans from rich citizens. Consider the plight of one Richard Reed, who did not contribute to one of Henry VIII's levies:

> The English army was then in the field on the Scots border. Reed was sent down to serve as a soldier on his own charge; and the general . . . received intimations to employ him on the hardest and most perilous duty, and subject him, when in garrison, to the greatest privations, that he might feel the smart of his folly and sturdy disobedience.[12]

The Stuarts continued the practice of expropriation. As late as 1672, in the infamous stop on the exchequer, Charles II suspended debt payments to bankers amounting to about £1.3 million, at a time when annual crown income was less than £2 million.[13]

Yet soon after, England had a constitutional monarchy. In the Glorious Revolution of 1688, the Stuart king, James II, was overthrown and replaced by William and Mary. The new monarchs agreed to a Declaration of Rights. The crown recognized the legislative supremacy of Parliament and also the need for parliamentary consent for a standing army in peacetime. Furthermore, judges were protected from arbitrary dismissal, strengthening individual liberties and the property rights of the citizens against the crown.

The consequences for the English government's ability to borrow were extraordinary. In 1688, government debt was about £1 million, about 2 or 3 percent of GDP. Much of the debt was short-term (recall that creditors lend only short-term if uncertain of the motives of the debtor), requiring between 6 and 30 percent a year in interest, at a time when the Dutch government was able to borrow long-term at 4 percent per year.[14] By 1697, government debt had multiplied seventeen times to about 40 percent of GDP, a significant portion of which was long-term. The proximate cause of the increase in government debt was war with France, but it also reflected the greater willingness of investors to supply the government with debt. Even while government debt mounted, interest rates came down, from 14 percent soon after the revolution to about 6 percent in 1697.

The now conventional explanation is that by constitutionally enhancing the "countervailing" power of Parliament and the judiciary, the crown offered investors the credible commitment that it would not attempt to expropriate them.[15] Parliament represented both the moneyed interests of merchants and financiers (the Whigs) and the landed gentry (the Tories). Given its composition, the increase in its power as a result of the curbs on the power of the king made property and financial contracts much more secure. In turn, investors obtained the confidence to invest. Thus, the argument goes, the internal constitutional limitations on the English crown's powers allowed it to raise large sums at short notice, giving it external strength and transforming England into a European nation of the first rank.[16]

There is, however, something incomplete in the argument that the government could show its commitment to respect property by setting up a more democratic political process, which kept the arbitrary powers of the government in check. If it were so easy to offer a credible commitment, why did other governments, especially those of other nation-states like France and Spain that were perpetually in financial need, not do so?

One possibility is that their situations were different. For instance, it could be argued that England's government could be tamed more easily because it had no standing army to carry out its arbitrary orders, and finance for raising an army had to be approved by Parliament. Since many members of Parliament were also property owners, Parliament was unlikely to approve the raising of an army that could be used to expropriate the citizenry. By contrast, the French and Spanish kings had standing armies: external threats were more proximate, and they did not have the luxury of time provided by a Channel separating them from their enemies. Thus, the argument must go, these monarchs could not set up credible internal constraints on the power of their governments, even though they, too, desperately lacked for finance.

Too much, however, could be made of these differences in geography. It is difficult to believe that the absence of a standing army in England was the primary reason for the English king to be better able to curb his own powers. After all, even if England, surrounded by seas, was not as exposed to sudden foreign attack as France or Spain, the English king did have a smaller standing police force to keep internal peace and did use it to expropriate the citizenry. Or to see it another way, even if the constitution mandated that the king needed Parliament's permission to raise an army, he could simply have ignored constitutional niceties once he was allocated the funds and turned the army against Parliament. The loyalty of the army would then have depended on who could give it a better deal in the long run. (After all, ancient Rome, too, tried to keep popular generals and their armies far from the center of power, but eventually the praetorian guard chose many of the later emperors.) That the king did not, or could not, attempt to turn the army suggests that other factors were at work.

Put yet another way, the great lords who surrounded the feudal monarch had powerful armies. Yet constitutionally bound government, and respect for property, emerged only after the demise of feudalism. Why only then and not before? There seems something missing in the argument that governments became better able to borrow by setting up the checks and balances on themselves that would curb their own baser instincts. What was the power that bound them?

Perhaps it is more fruitful to question whether it is possible for any government to set up countervailing power, especially the kind set up through constitutions. An alternative view is that the interactions between powerful national players are rarely governed by constitutional rules since, at the national level, most rules can be changed. Political power is not easily conferred by legislative fiat or a change in the constitution. Instead, it has much deeper roots, some lying in the ownership of property itself. It is more fruitful to think of the devolution of political power and the security of property as intertwined processes in which secure property eventually became the fount of political power.

Pursuing this line of argument, Parliament did not become powerful in England as a result of constitutional changes brought about in the Glorious Revolution of 1688; it was already powerful, as evidenced by its ability to depose two Stuart kings (Charles I and James II) in quick order. This then means that the constitutional changes largely reflected the power relationship that preexisted these changes, while the conflict between the Stuarts and Parliament was only a last-ditch stand by the king against an inevitable passing of the balance of power. Of course, constitutional change made the devolution more secure against reversal. Our point is that it was the culmination rather than the source of the transfer of power. Let us now explain.

The Decline of the Aristocracy and the Rise of the Market

A constitution is simply words on a piece of paper, and sometimes not even that. Parliament commanded no armies directly. How did it gain more power over the monarchy than did the powerful feudal lords with their loyal retinues who surrounded the medieval monarch? To see how, we have to delve deeper into history. The first piece of the answer is the decline of the great lords.

Henry VII, the Lancaster pretender to the throne, defeated Richard III unexpectedly at Bosworth Field in 1485, thus ending the War of the Roses between the House of York and the House of Lancaster. Given Henry's questionable claim to the throne, he set about eliminating serious threats to it. One way was to directly attack the most powerful of the lords—and since power stemmed from landholdings, confiscate their land and sell it off in pieces so that no successor would pose a similar threat. Henry VIII continued this policy, executing, among many others, the Duke of Buckingham, who was the highest and richest among the nobility. The Tudors also took care not to create any new concentrations of power: they created no new dukes during their reign.[17]

While some of the most powerful lords were dealt with on trumped-up charges, not all could be eliminated in this way. The source of a lord's coercive power came from his band of armed dependents. Since there was not much of a market for food or land, the surplus produced by a lord was used to feed a retinue of servants and marginal tenants.[18] He offered them protection against other roaming bandits (or equivalently, in those times, other lords) and rented out land to them at low rates. In return, they offered their loyalty and arms to the lord, wearing his livery as a sign of their allegiance. The lord used his armed band to intimidate courts, rivals, and even the king.

To deal with these armed bands, Henry VII passed a series of acts asserting that the prime loyalty of every subject was to him, the king, and not to the subject's local lord. He forbade the employment of royal officials by others. And he started enforcing an old law restricting the use of livery to household servants, making examples of those lords who continued to maintain a personal militia.

In the meantime, there was another equally compelling reason for the lords to disband their militias. As the market for food expanded, the surpluses generated by the land could be sold instead of given to servants and tenants. Feeding the retinue was no longer free. And as rents for land increased, and a market for land sales started flourishing (more on this shortly), lords started feeling the true cost of maintaining inefficient but loyal tenants. The more efficient tenants also felt the cost of spending time in the service of the lord rather than in the more profitable occupation of tilling their fields. They much preferred to pay a market rent in cash rather than pay a below-market rent and have further feudal obligations. Thus, as markets expanded, nonmarket obligations like military service came under pressure, a phenomenon we will see again and again under many guises.

Moreover, long years of peace under the Tudors left the lord unable to use his militia even to fulfill his traditional feudal obligations to the king. As the costs of maintaining militias became more apparent and the benefits declined, some lords disbanded their militias. The process became self-reinforcing. Since one of the benefits of a militia was protection against the militias of other lords, fewer militias meant even fewer benefits. Thus, over time, lords lost their coercive power due to pressure from the monarchy and from economic forces. A "Duke of Buckingham in the early sixteenth century, with his castles, his armories, and his hundreds of armed retainers," gave way to "a Duke of Newcastle in the mid–eighteenth century, with his Palladian houses" and his political connections.[19] The Tudors and the market they helped create had effectively crushed the coercive power of the aristocracy.

The Rise of the Squirearchy

What took the place of the aristocracy? The great confiscations by the early Tudors, culminating in the dissolution of the monasteries, brought a huge amount of land on the market. Some of this land was granted away, but much of it was sold, with great benefit to the crown's coffers. Because they had a direct interest in the market value of the land, the English monarchs amended the law to give buyers better title to the land, allowing them to sell it further if necessary. The flourishing market for land had a number of effects in addition to what we noted earlier. First, the more prosperous farmers, the ones who generated substantial profits from their land, could buy more, while those who did poorly sold their land or had it seized and sold by creditors. Second, farmers who had scattered strips could consolidate their landholdings and manage the consolidated land better.[20] Third, prosperous professional men like lawyers and merchants could buy land, the age-old symbol of status, and bring modern management techniques to it.[21] Land moved into the hands of more able farmers and more competent managers.

The consequence was the emergence of an intermediate class between the lord and the peasant, the squirearchy (or alternatively, the gentry), which was more intimately involved with the land than the former and more apt to take risk with new techniques than the latter. The archetypical member

> was not tempted by great possessions into the somnolence of the rentier; was less loaded than most noble landowners with heavy overhead charges in the shape of great establishments; did his work for himself, instead of relying on a cumbrous machine to do it for him; owned, in short, his property, instead of being owned by it.[22]

He was thus much more able to exploit the land he farmed, and much more closely linked to it, than either peasant or lord.

When landholdings were vast, the skills required to manage that land and generate revenues were supervisory skills: the feudal lord employed overseers who supervised a steep hierarchy at the bottom of which was the peasant. While the peasant had the capacity to get to know the land well and get the most productive value from it, without ownership, he had little incentive or ability to do so. In fact, in the early Middle Ages in England, and till quite late in other countries, serfs were not allowed to own property, had to pass on their earnings to their master, and were bought and sold with the land they tilled.[23] Moreover, to reduce the need for management, the individual peasant often had "no choice of date or of crop; he must plough and reap with the rest, and sow the same seed as they."[24]

While the great lord probably was tutored since early childhood to drive overseers and supervise his estate, he did not have an intimate relationship with the land: it was too vast for any one man to get to know well. Management was often simply the maintenance of tradition, which few lords transcended. As a result, the revenues generated from the land did not really depend on whether this particular lord owned it or whether some other person, who was equally capable of driving overseers and sticking with custom, owned it. In economic parlance, the income from the land to the lord was a pure rent: it derived simply from his ownership of the land, and there was little other economic link between the property and the owner.

Not only was property loosely linked to the lord, but the extent of security of property would have made little difference to the size of the revenues generated. Since the peasant exerting the effort did not own the land and farmed it at the pleasure of the lord, greater security for the lord's ownership did little for the peasant. Of course, the lord may have had some additional incentive to make improvements to the land if he knew his tenure was secure, but given the kind of extensive agriculture he practiced, these would not have added substantially to revenues.

Given all this, the lord owned his extensive holdings only because he had a sufficient armed force to bloody the monarch's nose. If the monarch did not fear questions about his own legitimacy when he expropriated other inherited land, if he did not fear that other lords would band together against him, and if the resistance this lord could mount to an assault was limited because his band had withered away, property could, and would, change hands whenever the monarch desired it. The inefficient structure of ownership was itself the cause for the insecurity of property. From the perspective of the monarch, one lord was just as good as another because each one's supervisory skills allowed them to generate approximately the same surplus for taxation. The only security to property was then the favor of the sovereign. Property simply could not be secure when the owner was so replaceable.

The gentleman farmer, owning smaller (but not economically unviable) plots, was different. First, the very origins of his land, typically acquired through purchase using his own accumulated wealth rather than through inheritance or custom, indicated that he had a competency that was required of neither lord nor peasant. Second, on land he farmed himself, he was likely to make the decisions on what to plant and where, experiment with different crop rotation and irrigation techniques, understand how the weather mattered every season and which clump of trees provided beneficial shade, and so on. Both because he was competent and because he was closely involved in managing his land, the gentleman farmer was very effective in exploiting the land he farmed. In addition, he would also be more able to rent land out well, since his intimate knowledge of the land's possibilities would allow him to pick appropriate tenants.

In short, the burgeoning market for land moved land to the highest-value user, the competent gentleman farmer. And as he became more familiar with it, his ability to generate value only increased, so that he was, given the circumstances of the times, far and away the most economically efficient owner of the land. Unlike the great lord, the intrinsic value of the land he owned would be far less if the gentleman farmer were expropriated, for his skills would then be unavailable to manage it. It would be better for a farsighted government to negotiate a steady tax from each of these farmers than to expropriate any one of them. In addition, security of property would enhance the taxes the gentleman farmer would pay because he would then have a greater incentive to invest in the land and create value.

While these economic concerns may not have been foremost in the Tudor monarch's mind, the great lords were. In a further attempt to undercut the power of the lords, the monarchy devolved more and more of the duties of tax collection and dispensing local justice to the gentry.[25] But this then made the gentry even more indispensable to the monarch:

> The plain truth was the law, as they [the gentry] practiced and understood it, and the local administration of England, had made the ordinary life of the country depend at every point on them, and hardly at all upon the Crown. The entire machine—law courts, parishes, poor law, city and country—could run very well without the king; but it could not run without the gentry. In other words, the gentry was essential to the power of the king, but he was not essential to theirs.[26]

143

In short, even while the gentry were becoming economically more powerful, they were also becoming critical to land administration. From the perspective of the overall productivity of the agricultural sector, this was probably a good thing, for their administrative indispensability enhanced their sense of security in their property, which undoubtedly made them more productive and further reinforced the security of their property.

The rise of the gentry was a steady process. By one count, there were one thousand esquires in Henry VIII's time (there is a certain latitude in who precisely qualified as an esquire, though typically this referred to the gentry), and this number had expanded to sixteen thousand by Elizabeth's time. There is no doubting the fact that the steady rise in productivity of English agriculture dates from the time of the emergence of the gentry. Early historians thought it uncontroversial that the emerging gentry were much more productive than the lords and peasants they displaced.[27] Since then, ideology has embroiled the debate on who exactly was responsible for the increase in productivity, though there have been recent attempts to use large-sample data to extricate the facts from controversy.[28] The data suggest that the emerging gentry in the sixteenth and seventeenth centuries did contribute substantially to the productivity revolution.[29] The wealth of the gentry expanded in tandem. By 1600, it was rumored that the gentry were three times richer than the church, nobility, and rich peasantry put together.[30]

So the decline of the aristocracy was accompanied by the rise of the squirearchy. We will argue that the squirearchy was more able to curb the power of the monarchy than were the great lords. How did this happen? After all, the squires were individually less powerful, and collectively more dispersed, than the great lords. What bound them together against the king?

Parliament and the Origins of Property

Large, dispersed groups have a harder time coordinating actions than narrow, focused ones, a point we come back to in later chapters. Despite being numerous and dispersed, significant portions of the gentry could come together. The origins of their property gave the gentry a common interest in defending it, while Parliament provided the common meeting ground where their actions could be coordinated. The gentry were thus able to overcome the impediments to collective action that typically plague large groups. Let us explain in greater detail.

In dissolving the monasteries, Henry VIII was taking on the might of Rome. Opposing forces could well question the legitimacy of his reign and could threaten it if given the appropriate backing of the holy church. He needed allies, and he found them by distributing church lands to the gentry so that "being bound by the same ties of private interest, they might always oppose any return to the dominion of Rome."[31] In the words of a British historian,

> the participation of so many persons in the spoils of ecclesiastical property . . . was of no slight advantage to our civil constitution, strengthening, and, as it were, infusing new blood into the territorial aristocracy, who were to withstand the enormous prerogative of the crown. For if it be true, as surely it is, that wealth is power, the distribution of so large a portion of the kingdom . . . must have sensibly affected their weight in the balance. Those families . . . which are now deemed the most considerable, will be found, with no great exception . . . to have acquired no small portion of [their estates] . . . from monastic or other ecclesiastical foundations.[32]

In consolidating opposition against Rome to protect their own position, therefore, the Tudors also consolidated opposition to future kings. Many among the gentry were especially wary of monarchs who had Catholic leanings or who sought ties with other Catholic monarchs.[33] The troubles faced by King Charles I (executed) and James II (deposed) were, in no small part, due to this.

Parliament provided the coordination the dispersed gentry needed to assert its recently acquired economic power. Parliament, historically, had been the institution whose consent the king needed to impose new taxes. It was the mechanism by which the king negotiated with his principal sources of taxes, and it was not easily dispensed with, especially once the king came to rely on the squirearchy to collect his taxes. This does not immediately mean that Parliament could stand up to the monarch. The early Tudors exerted almost absolute dominion over Parliament.[34] Elizabeth only had to pass the word to Parliament not to discuss a subject for it to desist. Her chancellor, on confirming a new speaker of the House of Commons, warned him against the House of

Commons' meddling in anything touching on "her majesty's person or estate, or church government."[35] His warning was obeyed scrupulously.

But as the gentry grew in wealth and power, and as they saw signs of revival of Catholicism, their opposition strengthened. Parliament had already become fractious toward the end of Elizabeth's reign, complaining vociferously about the creation and sale of monopolies over such essentials as salt. By the time of her successor, James I, Parliament was actively voting down the king's proposals and standing up for the right to free speech and the liberties of its members. James vainly threatened his Parliament: "I am a man of flesh and blood, and have my passions and affections as other men; I pray you do not go too far to move me to do that which my power may tempt me unto."[36] But Parliament ignored him.

A simple economic calculus would explain why Parliament had become so confident. Suppose matters came to a head between the king and the Parliament about property or, equivalently, taxes. While honor and custom would sway a few, many citizens, especially those who were being recruited to fight, would decide on the basis of their pocket. The newly recruited militias would give their loyalty to those who would pay them regularly and well. As the saying goes, *Pecunia nervus belli,* or "Money is the sinews of power." The king could promise to declare his opponents traitors, seize their lands, and use the proceeds as well as his own wealth to pay those who sided with him. Parliament could promise to do the same thing in reverse. So the side that would attract the greater following would be the side that could promise the militia greater wealth, both of its own and from seizing that of its opponents.

For reasons discussed earlier, the gentry were especially good at managing and generating wealth from their land. The king and the great lords had no such ties to their land. Far less would be lost if the king and the great lords were relieved of their holdings and the gentry retained theirs, than if the reverse happened. So the gentry clearly had the ability to promise militias more. There were, of course, other factors that added to their ability to attract a following. Much of the land tax collection machinery was in the hands of the gentry, so they were better prepared to fund the war while it was in progress. Furthermore, they were men with strong ties to the local population, while the king and lords were remote. The fundamental point, however, is that the balance of power had changed. If the monarchy were not farsighted enough to see this, it might very well take a civil war, a beheading, and a revolution to convince the monarchy that power had indeed shifted hands! Certainly, there were men in the midst of these revolutionary times who saw that matters had changed. Thus, Henry Neville, a member of Parliament, exclaimed to the House of Commons in 1658:

> The Commons, till Henry VII, never exercised a negative vote. All depended on the Lords. In that time it would have been hard to have found in this house so many gentlemen of estates. The gentry do not now depend on the peerage. The balance is in the gentry. They have all the lands.[37]

As an elected Parliament gained power over the monarch, the conditions for a constitutionally limited government were finally in place.[38] The Glorious Revolution formalized this state of affairs and enshrined the concept that taxation could not be arbitrary and required the consent of the people's representatives. Less than a century later, this principle was reiterated in the American Declaration of Independence.

Recapitulation

Let us recapitulate. There were three critical steps on the way to a government that respects property rights. The first was the decline of the coercive power of the great nobles. This ensured that raw physical might no longer determined economic outcomes and that ownership was not the prerogative of an inefficient few. The second was the emergence of an intermediate class, the gentry, who were not just economically powerful as a class but also efficient exploiters of the land they owned. The third was the existence of Parliament as a coordinating institution. Without it, the dispersed gentry would have struggled to assert politically its new economic power. Thus, the Parliament, weak in the Tudor years when the gentry was emerging, became strong when the gentry became wealthy. The power of the Parliament was also strengthened by the commonality of interests among the gentry. Most derived income from land, and many owned land that was previously expropriated from the Catholic Church.

Thus, the emergence of property rights in England was due to a fortuitous combination of factors. Were all of these factors necessary? James Harrington, an Englishman who was a contemporary of Oliver Cromwell and studied the sources of power in his 1656 book *Oceana*, believed that the redistribution of land through the great Tudor expropriations (and the land sales by Stuart monarchs as they attempted to fund their extravagances) was solely what changed the balance of power. This belief in property as the fount of power—because those who have property have the ability to pay armies—is clearly enunciated in one of Harrington's pamphlets:

> All government is founded upon overbalance in propriety. [That is, governmental power derives from property; the man or men whose property exceeds (overbalances) the total wealth of others in the state controls its government.]
>
> If one man hold the overbalance unto [over] the whole people in propriety, his propriety causeth absolute monarchy.
>
> If the few hold the overbalance unto the whole people in propriety, their propriety causes aristocracy or mixed monarchy.
>
> If the whole people be neither overbalanced by the propriety of one, nor of a few, the propriety of the people (or of the many) causeth the democracy or popular government.[39]

There is a long tradition for the belief that widely distributed property leads to democracy and civil society. Some societies have suggested maximum limits on what can be owned, while others have suggested minimum limits: the Roman republic had an "agrarian law" that limited the land any one person could own. Jefferson's draft constitution for Virginia, written in 1776, required that each adult have fifty acres of land.[40] Yet the argument that property is power is, at some level, circular. To claim that property leads to power is to presuppose that the government respects allocations of property. Else why could the government—which enforces property rights—simply not declare the property rights of the rebels null and void if it feels that they would fund armies against the government?

If we were to stress a single most important factor in the emergence of property rights, it would not just be the wider distribution of property but also the economic (or social) ties between the property and the owner, which is all that would persist in an atmosphere of anarchy. Thus, Harrington omits a vital step in his arguments: the sale of seized land and the flourishing subsequent land market led to property's being held by those who could manage it much better. It was this—the economically efficient holding of property—that enhanced the security of property, because the efficient holders had the economic power to defend their property against others. In addition, of course, the ability for the gentry to coordinate action through Parliament helped convert their dispersed, but substantial, economic power into political power.

Would it have been enough to open a market for land? Was the expropriation of the great lords and the monasteries necessary for the wider distribution of power? While it is hard to answer such counterfactual questions categorically, we believe that the expropriations, despite violating property rights, somewhat paradoxically helped build future limitations on the monarchy. For one, the expropriations did redistribute wealth directly, spreading economic power. More important, the lords and monasteries owned a significant portion of the land in their localities. They were local monopolists. Even if smaller properties were more efficiently managed, like all monopolists, they may have preferred holding on to their land, managing it inefficiently, but squeezing monopoly profits out of the local populace. Thus, a market for land might not have moved land into more efficient hands were it not for the expropriations, which were a sort of antitrust action.

Our argument also suggests why government was much more participatory in the cities than in the nation-states. In the city-states, the dominant source of wealth was not land but trade and manufacture. The surplus generated by these activities was clearly closely tied to the expertise, incentives, and relationships of the owner of the business, much as land was tied to the commercial farmer. It made economic sense to respect property rights within the city and to give *citizens* (a word that originates from the French *cité* and was originally applicable only to residents of a city) the sense of security by allowing them to participate in government. As the old saying goes, *Stadtluft macht frei,* or "City air makes free."

Clearly, the cities grew along with business, and there is no reason to believe that respect for property was highly developed in the early life of a city. But over time, the quantum of business grew, and businessmen demanded, and obtained, respect for property as well as participation in city government.

In the nation-states, by contrast, the dominant source of revenue was land. As long as property holdings were concentrated, the nation-state could not commit to respect property. Even if manufacture or trade started up, it would be hard for the nation-state to show respect for business property when business output formed only a small fraction of total output. Thus, it was only after the breakup of the feudal estates or after extensive land reforms that the group of gentry emerged who not only were strong advocates of the institution of private property but also forced government to respect it. This then paved the way for competitive industry to emerge. Of course, once industry became sufficiently important, the pattern of landholdings might become less important to the security of property.

English history offers some evidence of this sequence. One of the rights the king attempted to usurp for himself as industries grew was the right to grant industrial monopolies. Consider the following case, which vividly demonstrates that these monopolies contributed to the insecurity of property, the arbitrary power of the king, and the ruin of economic activity. In 1614, a scheme was concocted to

> take from the Merchant Adventures [a trading company] their rights to export unfinished woolen cloth to the Netherlands and to give to a new company the exclusive right to export cloth. . . . It was estimated that the export of entirely finished cloth . . . would bring in an additional profit of 600,000 to 700,000 pounds a year to those engaged in the cloth trade. Of this the king was to have 300,000 pounds for his grant of the franchise to the new company. The Dutch . . . refused [to let in] the English finished cloth, and the new company came to a quick end. Yet before the Merchant Adventurers could recover their old rights, which they did at a cost of between 60,000 and 70,000 in bribes to James' officials, the entire cloth trade had been disorganized. . . . As late as 1620 the English merchants were exporting only half as much cloth as they had sent abroad in 1613.[41]

Parliament saw the danger to the security of property (and its own power) from these monopolies and, in 1624, passed the Statute of Monopolies, which forbade the issuance by the king of patents of monopoly to individuals except in the case of new inventions. The antimonarch Parliament that served between 1640 and 1660 went further and virtually ended the practice of granting monopolies to corporations as well as individuals.[42] So in addition to protecting the rights of landowners, the power of the landed gentry acting through Parliament placed constraints on the arbitrary powers of the king over industry.

Eventually, of course, industry became the source of security to property. Even though the landed gentry were instrumental in breaking the power of the monarchy, eventually, they used Parliament to further their own interests. The emergence of small and medium-sized farmers in the sixteenth and seventeenth centuries—the yeoman revolution—gave way to Parliamentary enclosures and the landlord revolution in the eighteenth and nineteenth centuries. While the former movement was progressive and enhanced productivity, the latter redistributed wealth to the newly politically powerful.43 By then, however, industry had come into its own—as evidenced by the battle over tariffs on food that it eventually won—and power shifted to new defenders of property.

Other Countries

We have focused on England because it is the canonical example of the emergence of constitutionally limited government. It is useful to see briefly whether other countries that developed constitutional government fit the mold.

France is often the canonical counter to Britain. Historians have puzzled over why France did not achieve constitutionally limited government until the nineteenth century. One reason is simply that the nobility and the church in France were all too strong before the French Revolution. Even a powerful king like Louis XIV only played the grandees off, one against the others. When he died, they regained their power.44 Since French kings could not suppress the great lords, they tried to enlist the peasantry's support by protecting their property rights against encroachment by the lords.45 So the peasantry in France held a substantial portion of the land, but in small, relatively inefficient holdings.46 Land sales also did not take off, in part because the king had no incentive to make alienation easy, for that would allow the peasants to sell out to, or be dispossessed by, the lords, and in part because, unlike England, there was no initial grand sale of expropriated land to jumpstart the land market. So the gentry did not emerge as a class. Finally, since the king levied and collected taxes through a centralized bureaucracy directly from the peasants, he really had no need to summon any form of Parliament on a regular basis.

The French Revolution and the confiscation and sale of the properties of the church and the aristocracy had some of the effect in France that the Tudor expropriations had in England. It reduced the land and power of the nobility, strengthened the then minuscule French gentry as well as the rich peasant farmer, created a national market for land and food by abolishing internal impediments to trade, and created a more permanent institutional structure of representative government. As a consequence, the productivity of French agriculture increased substantially in the nineteenth century.[47] The political and economic effects of these changes were undoubtedly critical in fostering the late, but substantial, French industrial revolution.

If our arguments hold generally, then they should not be valid just historically but also more recently. Very crudely, our arguments suggest that in predominantly agricultural countries, the security of property— clear laws facilitating the ownership of property and its sale as well as a judiciary and a government that respect them and enforce rights— should be low where land ownership is highly concentrated. Not only do big landowners have the ability to defend their property through private armies or through their influence over the local apparatus of the state, but they also have no incentive to see the infrastructure of a free market emerge to challenge their power.[48]

Statistical analysis suggests that the prediction seems to be borne out by the data. When a country is heavily dependent on agriculture, a high concentration of land ownership does seem to be associated with a lower level of protection of private property.[49]

This leads us to a final question. If wider (but not too wide) distribution of land led to participatory politics and respect for private property, why did every country not undertake land reform? Why till 1861 were the vast majority of Russian serfs tied to the land and without protection from their overlords and from the government? Why did it take the French Revolution, the Napoleonic conquests, and the revolutions of 1830 and 1848 for land to be distributed in continental Europe in a way more conducive to intensive commercial farming and greater respect for property rights?

One reason may be the nature of the land in some countries. Some lands lend themselves to intensive farming, while others lend themselves to a mode of agriculture such as plantations that is more extensive. This may partly explain why Costa Rica has had a more democratic history than Colombia.

The argument that the necessary technology of production does not permit an ownership pattern favorable to the emergence of strong property rights applies not only to land but also to industry. When industry consists of large monopolies, which exist only because the government affords them privileges, the government is likely to have little respect for property. For example, firms in extractive industries have value largely because of their rights to extract and really do not utilize huge amounts of human ingenuity. In countries that are abundant in natural resources—such as Zaire—the government can extract large amounts of money simply by withdrawing a mining privilege from one company and auctioning it off to another. Of course, eventually bidders realize they will have to factor in the cost of future bribes that will be needed to keep their privileges. The outcome, however, is that the government will have little incentive to respect property rights. Only a few countries have overcome the curse of being richly endowed with mineral resources.

But the most important reason why countries did not attain the appropriate distribution by design may be that the self-interest of the government and the nobility did not permit land reform, even if it would benefit the country as a whole. Certainly, an individual lord could not hope to gain by dividing up his land and selling the pieces to the peasants who farmed it. If other lords did not follow suit and force an eventual change in the climate of property rights enforcement, our revolutionary lord would find that the peasants to whom he had sold land enjoyed even less security of tenure now that the lord was not present to protect them. Moreover, any wealth the lord gained from the sale would itself be up for grabs, now that he could not hold out the prize of grain or below-market rents to enlist the support of his peasants in battle.[50]

The sovereign might also not have had the incentive to move to distribute land widely. After all, even if property rights became more secure, and the land became more productive, he would lose power. In many cases, it would be in the monarch's self-interest to continue coercive-extractive policies, even if detrimental in the long run for the country—as Louis XV is famously supposed to have said, "France will last my time."

The effects of the initial distribution of land may persist long after the distribution is no longer optimal, as we noted in the introduction to the book. For example, even after the emancipation of indentured or slave labor reduced the profitability of the large Latin American haciendas, the owners did not disband them. The need to maintain a ready pool of unskilled, poorly educated labor may explain why many of these hacienda-dominated countries did not pursue universal education and economic and social rights as vigorously as others did.[51]

If initial distributions of landholdings tend to persist in the absence of forcible reform, the legacy of history may explain why some countries, or even parts thereof, were lucky while others were not. For example, northern Italy and southern Italy are extremely different in their economies, today northern Italy being much more progressive than southern Italy. Estates were much larger in the South and the peasants far poorer. A number of historical factors, including the Norman conquest of the South in the eleventh century and the greater devastation caused by the plague in southern Italy in the fourteenth century, could account for the differences in land distribution.[52] In turn, these differences may partly explain the disparity in economic progress between the North and the South that persists even today.

The legacy of historic land distribution patterns seems to be important in India also. Areas in which property rights over land were given over to large landlords by the British in colonial times have significantly lower agricultural investment, lower agricultural productivity, lower rates of literacy, and higher rates of infant mortality in recent years.[53] The growing disparity between the booming west and south of India and the relatively stagnant central and northeast areas is probably, in some measure, a legacy of history.

Similarly, some former colonies of European powers developed stronger respect for property rights earlier than others: the initial European settlers migrated en masse to a colony if the climate was hospitable and the land disease-free—leading to the emergence of a group of yeoman farmers who formed a solid base for representative, constitutionally bound government. By contrast, landholdings in a colony were much more concentrated, and industry much more extractive, if the land was inhospitable so that only the minimum number of Europeans migrated to oversee large holdings worked by native labor.[54] These latter countries would have had to await the emergence of a viable manufacturing and trading class to establish secure property rights, but the emergence of that class would itself be held back by the absence of property rights and finance.

Finally, some governments care more about their own power than the prosperity of their citizens, giving us examples of the consequences of inappropriate redistributions of property. Fearful of their role in supporting the institution of private property, Stalin exterminated the yeoman farmers in Russia, the kulaks, in the 1920s and 1930s and gathered their land into large collective farms. The collectivization of Russian land caused enormous losses in agricultural production—but served the intent of removing the yeomanry, a strong force for private property, completely from the Russian landscape. Government could move ahead with communism unopposed.

More recently, formerly socialist economies have attempted to figure out how to distribute state-owned property to private citizens so as to ensure a smooth transition to capitalism. Some economists have argued that it does not really matter who owns the property; all that matters is that property find its way into private hands.[55] Our arguments suggest otherwise. Property in the wrong hands, especially if concentrated, can be very detrimental both to reducing the power of the state and to the emergence of free markets. The Russian republic provides one clear illustration. In an underhand deal to win support for the 1996 presidential election, Boris Yeltsin agreed to give a few powerful operators some of the best Russian companies at bargain-basement prices. This was just the most egregious of events by which Russian industry and finance became dominated by a few, whose primary competence was contacts rather than business acumen. It is little wonder that these "businessmen" came to be known as oligarchs, reminiscent of the reactionary feudal lords who stood in the way of capitalism.

Not only do these oligarchs oppose the development of free markets and free access to finance, but they also offer little countervailing force to a powerful state. Since their empires are not built on competence, they can be taken away as easily as they were acquired. The government of Vladimir Putin has, in fact, cut some of these oligarchs down to size and assumed significant power. Whether the oligarchs are replaced by others in a game of merry-go-round or whether the oligarchs are done away with so that a truly competent and competitive business class emerges is a matter to be seen. In that lies the future of Russian democracy and free market enterprise.

Summary

Historically, the greatest obstacle to the development of free markets, especially free financial markets, was the rapacity of governments. We have argued that the emergence of a class in England that individually was large enough to farm commercially and take risks but was not individually strong enough to protect itself created the demand for a constitutionally limited state. Institutions like Parliament and the administrative machinery served to coordinate this class and give it political power, which then resulted in the limitations on government it sought.

These safeguards were extremely important to ease the path of government finance. Unlike with land or industrial assets, most financial assets are held passively: the holder has no great expertise in generating value from those assets. Since the government suffers only a loss of reputation if it expropriates the cash or gold held by its citizens or if it repudiates the debt it owes them, the holders of financial assets are the first to be targeted by a government in need. It is rare for a troubled modern government to take the land farmers own or the machines firms have to pay its bills, but it is perfectly willing to pay public creditors only a fraction of the amount it owes. Finance therefore has to come within the perimeter of defenses built against the government by other forms of property for it to flourish.

But when investors feel safe, a country can benefit greatly because it can borrow to fund national enterprise and not be limited by what it can raise in the short run through taxes. As historian Richard Ehrenberg, writing in the early part of the twentieth century, puts it, "England would not have been the Great Britain of today, it would not have conquered half the world, if it had not incurred a national debt of 900,000,000 pounds between 1693 and 1815."[56]

The emergence of representative government is, however, only the first battle toward financial freedom. By becoming representative, government can obtain a greater latitude to borrow and can reduce the threat its people face from it. But it need not make the government interested in broadening access to finance. Government, even in a democracy, can be captured by a small, well-organized class that has little interest in seeing broad-based access to finance. This is what we turn to now.

CHAPTER SEVEN

The Impediments to Financial Development

THE FIRST STEP in the long march toward a first-rate financial system is to tame the government, to make it more respectful of its citizens' property so that citizens can create wealth in security. The devolution of the ownership of property toward those who can best use it is a crucial step in this process. Power invariably moves to the people as property becomes more efficiently and widely distributed.

This is just the first step. The most appropriate government for the financial sector is not necessarily a passive one. For instance, at minimum, the government has to enforce private contracts. But often, it may be called upon to do more. The cost to aggrieved parties of initiating enforcement is often so large as to make contractual protections worthless. A small shareholder, who buys a few shares in the market, will find it prohibitively expensive to enforce her rights against violation by the firm's insiders. Without a supervisory agency or some other mechanism to mitigate wrongdoing by insiders, minority shareholder rights will not be protected and outside equity financing will remain small.

More generally, markets do not arise in a vacuum. To function, they need infrastructure. Much of this infrastructure benefits every market participant, regardless of whether she has contributed to build it or not. Uniform standards in information disclosure, for instance, benefit both firms and investors, but no firm or individual will want to incur the entire cost of creating the standards or enforcing them. Market infrastructure is thus what economists call a public good: it benefits many, not all of whom can be charged for the benefits they get.

This does not immediately mean the government has to step in to provide the public good. Private parties provide public goods sometimes, especially when they can capture a large enough share of the benefits to pay for the public good's cost. Our university, for instance, captures enough of the benefits from additional security on campus that it pays for a private police force to patrol the area. In the same way, the New York Stock Exchange benefits enough from a reputation for good governance of its listed companies that it imposes its own strict standards of disclosure and governance on them. Nevertheless, in many situations, no easily organized group of participants captures enough benefits from the public good to provide it. Because too many beneficiaries have no incentive to pay and prefer a free ride, the private provision of public goods is often insufficient.

Whenever these coordination and free-riding problems are present, the government can play an active role in promoting the infrastructure needed for finance (and markets in general) to develop. But just because government *can* do good does not imply that it *will* do good. Governments in even the most democratic societies may not closely reflect the will of the public or its best interests: the same coordination and free-rider problems that suggest a need for organized intervention also impede the public's ability to direct that intervention toward its own greater good.

The reason is that even though democratic governments respond to pressures, the average individual, who is an anonymous member of a large, heterogeneous group, does not have the incentive to exert himself to see that his preferred policies are enacted. Instead, he usually prefers that others exert themselves for the cause. But when everyone thinks this way, committed lobbyists from small, homogeneous, motivated pressure groups—rather than the larger public—end up determining the political agenda. Therefore, while the first step to financial development is to contain the excessive power of the government over its citizens, the second step is to contain the power of small pressure groups over the government agenda. Who these groups are and why they want to hold back finance is the subject of this chapter. How to reduce their influence is the focus of the next one. But first, let us ask why organized intervention is needed to set up market infrastructure.

The Need for a Central Authority

In Chapter 1 we have already discussed how court inefficiencies and delays can jeopardize lending. More generally, market transactions require a central authority to enforce them promptly and at low cost. To see the importance of such an authority, consider how Poland and the Czech Republic attempted to create equity markets after the fall of the Berlin Wall.

The two countries, starting with a similar level of economic development, took very different paths.[1] Vaclav Klaus, the Czech Republic's libertarian prime minister, strongly believed in the market's ability to organize itself. Driven in part by ideology, the Czech Republic embarked on a massive privatization plan before setting up a robust market infrastructure. The Polish government, by contrast, proceeded more gradually. It first introduced very strict disclosure standards. Then it created the analog of the U.S. Securities and Exchange Commission (SEC), whose task was to ensure the enforcement of these disclosure standards as well as other rules meant to protect minority shareholders. Only later did it proceed with privatization.

Several years later, events seem to vindicate the Polish approach. While the Czech stock market started bigger, it quickly lost momentum as small investors began to realize that they lacked effective protection. Stories of investors' being defrauded by insiders, and of large institutional investors' allying with corporate insiders against minority shareholders, became common. Of course, eventually small investors become sophisticated enough to demand safeguards, but by then, they had been burned. According to an estimate, corporate insiders in the Czech Republic, on average, capture 58 percent of the value of a company for themselves over and above their legitimate shareholding, compared to an insignificant 1 percent that is captured in the United States.[2]

First impressions count: Once investors become convinced the market is unfair, extensive reform may not be enough to bring them back. It may not be possible to get investors to pay attention to the reform, so that they can be convinced that things have changed. The consequence of the investors' unfortunate initial experience was that Czech firms lost an important source of financing. Between 1996 and 1998, no companies raised funds through public share offerings.[3]

By contrast, the initially smaller Polish market quickly grew to surpass the Czech market, as the Polish authorities showed their willingness to prosecute violations of small shareholders' rights. Consequently, the value captured by insiders in Poland was a much lower 12 percent of the value of a company.[4] Knowing that their rights were better protected, investors gained confidence in the Polish stock market, and both new and existing companies were able to raise capital (U.S. $2.5 billion in the period 1996–1998).[5]

The point is that dispersed investors may find it prohibitively costly to become informed or to enforce their rights; hence, they need an organization like the SEC to represent them and laws to protect them. As another example, consider the effects of the 1933 Securities Act, which mandated the disclosure of corporate information with the accompanying threat of punishment for violations. Following the passage of the act, investors priced equities in the United States more accurately.[6] Mandatory disclosure—one explanation goes—made the information that firms disclosed more credible. As investors became more informed, the volatility of securities prices was reduced. Over time, the reduction in price fluctuations benefited ordinary investors, enabling them to make better investment decisions and reducing the ability of informed but unscrupulous traders to take advantage of them.

Interestingly, the NYSE had many of the rules that were required by the Securities Act of 1933 even prior to the act. So one argument about what was lacking is that it was the force of the law behind these rules, and the Securities Act certainly provided this. More generally, firms in countries that have better statutes protecting shareholders tend to have higher market values relative to book value, suggesting that investors expect to get more of the money firms generate and are thus willing to pay a higher price for these stocks.[7]

Of course, the existence of laws on the books does not mean they are enforced. While, at the end of 1998, laws prohibiting insiders from trading on privileged information existed in 87 of the 103 countries with a stock exchange, only 38 of them prosecuted violations.[8] The enforcement of laws prohibiting insider trading can benefit the ordinary investor because she does not have to worry about losing out by trading with someone with inside information. With lower costs of trading equity, shareholders will demand a lower return from firms, allowing firms to raise funds more cheaply. Indeed, after the law against insider trading starts being enforced, the rate of return shareholders demand in a country falls, implying that shareholders demand less as a compensation for risk when they know that they will not be cheated. So another argument for why the Securities Act of 1933 "worked" is that enforcement by the federal government was seen as more credible because it may have been seen as less subject to capture by insiders on the exchanges.

A central authority also solves coordination problems. For instance, study after study has shown that better accounting standards help make firms more transparent, making it easier for them to inspire confidence in investors. Of course, firms can adopt a policy of better disclosure by choosing a transparent accounting standard on their own: nothing prevents a German firm from also disclosing its accounts using more transparent U.S. standards. But without sanctions for improper disclosure or omissions, this would just be cheap talk, of very little value as a signal. Moreover, each firm would have the incentive to choose a method of disclosure that puts it in the best light. This would be problematic because disclosure serves two purposes: informing the investor about the firm and giving him a standard with which to compare it to other firms. If each firm chose its own idiosyncratic method of disclosure, comparability across firms would be lost—a problem that is apparent among the private equity funds, where investors complain about the difficulty of comparing fund performance when each fund can choose the method of disclosing performance that it prefers.

Of course, there are benefits of competition among standards, and eventually one standard will drive out another. The central authority may insist on the wrong standard, either because it is mistaken or because it is influenced by a particular group of self-interested firms. Nevertheless, the virtues of ready comparability stemming from a single, even if biased, centrally imposed standard can help avert the confusion from competing, even if slowly convergent, standards.

Why the Government?

Some of what we have listed above can be done both by the government and by organized private bodies. But in many instances, the government enjoys a natural comparative advantage. Certain penalties, such as exclusion from future activities, can be enforced by private organizations, but there are limitations on how much punishment they can inflict. For one, certain harsh remedies like incarceration are, in civil societies, a monopoly of the government.

Equally important, private sanctions can always be negotiated down. A trader who violates the rules of the Securities Dealers Association can attempt to persuade the association to change the rules that led to his exclusion or, easier still, find a loophole. If he is a prominent member, he may have some success doing so, with the association preferring the easier route in the short term despite the longer-term loss of reputation. By contrast, a violation of securities laws will lead to penalties, with the government prosecutor having only narrow room to negotiate. Changing laws is a much costlier and more cumbersome process than changing association rules—one reason why the law is more likely to be enforced. Another reason is that a federal prosecutor will be more distant from the trader than exchange officials, making him more likely to enforce the rules.

Of course, in corrupt economies in which the government bureaucrat is willing to "negotiate" everything, the government may be worse than the Dealers Association because, unlike the association, the government bureaucrat has little to gain privately by punishing transgression. However, once a government progresses beyond the predatory phase, as discussed in the previous chapter, it should well be capable of harsher sanctions than private associations.

The second area in which governments might be better is in imposing an agreement on all, not just the narrow parties to a contract. Consider, for example, the concept of limited liability discussed in Chapter 2—the idea that a firm (or an individual) can walk away from its debts if unable to pay. While it may seem commonplace today, there was a time when it was thought that limited liability was a fraud perpetrated on the unsuspecting public investor by those who had influence enough to obtain such protection from the sovereign. It was felt that under limited liability, the rich lured the poor investor into a venture under the pretext that it was well capitalized and then left the venture to its own devices at the slightest hint of trouble without bearing any of the costs. An editorial in the *Times of London* in 1824 thundered:

> Nothing can be so unjust as for a few persons abounding in wealth to offer a portion of their excess for the information of a company, to play with that excess for the information of a company—to lend the importance of their whole name and credit to the society, and then should the funds prove insufficient to answer all demands, to retire into the security of their unhazarded fortune, and leave the bait to be devoured by the poor deceived fish.[9]

But limited liability, as we have argued, is essential in a modern stock market, in which large sums have to be raised from a dispersed set of investors. It is, however, not simply a contract between two parties. Limitation of liability would be for naught if the owner's liability were limited only vis-à-vis parties with which the firm wrote contracts but unlimited vis-à-vis third parties. No one would buy shares if the buyer's entire wealth were at risk from suits by individuals who bought a defective product made by the company, or by the government attempting to recover the costs of environmental cleanup. This is why a stockholder enjoys limited liability even against noncontractual parties who have claims against the firm. Such a legal device, absolving the owner of any liability greater than the amount invested, and under a variety of circumstances, is a form of property right, held against one and all. Its universal applicability is impossible to achieve through private contract; it requires legitimization by the government.

More generally, finance makes use of a number of legal constructs such as priority (of debt), security (collateral), and bankruptcy, which attempt to specify property rights. But property rights are not simply a contract between two parties; they are a set of rights the individual holds against all comers, whoever they may be. For example, traditional Roman law defined the ownership of a piece of land as an unlimited right *usque ad inferes et usque ad sidera* ("from the center of the earth to the stars"). Such rights need the broad support of society through its agent, the government. Private contracting cannot substitute here.

In summary, we believe that there is a role a central authority can play in setting up the infrastructure for the financial system, and sometimes, but not always, the best institution to play this role is the government. An analogy may make our stand clear. Think of a downward-sloping field that needs to be irrigated. The force of gravity, if allowed to work, enables water to flow everywhere. This is the libertarian view. But there typically will be obstructions in the field, and channels will have to be cut to enable speedy irrigation, even if, given enough time, water will seep through everywhere. This is the interventionist view.

A more moderate libertarian view is that sometimes channels are needed, but farmers can organize privately to dig them. By intervening, the government will impede such private efforts. The interventionist recognizes the possibility that farmers may organize privately but argues that it will take time, there will be some tasks that are beyond private organizations, and perhaps most important, it may be prohibitively costly for the public to overcome the costs of organization and free-rider problems to create the necessary private organizations.

Thus far, we seem to have espoused the interventionist cause. But now it is time to recognize that the very forces that impede private organizations from voluntarily forming to undertake large public works will also prevent public organizations like the government from working in the public interest. Instead, even in a democracy, governments may work in the interest of a privileged few rather than the larger public and dig the wrong channels. This is what we now turn to.

Why Might the Wrong Channels Be Cut?

Given the undoubted benefits of financial development that we have documented, one might think that, in democracies, there would be strong political support in favor of finance and the government would be directed to create the necessary infrastructure. Unfortunately, this is not the case. Even in a democracy, not all voices are heard equally loudly, and policy making is often captured by powerful special interests that thrive because of the peculiarities of democratic governance. But what group has a vested interest against financial development? And how does it succeed in controlling the political agenda?

In order to illustrate the political obstacles to financial development, we will first explain which groups are likely to capture the government's policy agenda, and then we will argue that such groups often have an antifinance bias in countries with an underdeveloped financial sector. In many ways, the arguments we present are not specific to governments: they apply equally to private organizations formed for public purposes, as long as the large mass of people influenced by the organization's actions are dispersed and unable to coordinate actions.

Two economists, Mancur Olsen and George Stigler, argued in separate works that small, focused interest groups have disproportionate power in a democracy.[10] These ideas, which have taken firm root at the University of Chicago, are simple but powerful.[11] An example should make the underlying rationale clear.

In many cities in the developed world, the number of taxis on the road is strictly regulated. Most cities give out a certain number of medallions, each of which gives the owner the right to run one taxi. In New York, this number is precisely 11,787, and no new medallions have been issued in the last fifty years. Anyone who wants to operate a taxi has to buy a medallion from an existing owner. If the number of medallions is scarce relative to the demand for operating taxis, the price of medallions will rise since their supply is strictly limited. Prices of medallions can indeed be very high (over $200,000 in New York), suggesting that demand far exceeds supply.[12]

From an economist's perspective, this is an aberration. The high price of medallions suggests that there are potential entrants who would like to run taxicabs but are not allowed to. Such restrictions on the operation of the market seem unseemly. Yet the public rarely protests, even when it is habitually inconvenienced by the near impossibility of finding taxis.

When City Hall is asked, it will usually explain the restrictions on medallions as some combination of aesthetics, environment, and quality of service. More licenses for taxicabs would lead to more crowded streets and less-civil drivers. Moreover, cutthroat competition among drivers would not be good for the general public since medallion owners would have a lower incentive to maintain their cars or hire well-mannered, knowledgeable drivers.

These arguments are specious. Most cities do not impose minimum qualifications for taxi drivers. Medallion owners have no greater incentive to hire better drivers (or maintain cars) simply because their business is protected from entry: if anything, they have less incentive than if they faced competition. The real reason to restrict competition is the obvious one: medallion owners benefit from it.

How can the medallion owners get away with it? The answer is simple. Governments in democratic countries respond to pressure. Organized groups can exert more pressure than unorganized groups: they can pay for television advertisements, they can speak to City Hall functionaries, they can contribute influential amounts to campaigns . . . Which groups are the easiest to organize? A small group such as the owners of taxicab medallions has common interests and meets regularly at industry functions. It can quickly put together an agenda on which each member can agree. By contrast, the general public consists of people with widely differing motives and tastes. Everyone comes from different locations. It is hard to get everyone to meet, let alone speak with one voice.

Customers benefit from a competitive taxi market. But each one of them receives only a small benefit from an increase in the number of taxis, often too small to justify any political involvement. Furthermore, customers are dispersed, with many living out of town, so that the cost of coordinated action becomes prohibitively expensive. It is also costly for any one of them to inform himself about the details of the issue—whether the taxi owners and City Hall really have a sound economic case or whether they are camouflaging greed with high-sounding economics. Such rational ignorance is exacerbated by the ease with which any individual customer can hide among the large numbers of fellow customers and attempt a free ride on their political activities.[13]

By contrast, each taxi owner is greatly affected by entry and has the incentive to become well informed about his political options. Owners therefore form a small and well-identified group, which can easily act in a coordinated fashion. As a result, even in a democracy, their interest often prevails, despite the inefficient entry restrictions they advocate.

Economists cannot see inefficiency without asking whether there could be a better way. If the taxi owners are so politically powerful, could they not agree to forgo their privileges in return for a payment by customers? After all, everyone would be better off. Unfortunately, such bargains do not take place. One reason is that if such an offer were made, the public would no longer be ignorant. The arguments the taxi owners make for maintaining restrictions on the number of medallions would be revealed as specious (after all, they are willing to forgo restrictions for money, so it cannot be that society will embark on the road to perdition if the number of medallions is increased). Not being ignorant any longer, the public could vote to expand the number of medallions, leaving the taxi owners worse off. More generally, political privileges are often so tenuous that they cannot be traded, because the act of trading them will destroy them.[14] Now let us try to understand how such a framework can explain why financial development may be retarded.

The Small Groups against Financial Development

Financial development appears to be so beneficial that it seems strange that anyone would be opposed to it. However, financial development is not always win-win. It could pose a threat to some.

Consider, for instance, established large industrial firms in an economy, a group we will call industrial incumbents. In times of stability, these incumbents typically do not need a developed financial system to ensure their access to resources. They can finance new projects out of earnings from existing businesses—as most established firms do—without accessing external capital markets. Even when their business does not generate sufficient cash to fund desired investments, they can offer the assets they already own or their reputation as collateral against which they can borrow. Typically, as we have seen, even a primitive financial system is geared to providing funds against collateral or reputation—so industrial incumbents rarely suffer from a lack of funds even if the system is underdeveloped.

Indeed, they may be hurt by financial development. To begin with, we have seen in Chapter 5 that financial development breeds competition, and competition erodes incumbents' profits. Financial development also requires more transparency, which will directly hurt incumbents' traditional ways of doing business through contacts and relationships. Consider some examples. In 1991, the Bronfman family was permitted by the Canadian tax authorities to move 2 billion Canadian dollars to the United States without paying capital gains taxes. When the auditor general complained that the transaction "may have circumvented the intent of the tax code," the government finance committee attacked him for violating the Bronfmans' right to privacy.[15] In a similar vein, in India, a borrower can take money from one state bank, default, and obtain a fresh loan from another state bank. Banks do not share information about defaulters, in part because there is a law (which is finally being repealed) preventing widespread dissemination of information about defaulters. The privacy of defaulters and their right to maintain access to the public till are deemed more important than the public's money, but this is, of course, natural in an economy dominated by incumbents.

Incumbent financiers may also not fully appreciate change. While financial development provides them with an opportunity to expand their activities, it also strikes at their very source of comparative advantage. In the absence of good disclosure and proper enforcement, any financing that is not against solid collateral is "relationship-based." The incumbent financier gathers information from his wide-ranging informal contacts rather than from publicly available sources. He recovers payments not by using the legal system but by threatening and cajoling, using the many informal levers of power he has developed over the years. Key, therefore, to his ability to lend are his relationships with those who have influence over the firm, such as managers, other lenders, suppliers, and politicians. Equally important is his ability to monopolize the provision of finance to a client so that his threat to cut off credit carries weight. Such monopolies are more likely if there are no public records of a client's repayment history so that the client is locked in to his financier because only the latter knows his credit history: any other financier approached by the client would be wary of lending, wondering whether he was being approached only because the incumbent financier had deemed the client too risky.

Opaque borrower histories and inadequate legal infrastructure provide formidable barriers to entry behind which the incumbent financier adapts to enjoy large profits. By contrast, disclosure and impartial enforcement tend to level the playing field and reduce barriers to entry into the financial sector. The incumbent financier's old skills of being well connected become less important, while new ones of credit evaluation and risk management become necessary. Financial development not only introduces competition, which puts pressure on the incumbent financial institution's profitability and its relationships, but it also makes the financier's skills—his human capital—redundant.

In short, free markets tend to jeopardize ways of doing business that rely on unequal access. Thus, not only are incumbents likely to benefit less from financial development, but they might actually lose. This would imply that incumbents might collectively have a vested interest in preventing financial development.

They may also have the ability to affect policy: incumbents are a well-defined, focused, small group. In small countries, they have attended the same elite schools, frequent the same clubs, and often intermarry. They may be able to keep finance underdeveloped because those who benefit most from development, potential entrants, are small, poor, and unorganized, while the vast ill-informed majority do not know enough, or feel enough pain, to stir out of their complacency.

But this raises a question. Rich incumbents have other ways to protect their market share. Why choose to leave financial markets underdeveloped to do so? After all, this could end up hurting the incumbents, who might occasionally need external finance. Why not ban entry into industry or finance outright? Such a ban could be better targeted at rank outsiders, leaving insiders to enjoy the benefits of a more developed system.

There are, however, some advantages for incumbents from leaving finance underdeveloped as opposed to directly banning entry. First, direct entry restrictions often require very costly enforcement. Enforcement becomes particularly difficult, if not impossible, when the product whose market is restricted has many close substitutes. Enforcement is further complicated by the possibility that entrants can innovate around banned items. Each new threatening innovation has to be identified, categorized, and then banned. The bureaucracy that implements this "License Raj" will absorb a substantial part of the profits on its own and may compete for power with incumbents. By contrast, leaving finance underdeveloped is an act of omission, with few of the costs entailed by an act of commission, such as the use of the apparatus of the state to stamp out entry. Malign neglect may be as effective as active harassment but much easier to implement!

Second, the active enforcement of restrictions on entry is a very public, and therefore politically transparent, process. In a democracy, citizens have to be convinced that restrictions on entry benefit them, and this is a hard sell when they are faced with the poor service and extortionate prices of the local monopoly. By contrast, the malign neglect that leads to financial underdevelopment is less noticeable—it goes with the grain to have comatose bureaucrats who do not act rather than have overly active ones—and can be disguised under more noble motives. For example, the requirements that firms that list have to be profitable for a number of years before listing can be sold to the public as a way of protecting them from charlatans rather than as a way of preventing young, threatening, albeit unprofitable, entrants from raising finance. The requirement also obviates the need to improve accounting standards, something that would tend to level the playing field between the established and the fledgling.

Third, the more technical the barrier to entry is, the more costly it is for the general public to overcome their rational ignorance and find out whether it is justified. While most people can appreciate that a flat ban on entry has perverse effects, the same cannot be said for more technical norms that restrict access to finance. Take the above-mentioned listing requirement. For most voters, it would take considerable effort to find out whether it is justified: after all, are they not being protected from charlatans? If it is rational for the public to stay uninformed about technicalities, incumbents will find it easier to use that route to get their way.

Finally, the problem with entry restrictions is that they do not give a clear rule about which of the incumbents will get the right to monopolize new areas of the economy that emerge as a result of innovation or expansion. The fight over the right to enter these areas, especially when outsiders join in, can be messy, costly, and very public. It also will take profits from incumbents and give them to the bureaucracy that administers the system. By contrast, when the financial market is underdeveloped, the set of potential competitors for any new business is well defined and small—restricted to those incumbents that currently have financial surplus. This is the reason why, in less-developed capital markets, diversified business groups are dominant.[16] Because they have internally generated funds, these incumbents naturally enter new sectors even when they have no specific expertise in that area. Opportunities are allocated to those that happen to have resources, without a messy fight.

In short, while votaries of free markets like George Stigler have pointed out that regulations often are instituted to protect the regulated from competition, they also tend to be dismissive of the need for any regulation at all to create a market. By contrast, as we argue in the beginning of this chapter, some regulatory and supervisory infrastructure is needed for a competitive market to flourish. If so, private interests can be opposed to that regulation. Lack of regulation can be as protective and as much of an entry barrier as excessive regulation or outright prohibitions on entry!

This is not to say that direct entry restrictions are not used. Around the world, to start a generic business, an entrepreneur typically needs to follow ten bureaucratic procedures, requiring sixty-three days, with a cost equal to one-third of the average per capita income.[17] In some countries, however, the restrictions are more severe. In Bolivia, the number of procedures is twenty, with a cost equal to 2.6 times the average per capita income. These regulations do not seem to be used to screen out bad producers or protect the environment but rather to restrict entry. Of course, if the true objective is to limit entry, then it is efficient to use multiple methods, including keeping finance underdeveloped.

This is, in fact, what happens. If incumbents use multiple methods, and financial underdevelopment is similar in purpose to bureaucratic entry barriers, their use should be strongly positively correlated. They are! Countries requiring a lot of procedures to start a business also tend to have an underdeveloped capital market, with a low equity market capitalization to GDP ratio.[18] This negative relationship suggests that financial underdevelopment is another form of entry barrier.

Summary

It is useful to reflect on the different points we make about power in the previous chapter and in this one. We argued in the previous chapter that the taming of the government did not take place when the lords and their associated retainers had coercive power. Instead, it seemed to take place as their concentrated coercive power gave way to the economic power of the gentry and as property migrated into the hands of those who could use it well. Not only did proprietors have the economic power to defend their interests (and with coordinating institutions like Parliament, the ability to translate economic power into political power), but it was also in the sovereign's own interest to respect property rights and allow more participation in governance, for that would help him ensure that owners created the most economic surplus. They then paid the most taxes into the treasury coffers. These taxes could form a far more lucrative and stable form of revenue than periodic expropriation. Thus, wider and more efficient property holdings led to more participatory governance and more respect for private property rights.

But even if the government does become participatory and more respectful of property, there is no guarantee that it will work in the public interest. Small, well-focused groups can sway government policies toward their interests at the expense of the public. Since financial markets rely on the government for good policies, these policies may never be enacted when well-organized incumbents oppose them. This then leads naturally to the question "When are the special interests opposed to financial development overcome?" That is the subject of the next chapter.

CHAPTER EIGHT

When Does Finance Develop?

Is FINANCIAL development doomed never to take place because incumbents are so powerful? Clearly not! Some countries have enjoyed strong financial systems at certain points in time, and there has been a worldwide boom in the financial sector in the last few decades. This must mean that sometimes incumbents cannot get together to block development, and even if they do so, the tyranny of incumbents can be broken and development unleashed.

One reason, as our earlier comparison of Brazil and Mexico suggests, is political change. The ideas of the French Revolution, distributed via Napoleon's conquests throughout much of western Europe, picked up momentum with the revolutions of 1830 and 1848. By the 1850s and the 1860s, governments in Europe had become much more participatory. Arguably, the Napoleonic land reforms had the effect of diminishing the power of the then establishment, the landed nobility, and giving more political power to rich peasants, would-be industrialists, and financiers. With the growing economic importance of the business and professional class, financial reform followed quickly. For example, firms were allowed to incorporate freely with limited liability in France in 1863, Spain in 1869, Germany and Belgium in 1873 . . . Stock exchanges also emerged around this time. Many new firms were formed, and new financial institutions like the Crédit Mobilier in France sprang up to take on the establishment and provide credit to the upstarts.

A second reason for incumbents not to oppose development blindly is that they themselves can benefit from financial development when their investment opportunities are high relative to their ability to finance them. A sudden expansion in required scale, perhaps because of an opening of new markets for their products, increases their demand for financing. Alternatively, a sustained period of poor economic conditions may deplete incumbents' reserves of cash, forcing them to seek finance and allowing them to be more amenable to financial development when the economy turns up.

Finally, and perhaps most important, increased competition resulting from forces beyond the control of incumbents—in particular, competition as a result of technological changes and competition stemming from open borders—can reduce incumbents' incentives to use financial underdevelopment as a barrier to domestic entry. We now examine all these in greater detail.

Political Change and Financial Development:

The Story of Crédit Mobilier

It is perhaps best to illustrate the impetus given to development by political change with a brief sketch of the rise and fall of the Société Générale de Crédit Mobilier in France in the second half of the nineteenth century.

The fall of Napoleon in 1814 (with a brief comeback in 1815) heralded a long period of relative peace in continental Europe. The industrial revolution picked up speed, and soon there was a tremendous need for credit to fund the expansion. But even in France, one of the most technologically advanced countries in western Europe, the financial system was grossly underdeveloped.

At the center of the financial system in France stood the Bank of France. It had been started by Napoleon, who was influenced by the success of the English government in mobilizing credit from the Bank of England. Napoleon, too, sought a ready source of credit for his military adventures with the Bank of France. But unlike the Bank of England, the Bank of France had "difficulty placing its shares in spite of the personal example of the First Consul and his decree requiring government agents to purchase shares and deposit their surplus funds in the Bank; almost two years elapsed before the entire capital was paid in."[1] Perhaps one reason the bank had such great difficulty raising money even at the height of the French Empire's success was that it was little more than an extension of an all-powerful government, and it had no ability to refuse the extensive demands made on it. The initial reluctance of private investors to trust it with their money proved justified. With the fall of the empire in 1814, the bank went into virtual liquidation.

This established financial institution was, however, too valuable a tool for the government and the establishment to simply let die. While there were some moves to privatize the bank at this point, the Restoration government in France preferred having it under its own control. As Baron Louis, the then finance minister, told the representatives of the bank, "You want to be independent, but you will not; you will have a governor, I will name him, and he will not be the one who currently occupies the post."[2]

From the beginning, the Bank of France stood as a bulwark against financial development because it feared the competitive threat to its own position.[3] The bank opposed the setting up of joint stock banks. In part, this was because many of the grandest proposals were influenced by the doctrines of the eccentric philosopher Henri de Saint-Simon. Saint-Simon believed that the hereditary nobility and the landed aristocracy were parasites and the future lay in the hands of industrialists and bankers. The free flow of credit to industry was the key to progress, and his more sensible and enterprising followers proposed schemes marrying banking and industry. But the government of the Restoration (correctly) feared that these proposals struck at its own legitimacy—after all, the hereditary nobility and the landed aristocracy were its political base.[4]

It therefore took successive political revolutions to overcome the forces of incumbency. Even though the Revolution of 1830 weakened the aristocracy and put progressives in government, the Bank of France retained enough influence to oppose innovations, especially the founding of new financial institutions. The Revolution of 1848 further weakened the establishment, and a grievous blow was struck by the coup d'état that brought Louis Bonaparte to power. The new government was fully aware that the financial establishment, especially the Rothschilds and the Bank of France, had close connections with the Orleanist monarchy that had just been overthrown. So it made haste both to constrain the powers of the established financiers and to build up counterweights. One of the decisive actions it took was to force the Bank of France to extend more credit to emerging industries like the railways (which did not have ties to the ancien régime). It also authorized new kinds of financial institutions such as mortgage banks. Soon, France had a national market that could supply mortgage financing to even the smallest borrowers at reasonable prices. But perhaps the boldest move was to authorize the formation of the Société Générale de Crédit Mobilier in 1852.

The promoters of the Crédit Mobilier were Emile and Isaac Pereire, brothers who had been strongly influenced by Saint-Simon's economic ideas. They had a vision of a vast financial conglomerate that would be financed through equity and bond issues and would diversify risk by lending to a variety of industries. By controlling the flow of credit to these industries, it would be able to fine-tune production and thus make sure that all parts of the economy moved in harmony, without periods of overcapacity and unemployment. The liabilities of this giant intermediary would be safe and liquid because it was so well diversified and because it was governed by the most reputable captains of banking and industry (including, of course, the Pereires).[5] Thus, the Crédit Mobilier was part trust fund, part bank, part cartel. Modern banking theory would suggest that some of its functions were incompatible. Nevertheless, to the government of the Second Empire, it looked like the very institution to challenge the dominance of the Bank of France and the Rothschilds.

The proposal for the Crédit Mobilier was predictably opposed by James Rothschild, who wrote a letter to the government characterizing the scheme as fraught with speculation, irresponsibility, and monopoly.[6] Nevertheless, there was great support for the venture among the public, so much so that a market developed in its shares even before issue, when they fetched a price that reached four times the par value of the stock.[7] Since it had the support of the government, and because it had caught the public imagination, it was impossible to stop the Crédit Mobilier from being set up.

It soon had enormous impact, not just in France but also in continental Europe. In its first year of operations, it bought a large stake in the Crédit Foncier, the newly created national mortgage bank, with which it shared directors and coordinated operations. It financed through direct lending and underwriting a number of railroads and merged some of them together. It reorganized the coal industry in Loire and participated in setting up the Darmstädter Bank, which was modeled along the lines of the Crédit Mobilier itself, in Germany. It financed a number of other undertakings in France and neighboring countries and subscribed to a government loan.[8] The economic historian Rondo Cameron provides a measure of the rapid growth in its importance to the French economy. By 1856, four years after it commenced operations, it handled all financial operations for sixteen large financial and industrial enterprises, with a combined capital of 1 billion francs, over one-fifth the capitalization of the Paris Bourse.9 It had considerable effect on the formation and financing of large-scale enterprises, and soon every government in western Europe considered setting up its own version.

Some of the best-known banks in France today were set up during this period of ferment when the government encouraged rather than opposed new business formation. The Crédit Lyonnais incorporated under the new limited-liability laws in 1863 and the Société Générale in 1864. Numerous new joint stock banks were set up in other countries of continental Europe.

Parenthetically, such periods of economic and political ferment are extremely important. After all, the entrant of today becomes the incumbent of tomorrow. If the leaders of the financial and industrial sectors emerge extremely competitive from such episodes, they are less likely to press for inefficient regulations hampering entry.

Despite serving as an example—and in many cases, a catalyst—for financial development, the Crédit Mobilier itself faced increasing problems. These had to do with the way it was financed and the control its opponents had over it. The firm was set up initially with substantial equity capital. It could also issue short-term debt and take deposits from the companies it had promoted (its affiliates). These, and its ability to recover loans made to, or to sell the securities it held in, affiliate companies in the booming market, were sufficient for it to provide financing to new ventures when times were good. But with the depression of 1857–1858, many of these sources dried up. Instead of affiliates' being net sources of funds, they became net drains, requiring large loans to help them through the troubled times. As public financial markets dried up, the Crédit Mobilier became their only hope.

Moreover, instead of following sound banking practice and maintaining a diversified portfolio, the Pereires became infected with the hubris that often strikes successful financiers—that anything they touch will turn to gold. One of their early promotions was a company set up in 1854 for urban reconstruction in Paris. The Société Immobilière, as it became known, soon became enmeshed in another one of the Pereires' projects, the proposed Suez Canal. Anticipating that its opening would transform Marseilles into one of the world's largest ports, the société bought large tracts of land around Marseilles and started developing them with funds from the Crédit Mobilier. But investment in land, especially when the principle is "build it and they will come," is fundamentally illiquid. By 1865, the Crédit Mobilier had 55 million francs in loans to companies, of which fully 52 million were to the société.

Crédit Mobilier's fundamental problem now emerged. It had little ability to fund illiquid investments because the government controlled its access to long-term funding. And the government was influenced by Crédit Mobilier's rivals, the Bank of France and the Rothschilds, who, seeing that the government of Louis Bonaparte was likely to be around for some time, had wormed their way back into its favors.[10] So when, in September 1855, the Pereires announced a long-term bond issue, the government asked it initially to postpone the issue to avoid burdening the capital market with excessive issues and then forced it to postpone the issue indefinitely.[11] The Pereires did not help their case by repeatedly attacking the policies of the Bank of France. So when again, in 1863, the Pereires proposed doubling the capital of the Crédit Mobilier, the proposal was again turned down.

As its loans to the Société Immobilière grew, the Pereires finally got permission to raise new capital, in return for a number of modifications in its statutes, restricting its freedom of action further. But it was already too late. The new capital was simply poured into the bottomless pit of the Société Immobilière. Shareholders grew restive, and Crédit Mobilier's share price plummeted. On the verge of bankruptcy, the Pereires found other financial institutions reluctant to lend and approached the Bank of France for a loan to extricate themselves from the mess at the Société Immobilière.

As Rondo Cameron puts it, "The first reaction of the regents [of the Bank of France] was outrage and indignation. That they should be asked to save the men and institution that for 15—nay, 37—years had by both word and deed attacked and attempted to overturn their privileges and position!"[12] Eventually, however, the Bank of France felt that the total collapse of a large institution like the Crédit Mobilier could have repercussions on the whole economy and decided to intervene, at the very least to ensure an orderly liquidation. In return, it demanded the resignation of the Pereires brothers from their posts. Somewhat ironically, it was a former governor of the Bank of France who replaced Isaac Pereire as chairman and presided over the restructuring of the firm. While the Crédit Mobilier did not really expire till the Great Depression in the 1930s, henceforth, it was a shadow of its former self.

The demise of the Crédit Mobilier contains, in many ways, the classic cautionary lessons on how to run a financial institution. Diversify, do not throw good money after bad, match assets with liabilities, maintain liquidity, or at least make sure you have friends who are willing to supply liquidity when you are in need . . . All these lessons were ignored. The Crédit Mobilier may not even have been particularly good at financing its clients: its clients were not particularly damaged by Crédit Mobilier's demise, suggesting either that it was never very special or that its clients had seen the handwriting on the wall and had acquired alternative sources of finance by the time it became incapable of lending."[13]

Nevertheless, the story of the Crédit Mobilier also reflects how important political change is to financial reform. It shows how an upstart financial institution, by devising new financial and industrial arrangements, can shake up the entire financial and industrial establishment, far more perhaps than direct political intervention ever could. It also shows that the establishment will follow the upstart's lead if its strategy is of any value and may eventually beat it at its own game. So even if the upstart is short-lived, it can forever change the practice of finance. In order to preserve their position in Austria, for example, the Rothschilds were forced to set up a Crédit Mobilier–like institution, the Creditanstalt, which was at the center of the Austrian financial system till the Great Depression.[14] In more recent times in the United States, we have seen how the financing of hostile takeovers by Drexel Burnham Lambert eventually led top-tier commercial and investment banks to overcome their own scruples about antagonizing the blue-blooded industrial establishment. They were forced by the competition from upstart Drexel to finance the takeover of such hoary firms as Singer and RJR Nabisco, against the desires of the incumbent management.

The comparison is particularly apt. Like the Crédit Mobilier, Drexel Burnham Lambert, too, stepped on many toes and found it had few friends in the establishment when it ran into difficulty. That the Federal Reserve did not find it imperative to orchestrate its rescue cannot be unrelated to the number of enemies Drexel made through its financing decisions. *Plus ça change, plus c'est la même chose!*[15]

New Opportunities and Financial Development

The new financial and industrial firms that emerge during a period of political change eventually do become established incumbents—if they do not die first. But they do not always want to use their powers to kick away the ladder of financing that took them to their perch: industrial incumbents will also benefit from financial development when their investment opportunities are high relative to their ability to finance them. A sudden expansion in required scale, perhaps because of an opening of new markets, increases their demand for financing and hence their willingness to press for financial development. Efficient producers are especially likely to see opportunity rather than threat in new markets.

In the 1850s and 1860s, the dramatic reduction in the cost of transportation suddenly expanded the potential size of the market that each firm could service. In order to enable their firms to penetrate foreign markets, countries started espousing the cause of free trade. They also moved to the gold standard. The fixing of exchange rates in terms of gold allowed producers to be more certain of the prices they would get for exports (as well as the costs of their imported inputs), thus allowing them to produce for trade with greater confidence. The gold standard also encouraged intercountry flows of capital, which benefited both capital-rich countries like England that could invest their surplus and capital-poor countries like Sweden that could industrialize rapidly using foreign capital. Thus, the expansion in markets also led to an expansion in the need for financing as well as in the supply of financing.

Incumbents' attitude toward financial development can change over time, as financing needs change. In continental Europe, for instance, World War I represented an important turning point in these needs, especially for heavy industry. Before the war, high investment needs made heavy industry very dependent on external financing. As a result, the cause of financial development was strongly supported by powerful industrial firms in these countries. After the war, however, inflation and war profits freed many of these firms from the need to raise funds on a continuous basis. For example, Ansaldo, an Italian producer of heavy machinery, was very dependent on bank financing before the war. After the war, it was flush with cash, so much so that it twice attempted to take over the very bank that had financed its development before the war.[16] In short, changes in the financing needs of major players (rather than the needs of the larger public) can contribute to a significant shift in the political attitude toward finance.

New Technologies and Competition from the Outside

Technological change can also make it less profitable for incumbents to keep out potential local entrants. This is because technology can make it possible for competition to seep in from across political borders. Because political entry barriers are no longer airtight, incumbents may also abandon their support for other forms of entry barriers, including financial underdevelopment. An example of a regulatory entry barrier in the United States that succumbed in large part to the competitive pressure brought about by technological change is the law prohibiting banks from opening branches.

The United States Constitution prevented its constituent states from issuing their own money and from taxing trade between states. As a result, early in their history, states had to look for new sources of revenue. One important source was banks. States restricted entry into banking: a bank charter purchased on payment of a substantial fee to the state was required to undertake banking business in a state. Furthermore, states often held shares in banks and also taxed their profits.[17]

Bank profits were therefore a disguised tax on the people, with private bank owners making profits and passing a significant portion on to the state in the form of taxes and dividends. The state could maximize taxes by maximizing bank profits. This would imply giving a bank charter to only one bank for the entire state. But that would put too much power in the hands of one bank. Equally inconvenient from the state's perspective was to give charters to many banks, for that would force them to compete away profits, thus allowing the undeserving public rather than the needy government to get the benefits.

States therefore decided on a halfway measure. More than one bank would be given charters, but banks would not be allowed to open multiple branches within the state. Some states even had unit banking laws, restricting each bank to just one branch. The effect of these restrictions was to give each bank a monopoly over a small area surrounding it, enabling the bank to make profits. But they also ensured that the state was not beholden to one bank. Thus, restrictions on intrastate branching became the norm. Moreover, since states did not receive fees from banks incorporated in other states, they prohibited out-of-state banks from operating within their borders.

In general, these restrictions were extremely inefficient. By preventing good banks from expanding, and all banks from diversifying beyond their local territory, the branching restrictions made banks, on average, less cost-effective and more risky. Yet the restrictions persisted, initially because the state needed them to raise revenue, and later, because the small banks that emerged as a result needed them to survive and were willing to pay the state's legislators to ensure that the status quo prevailed.

This illustrates an important point about entry restrictions. Once the restrictions are in place, some constituencies will emerge that owe their existence to the restrictions and are not competitive enough to survive without them. There will be a natural tendency for these constituencies to grow more powerful over time: as time passes, those that are hurt by the restrictions will wither away, reducing the opposition. Restrictions will also provide the current and prospective profits with which the incumbents that benefit can pay for their political defense. By contrast, opponents of entry restrictions have nothing to offer supporters but competition. Competition erodes, rather than shores up, the prospective profits needed to pay for political assistance. Is it any wonder, then, that anticompetitive forces are so powerful?

In the case of branching restrictions, the natural supporters were small banks, which survived at an inefficiently small scale only because the branching restrictions protected them against large, cost-efficient banks. Other financial institutions such as insurance companies also supported restrictions because they feared that large banks would enter insurance and would be very effective at distributing insurance through their branches. Large banks were opposed to branching restrictions because they prevented their natural growth and diversification. It stands to reason that small banks and insurance companies would col-lude to keep in place the restrictions on intrastate branching. Through much of the twentieth century, their preferences prevailed. Starting in the early 1970s, however, many states relaxed their restrictions. What made them do it?

The answer is technology.[18] Branching restrictions help a bank create a local monopoly for itself only if it is hard for other banks to do business with the bank's customers at a distance. But technological innovations erode the effects of distance. Automatic teller machine networks enable a bank to provide cash to its customers no matter where they are, with-out having a local branch. Credit-rating agencies maintain detailed and timely records on customer creditworthiness so that a bank without a local presence can make loans to individuals without being subject to undue risk. In short, technological advances allow banking business to be conducted at a distance, eroding local monopolies and making them less valuable to maintain.[19]

While the broad timing of the deregulation across the various states in the United States, starting in the 1970s, corresponds to when these major technological advances became commercially important, there were differences among states as to when each one deregulated. The timing of when a particular state deregulated offers evidence of the strength of the private interests against deregulation in that state. The removal of restrictions on branching occurred sooner when the state had fewer small banks and more small, bank-dependent firms (which had a strong interest in facing more competitive banks). Also, the presence of a large insurance industry in that state led to delays in deregulation.[20]

Deregulation also had the predicted consequences. Small banks lost market share, and in states where banks could enter the insurance sector, the insurance sector shrank. But in general, borrowers benefited because they obtained lower average interest rates on their loans, and the state economy benefited because growth rates of state income increased (as we have noted earlier).[21] Special-interest groups were indeed holding back economic progress, and technological change may indeed have been the only way that their incentives to oppose entry could be altered.

Openness and Financial Development

We have just seen that technological change can put pressure on incumbents to alter archaic financial regulations, since these become less useful in preventing competition. Another instance in which incumbents find financial underdevelopment less useful as a tool is when an economy is, or becomes, open to the entry of foreign goods and capital. The easiest way to think about this is as follows: Incumbents can manipulate the political process in order to suppress domestic competition. But open borders subject them to competition from entities that are not governed by the domestic political process. This has a number of consequences.

For one, there are fewer profits to protect in the system: given that the economy is open, incumbents cannot use domestic political action to restrain foreigners. Moreover, given that prospective profits from restraining domestic entry will be limited (how much damage can domestic entry do when one is bearing the full brunt of the foreign peril?), both the incentive to keep restraints in place as well as the ability to pay politicians for their support diminishes. Finally, in the face of foreign competition, even established domestic incumbents find a need to rely on the domestic infrastructure—for example, established firms finally find that the high cost of domestic finance hurts. So not only do they not want to oppose financial development, they become active supporters.

Of course, whether a country's borders are open is itself, in part, a political decision. We will not examine that decision in this chapter, because it is part of a larger question of whether a country's economy is willing to be market-oriented, which is the focus of subsequent chapters.

We have been a little quick thus far in arguing that openness fosters competition, which, in turn, fosters financial development. Some forms of outside competition may, in fact, make incumbents even more eager to suppress financial development. It is therefore useful to examine separately the effects of a country's openness to trade (that is, to competition in goods and services) and the effects of its openness to capital flows (that is, to competition in the financial sector). It is also illuminating to separate out the reactions of industrial incumbents from financial incumbents.

Consider first a country that is open to trade alone. While foreign markets bring opportunity, openness also brings foreign competitors to domestic markets. Foreign entry drives down domestic profits. Lower profits mean that established firms have lower cash flow from operations, making them more dependent on external finance. At the same time, outside opportunities (or the need to defend domestic markets against superior foreign technologies) increase the need for incumbents to invest more and to manage their risks better.

Such competition was responsible, in part, for the liberalization of the financial sector in Spain in the aftermath of its accession to the European Community in 1986.[22] Till then, the domestic financial system in Spain was dominated by a cartel of the seven largest banks, which controlled 72 percent of deposits and was able to maintain the cost of credit significantly above the European average.[23] The increasingly competitive environment resulting from the entry into the European Union highlighted the disadvantages imposed on the industrial sector by the financial system, forcing a major shift in policy. In 1988, the socialist government of Felipe González approved a major reform of the capital markets, a proposal by an ad hoc government commission that had been ignored for over a decade. That a socialist government pushed for the development of financial markets when its right-wing predecessor did not suggests that, under the pressure of foreign competition, ideology may play a very limited role.

What happened in Spain is probably an exception. Just because incumbent industrial firms need external finance does not mean the country will improve transparency and access to finance. In fact, given their greater need for finance, industrial incumbents may press for greater financial repression so that the available finance flows their way. Financial incumbents also may be unwilling to trade the increased competition in the financial sector (from greater transparency and access) for the additional industrial clientele that reforms may generate. It may be far more profitable to support the existing relationships with industrial incumbents and ply them with the greater amounts of capital they now need.

Instead of pressuring the government into improving the quality of the domestic financial system, therefore, industrial incumbents may petition it for further loan subsidies in the face of foreign competition. Government lending is pernicious for two reasons. First, it responds to political needs rather than economic opportunity. Second, cheap government funding tends to crowd out a public capital market since investors do not have the benefit of subsidies and cannot supply funds at the same rate. Funds will tend to be intermediated by the banking sector, which can petition the government for a share of the subsidies. Since the banking sector cannot compete with the government without subsidy, it will become little more than a government agency in charge of distributing credit according to government plans, even if not directly owned by the government.

This is in fact what happened in France after World War II. At the end of the war, French industry was largely composed of small and medium-sized firms. They had been isolated from international competition during much of the interwar period. Unlike in other countries in Western Europe, agriculture was still a dominant employer in the economy. Over the next thirty years, internal and external competitive pressures forced the economy to be transformed in two important ways. First, agriculture gave way to industry, and second, industry restructured and consolidated so that it came to be dominated by large firms.

Outside competitive pressures forced industrial change, but instead of allowing the financial markets free rein in effecting these changes, the government decided, for reasons we explore in more detail in the following chapters, to control the pace of change by taking over the financial sector.

For example, the French government intervened extensively in the labor-intensive textile industry. Even though the average firm was small relative to producers in other European countries, and even though it used outdated machinery, the government blocked new plants that would have higher productivity and potentially bid up wages. It directly subsidized wages to prevent layoffs and imposed a number of restrictions to prevent foreign competition. A fund was set up exclusively to provide monies that would preserve the small-scale nature of the textile industry.[24] Thus, initially, the objective seemed to be to preserve the industry in its antiquated form by providing finance.

Over time, economic forces did play themselves out, albeit slowly. Employment in the industry dropped, aided by government funding that helped smooth plant closures. The thrust of government intervention now turned to facilitating mergers, again with the carrot of government-directed credit. While government intervention certainly prevented the rapid layoffs that would have occurred if the industry had been exposed to competition, it also prolonged the pain and allowed the industry to become much less productive than its Dutch or German counterpart. And when, in the early 1970s, new competition emerged from developing countries, the industry was particularly unsuited to meet it. This unleashed yet another bout of government intervention, more aggressive than in the past, as decisions on what firms to rescue were made, not by creditors but by the government.[25] Intervention invariably creates its own future justification.

Government intervention in the allocation of credit was thus pervasive. As late as 1979, a Bank of France publication reported that 43 percent of all credits to the economy were made with some kind of privilege or subsidy, and 25 percent of corporate lending was subsidized directly.[26] Much of the control emanated from the treasury, a small group of approximately one hundred bureaucrats comprising the elite of the elite. As a French businessman who began his career in the treasury remarked:

You live with a profound belief that France is the center of the world, that Paris is the center of France, and the Trésor is the center of Paris. . . . The Trésor's influence and prestige extend into every part of France. It represents the State inside the three largest banks: Crédit Lyonnais, Banque Nationale de Paris, and Société Générale. It also has a viselike grip on the finances of the French public sector, one of the biggest in the West, and on government subsidies.[27]

In short, governments may intervene to mitigate the effects of outside competition, and this may further reduce the transparency of, and the access to, the financial system. Thus, openness to trade flows (that is, industrial-sector openness) alone may not be enough to convince either, or both, dominant interest groups to support financial development. This suggests that there were other factors in the Spanish experience that made it different from the earlier French experience, so that external competition spurred financial development in the former and government intervention in the latter.

It is when both cross-border trade flows and capital flows are unimpeded that industrial and financial incumbents will have convergent incentives to push for financial development. Industrial incumbents, with depleted profits and the need for restructuring operations to meet competition, will require funds. But it is important to note that, with free cross-border capital flows, the government will not be able to respond by stepping up the flow of credit to incumbents: as product markets become more competitive, the risks in, and information requirements for, lending will increase. The potential for large errors from the government's directing the flow of credit will increase. Moreover, the ability of the government to provide large subsidized loans to favored firms will decrease as mobile international capital forces governments to maintain a balanced budget. The government's role in the financial sector will diminish.

This is, in fact, what eventually happened in France. During the 1950s and 1960s, the French government limited the political price it had to pay for the extensive subsidized credit it doled out, financing the credit through an expansion in the money supply. This meant that instead of paying taxes to finance the government's large expenditure, citizens financed it by accepting higher inflation and thus a lower value for their holdings of money. During this period, France was forced to devalue the franc three times (without counting the tariffs introduced in

1954, which were meant to mimic the effect of a devaluation).[28] But these devaluations were few and far between and were swallowed by the public.

Matters came to a head in the 1980s. Even though François Mitterrand came to power in 1981 with a program to increase subsidies and the state's role in the economy, the environment had changed. With the breakdown of the Bretton Woods agreement (more on this later) in the 1970s, international capital mobility had increased. With the accession of Mitterand's socialists to power, capital started fleeing France, partly because the rich were escaping before the anticipated confiscatory policies of the socialists and partly because the sensible foresaw that the exchange rate would come under pressure as the socialists continued loose budgetary policies. Almost inevitably, the French devalued in October 1981, then did so again in June 1982. By March 1983, France was again on the brink of running out of reserves as it tried to defend the franc.

The additional external pressure from free capital flows forced the socialist government to do an about-face. Recognizing that either it had to completely close down the economy to trade and capital flows or else it had to balance its budget and cease meddling in the functioning of the economy, it chose the latter. Only a few years after having nationalized the entire banking sector, the French socialists became strong supporters of a free market French financial system, so much so that in 1986, they inaugurated in Paris that ultimate symbol of a market economy, a futures market!

With the diminished role of the government, competition in the industrial sector and in the financial sector can reinforce each other when the economy is open to both trade and capital flows. The healthiest industrial incumbents will be able to tap the now open foreign markets for finance. These firms, able to compete in international markets, may not be much worried, or affected, by domestic entry and thus may not oppose domestic financial development. While the not-so-healthy industrial incumbents may be the hardest hit by foreign competition, there are reasons why they, too, may not oppose financial development and may in fact support it: they will need finance. And their existing financiers will be reluctant to lend to them on the old cozy terms.[29] Difficulty in financing will lead these firms to push for greater transparency and access so that their own access to finance improves. Unlike the case when the country is only open to capital flows, industrial incumbents now will also push for financial development. The accompanying threat of domestic industrial entry will now seem relatively minor, given the competitive state of the markets for goods and services.

Moreover, as the domestic financial sector loses some of its best clients, domestic financial institutions will want to seek new clients among the unborn or younger industrial firms that hitherto did not have the relationships to obtain finance. Since these clients will be riskier, and less well known, financial institutions will have no alternative but to press for improved disclosure and better contract enforcement. In turn, this leveling of the playing field will create the conditions for more entry and competition in the financial sector.

This then gives us the missing link for the Spanish experience. The salutary combination, not only of open borders to trade but also of prospective cross-border capital flows as a result of increasing European monetary integration, and not the former alone, gave strong impetus to the financial-sector reforms in Spain to which we referred earlier. European monetary integration has also provided a tremendous boost to stock markets around continental Europe, so much so that the Deutsche Bourse from Germany, a stock market from a traditionally bank-dominated country, seriously considered being the senior partner in a merger with the London Stock Exchange.

Other influences will kick in over time. As the domestic financial incumbents improve their skills, they will seek to compete abroad. As they look for new clients outside, they will be forced as a quid pro quo to increase access for foreigners and dismantle domestic regulations that give them their privileged competitive positions. For example, the German government banned lead underwriting of deutsche mark bonds by Japanese financial institutions until Japan agreed in 1985 to allow foreign securities firms to act as lead underwriters for bonds denominated in yen.[30] Foreign financial firms that enter the domestic market are likely to be another powerful constituency for financial development. Since they are not part of the domestic social and political networks, they would prefer transparent arm's-length contracts and enforcement procedures to opaque negotiated arrangements. It is not a coincidence that these are the very requirements of would-be domestic entrepreneurs who are also outsiders to the domestic clubs.

The Japanese corporate bond market offers a good example of financial development's being forced from the outside. In 1933, the Japanese banks, with the blessings of the Ministry of Finance, formed a Bond Committee, which determined which firms could issue bonds, on what terms, and when. The committee established a collateral principle— "Corporate bonds shall not be issued without sufficient collateral"— and required that only banks should serve as trustees of the collateral, in return for a substantial fee. This effectively brought all corporate debt financing under the control of banks, which, in turn, were given directions by the government on whom to favor.

The most important players had little incentive to object to the Bond Committee when it was set up, even though it significantly restricted the access of firms to the corporate bond markets.[31] Each individual firm might have been better off if it could have obtained arm's-length bond financing also instead of being restricted to bank financing. But initially no one wanted to upset the main bank and risk losing access to credit if economic conditions deteriorated. And restrictions on financing also restrained entry, and therefore competition, in the industrial sector. Therefore, as a collective, firms did not oppose change.

With the exception of the securities firms, other financial institutions also benefited, because they could charge higher rates for long-term financing, so they did not challenge the banks. The important securities firms were co-opted. Even though there were hundreds of securities firms, the big four—Nomura, Nikko, Daiwa, and Yamaichi— took turns lead-managing whatever issues were permitted and captured 75 percent of underwriting commissions.[32] If they challenged the Bond Committee, their oligopoly might be threatened as well as the cozy fixed commission they enjoyed. The Japanese government was happy with the status quo because it could be confident that there would be no unpleasant defaults in the bond market and because, as a consequence of the restrictions, money flowed through the banking sector, where it was easier to direct. The only clear sufferer was the individual investor, but she could be ignored: as with all situations in which those who bear losses are small and dispersed, it was very hard for individuals to overcome inertia and free-rider problems to organize and fight the system.

With all the important players happy with matters, change had to come from outside. International capital flows were the source of this change. As it became easier to borrow abroad in the 1970s, mature Japanese firms attempted to reduce their costs by replacing bank debt with public debt. For this, they went to the Euromarket—an offshore financial market that was not under the control of the Japanese government—where there were no collateral requirements and there was a wide range of instruments, maturities, and currencies in which they could issue. From accounting for only 1.7 percent of Japanese corporate financing in the early 1970s, Euromarket issues went on to account for 36.2 percent in 1984.[33]

Initially, Japanese banks tried to keep domestic restrictions on bond issuance—because they did not have the right to underwrite bonds in the domestic market—while they attempted to participate in underwriting some of the Eurobond issues. Japanese securities firms were opposed to this because they felt that banks would use their muscle to strong-arm clients into using them as lead underwriters. Perhaps more important, they feared that this would be a way for banks to eventually demand domestic underwriting powers. So Japanese banks and securities firms fought over clients in the Euromarket. The conflict, however, benefited the firms because there was no concerted attempt to hold them back from issuing in the Euromarket.

Meanwhile, there had been foreign pressure in the domestic market. In 1978, the U.S. retailer Sears requested permission to issue unsecured bonds in Japan. The Japanese government had little ability to deny the issue without inviting retaliatory action, especially when a Japanese retailer, Ito Yokado, announced that it would issue unsecured dollar bonds in New York later that year. The face-saving measure the Japanese government adopted was to draft conditions for firms to be eligible to issue unsecured bonds tailored so that forty foreign firms and only two Japanese firms, Toyota and Matsushita Electrical, qualified. In March 1979, Sears became the first firm to issue unsecured corporate bonds in Japan since 1933. Soon after, Matsushita Electrical followed.[34] The collateral principle had been breached!

Despite the increase over time in the number of firms that met the criterion for issuing unsecured bonds in the domestic market, there were still enough restrictions—such as a single issue date each month and the requirement that firms could not issue more than twice their net worth—that the domestic market continued to be unappetizing. The Bond Committee continued to oppose the establishment of bond-rating agencies for fear that its rules would be rendered redundant. After all, it had thus far succeeded in keeping Hitachi, with a top-quality AA rating in foreign markets, from being eligible to issue unsecured bonds in the domestic market.

However, as droves of firms continued to flee to the Euromarket, banks came around to the view that it might be better to trade some of that underwriting business in return for giving up their ability to act as spoiler in an increasingly irrelevant domestic bond market. So in the late 1980s, banks agreed to a horse trade whereby they agreed to relax the criteria for which firms were eligible to issue unsecured domestic bonds in return for the ability to act as lead underwriter for Japanese corporate issues in foreign markets.[35]

Thus, competition from the Euromarket forced changes that allowed Japanese firms to tap domestic Japanese bond markets. It was not so much that the political power of various parties was changed, but the appeal of the status quo was reduced as profits evaporated, and incumbent financial institutions gave up their opposition to change. The primary virtue of competition from outside markets and institutions is, then, that foreign competitors are not part of any domestic cartel and therefore offer an opportunity for the public interest to prevail.

The Systematic Evidence

Thus far, we have provided anecdotal evidence supporting our thesis of how financial development takes place. A more systematic analysis of the patterns of financial development across countries and over time also supports our basic thesis. There was a surge in financial development in most European countries during the second half of the nineteenth century. During this period, the so-called bourgeois revolutions, bolstered by land reform, increased the political influence of the emerging industrial class. At the same time, the reduction in transportation costs, with the consequent expansion of markets, created great opportunities for investment and thus great needs for finance. This fortunate convergence between political change and the need for finance created the ideal conditions for financial development. Following the example of France under Louis Bonaparte, governments started to actively promote the development of their financial sectors. As a result, by the beginning of the twentieth century, advanced countries in Europe reached very high levels of financial development, higher than what we have seen as recently as 1980.

FINANCIAL DEVELOPMENT IN 1913 AND 1980

COUNTRY	DEPOSITS TO GDP		STOCK MARKET CAPITALIZATION TO GDP		EQUITY FINANCING TO FIXED INVESTMENT	
	1913	1980	1913	1980	1913	1980
Austria	1.12	0.62	0.76	0.03		0.00
Belgium	0.68	0.39	0.99	0.09	0.23	0.03
Canada	0.22	0.47	0.74	0.46		0.04
Denmark	0.76	0.28	0.36	0.09		0.01
France	0.42	0.45	0.78	0.09	0.14	0.06
Germany	0.53	0.30	0.44	0.09	0.07	0.01
Italy	0.23	0.59	0.17	0.07	0.07	0.04
Japan	0.13	0.48	0.49	0.33	0.08	0.01
Netherlands	0.22	0.25	0.56	0.19	0.38	0.01
Norway	0.65	0.30	0.16	0.54		
Sweden	0.69	0.48	0.47	0.11	0.08	0.00
Switzerland	0.93	0.69	0.58	0.44	0.03	
United Kingdom	0.10	0.14	1.09	0.38	0.14	0.04
United States	0.33	0.18	0.39	0.46	0.04	0.04
Average	0.50	0.40	0.57	0.24	0.13	0.02

Source: Rajan and Zingales (2003)

Consider the accompanying comparison between three different indicators of financial development in 1913 and in 1980 for a number of developed countries. The indicators are measures of financing (such as stock market capitalization) divided by measures of economic activity (such as gross domestic product).

One way to measure financial development is to look at the role played by banks in intermediating funds. This is what our first indicator, the ratio of deposits to GDP, captures. That this ratio dropped by 20 percent between 1913 and 1980 suggests that banks played a relatively bigger role in the allocation of savings at the beginning of the twentieth century.

Of course, it would be simplistic to draw any conclusion about financial development on the basis of this information alone. As financial markets develop, banks lose some of their importance; thus, the evidence could reflect the greater importance of financial markets in the latter part of the twentieth century. But this is not the case. If we use a similar indicator to measure the development of equity markets (the ratio of stock market capitalization to GDP), we find that in 1980, equity markets were less than half the size they were relative to GDP in 1913. In fact, for all countries except the United States and Norway, the ratio of stock market capitalization to GDP was smaller in 1980 than in 1913.

Even this measure is not perfect. For example, in 1980, Norway had a very high stock market capitalization to GDP ratio, not because the equity market played a big role in financing industry there, but because Norway found oil in the North Sea. Coupled with the second oil shock, which multiplied oil prices in 1979, the value of Norwegian oil companies increased tremendously. More generally, the level of equity market capitalization may reflect other factors besides the importance of the equity market in financing firms.

However, our third indicator, the fraction of investments financed through equity issues, also suggests a pattern similar to the first two.[36] In all countries except the United States, equity issues were a more important source of investment funding in 1913 than in 1980. On average, the fraction of investment financed with equity dropped from 13 percent to 2 percent over the period (and even in 1990, it had not reached the level it had reached in 1913). Overall, the different indicators give a remarkably consistent picture: in most countries, financial systems were highly developed in 1913, certainly in comparison with the picture in 1980.

There was, however, a fair amount of diversity across these countries. The equity market in 1913 was much more important in England, Belgium, and France than in the United States. The differences cannot be explained on the basis of differences in economic development alone. For example, per capita income in Japan was only one-fourth that of the United States, but its equity market was much more developed. What explains these differences across countries? What explains why these differences changed over time? And what explains the decline in all measures of financial development between 1913 and 1980?

One possible explanation is that the incentive and the ability of domestic incumbents to hold back domestic financial development was different across countries and over time because of differences in the degree of openness of the country's goods and financial markets. We can check this. If our conjectures are right, a country's domestic financial development should be positively correlated with its degree of openness to product and capital flows.

The twentieth century had two periods when the world was relatively open to capital flows. One was the period we have just examined, the beginning of the twentieth century. At that time, many countries adhered to the gold standard, making gold effectively the common currency of international trade and finance. Cross-border flows of capital were relatively unhindered, and capital traversed the globe looking for the highest return, whether it was to be found in Brazilian silver mines or Indian railways. Our analysis suggests that during this period of plentiful capital flows, incumbents would have had the least political will and strength to oppose financial development in countries that had the fortune to trade extensively. Thus, for any level of demand for finance, countries that were more open to trade at that time should have had much better-developed financial markets.

Consider, therefore, a plot of the size of a country's equity market in 1913 against its openness to trade multiplied by the extent of its industrialization.[37] Countries that were more open to trade did, in fact, have bigger equity markets for any given level of industrialization (which is a proxy for the demand for finance).

Of particular interest is the United States, which despite being among the most industrialized countries in the world at this time, has a relatively underdeveloped equity market because it was relatively closed to trade.

We can graph other measures of the ease of access to finance in a country, such as the number of exchange-listed companies or the quan-

MARKET CAPITALIZATION AND OPENNESS IN 1913

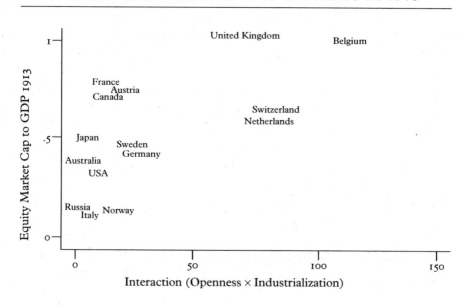

Interaction (Openness × Industrialization)

tity of public corporate issues, and we find a similar pattern: before World War I, countries that were more open to trade had better capital markets.

Cross-border capital flows fell precipitously, for reasons we will come to, in the decades between 1930 and 1980 and started increasing only in the last part of the century. By the end of the century, they had regained the levels (relative to measures of economic activity such as world gross domestic product) that they had at the beginning of the century. A graph for 1997 similar to the one presented here for 1913 shows a similar pattern. Countries that were more open to trade at the beginning and the end of the century had deeper financial markets.

More analysis of the data suggests that the positive relationship between trade openness and the size of a country's equity market is much weaker, or nonexistent, in the period between 1930 and 1980, when cross-border capital flows were much smaller. Thus, both cross-border trade and capital flows may indeed be necessary for financial development.

Of course, all we have documented are correlations between openness and the size of capital markets. Econometric techniques show that the former is likely to cause the latter.[38] Even so, this is only an indirect verification of the possibility that open borders curb the power of incumbents. The skeptical reader will want more direct evidence that openness influences financial development—in particular, that it works because it curbs the power, or alters the incentives, of incumbents.

There is such evidence. As described earlier in the book, *Forbes* magazine publishes a list of billionaires around the world every year, classifying them as those who inherited their wealth or those who created it through their own entrepreneurial efforts. We have argued that it is easier for a poor but talented entrepreneur to make it on her own in a developed financial system in which there is widespread access to finance. So in a developed financial system, the fraction of self-made billionaires should be higher. Conversely, in an opaque system, which protects incumbents against competition, it is easier for heirs, however incompetent, to retain their fortunes. As we described in Chapter 5, self-made billionaire wealth is higher in countries with a more transparent and developed financial system. More important, countries with lower barriers to foreign direct investment have a lower ratio of inherited billionaire wealth to GDP and a higher ratio of self-made billionaire wealth to GDP.[39]

Lower barriers to foreign competition and lower incumbency seem to go together. It is unclear how much this is because countries dominated by incumbents create high barriers to competition penetrating from outside and how much it is because foreign competition erodes the economic might of incumbents. Regardless of the mechanism, the conclusion is clear: foreign competitors seem to make common cause with domestic entrants in making life difficult for domestic incumbents.

This conclusion is bolstered by evidence of the impact of the enactment of the Canada–United States Free Trade Agreement (FTA) in 1988.[40] The FTA lowered trade barriers between Canada and the United States and, perhaps more important, eliminated all kinds of discriminatory taxes on investors that had previously limited capital flows between the countries. The agreement was unexpected. Canada and the United States had reached the final stages of negotiations on freeing trade several times before but had balked. This time, the conservative government of Brian Mulroney, which favored free trade, called for a snap election on the issue. Polls did not augur well for the conservatives, but they astounded everybody by being elected with a clear mandate. Since markets were surprised by the election results, one way to see how the FTA impacted various kinds of firms is to see how their stock price reacted on the announcement.

The stock price of firms controlled by heirs of the original founder— our classic incumbents—was most adversely affected by the election results, while the stock price of entrepreneur-controlled firms went up. The market's verdict was unmistakable: open borders are indeed inimical to entrenched incumbents.

Summary

We ended the last chapter pointing to the powerful forces arrayed against finance—the forces of incumbency opposed to the changes unleashed by free access to finance. There are some circumstances in which these forces can be overcome—for example, when a society undergoes significant political change. There are also circumstances in which the self-interest of incumbents becomes aligned with the public interest. One is when new markets open up or new technologies become available. Incumbents, faced with significant new investment opportunities, cannot rely on traditional funding sources (such as internal cash) and may press for better access to finance. Similarly, when a country's borders open up to external trade, industrial incumbents might have depleted profits while needing to make massive investments to compete with foreigners.

Unfortunately, it is not clear that finance will develop even when industrial incumbents are in need. Incumbents may skew access to finance even more, especially if they can co-opt the government. History suggests that finance is likely to develop only when the government's ability to play favorites is limited. The opening of a country's borders to capital flows (and not just to trade) ensures some of the required discipline on government actions. This then suggests that it is the fortuitous combination of a need on the incumbents' part for financing as well as the discipline on government intervention stemming from borders open to capital flows that channels political efforts toward improving financial infrastructure. The explosion in financial markets around the world in the last three decades is intimately bound with the greater openness in the world economy.

Thus far, we have discussed the conditions under which the political opposition to financial development will be overcome. But once some financial infrastructure is in place, will countries continue to have healthy financial sectors? The evidence here is far from reassuring. Financial markets in countries around the world shrank between 1930 and 1980. What explains this reversal? In part, we already have the answer: cross-border capital flows diminished to a trickle during much of this time. This then provided the setting in which incumbents could reassert their interests and suppress finance. But why did countries close their borders to capital flows? Could it happen again?

We have hopped backward and forward through history thus far. But to answer these important questions, we have to shine a light on the period 1930 to 1980. We have to understand the economic and political environment at that time and the alternative to the market economy that emerged. And we have to understand why that alternative broke down and the problems it has left for us. This is the subject of the chapters that follow.

PART THREE

THE
GREAT
REVERSAL

CHAPTER NINE

The Great Reversal between Wars

GOVERNMENT respect of property rights is the first step toward the development of financial markets. As we have seen, this respect best arises when property is owned by the most competent and specialized. When, in addition, it is widely distributed, representative government arises. But even in a democratic form of government, there is no guarantee that policies will reflect the needs of the people. Incumbents can capture the policy-making process and enact antimarket legislation. Revolutionary political or technological change can loosen incumbents' hold on markets, but these are rare occurrences. In the natural course of events, it is competition from outside that curbs incumbents.

If, however, markets rely on open borders to limit the power of domestic vested interests, then we have to ask how politically stable open borders are. Countries tend to remain open when the rest of the world is open. France, as we have seen, faced a defining moment in 1983, when the socialist government had to decide whether to close its borders to capital flows. It chose to remain open because it feared jeopardizing its strong trade links to the rest of Western Europe. Similarly, during the Asian financial crisis in 1998, most affected countries chose to remain open because the rest of the world was unaffected and continued to be open to trade.

There are good reasons why, once a country opens its borders, those borders tend to stay open unless many other countries begin closing their borders. Those that benefit from openness—exporters, importers, multinational firms—gain power and develop their own political constituencies in open countries. Not only do these firms rely on foreign sources for their supplies, but they are also keenly aware of the extent to which the foreign markets for their products can be destroyed by tit-for-tat policies by foreign governments. They then form a countervailing force to those who would want to close borders. Moreover, if other countries are open, a country's borders are bound to be porous no matter how determined it is to close them down. The economic pressure for cross-border trade will eventually force goods and capital across barriers erected by all but the most austere police states. So both the configuration of power and the permeability of borders will favor the continued openness of a country when the rest of the world is open.

Matters are different when there is incipient pressure in many countries to close down. The constituencies favoring openness will be economically weaker, and thus less politically powerful, when other countries close down. They are also less likely to have an incentive to fight for openness when they see their foreign markets vanish. Moreover, when the collective political will of countries is focused on stopping cross-border flows, it indeed becomes much easier to stop them.

So openness is what economists call a strategic complement: countries want to have less of it when other countries have less of it. Therefore, once some cataclysmic event causes some countries to close their borders, the process can cascade. During the Great Depression, many countries closed their borders to both trade and capital flows. It is important to understand why, and whether it can happen again. Hence, in this chapter, we analyze the historical events surrounding the Great Depression, starting from the economic and political environment at that time, and concluding with a discussion of the forms the antimarket reaction assumed. In Chapter 10, we explain why the antimarket reaction was so strong at this time and why free financial markets gave way to strongly cartelized or government-controlled financial systems. Finally, in Chapter 11, we describe the deficiencies of these systems and obtain a more rounded explanation for why markets have become free again. We travel over some territory that we have already covered, but with a much sharper focus on attempting to understand when financial development can be reversed.

The Gold Standard

In the early years of the twentieth century, the political institution underlying the triumph of markets in most of the developed world was the gold standard. Not only did the gold standard facilitate trade and capital flows, but it also imposed tight budgetary discipline on governments, which made it difficult for them to intervene much in economic affairs.

A country on the pure gold standard essentially used gold for circulating money. If paper money or coins made of other metals circulated, enough gold was maintained in the vaults of the central bank to convert these into gold on demand. It was critical to the working of the gold standard that countries remain committed to maintaining the convertibility of their currency into gold at a constant rate. Once these commitments were credible, it was as if the whole world used a single currency, gold. Because a common currency reduces uncertainty about prices and costs across borders, it leads to an expansion in the volume of cross-border trade and investment. The gold standard was the primary reason countries were so open to trade and capital flows in the early part of the twentieth century.

But the gold standard also limited the range of policies a country's government could implement. Consider, for example, how a trade imbalance could be rectified. If a country's imports of goods and services exceeded its exports, it ran a negative balance of trade, which either ate into its reserves of foreign exchange and gold or forced it to borrow from foreigners. If a country's reserves were insufficient, or foreigners were unwilling to lend, it had to reverse its trade deficit and run a surplus. Under the gold standard, a country could not simply depreciate its currency, making exports cheaper and thus increasing their quantity. Since the exchange rate was fixed, the only way for a country with a persistent negative balance of trade to sell more outside was to produce goods more cheaply by allowing domestic wages and prices to fall, so that the country could become more cost-competitive. Thus, the inability of governments to allow the exchange rate to depreciate gave them one less tool with which to cushion adverse economic events.

But the straitjacket was even more confining. If the country's banking sector suffered a serious crisis of confidence, the central bank could not lend freely at a low interest rate for fear that the exchange rate would be affected. Instead, it had to hope that confidence would be magically restored or that somehow foreigners would step up to lend freely. Governments were not just impotent under the gold standard; they were dependent on the benevolence of foreign governments that had exchange surpluses to lend.[1]

World War I and Its Aftermath

Until World War I, the gold standard worked reasonably well. Its strait-jacket restricted incumbents' ability to distort the rules of the game in their favor, and governments intervened very little in the economy. Moreover, classical economics, with its emphasis on letting market forces find their way, was convenient, at least for those in power, for it imposed the burden of any adjustment on workers, who were forced to accept the lower wages necessary for a country to regain competitive-ness.[2] This was only possible because labor was politically weak. Most countries had only recently moved to universal franchise, and both labor parties and unions were subject to constant harassment. Workers them-selves were poorly educated and were slow to absorb the radical ideas that socialist intellectuals were then debating.

That World War I jolted society the world over is probably an under-statement. From the perspective of political economy, however, two consequences were particularly important. First, the need to coordinate war production had led to significant wartime centralization of produc-tion throughout the economies of continental Europe. The reason for wartime centralization was simple. A decentralized market economy produces for those whose needs can be backed with cash. Military needs during the war were paramount, but it would have been prohibitively costly for the government to continuously outbid private consumers all the time. The military command soon came to believe that the best way to manage was to ban certain forms of private consumption, set prohib-itive prices for others, and commandeer production toward war goals—in other words, suppress prices and the private market in favor of a command-and-control system along the lines of the military. They had willing allies. The historian William McNeill describes the control of the war effort in Germany after 1916 thus:

> [T]he generals in charge often became impatient with the financial claims and controversies that continually embroiled and sometimes obstructed prompt and deferential obedience to their demands. As shortages rose, one after another, the generals relied more and more on big labor and big business to remodel the economy according to military needs. Each party got more or less what it wanted: more munitions for the army, more profits for the industrialists, and con-solidation of their authority over the work force for union officials.[3]

In many countries, prices were centrally controlled and resources allocated to those uses that were deemed critical to the war effort. Centralization was aided by the cartelization of industry, of the banking sector, and of the workforce because this reduced the number of parties with which the central authority had to negotiate. The reliance on hierarchical command rather than prices to determine the allocation of resources seemed to work, at least for a while. This is not surprising. With a clear objective, such as delivering munitions, and with incentives provided by patriotic fervor, the price mechanism can be suspended for a while without severe costs. Eventually, of course, the task of running a complex economy from the center overwhelms even the most competent management. Severe distortions did build up in the wartime economies. Nevertheless, the relative success of centralized economies suggested that government intervention was not all bad, and many saw it as an attractive model to which to return during the years of the depression.

The second consequence of the war was that the working class became more aware of its power. The trenches during the war served as classrooms, where the working class absorbed more radical ideas. The senseless carnage of a war that left all the main combatants worse off led many to doubt the caliber and motives of their political leaders. Socialist intellectuals now found a receptive following among labor. Organized and awakened labor would no longer continue unquestioningly to absorb the costs of adjustment to macroeconomic imbalances.[4]

With the end of the war, economies had to change significantly to reorient themselves to civilian production and market-determined prices. They also had to rectify the distortions that had built up during the period of centralized control. Industrial strife increased as workers were unwilling to absorb the entire brunt of the adjustment once again.

In spite of this increased resistance, the power of the preexisting order was so strong that countries paid the price to return to a version of the gold standard. By the late 1920s, the gold exchange standard was effectively in place in much of the world. But economies had been stretched by the effort, and according to some economic historians, this may have sown the seeds for what was to come.[5]

The stock market crash of 1929 in the United States and the ensuing recession in the United States were the proverbial straw. With the single biggest consumer in the world contracting, exports plunged all around the world. Balance-of-payment problems worsened in Europe, Japan, and Latin America. With cross-border lending also slowing to a trickle, the required adjustment for a country under the gold standard was clear. Its domestic wages and prices had to fall so that it could start exporting more and generate the necessary surpluses. But with labor no longer willing to accept significant wage cuts, the next "best" way for politicians to restore the balance of trade was to ban imports and subsidize exports. The United States was in the forefront of this movement with the notorious Smoot-Hawley bill. Of course, if every country did this, world trade would collapse, and it did. The world entered a downward economic spiral, and recession turned to depression.

Moreover, as prices fell, debtors had to sell more goods just to generate enough to pay off their fixed debts, so debt defaults increased. Losses at financial institutions mounted, and the threat of a financial crisis put pressure on central banks to intervene and bail out the system. Again, under the gold standard, central banks could not lend freely to bail out the banking system without jeopardizing the exchange rate.

Faced with severe economic conditions, there was pressure for governments to do something. Political conditions made it impossible to give markets the time to sort things out on their own and remedy the mess that some would argue political interference had created. As John Maynard Keynes famously wrote, "In the long run we are all dead." The pressure grew for more intervention that would ease the growing pain. A frightened electorate threw out governments that waited passively for markets to recover. Newly elected politicians were anxious to do something.

The Political Response to the Depression

In general, politicians blamed unbridled competition in the 1920s for what, from the vantage point of the depression years, seemed like excessive investment by industry, excessive lending by banks, and excessive speculation in the stock market by all and sundry. The antimarket sentiment was reflected in statements made by politicians from very different persuasions. For example, one of the attractions of Nazism was that it would tame the market and place it at the service of national goals.[6] Hitler felt that economic problems could be overcome by political will alone. He wrote, "The Volk [nation] does not live on behalf of the economy, its economic leadership, or economic and financial theories, but rather, finance and economy, economic leadership, and every theory exist only to serve in the struggle for our people's self determination."[7] Hitler, as had many rulers in the past, found a convenient scapegoat in the Jews for the financial troubles besetting the economy, but the sympathetic ear he found in the German people cannot entirely be unassociated with his willingness to bring the market under political control.

Competitive markets weighed equally on Franklin Roosevelt. In his inaugural address, he, too, blamed the market, finance, and the "outworn tradition" of classical liberal economics for the state the economy was in:

> Our distress comes from no failure of substance. . . . Plenty is at our doorstep, but a generous use of it languishes in the very sight of supply. Primarily this is because the rulers of exchange of mankind's goods have failed through their own stubbornness and their own incompetence, have admitted their failure and abdicated. Practices of the unscrupulous moneychangers stand indicted in the court of public opinion, rejected by the hearts and minds of men. . . .
>
> . . . The moneychangers have fled from their high seats in the temple of our civilization. We may now restore that temple to the ancient truths. The measure of restoration lies in the extent to which we apply social values more noble than mere monetary profit.[8]

He, too, felt it a duty to intervene. In a fireside chat in 1934, he said:

> Men may differ as to the particular form of governmental activity with respect to industry and business, but nearly all are agreed that private enterprise in times such as these cannot be left without assistance and without reasonable safeguards lest it destroy not only itself but also our processes of civilization.[9]

But Roosevelt claimed that by intervening, he was only restoring the ideals of the free market because he was fighting monopoly. (Parenthetically, democratic governments always claim to interfere with markets to combat monopoly and reduce risk, two popular but generally incompatible objectives.) In his acceptance of the Democratic Party's presidential nomination in Philadelphia in 1936, he said:

> Throughout the Nation, opportunity was limited by monopoly. . . .
> For too many of us the political equality we once had won was mean-

ingless in the face of economic inequality. . . . A small group had concentrated into their own hands an almost complete control over other people's property, other people's money, other people's labor— other people's lives. For too many of us life was no longer free; liberty was no longer real; men could no longer follow the pursuit of happiness.[10]

Since the market seemed to be inflicting pain on the many for the profit of a few, Roosevelt concluded:

Against economic tyranny such as this, the American citizen could appeal only to the organized power of Government. . . . Better the occasional faults of a Government that lives in a spirit of charity than the consistent omissions of a Government frozen in the ice of its own indifference.

In summary, politicians with stripes as different as Hitler and Roosevelt knew that something had to be done. Their explanations for what had happened differed, as did the means they sought to employ, but the belief that the government had to replace the failed market was almost universal.

The response of governments to the problems of the depression varied in their details but typically had three common themes. The first was to abandon the gold standard. As Roosevelt declared in his message to the World Economic Congress in July 1933, "The sound internal economic system of a Nation is a greater factor in its well-being than the price of its currency in changing terms of the currencies of other Nations."[11] In Roosevelt's view, the pain engendered by the gold standard was no longer worth the price. With the greatest economic power in the world withdrawing its support, the gold standard was history.

With no external discipline on the extent to which governments could intervene, they were now free finally to remedy what they saw as obvious defects of the market. So the second theme was to curb competition, from both external and internal sources. Foreigners had access to domestic markets in the past because powerful domestic incumbents saw opportunities in trade. With export markets no longer proving attractive, there was no reason to allow foreigners into the domestic market. Foreigners were the easiest targets because they had no political voice. Imports of goods and people were curbed through prohibitive tariffs and restrictive immigration policies.[12]

Domestic competition was also problematic. The head of the National Recovery Administration (NRA), set up during the depression in the United States, argued that employers were forced into layoffs during the depression as a result of "the murderous doctrine of savage and wolfish competition, [of] dog-eat-dog and devil take the hindmost."[13] As Roosevelt put it in introducing the National Industrial Recovery Act, cooperation among firms was needed to push up wages and employment. But

> One of the great restrictions upon such co-operative efforts up to this time has been our anti-trust laws. They were properly designed as means to cure the great evils of monopolistic price fixing. They should certainly be retained as a permanent assurance that the old evils of unfair competition shall never return. But the public interest will be served if, with the authority and under the guidance of the Government, private industries are allowed to make agreements and codes insuring fair competition.[14]

In short, the government offered its blessing to industrial cartels. The government's desire to curb competition especially hurt new entrants. By contrast, it was most welcome to domestic incumbent firms, which, freed from foreign competition, were happy to reach agreements with other incumbents and do away with new entry into domestic product markets.

An example of the kind of measures adopted was the federal regulation of trucking in the United States. The Motor Carrier Act of 1935 was designed "to protect the public interest by maintaining an orderly and reliable transportation system, by minimizing duplications of services, and by reducing financial instability." The act exempted the trucking industry from antitrust laws and required all interstate motor carriers to file their rates with the Interstate Commerce Commission (ICC), which had the authority to set minimum rates and suspend rate cuts. Similarly, the ICC had the power to regulate entry into the industry through the grant of operating certificates. The ICC followed a policy of not granting authority to serve a route already served as long as the existing carriers provided adequate service. In other words, the onus was on a potential entrant to prove that the incumbent was doing a terrible job and not that the job could be done better. Needless to say, entry was very limited.[15]

The act limited competition not just within the industry but also between trucking and the railways (which had the same regulator). The sizable profits that resulted for incumbents can be gauged by the price of operating certificates—the ticket to becoming an incumbent—which was 15 to 20 percent of annual carrier revenues.[16] Other organized interest groups also benefited.[17] For example, after trucking was eventually deregulated in the late 1970s, the premium earned by unionized trucking employees over nonunionized employees fell from 50 percent to 30 percent.[18]

If prices were no longer set in a competitive market, something had to take the place of the market in channeling resources. The centralized control of the economy, only recently disbanded after World War I, provided an attractive alternative, especially given the seemingly total inability of the market to resuscitate itself. For example, the NRA sought to set prices, control overproduction by allocating production quotas, and thus stabilize wages. Its model was the War Industries Board of 1917–1918.[19] While the NRA itself was declared unconstitutional by the United States Supreme Court in 1935, centralized control of industry became firmly entrenched in other countries, especially Germany, Italy, and Japan. So the third common theme was a return to the corporatist management of the economy, with the government allocating resources from its lofty vantage point and substituting for the market.[20]

It is not necessary for us to enter into the still-unsettled debate about whether intervention was needed or not. Economists still argue over the true causes of the depression—whether it is a classic example of the complete failure of markets or a canonical example of the opposite, a failure of government. What is obvious is that in the depths of the depression, with the economy in disarray, the stock market having crashed, export markets moribund, firms failing in the thousands, the banking system in collapse, and unemployment at unprecedented levels, the public did not believe the free market system worked.

These conditions, as we explain in greater detail in the next chapter, created the fertile ground for an unlikely coalition between the needy and the incumbents. Even when there is a generalized promarket consensus, incumbents succeed in carving out exceptions and protections. But when this consensus breaks down, it is especially hard to resist their influence. Riding on the coattails of the popular revulsion against markets, incumbents reestablished positions that had been much weakened by competitive and open markets.

That the legitimate desire to provide some relief to the growing masses of the needy served as a smoke screen for wealthy incumbents to protect their interests is also suggested by a central item on the reform agenda at this time: control over financial markets. Since this was an effective way to establish control over competition, it was natural that political attention would shift toward the financial markets and institutions. Because the financial sector was in disarray, political intervention could be effectively disguised as an attempt to introduce stability into the system. Clearly, commercial and investment banks would be opposed to controls that would reduce their profitability. If foreign capital had been flowing freely, the possibility of seeing business go to foreign financial institutions or foreign markets would have made the domestic financial institutions extremely reluctant to accept constraints on their activities. Since cross-border flows had virtually stopped, this was not a concern. Moreover, government controls brought with them the prospect of government-enforced cartels, which could enhance rather than reduce profitability.

The precise manner in which intervention took place, as well as the identity of the incumbents who benefited most, differed from country to country, but the outcome was similar: financial markets became less competitive, and only a privileged few retained access to finance.

The Consequences: The Great Reversal

It is useful to start with the effects on a market that is particularly sensitive to political winds and is a bellwether of the case of access to arm's-length finance: the equity market. In the accompanying table, we report for a number of years the fraction of total fixed investment in a country that is financed through equity issues. In spite of missing data, there is a clear trend. With the exception of Japan, financing through equity offerings plummeted in the 1930s, not only relative to the extraordinary levels reached in the boom year of 1929 (and equity issues are usually plentiful in boom years) but also relative to the more normal level in 1913. Clearly, some of the fall can be attributed to the depression and the Second World War, but the fall was not reversed after the war and may have reached its nadir in 1980, long after the war ended. Interestingly, this pattern is also seen in a country like Sweden, which escaped both world wars.

EVOLUTION OF EQUITY ISSUES

Amount of funds raised through public equity offerings by domestic companies normalized by total national investment.

COUNTRY	1913	1929	1938	1950	1960	1970	1980
Austria	—	0.07	—	—	0.04	0.07	0.00
Belgium	0.23	0.85	0.03	—	0.09	0.08	0.03
Canada	—	1.34	0.02	0.03	0.03	0.01	0.04
Denmark	—	0.03	0.01	—	—	—	0.01
France	0.14	0.26	0.03	0.02	0.04	0.04	0.06
Germany	0.07	0.17	0.06	0.00	0.04	0.02	0.01
Italy	0.07	0.26	0.03	0.02	0.08	0.02	0.04
Japan	0.08	0.13	0.75	—	0.15	0.03	0.01
Netherlands	0.38	0.61	0.45	0.02	0.02	0.00	0.01
Sweden	0.08	0.34	0.06	0.01	0.03	0.00	0.00
United Kingdom	0.14	0.35	0.09	0.08	0.09	0.01	0.04
United States	0.04	0.38	0.01	0.04	0.02	0.07	0.04
Average	0.14	0.40	0.14	0.03	0.06	0.03	0.02

Source: Rajan and Zingales (2003)

Other indicators of the health or size of financial markets suggest a similar story. Financial markets shrank in size starting in the 1930s and had not recovered by 1980. To understand how this market reversal occurred, we now take a closer look at three countries that represent three different ways in which the government, under the influence of incumbents, intervened in financial markets: Italy, Japan, and the United States.

The Private-Public Nexus in Italy

Italy represents an example of how incumbents used public money to protect themselves and their positions in an economy severely affected by the Great Depression, with consequences that lasted for the following sixty years.

Even before the onset of the Great Depression, the Italian economy had been weakened by Benito Mussolini's decision in 1926 to revalue the lira. The ensuing deflation was severe. In one year, the total credit extended by the central bank to the banking system shrank by 36 percent.[21] To compensate for the shortage of domestic liquidity, banks borrowed abroad. In 1930, however, foreign credit became scarce, and domestic deposits started to shrink. This triggered a severe liquidity crisis in the banking system, because its assets were tied up in long-term credit and equity investments. One after another, the major banks asked the Fascist government for support.

Following a pattern it had set in earlier bailouts of smaller banks, the government set up a holding company, which it financed together with the central bank. This company acquired all the corporate shares held in the portfolios of the banks at the higher historical, not current, prices. Thus, the government not only provided liquidity to the banking system, but it also absorbed part of its losses.[22] It also became the largest shareholder in a number of firms. Many of the industrial firms thus acquired were themselves on the verge of failing and benefited not just from the rescue of their banks but also from the direct infusion of public money. The two largest banks (Credito Italiano and Banca Commerciale) had acquired a substantial quantity of their own shares in an earlier failed attempt to support their own share prices. So with this operation, the government acquired a controlling interest not only in industrial firms representing 42 percent of the capital of all Italian corporations but also in the two most important credit institutions.[23] The cost of the entire bailout was a staggering 10 percent of GDP—the comparable amount in the United States today would be $1 trillion.[24]

Unlike with similar bailouts in Germany and Austria, the Italian government did not sell many of its newly acquired companies back to the private sector. Of the few it sold, the most egregious case of privatization was the sale of a controlling block in a gas company, Italgas, to a group of Turin industrialists at less than one-fourth of its market value.[25] But in general, however, there was very little pressure from industrialists on the government to reprivatize.[26] In part, as the Italian economic historian Gianni Toniolo points out, many of the companies the government had taken over were in capital-intensive sectors and were not very economically attractive because they had highly cyclical revenues and were dependent on military demand. As long as the state continued to run these plants, the private sector obtained the essential inputs it needed, such as steel, without the necessity of absorbing losses in these unprofitable areas.[27]

Equally important, however, is that even though the public taxpayer had paid for the bailouts, the firms were not nationalized in the traditional sense of the word. The banks and many of the largest manufacturing companies whose control was acquired during the bailouts continued to be listed on the Milan stock exchange and were special only in that they had the government as the main shareholder. But the government did not intervene directly in their running.

Instead, it created an autonomous company, the Istituto per la Ricostruzione Industriale (IRI), to hold and control these stakes. During the Fascist period and for the first two decades after the war, the government's control over IRI was minimal. The first head of the IRI was not even a member of the Fascist Party.[28] Furthermore, even though the head was appointed by the government, he had little control over his operating firms, which were run as separate fiefdoms, accepting only general directives about financing from the center.[29] As an example of how little control the Fascist government had, one of IRI's subsidiaries, the Banca Commerciale, employed many anti-Fascist leaders in its research department, and these leaders came to play a very important role in Italian politics after World War II.[30]

The point is that after bailing out a substantial portion of the private sector at an enormous cost to taxpayers, the state neither sold its stake back at a fair price nor took active control. The private sector retained control without having to pay for it. Not only did existing managers keep their jobs, but also many of the board members, who represented the interest of the previous owners, retained their seats. Public ownership and control was a facade for a much more complex intertwining of the private and public spheres. For example, Giovanni Agnelli, who owned Fiat, was a director of Credito Italiano, one of the IRI banks, from 1946 to its privatization in 1994.[31] He also sat on the board of Mediobanca, IRI's investment bank, between 1962 and 1991.

As a result of such links, shares that had been acquired with taxpayers' money to save the banking sector were voted in such a way as to protect and enhance private interests. There is no better illustration of this than Mediobanca, the shadowy IRI investment bank that, till recently, had a hand in almost every major corporate finance decision in postwar Italy. Mediobanca was created with government money to provide long-term finance to firms. As its founder and long-term chairman Enrico Cuccia declared to a leading industrialist when Mediobanca was founded, "Together we will rebuild not just Italy, but capitalism itself. The state will put up the money, you [will provide] the entrepreneurship."[32]

Approximately 68 percent of Mediobanca's shares were owned by the three banks controlled by IRI, 3.75 percent was owned by a group of leading industrialists, while the remaining shares were sold on the Milan Stock Exchange. Despite the absolute majority of shares owned by IRI, Mediobanca was governed by a voting trust in which the 3.75 percent owned by the industrialists and the 68 percent owned by IRI had equal voting power.[33] The stated reason for this agreement was "to protect Mediobanca from the shareholder of the shareholders"—that is, IRI—and "shield the financial institution from political interference that could have been exerted through IRI."[34]

Fairly soon, Mediobanca went far beyond its mandate to provide long-term finance to industry. It held enough shares in all the large family-owned firms that its votes were needed for any major decision. It thus protected them from unwanted takeover threats. In fact, Guido Carli, the governor of the Italian Central Bank between 1963 and 1978, called Enrico Cuccia "the sentinel who, as always, protects the empty barrel of Italian capitalism."[35] That government money provided the protection while the public shareholders suffered from the misgovernance of less-than-competent families with no recourse was the least of Cuccia's concerns. It is not surprising, then, that unlike other countries where the private sector actively pushed for privatization, the industrialists in Italy were content with the prevailing state of affairs, and the IRI, set up as a temporary stopgap measure in the 1930s, owned a large fraction of corporate Italy into the 1990s.[36]

Paralleling these developments in the ownership and control of firms were changes in access to financing. The governor of the Bank of Italy headed a "Committee for the Protection of Savings and the Granting of Credit," which had to approve all equity and bond issues. This committee was also given the power to determine bank lending and borrowing rates, the price of bank services, and the allocation of bank liquidity.[37] In short, all financing decisions were centrally determined.

Inevitably, the financing that was allowed reflected a desire for stability rather than competition. The number of publicly traded companies (a good indicator of the ease of access of new firms to arm's-length financing) remained below its 1929 peak until 1986.[38] The average age of the companies going public was an elderly fifty-three years in the period 1968–1981 and thirty-five years in the period 1982–1992.[39] Young entrants clearly did not have easy access to finance.

With entry by threatening businesses discouraged and competition among financial institutions "managed," finance allowed neither creation nor destruction. Many of these cozy arrangements persisted long after the depression was over, right into the 1990s. In fact, the system of state ownership and private control might have continued much longer were it not for two outside forces. First, Italy, which was among the founding members of the European Community, had difficulty in satisfying the strict criteria laid down in Maastricht for qualifying for the European Monetary Union. Both its debt and its public deficit were extremely large. In order to reduce both, the Italian government was forced to privatize its holdings in state firms to raise funds. Second, European Union rules prohibited government subsidies even to state-owned companies and thus made it hard for these unwieldy conglomerates to continue living off taxpayers' money. Once again, it was only thanks to external pressure that the power of domestic vested interests was overcome.

The Demise of Financial Markets in Japan

Japan is similar to Italy inasmuch as the large Zaibatsu (translated as "financial clique") banks seized the opportunity provided by the Great Depression to push forward a consolidation of the banking sector they had wanted since the end of the nineteenth century. The main difference is that incumbents' interests matched well with the Nationalist government's desire to concentrate the financial system in the hands of the few, so that it could better guide the allocation of resources toward the looming war effort. The effect of their maneuvers, however, outlasted the Nationalists' grip on power and survived well into the 1980s.

Before World War I, Japan was making rapid strides toward developing strong financial markets. Until 1918, there were no restrictions on entry into banking, provided a new bank could meet minimum capital requirements. There were over one thousand banks when World War I began, and by 1920, there were over two thousand banks. The five large

Zaibatsu banks accounted for only 20.5 percent of the deposits before the war.[40]

While bank competition helped Japan's development, it did not please everyone. As early as 1892, the chairman of the Tokyo Bankers' Association asked the Ministry of Finance "to impose minimum capital requirements on banks as a way of erecting barriers to entry and limiting competition in the banking industry."[41] Until 1927, however, the opposition of the Lower House (Diet), sensitive to the interest of small banks, prevented the passage of any such legislation.

The banking crisis of 1927, triggered in part by political maneuvers, gave the large banks an opportunity to overcome the resistance of the Lower Diet. The Bank Act of 1927 fulfilled the wishes of the largest banks, by requiring that deposit-taking institutions reach a minimum capital level of 1 million yen within five years. By 1932, at the end of this five-year period, there were only 538 banks.[42]

At the same time as the banking system was becoming more concentrated, the government's control over it was increasing. This became especially pronounced as the government sought to direct funds toward supplying the war effort against China in 1937. The government could best prevent firms that were not critical to the war effort from obtaining financing by suppressing small banks and arm's-length financial markets, both of which were hard to control. These motives coincided with the large banks' interests in suppressing competition from other sources of finance.

The coalition between large banks and the government thus transformed the once competitive Japanese banking system into a concentrated "main" bank system. By 1945, after a period of bank mergers promoted by the Ministry of Finance, only sixty-five banks survived.[43] The five Zaibatsu banks' share of total deposits, which before the First World War had been just 20.5 percent, had increased to 45.7 percent by 1945.[44]

This private-public nexus also played a part in the demise of the vibrant arm's-length financial markets. In 1929, 26 percent of the liabilities of large Japanese firms' balance sheets consisted of bonds while only 17 percent was bank debt.[45] As bond defaults increased, a group of banks together with trust and insurance companies used the poor economic conditions as the excuse to agree in 1931 to make all subsequent bond issues secured in principle. This immediately made it harder for their clients to issue public debt and made them more dependent on their bank for financing. With the acquiescence of the Ministry of Finance, the agreement was formalized in 1933 through the formation of the Bond Committee we have encountered earlier. Giving banks the responsibility for determining firms' right to access the public bond markets was like giving a fox that resided in a chicken coop the right to determine which chickens could leave.[46] The obvious outcome was that a flourishing bond market was killed off. By 1936, bonds were down to 14 percent, while bank debt was up to 24 percent of the liability side. By 1943, 47 percent of liabilities were bank debt, while only 6 percent were bonds.

The equity markets were similarly choked through fiat. The attitude of the government toward shareholders is illustrated by the following statement by a bureaucrat:

> The majority of shareholders take profits by selling appreciated stocks, sell in times when the price is expected to fall, and often seek dividend increases without doing anything to deserve them. If these shareholders control the directors of companies, influence strategies, and seize a substantial amount of profits, then the system of joint stock companies has serious flaws.[47]

The Temporary Funds Adjustment Law crimped equity issues in 1937 by mandating that companies seek permission before issuing. The Corporate Profits Distribution and Fund Raising Order required firms to seek government approval for increases in dividends if the level of payout was greater than 10 percent, thus making equity unattractive. Still later, the Munitions Companies Act brought companies under the control of government bureaucrats, and they were allowed independence from the shareholders as long as they "worked in the interests of the nation." Thus, new stock issues, which accounted for 60 to 75 percent of net industrial funding in 1935 and 1936 fell to 20 percent of funding by 1944–1945.

Japan illustrates yet again the point that the arrangements set up by incumbents persist long beyond the immediate crisis that is the ostensible reason for them and long after the demise of the governments that aided and abetted. Once the banks had power, they were unlikely to give it up easily. Despite their best efforts to break up the bank firm combines established during the period of militarization, the postwar

American occupying forces could not prevent their reemerging as the Keiretsu, or main bank system. During the war, the government assigned each munitions company to a "main" bank, which would be responsible for ensuring that no financial need went unmet. Of the 112 companies that had descended from wartime munitions companies, the financial institution designated by the government during the war was still the largest lender and one of the top-ten shareholders in 61 of the firms in 1974. In fact, 88 of the 112 companies still had close ties to their designated institution over thirty years after the war![48]

Similarly, as discussed earlier, the Bond Committee, set up ostensibly to improve the quality of bond issuance during the depression, survived until the 1980s. Even as Japanese industrial firms invaded the rest of the world in the 1970s, their bond markets remained minuscule. As we have seen, it was only in the early 1980s, as Japanese firms decided to borrow abroad rather than depend on their antiquated financial system, that Japanese banks had to loosen their stranglehold. The powers of the Bond Committee were curtailed. The markets had their revenge as the banks paid the price for years of being shielded from competition, made terrible credit decisions, and drove Japan into an economic crisis that still persists.[49]

The Experience in the United States

The U.S. experience represents a useful counterexample. In spite of similar pressure from incumbents, the United States succeeded in limiting the extent to which the financial system (and the economy in general) became cartelized. This is not to say that there were no examples of regulation introduced to limit competition and favor the incumbents— we will shortly describe one of the lesser-known examples in detail—but that the efforts had more limited success than in Italy or Japan. The causes of this different outcome are worth analyzing if we want to avoid future reversals.

The United States was more federal in character. States had a say, and there was political competition among states. Even though barriers had been erected to the flow of goods across national borders, the United States had a nationwide market for goods and services. So state legislation would not restrain the actions of out-of-state competitors and, thus, could only end up hampering local companies. In addition, powerful local politicians, who favored local incumbents, opposed the centralizing tendencies that were rampant in other countries. This was particularly reflected in the financial arena, where there was an old tradition in the United States of opposing the concentration of East Coast financial power.[50]

Another moderating influence was that the 1920s in the United States had been a period of unfettered entry and competition, especially in the financial sector. No single type of institution dominated the financial sector. So any legislation that emerged would necessarily be a compromise among different interests. Finally, checks on political expediency such as the legislative oversight exercised by the Supreme Court also helped moderate outcomes.

That the United States escaped the wholesale antimarket changes that took place in other countries does not mean that political interests were not at work. But because political power was more widely distributed, the legislation that emerged did not reflect the interests of just one set of incumbents. For example, small banks obtained federal deposit insurance, which ensured their stability and capped their funding costs. Large banks had been trying to coordinate limits on deposit interest payments since at least 1905.[51] The Banking Act of 1933 (also known as the Glass-Steagall Act) gave them what they wanted by prohibiting interest payments on demand deposits and limiting interest payments for time deposits. Investment banks benefited from the securities and banking legislation passed in 1933 and 1934. Not only were commercial banks prohibited from underwriting corporate securities, but legislation also reduced competition within the investment banking industry.

It is worth dwelling on this last point, for it goes counter to the belief that the securities legislation in the early 1930s, with its emphasis on disclosure and transparency, was entirely focused on laying the foundations for a vibrant, competitive financial system. It may have broadly done that, but particular interest groups also shaped the legislation for their own benefit. The legislation on securities issuance offers an example of how seemingly innocuous changes in laws can limit competition severely.

Perhaps the institutions that saw their business affected the most by competition during the 1920s were top-tier investment banks, firms like J. P. Morgan and Kuhn Loeb. Before World War I, only wealthy individuals and institutions invested in securities. In this world, prior relationships—in particular, with foreign investors—were key to an investment bank's ability to place new security in a reasonable time framework. As a result, a few prestigious houses dominated the underwriting of new securities.

The war changed everything. To finance the war effort, the U.S. government issued more than $21.5 billion in bonds over two years, at a time when the total amount of corporate securities issued in the previous ten years was only $16.6 billion.[52] To place this large quantity of bonds, commercial and investment banks had to sell to people who had never invested in securities before. From 1917 to 1919, the number of investors who held Treasury bonds exploded from 300,000 to 21 million. National City Company (the precursor to today's Citibank) pioneered retail sales to the middle-class investor and even had a network of salesmen who went door-to-door. These new distribution techniques substantially increased the speed with which new issues could be placed. They also increased competition in the underwriting market.

The predominant way securities were underwritten then, as now, was through syndicates. The lead underwriter for an issue put together a syndicate of underwriters. Syndicate members were bound by an agreement to sell the security at the same time and at the same price. The syndicate effectively combined the investor lists of various houses, thus broadening the market for a security.

As competition increased, however, syndicate members began to seek an advantage over their rivals by violating the provisions of syndicate agreements that specified the timing and the price of the distribution. Not only did they jump the gun, but worse still, they offered investors a better deal by giving discounts, thus undercutting everyone's profits. In the past, such deviations could easily be identified and punished by the lead underwriter: the market was small, everyone talked to everyone else, and most of the cultured syndicate members understood the value of genteel cooperation. But with the explosion of the securities business and the large volume of issues coming to market, the top-tier houses had no option but to access the retail market by including the new breed of securities dealers in their syndicates. These did not feel bound by tacit agreements not to compete, and detecting their violations became all but impossible in the expanded market.

Even while money-minded newcomers undercut the profitability of their syndicates, the old houses also faced competition from banks that integrated commercial banking with investment banking like National City. These banks could not only sell to the retail investor through their branches but were also reputable enough to be lead underwriters. Given their sales networks, these fully integrated "universal" banks were not as reliant on syndicate agreements to ensure the profitability of their underwriting. Their share in the corporate underwriting business increased continuously during the 1920s.[53]

The old established houses looked for respite from competition, and the legislation drafted in the 1930s in response to the stock market crisis gave them the opportunity. The Securities Act of 1933 mandated greater transparency and disclosure in underwriting. But in doing so, it also served the purpose of reducing competition in underwriting.[54] For example, it eliminated the possibility of underwriters' selling securities prior to the date agreed upon by the syndicate by making it illegal to do any publicity before a registration statement is filed with the SEC. Since the lead underwriter can easily control this date (the registration does not become complete until the final price is fixed), the act provides the lead underwriter with the legal means to prevent preoffering solicitation. The Securities Act also eliminated the problem of secret undercutting by making it illegal to grant undisclosed discounts.

By eliminating the challenges to syndicates and restoring their profitability, the Securities Act favored the traditional investment banks. Perhaps equally favorable to them was the Glass-Steagall Act, which forced their chief competitors, commercial banks, to get out of the business of underwriting. All this legislation led to a significant increase in the degree to which a few traditional players dominated the industry, a dominance that continues to this date.

The political process by which the investment banks obtained this favorable legislation is also worth noting. The Senate Banking and Currency Committee conducted hearings between 1932 and 1934 into abuses in the financial system. The hearings, named after the chief counsel, Ferdinand Pecora, highlighted a number of cases that suggested that bankers behaved in an ethically unsound way, when not actually perpetrating fraud. These cases were meant to highlight only the tip of an iceberg of abuse and were instrumental in preparing the public for the legislation that followed. Even though no segment of the financial sector escaped unscathed, the Pecora Committee particularly went after the commercial banks.

One charge that should resonate in these times was that the combination of commercial banking and underwriting was fraught with conflicts of interest. Since a commercial bank had loans outstanding to firms, it could favor the interests of its own owners in the following manner: if it had bad news about a firm to which it had lent, it could use its underwriting arm to certify and distribute securities on behalf of the firm to an unsuspecting public and get the firm to use the proceeds to repay the outstanding bank loan. Thus, the bank's owners would escape booking losses on a bad loan. Similarly, its access to its own unsophisticated depositors could be misused, since these depositors could be sold securities that no one who had any reasonable market experience would touch. It was argued in the Pecora Committee that the conflicts of interest inherent in combining lending and underwriting could, and did, lead to an abuse of trust. The view that banks had betrayed the naive retail investor resonated among a public that had lost tremendous sums and led, almost inevitably, to the separation legislated by the Glass-Steagall Act.

The truth is that none of the allegations has stood up to modern scrutiny. Not only is there little evidence of the purported abuses in the specific cases examined by the Pecora Committee, but an examination of a much wider sample of cases indicates that, on average, the banks did not sell any worse securities than comparable investment banks.[55] In fact, through much of the 1920s, universal banks had been distancing their underwriting arms from their lending arms voluntarily, so as to reduce the appearance of conflicts of interest.[56] The legislation separating commercial from investment banking was politically, not economically, motivated.

So why was the Pecora Committee so one-sided? Some see the Glass-Steagall Act as part of a continuing American tradition of not letting any financial interests get too powerful.[57] Perhaps the Pecora Committee was just an instrument in this process. Others have argued that Senator Carter Glass, a prominent member of the committee, wanted to get commercial banks out of the securities business, for they had violated his long-cherished belief that commercial banks would be stable only if they made short-term, self-liquidating loans.[58]

There is a simpler political answer.[59] The top-tier investment houses were better connected politically. Furthermore, they had not had as much contact with the lay public, and therefore there was less value in offering them as sacrificial scapegoats to a public baying for someone's head. They were also more respectful of, and cooperative with, the committee. Finally, the Roosevelt administration needed a great deal of information in a short period of time to draft the necessary legislation. The traditional investment banks, already well connected politically, offered to provide this information and thus acquired some ability to influence legislation (and the committee). Perhaps momentous legislation does indeed spring from such mundane causes!

Summary

In this chapter, we have argued that the incentives of incumbents to oppose financial development are muted when a country is open. But what determines the decision to be open? How is it affected by incumbents' interest? While the same groups that oppose financial development also tend to oppose openness, the decision of a country to be open is also influenced by its neighbors. The constituencies favoring openness will be economically weaker, and thus less politically powerful, when other countries close down, since they lose the incentive to fight for openness when they see their foreign markets vanish. For this reason, world economic downturns, such as the Great Depression, can precipitate a reaction in many countries that can lead to a closing of borders. This simultaneous closing down of borders provides incumbents with the opportunity to reassert themselves.

An economic downturn also increases the number of the needy and the consequent political pressure to act. This pressure provides incumbents with a noble mantle behind which to hide their baser interests. We have illustrated how crisis provided cover for the resurgence of incumbents through the experience of three different countries. In Italy, what was presented as an attempt to stabilize the banking system was really a way for the private sector to rescue itself using public money. In Japan, large banks and the military government colluded to dominate the financial sector. While the military government collapsed at the end of the war, the banks acquired their own empires and survive (albeit barely) today. In the United States, there was more political give-and-take, and as a result, the financial system retained some degree of competition. Nevertheless, competition within various segments of the financial sector fell, and access to financing became more limited.

Especially noteworthy is that in all these countries, the privileges obtained by incumbents long survived the governments that were persuaded to put them in place. Many of the restrictions on competition, introduced in the political heat of the times, took over half a century to undo.

Incumbents were able to turn back the markets against the wishes of the promarket constituencies that had grown during the times when the markets had flourished. In large part, this was because they were backed by those who had lost out as a result of the depression—the unemployed worker, the penniless investor, the elderly pensioner, and the destitute farmworker. Why did these people turn against markets during the depression? Is it possible that they might turn again? What lessons does this episode hold for our times? This is what we turn to next.

CHAPTER TEN

Why Was the Market Suppressed?

O UR ACCOUNT of the events surrounding the Great Depression and the consequent retreat of markets illustrates two points. First, the reversal in financial development was preceded by popular revulsion against markets. Second, the changed attitude toward markets provided a convenient cover for the resurgence of private interests against markets and competition. While the proximate cause of the reversal might have been the public disaffection with markets, the forms government intervention took and its duration are better explained by the machinations of the incumbents. It took over half a century to undo the constraints imposed on markets during these few years.

Could it happen again? To answer this, we have to understand better why significant segments of the public turned against markets in the 1930s. In some part, the reason was the severity and duration of the depression, especially when contrasted with the stability of the managed economy during the First World War or with Communist Russia, which appeared to be making great strides at this time. The stock market crash, the bank runs, the huge surge in unemployment, which in the United States amounted to over a quarter of the workforce, were severe blows. That capitalist economies were subject to booms and busts was not a revelation: the recurrent crises before World War I had already highlighted that. But the duration of the Great Depression undermined confidence that the system would eventually correct itself.

Equally important in the public's turning against markets, however, was revulsion against the unmanaged risks inherent in a competitive, free enterprise system. Competition and the process of creative destruction not only increase the efficiency of the economic system, as we have argued, but they also increase the amount of risk that individuals have to bear. Workers experience both the euphoria of plenty when their employer does well and the pain of layoffs when their employer fails. Their skills, honed over many years, can become obsolete in a trice if someone in a far-off land comes up with a better product or manufacturing system. Moreover, even as it increases risks, intense competition jeopardizes long-term economic and social relationships, which traditionally insulate people from temporary adversity.

Financial markets can insure some risks, but certainly not some of the most disruptive aspects of market-induced volatility. The risk of an entire industrial sector's becoming obsolete, the risk of protracted unemployment, the risk of a major downturn—all these are hard for the private sector to insure. Life will seem nasty and brutish to the unfortunates who are hurt by competition and left without opportunity or succor.

The sheer number of the distressed—the unemployed, the retiree who has lost her savings, the small-business owner who has seen his home repossessed by his creditors—obviously increases during economic crises, and so does their political power. In fact, their political power will increase more than proportionally with their number because, in times of crisis, the distressed can overcome the normal difficulties that dispersed groups have in coordinating their actions. Not only do skilled people, who are capable of organization, join the ranks of the distressed, but they also are well aware that there are many others who are as desperate as they are. Moreover, economic scandals are more likely to be uncovered in recessions, rendering the system even less legitimate in their eyes. The normal barriers to organization—the fear of acting alone, the absence of information about others and the lack of clarity about their intent, the existence of palatable alternatives—all fall at such times. The result is that the distressed organize and exert enormous pressure to address politically the adversity inflicted by the market. And their anger combines with the private interests of incumbents into a strong force against markets.

Could we face such a backlash again? There are parallels between the public distrust of markets then and now: a spectacularly successful energy company going bust (Insull then, Enron now), allegations that financial institutions were overly enthusiastic about stock in which they had an interest (Chase then, Merrill Lynch now), allegations of tax fraud by the most visible managers of the go-go era (Charles Mitchell of

National City then, Dennis Kozlowski of Tyco now). Matters, however, were substantially worse then. And certainly the economic system has changed considerably since the 1930s. But it is not without weakness.

The political pressure to curb the markets was particularly strong then because there were no buffers in place to cushion people from the blows inflicted by the market. Fortunately, policy makers in developed countries learned the lesson then that some amount of social insurance is necessary to reduce the uncertainty people face with a competitive market and to reduce the number of distressed in case of a downturn. Unfortunately, they learned this lesson in the midst of two great cataclysmic events, the depression and the Second World War, so that the system of insurance put in place then relied extensively on restrictions on the functioning of free markets. With markets' having become freer, it is no longer clear that the system of insurance put in place then is adequate.

It is perhaps useful to start by examining why politicians are so quick to impose restrictions on the workings of markets, despite their long-term adverse consequences. The decision on March 5, 2002, by U.S. President George W. Bush to impose tariffs on steel imports ranging from 8 to 30 percent offers a timely case study.

The Steel Tariffs

With total world consumption of steel at approximately 730 million tons in 2001, there is excess production capacity estimated at about 270 million tons in the steel industry.[1] Unless there is a sudden, unexpected explosion in the demand for steel, worldwide production capacity should be cut by one-third. In addition, the steel industry has also seen a sustained increase in productivity. In 1980, a ton of domestically produced steel in the United States required ten man-hours; today, the industry average is less than four.[2] For an industry whose demand is not expanding fast, such productivity gains have to be accompanied by a drastic reduction in employment. Employment in the steel industry in the United States has indeed fallen by more than 10,000 workers a year for the last twenty years, even while production has increased somewhat: in the year 2000, domestic shipments were 20 percent higher than in 1980.[3]

Not all is gloom in the industry. While some segments are shrinking, others are expanding. As Federal Reserve Chairman Alan Greenspan reminded Congress, "[W]e really have increasingly two steel industries in this country. One is based on the older technologies . . . and the other is the mini-mills, which are evolving at a very dramatic pace."[4] The labor productivity of mini–steel plants is seven times higher than that of integrated producers.[5] Not surprisingly, their share of U.S. capacity rose dramatically during the last two decades: from 15 percent of the U.S. production in 1981 to 50 percent today.[6]

In a situation of overcapacity, some producers have to close down. In a free market, it will be the most inefficient ones. In the United States, these are the old, integrated producers of steel, household names like U.S. Steel and Bethlehem Steel.

Closure is part of the process of creative destruction, and it is very healthy for the economy, for it clears the way for more efficient production and prevents weak firms from dragging the rest of the industry down with them. But it is also very painful for a few. It is of little consolation to the fifty-year-old steelworker to learn that he is the sacrifice demanded by the gods of efficiency. It is natural that he will blame the system and not his own skills or his luck, and he will do whatever he can to try to redress what he perceives as a fundamental injustice in the system. For this reason, thirty thousand steelworkers went to Washington to plead for help.

There are only 160,000 workers producing steel, while 9 million workers are in steel-consuming jobs. Despite being vastly outnumbered, U.S. steelworkers and firms gained the necessary political support to force the tariffs on steel imports. In light of our earlier description of the power of small, focused groups, this is not surprising. Since the cost of the adjustment falls disproportionately on particular groups while the benefit of having a more efficient system is very diffused, the political influence of the victims of competition is much greater than that of the beneficiaries. Old, integrated steel plants are located in states like Philadelphia, Ohio, and West Virginia that were closely fought in the all-too-close 2000 presidential election. Their unionized voters will be pivotal in the next election, as they may have been in the last. George W. Bush allegedly carried the mostly Democratic West Virginia in the 2000 elections because of President Bill Clinton's failure to do anything to help the steel industry.[7] It is clear that politics overcame George W. Bush's principles when he imposed steel tariffs.

What is surprising, however, is the form of support steelworkers obtained. Instead of direct compensation to workers who would lose their jobs, the U.S. government imposed tariffs to protect fewer than nine thousand jobs in the steel industry, which, according to a study, are likely to cost seventy-four thousand jobs in steel-consuming industries.[8] The tariffs will also cost consumers an additional $5 billion per year. And this is not a temporary lapse in policy making. The steel industry has consistently benefited from trade restrictions and government subsidies. The trade restrictions imposed in the 1980s are estimated to have cost consumers $6.8 billion a year, while the value of government subsidies received by the industry over the same period amounted to $30 billion.[9] The tariffs do not have effects only in America. Europe has already started levying its own tariffs so as to protect its steel industry from being overwhelmed with foreign steel denied entry into the United States. Thus, in addition to consumers in the United States, the ultimate losers also include steelworkers in poorer countries like Poland and Bulgaria and their dependents.

Why do politicians not provide direct help to individuals who are hurt by the process of creative destruction? Why do they instead interfere with the process by protecting inefficient firms, thus giving them the resources and the incentives to demand even further protection in the future? After all, it would be far cheaper for the United States to retrain each redundant steelworker, and offer him a hefty pension in addition, instead of imposing costly trade restrictions.

We see two reasons for such responses. One is a matter of form (how it looks), and the other is a matter of function (whom it helps). Consider form first. The costs of restricting competition are largely hidden. It seems victimless because it burdens foreigners, customers, and future potential entrepreneurs, none of whom is politically active (and some of whom are not even present). Steel-consuming industries will indeed protest about how much tariffs will cost the average citizen and how many jobs the industries will lose, but they have a reason to protest. Not only are their numbers potentially tainted by their biases, but they are also obscured by the economics underlying them, which the general public has little time, incentive, or ability to evaluate. From the government's perspective, the costs are off the balance sheet and will not add red ink to an already swollen budget. And from the perspective of workers who retain their jobs, restrictions on competition are only fair and do not impinge on their self-respect in the way that a government handout would have.

It is therefore in the interests of politicians to obscure the nature of the handout involved and present the case for tariffs as an optimal response by a concerned government. For example, Rep. Sherrod Brown of Ohio declared:

> Without immediate action by the President, the situation is dire. Inundated by *illegal* imports, 29 domestic steel companies have either declared bankruptcy or gone out of business in the last four years. . . . In order for the domestic industry to consolidate and survive, the federal government *must vigorously enforce U.S. trade laws.* [italics ours][10]

In fact, there is nothing illegal about steel imports. And when representative Brown calls for a vigorous enforcement of U.S. trade laws, he really means that the United States should invoke Section 201 of the World Trade Organization Agreement, also known as the Escape Clause, which allows countries to escape temporarily from their commitment to free trade.[11]

The alternative, a direct budgetary handout to displaced workers, would be far harder to get through politically. The costs would become very obvious to the average citizen, and she would wonder, "Why them and not me?" In other words, the change in form would short-circuit the public's tendency to remain rationally ignorant. And as the costs spill over into government budgets, politicians would have to make choices between the workers and other politically powerful constituencies that already have entitlements. Finally, the workers themselves would have to face up to the fact that they are indeed living off the benevolence of society, no matter how much it is in society's interest to be benevolent.

The second reason for these restrictions is function: while restrictions on competition are not the best way to protect workers' interests, they are certainly the way preferred by incumbent firms. The steel firms would not be helped if their workers obtained direct handouts. In fact, it would then become far easier to close the firms down. The thirty thousand workers bused to Washington are nothing but human shields used to protect incumbent firms' interests, at the expense of the vitality of the free market system.

The commingling between protection of people and protection of institutions goes beyond simply current jobs. One of the problems of large, integrated steel producers is the so-called legacy costs—that is, the costs of retirement and health benefits that existing firms have to provide to the six hundred thousand retired workers of the steel industry. There is no theoretical reason to entrust responsibility for worker retirement benefits to firms employing them. In the same way as they pay wages, firms could simply pay the necessary amount each month into a private or public trust fund, which would pay workers on retirement (what in modern parlance is known as a defined-contribution plan). But retired workers who depend on the firm for their benefits are another strong external constituency favoring the survival of the firm, which is why firms are unlikely to dispense easily with them. Incumbent firms have indeed erected an intricate defense of human shields to protect their interests.

What we will argue now is that while the unlikely coalition between capitalists and other sufferers from competition is always possible, it is particularly likely in economic downturns. Recessions reduce the benefits of, and thus the political support for, openness, weakening the strongest force for efficiency. At the same time, recessions increase the power of the distressed. Thus, economic downturns, especially downturns that occur simultaneously across a large number of countries, threaten the political stability of the capitalist system. This is what happened during the Great Depression and soon after, and the consequences of the antimarket reaction lasted for fifty years.

Why Is There More Support for Restrictions on the Market in a Downturn?

Unlike incumbent firms, the others who are hurt by competition are normally a dispersed group with an unfocused agenda. Thus, their ability to influence the political scenario is limited. But in times of economic crisis, several factors come together to give them more power. Their sheer number increases, and they have time on their hands. Equally important, the distressed share the common knowledge that many others are in the same hopeless situation and have similar beliefs about the rottenness of the system: scandals, real and otherwise, are typically uncovered in economic downturns, suggesting that the system might be corrupt (and it is easy for the distressed to convince themselves that the corruption is responsible for their state).

Furthermore, in downturns, acts of destruction, such as the closing down of firms and banks and the eviction of householders, predominate over acts of creation. While the "cleansing" may be necessary for the recovery, these are public events that can catalyze the distressed, already seething with resentment over the injustice of the system. They could well be jolted into organizing. Incumbents, who see an opportunity to channel the anger of the distressed against competition, also lend a hand to organize the distressed. And like an angry mob, once organized, the distressed can be used to achieve ends that go far beyond their original intent: they could become a threat to free markets.

Consider a city riot. While the circumstances under which riots start are complex, two conditions seem to characterize many of them: riots explode when there is generalized discontent and a catalyzing event. Generalized discontent alone is insufficient because the discontented face a severe coordination problem. If one person starts throwing stones at shop windows and turns out to be alone, he is treated as a common criminal and ends up in jail. But if a large number of people act simultaneously, the police will be overwhelmed, the protesters will be treated by the authorities as a political movement rather than a criminal gang, and few will end up in jail. Thus, events such as the 1992 acquittal of the policemen who beat up Rodney King trigger a riot not just because they increase the number of the discontented but also because these events are very public: they create the beliefs that allow people to conclude that others will be willing to act.

Political action by the victims of competition has some similarity to city riots. As long as each individual fears he will be campaigning alone, he holds back, since he knows that he will have to bear a large cost with no likely benefit. Economic crises not only create the general awareness that there are many more like him, with little to lose and everything to gain by organizing, but they also provide signal events around which the protesters can organize. For example, in 1931, unemployment in some areas of Chicago's South Side reached over 85 percent.[12] Many of the homeless unemployed drifted toward the lodging houses, where they were organized by the Unemployment Council. When funds for unemployment relief were cut by half, the unemployed marched in the streets, and the funds were restored.[13] Through the early years of the depression in the United States, many such protest organizations arose involving farmer groups, worker unions, and veterans' movements.

Second, times of crisis also tend to be times when corporate scandals come to light, undermining the legitimacy of the overall system. To understand why, we need to appreciate that corporate fraud often consists of a variant of a scheme devised by Charles Ponzi, an Italian immi-

grant from Boston. Ponzi became famous in the 1920s for offering phenomenal rates of return—for example, 50 percent on money invested for
forty-five days—to people willing to place money with him. He invested
their money ostensibly in some complex scheme involving postage
stamps that no one quite understood.[14] In truth, there was no such
scheme. He simply used the new money flowing in to pay interest on the
old money. As long as deposits were growing fast enough, his scheme
survived. Eventually, suspicious public authorities forced him to stop
taking deposits—at which point, the scheme imploded.

Similarly, much corporate fraud in developed countries, where outright theft is less of a problem, consists of Ponzi-like schemes—for
example, accelerating the recognition of future earnings to show higher
earnings today, hiding expenses and losses through various accounting
gimmicks, and hiding indebtedness in subsidiaries. Management's ability to conceal deceit depends on the firm's growing its way out of trouble. By contrast, the magnitude of the necessary deceit increases in bad
times as the firm's performance deteriorates. This then makes it harder
to conceal the problems, which is one reason why corporate scandals
tend to erupt in bad times. Enron collapsed, in part because all the creative accounting in the world could not help it conceal its mounting
losses.

Even perfectly legitimate investments sometimes have a dynamic
similar to the Ponzi scheme. As more and more investors got taken in by
the seemingly unlimited opportunities of the Internet in the late 1990s,
money poured into the sector, driving up prices and increasing the
return of earlier investors. The new money boosted the return for the
earlier money, seemingly justifying the premise of limitless wealth for
investors. But when the inflow of money slowed down, prices plummeted, and the entire phenomenon appeared to be a bubble. With the
benefit of hindsight, bubbles are easy to recognize. In the midst of them,
however, matters are murkier.

It is easy for politicians rummaging amid the carcasses of corporate
disasters to find "scandal." One can always find fault with business judgment. And when further prodding reveals evidence of seeming conflicts
of interest, what is actually reasonable business judgment given the
available information becomes cronyism or, worse, criminal wrongdoing. This is not to say that businessmen are without blemish (see the
next paragraph), only that outsiders are prone to believing that business
judgment is more scientific than it actually is. Much is attributed to

malevolence that should rightfully be attributed to uncertainty or even incompetence. The point, however, is that the political witch-hunts that start in downturns tend to further erode the legitimacy of the system of free enterprise and provide cover for antimarket actions.

Of course, the actions of some industrialists and financiers, confronted with a fall-off in performance, contribute to the feeling that the markets are rigged against the common man. On seeing their positions going awry, traders double up their bets hoping luck will favor them, in the process flouting their company's rules and even the law. Doing precisely this, Nick Leeson, a trader for Barings, took his bank down with him. In an attempt to maintain the phenomenal (and quite possibly legitimate) growth in earnings of its earlier years, the management of Enron resorted to accounting manipulation as the market turned more competitive and true profit margins fell.

With ruin staring them in the face, some businessmen might try anything, even if illegitimate, in the hope that the actions will stave off disaster. But since these are wild gambles, they typically do not succeed, and the subsequent investigations reveal the illegality of the actions. Other, perfectly honest businesses also get tarred.

Finally, the representatives of the people, perhaps compensating for their inertia when the scandal is developing or seeing a path to personal advancement, tend to overemphasize irregularities in their investigations. The insinuation is that these irregularities are the tip of the iceberg when, often, that is all there is. We have already mentioned the importance of the Pecora Committee hearings in setting the political stage for the New Deal financial legislation in the 1930s. While these hearings found little evidence that would directly support the ensuing legislation, they did uncover irregularities and possible tax fraud committed by Charles E. Mitchell, National City Company chairman. While only peripherally related to the issues being investigated, these findings contributed to the aura of illegitimacy surrounding the practices of the financial sector.

In sum, then, downturns help reveal patently illegal Ponzi schemes. Failure itself often tends to be seen as malfeasance rather than bad luck or incompetence: Ferdinand de Lesseps was lionized for successfully constructing the Suez Canal but was hauled into court as a swindler after the failure of his attempt to build the Panama Canal, even if he had possibly spent much more effort in setting the groundwork for the latter.[15] And the possibility of failure may lead normally honest businessmen into dishonest acts. Finally, as with the Pecora Committee hearings in the 1930s, some politicians may try to indict industry at large by highlighting a few unrepresentative acts. All these tend to diminish the legitimacy of the competitive system in the eyes of the victims of competition, a system they already view with jaundiced eyes because of what it has done to them.

As spontaneous organizations of the distressed emerge, professional politicians and political parties attempt to capture their energy toward their own electoral gain. Franklin Roosevelt, as we have seen, was not averse to using antimarket rhetoric to appeal to the distressed. And once the politicians capture power and there is a drive to legislate, incumbents are not far behind in directing legislations toward their needs. Thus, much as a riot can be exploited by a few to achieve goals that are not the intent of the mob—it is interesting how often riots that are ostensibly labeled "communal" in India turn into a targeted destruction of especially irksome rival businesses owned by the minority community—the political organizations of the distressed can be used by those who have a broader agenda.

The antimarket agenda of incumbents is particularly strong in global downturns, when the opportunities for trade and investment abroad are few, making openness less appealing. As protectionism increases, legislation pushed by the demands of the distressed and by incumbents has no need to be constrained by concerns about international competitiveness. It feeds into the natural instincts of politicians to avoid immediate and direct costs rather than the hidden costs of market restrictions. The market is easy prey.

Some caveats are in order before we conclude this section. We have argued that downturns lead to a coalescence of interests. This does not mean that one interest prevails—that, for example, incumbent businessmen fully succeed in capturing the agenda. Even while New Deal legislation in the 1930s attempted to create industrial cartels to eliminate price competition, it also brought in legislation giving unions legal status.[16] In practice, there will be give-and-take, but the common agenda will be for a coalition of incumbents, ranging from businessmen to union leaders to politicians, to suppress the free market.

It need not also be that interests dominate ideas. We do not deny the possibility that the world had become more humane and socially conscious in the 1930s and that some legislation was moved by well-meaning politicians who had the public interest at heart. Our point is that certain sorts of ideas have a better chance of finding fertile ground in which to germinate when the ground is fertilized with the right interests. In the 1930s, the dominant fertilizer was antimarket in character. Let us now describe the kind of economy to which it gave rise in the postwar period.

The Political Response

The Great Depression and the Second World War completely changed perceptions about the political viability of state intervention in the economy. The classical economists had preached that governments would make things worse if they intervened. Instead, the lesson politicians drew from the depression was that governments that followed the prescriptions of classical free market economists to do nothing and let the turmoil run its course were turned out of office. By contrast, those that broke with tradition and intervened to support prices and employment had some success and were reelected. In fact, in a number of countries, more than government-built bridges or roads, it was that most traditional of public works, preparation for war, which restored full employment. At the end of World War II, classical economics was in the political doghouse, while government intervention in the economy's working had become respectable.

People looked to the government to protect them from the vicissitudes of the now disreputable market. Developed countries set up explicit social security systems, providing old-age, unemployment, and health insurance. This created stable government employment that itself contributed to a sense of economic security. Government expenditures on subsidies and transfers, broadly programs of social insurance and redistribution, went up from 4.5 percent of GDP in 1937 to 8.5 percent of a much larger GDP in 1960.[17] While, in 1910, only 20 percent of the labor force in western Europe had some form of pension insurance, and only 22 percent had health insurance, by 1935, the percentages covered were, respectively, 56 percent and 47 percent, and by 1975, 93 percent and 90 percent, respectively.[18]

This system of insurance was set in place during the Great Depression and the immediately postwar years, at a time of stretched government budgets, with competing pressing organized demands for subsidy. There was no way a government could deliver on all its promises if the calls came all at once. Since the government was now the backstop to the market economy, and since its resources were stretched, it was natural that it would try to limit the potential calls on its purse. This meant finding allies that would participate in providing the people economic security. What better candidates than large, established corporations? After all, they had to have been successful to get to their current size. These firms also had enough scale to afford an administrative infrastructure that could provide and track employee benefits. But for these corporations to portray security to a people who had seen household names go under during the depression, their future survival had to be assured.

The solution to which most economies gravitated was the natural one. Given the disrepute the market was in, and the natural predilection of politicians to hide costs through market regulation, the political response was to make common cause with the firms' owners, managers, and unions and suppress competition. Therefore, the short-run steps that had been taken to deal with the problems of the depression became long-term policy. Industrial and financial cartels were allowed to form, and the resulting high profits for member firms and high wages for union members ensured industrial stability. In the long run, industries would ossify and need further protection (the Steel Tariffs of 2002 were just a mild version), but that possibility was too far beyond the politicians' horizons to matter.

The Rise of Relationship Capitalism

We shall call the system of managed competition that emerged post–World War II "relationship capitalism." Competition was restricted, in part, through regulatory bodies that set up entry barriers and mechanisms for firms to collude, as we saw in the trucking industry in the United States, and in part through grand, mediated, economywide agreements among relevant incumbent groups. In many ways, this simply continued the policies adopted during the depression. For example, in Sweden, labor, agrarian interests, industrialists and financiers, and the government came together in 1938 in Saljtosbaden to hammer out a pact. Labor obtained stable wages, policies for full employment, and social services; farmers obtained higher food prices and price supports; while the leaders of the private sector obtained industrial peace and respect for private property.[19]

Following this pattern, in the 1950s and the 1960s, the top leaders of the ruling Social Democrat Party, the labor unions, and the Federation of Swedish Industry came together every year to determine the country's economic and social program for the subsequent year in a private meeting at the summer home of the prime minister.[20] These agreements between trade unions and associations of employers ensured that no firm could attempt to undercut others to obtain a competitive advantage. Clearly, such arrangements hurt the public consumer, but they were acceptable because the consumer was also a worker. They also gave power to a few organized interests. In many countries, wages negotiated by unions were automatically extended to nonunion workers. Thus, even though, in France and Spain, only 10 percent of the workers were union members, the labor-industry agreement covered more than 70 percent of the workers.[21]

Large segments of the population were, of course, left out of this pact. Potential entrants and small and medium-sized firms did not have the state support that large firms had. Women and the young, who typically did not have long tenures in established firms, also received short shrift. But the system seemed to work, at least for a while. Not only did it offer more security than the competitive, market-oriented system that many countries had abandoned, but it also seemed to facilitate growth. For a while, it seemed as if one could have it all—growth with security. Harold Macmillan, the British prime minister between 1957 and 1963, led the Conservative Party to victory in the 1959 election with the slogan "You've never had it so good!"

In addition to direct regulation of competition—which could go only so far—the government relied on its control over finance to manage the economy. Its powers rested on three pillars. The first was the continuation of both active and passive policies that sought to repress domestic financial markets. Equity and bond issues became subject to government approval and were choked off. Similarly, many countries regulated initial public offerings of equity, requiring companies to have several years of positive earnings before listing. Young companies could clearly not meet this hurdle.

Passive policies toward the markets—the failure to create the infrastructure needed to make the market transparent and fair—were equally important. Before 1990, there were laws against insider trading in only 34 out of the 103 countries with a stock exchange.[22] More important, only 9 countries even bothered to enforce the insider-trading laws on their books. This state of affairs persisted even though, as we have seen, the enforcement of insider-trading laws substantially reduces the cost to companies of raising equity finance. The failure to mandate better disclosure standards or to endow the financial system with laws and administrative procedures to protect minority shareholders thus prevented all but the most established companies from accessing the equity market. As a result, even in the 1980s, the average age of a European company entering the equity market was forty years.[23] By contrast, in the United States, the typical venture-backed firm goes public today when it is just five years old.[24]

Massive state intervention in the allocation of credit was the second pillar on which government control over finance rested. Governments nationalized banks. Across a large number of countries, the government controlled nearly 55 percent of all bank assets in 1985.[25] They also offered subsidies to banks that made loans on preferential terms to priority sectors. Such directed-credit programs became common in both developed and developing countries in the 1960s and 1970s. In South Korea, directed-credit programs amounted to over 50 percent of total funds mobilized by the financial system in the 1970s.[26] In Japan, subsidized loans accounted for 71 percent of the financing of major industries in the reconstruction years immediately after the war and stabilized at a level of between 10 and 15 percent of financing for the rest of the century.[27] In France, three-quarters of all loans to business came from the state, the financial institutions (which were quasi-public), or nationalized banks and their subsidiaries.[28] Forty-three percent of all loans were subsidized by the state.[29] These figures are from 1979, after twenty-one years of uninterrupted rule by conservative governments and before François Mitterrand implemented his grand plan for bank nationalization!

State control of credit is not intrinsically bad. States may want to expand access to financing—after all, the nationalization of banks is often explained as necessary to allow financing to reach traditionally underserviced segments of society. In practice, however, large bureaucracies are extremely ineffective at funding small or young firms, and government-directed credit (at least the portion that is not frittered away in populist giveaways) typically goes toward the government itself and to established incumbents.[30]

The third and perhaps most important pillar on which government control of the financial system rested was restrictions on international capital movements. It is useful to see why these restrictions were so important to relationship capitalism and why, in the end, they failed. To their failure, which we describe in the next chapter, we owe in large part the revival of competitive markets in recent years.

The Bretton Woods Agreement

More often than not, economic theories have only an indirect influence on policy: they provide the cloak with which politicians can legitimize what seems reasonable given the mood of the moment. Governments intervened in the working of the economy in the initial years of the depression against the advice of the most respectable economists. But eventually, their actions were supported by perhaps the best-known economist of his age, John Maynard Keynes. In his pathbreaking book *The General Theory of Employment, Interest, and Money,* Keynes argued that it was quite possible for the demand for goods and services in an economy to fall below the economy's potential to supply them. The resulting excess supply—as evidenced in the unemployment of men and materials—would not automatically and quickly be cured by a reduction in wages and prices, in contrast to the prescriptions of classical economists. Instead, Keynes claimed, it was the duty of the government to step up at such times and bridge the gap between private demand and supply by providing demand of its own through the public works described earlier.

The emerging Keynesian consensus as the end of World War II came in sight was in accord with the public mood. It required governments to continue to play a substantial role in managing demand—in part, through social insurance schemes. But this seemed somewhat at odds with another important lesson learned from the 1930s. Perhaps the path of least political resistance for a government to increase the demand for goods manufactured domestically was to depreciate the exchange rate so that domestic goods would find a ready market abroad and to impose tariffs on foreign goods so that domestic demand could be forced to soak up only domestic goods. Of course, since all governments could play this game, these "beggar-thy-neighbor" policies eventually made trade seize up, and all countries were left worse off.

While free trade was in everyone's long-run interest, the United States was especially concerned about the short run. It, unlike other developed countries, had emerged from World War II with its industries and finances intact. It was especially worried that the rest of the world would erect barriers to keep out its goods and financiers. Therefore, it looked to set up a postwar system that would keep borders open.

The Bretton Woods agreement, concluded in New Hampshire in 1944, which set the stage for postwar economic reconstruction, was a compromise. It attempted to bind governments sufficiently so that their policies would not wreck international trade—something the United States strongly desired—while giving them enough autonomy to intervene to fine-tune domestic demand.[31] The route to the first objective was exchange rate stability: in order to prevent competitive devaluations, the agreement sought to peg exchange rates within a narrow band, giving countries the ability to adjust them only in case of "fundamental disequilibrium." The International Monetary Fund was set up to lend resources so that countries would have the ability to withstand pressures to devalue while they undertook the necessary adjustment in domestic policies.

The political mood, however, was not one in which European governments could ignore the domestic constituencies that had become organized during the depression. With fixed exchange rates, something else had to be sacrificed or the world would be back between the immovable object of the rigid gold standard and the irresistible force of organized demands for government intervention. The sacrificial goat was the cross-border flow of capital.

If capital flows were unrestricted, Keynes worried that governments would not be able to manage domestic demand easily. While he was concerned about the government's ability to set the level of interest rates, all kinds of government intervention would become more difficult.[32] For example, a government might want to "persuade" private banks to offer cheap funds to certain industries. Instead of providing direct subsidies, it might want to keep deposit interest rates low so that banks would still be profitable and use its many levers of power to direct the loans to favored borrowers. But if savers could simply flee the country toward higher world rates, this subsidization would not take place.

More generally, Keynes believed that free capital flows would limit the extent to which government policies could even hint at redistribution from the rich to the poor. As Keynes put it:

> Surely in the post-war years there is hardly a country in which we
> ought not to expect keen political discussions affecting the position

of the wealthier classes and the treatment of private property. If so, there will be a number of people constantly taking fright because they think that the degree of leftism in one country looks for the time being likely to be greater than somewhere else.[33]

Therefore, the compromise at Bretton Woods was to strive to open borders to trade but to keep them closed to certain kinds of capital flows. For not all cross-border capital flows were to be discouraged. It was essential for the stability of exchange rates that countries with a current account surplus finance countries with a deficit. Moreover, "productive" capital flows that could be employed in developing a country's real resources, such as foreign direct investment, were also to be encouraged. Thus, capital controls were meant primarily to prevent a twenty-year-old investment banker from moving money across the world to the country providing the highest returns—what government bureaucrats derisively term speculative capital.

Understanding and perhaps even sympathizing with the compulsions of European governments, the United States went against its bankers and agreed to controls on capital flows (though, in what proved to be important for the eventual demise of controls, in the hope of attracting capital that wanted to flee Europe, the bankers ensured that these controls were not watertight).[34] In the absence of the competitive discipline provided by cross-border capital flows, domestic financial institutions obtained a monopoly over finance. Productive firms that were not in political favor could not get finance. Capital controls also took away a significant source of budgetary discipline on governments, thus giving them leeway for constant intervention in the economy. As Keynes announced triumphantly, "Not merely as a feature of the transition but as a permanent arrangement, the plan accords every member government the explicit right to control all capital movements. What used to be heresy is now endorsed as orthodoxy."[35]

Who Were the Winners and Losers?

Who were the winners and losers in the relationship system? Unfortunately, the grand bargain that was at its center had so many cross-subsidies built in that it is often hard to disentangle who obtained the benefits and who really bore the costs. In general, however, incumbents—whether they were large firms, unionized workers, farmers, or the aged—gained at the expense of outsiders, such as would-be entrepreneurs, foreign firms, unorganized workers, immigrants, or the young.

Consider, for example, the system of pension and unemployment insurance in Italy until a few years ago. The pension system had two components: one provided by companies, the other provided by a state-run mandatory pension system. The contributions under the private pension system were under the complete control of the company's owner, who could use them as a cheap source of financing for his own enterprise. Workers thus bore a lot of the enterprise's risk without being compensated for it. Not coincidentally, this gave them a commonality of interests with their employers in suppressing competition. If we stopped here, we would conclude that employers benefited at the expense of workers. But this ignores the other dimensions of the retirement system.

The state-run mandatory pension system was extremely generous. It was a pay-as-you-go system that offered workers benefits that were much larger than the value of the past contributions they had made. New retirees obtained benefits equal to 80 percent of pretax wages earned in their last five years of employment, which meant that many were better off retired than on the job. And a low retirement age of fifty-five ensured that many did retire from their regular jobs, only to moonlight in the underground economy. And for those who were really impatient as well as mildly unscrupulous, the medical guidelines were loose enough to ensure a disability pension well before the normal retirement age.[36] Like a Ponzi scheme, such a system can work as long as there is growth in the economy. Since the initial postwar years were years of growth, workers gained on one side what they lost on the other, and companies were the net beneficiaries. The losers were future generations that would have to bear the cost of government profligacy. But the long run was never a concern in relationship capitalism because, after all, as Keynes had said, "In the long run, we are dead."

A similar pattern can be seen in the unemployment system. Until 1991, the main source of unemployment security in Italy was a law preventing companies with more than fifteen employees from firing workers without "just cause." While the unemployed were owed no formal payments, workers who lost their jobs received payments from the Cassa Integrazione Guadagni (CIG). The CIG was originally created in 1945 to supplement the wages of workers temporarily laid off from large manufacturing companies during the conversion from military production to peacetime production. Almost imperceptibly, the CIG was extended to other sectors of the economy and eventually covered permanent, and not just temporary, layoffs. Under this system, the government paid 80 percent of the salary of laid-off workers for a period of three months, extendable for no more than a year. In practice, the coverage period was often extended past the statutory limit, especially when a big company was involved.

Another alternative for a company was to force laid-off workers into early retirement. Not only did the state pension system have to absorb the loss of contributions, but it also had to support the retiree for more years. State-owned companies, such as the post office and the railway system, offered another line of support. These acted as "employer of last resort," especially in the South, where unemployment is endemic.

If we combine all these elements, the system did protect workers, especially those in large firms, from unemployment. It greatly benefited large firms, which had the flexibility to fire and rehire the same workers during different phases of the business cycle without facing any cost of retraining. But it was extremely onerous for rival medium-sized firms, which were large enough to be prevented from firing but not equally well protected by the CIG. And it was a drain on the government coffers.

Of course, the government eventually had to recover these costs from citizens through higher taxes and higher inflation. It could postpone the unpleasant burden somewhat by financing with debt, but eventually, there would be a day of reckoning.

Summary

Relationship capitalism emerged in much of the postwar world partly because of a general disillusionment with markets accompanied by a war-instilled faith in the power of government, and partly because incumbents rode upon the wave of reaction to craft a system that ensured their survival. The atmosphere of general distrust of the markets was based on experiences then that are eerily similar to the atmosphere in which the Steel Tariffs of 2002 were levied (though clearly, matters were much worse then)—a stock market decline, revelations of excessive enthusiasm by investment banks for peddling favored stocks, spectacular failures by high-flying firms of the previous go-go decade, and allegations of tax evasion and accounting fraud by their management . . .

The system had at its heart a grand bargain. Everyone on the inside had his or her small area of privilege. Enough people had privileges to lose if the system changed to ensure that the system had strong political support. The opportunity and risk inherent in the market system had been replaced by the privilege and stability of relationship capitalism.

Of course, privilege for one citizen is oppression for another. For every mature firm that was protected, an innovative would-be entrepreneur was denied entry; for every old white male worker who enjoyed a safe, well-paid job, a young female from a minority community was denied economic independence; for every pensioner who enjoyed a rich and fulfilling retirement, a poor child was not given the basic nutrition that would make him or her a productive citizen. This is not to say that these choices were conscious or that the system did not benefit some like the elderly who had been traditionally underprivileged. The problem was that there was no natural way in relationship capitalism to alter the system of privilege, so that those on the inside who started out underprivileged did not eventually became overprivileged. And for those on the outside, the denial of access became even more oppressive.

Eventually, however, changes in the external environment and the rigidities of the relationship system combined to bring about its downfall and led to the resurgence of markets that we have experienced recently. It is that to which we now turn. With that, we will have come full circle to today.

CHAPTER ELEVEN

The Decline and Fall of Relationship Capitalism

IN THE FIRST two decades after World War II, the system of managed competition that we refer to as relationship capitalism seemed to work well: both continental Europe and Japan, where the system had taken deep root, experienced phenomenal rates of growth in a politically stable environment. But the growth in the immediately postwar decades masked three serious problems. First, the relationship system did not encourage dramatic innovation. This was not necessary initially, when the primary task was reconstruction, but assumed much greater importance later. Second, with the market suppressed, there was no clear way to allocate the monopoly profits the system generated. Finally, the system had no easy way to effect destruction—so that resources could be transferred out of dying industries into sunrise industries. Events eventually uncovered these problems.

What brought the demise of relationship capitalism, however, was not just its inherent weaknesses but also the rising pressure for efficiency coming from international financial markets. The Bretton Woods agreement ultimately failed in its attempt to restrict cross-border capital flows. International capital movements, only a trickle in the beginning, became a flood. This created the political and economic conditions for the resurgence of competitive markets we have witnessed in the last quarter of the twentieth century. To understand all this, let us begin by seeing how relationship capitalism actually worked in the area of finance. There is a reason why we focus on this system. We believe that it, not socialism, has been the natural alternative to free market enterprise. To make a rational choice we have to understand its strengths and weaknesses better.

Relationship Finance at Work

Countries like Germany or Japan went much further and for far longer down the path of relationship finance than did countries like the United States or the United Kingdom. By the early 1990s, Germany was still largely a relationship-based system, while the United States and the United Kingdom had become truly market-based financial systems. So an examination of the differences between these countries in the early 1990s helps highlight how relationship finance differs from market-based finance. Crudely put, in the former countries, capital essentially circulated within a set of related firms and institutions, while in the latter countries, firms often have to raise money from, and return money to, arm's-length parties—hence, the terms *relationship finance* and *arm's-length finance*. Other terms have been used to describe these different systems: *Rhenish capitalism* versus *Anglo-Saxon capitalism* or *bank-based systems* versus *market-based systems*.

For example, in 1994, only 16 percent of borrowing by firms in the United States was from banks, while 49 percent was through the issue of securities (like bonds and commercial paper).[1] Unlike bank loans, securities are easily traded and are held by investors who typically do not want to have more than an arm's-length relationship with the issuing firm. By contrast, 80 percent of corporate borrowing in Germany was from banks and only 10 percent from securities markets. Banks, by the nature of their large illiquid holdings, tend to have much closer and longer-term ties with firms.

There were substantial differences on the equity side, too. Between 1991 and 1995, U.S. corporations annually issued equity amounting to 1.2 percent of GDP. By contrast, German corporations issued equity amounting to only 0.04 percent of GDP. Most telling, there were 3.11 initial public offerings per million U.S. citizens in 1995. The comparable number per million German citizens was only 0.08.[2]

Even the outstanding equity was held very differently. In 1994, individuals held about half the outstanding shares of U.S. corporations, though by 2000, this had fallen to less than 40 percent. Other nonfinancial corporations held only 14 percent of one another's shares, and banks held virtually zero. Thus the institutions holding corporate shares in the United States are primarily mutual funds and pension funds, which have an arm's-length investment relationship with the firms they own. In Germany, individuals held only 17 percent, while banks held 10 percent (and also cast the vote for a substantial fraction of the shares held by individuals). Other nonfinancial corporations held an astounding 42 percent of the shares. Thus, other firms and banks, which typically have a relationship that transcends more than shareholding, own a majority stake in large German firms. Because large institutions rather than individuals own shares in Germany, ownership is much more concentrated. The top five shareholders in Germany owned approximately 42 percent of shares in the average large corporation, while the number in the United States was only 25 percent.

The large shareholders in Germany tend to be much more protective of the management along some dimensions. Depending on how one counts, there were only four hostile takeovers of German firms in the second half of the twentieth century.[3] The reaction to German steel company Krupp's proposed hostile takeover bid for Thyssen (also German, also in steel) in March 1997 perhaps explains why. Thyssen immediately lashed out at Krupp's "Wild West" tactics (in other words, American-style arm's-length capitalism rather than the more traditional way of backroom consensus). Krupp's chairman came under vociferous attack and had to defend himself, among other things, from a volley of rotten eggs thrown by irate Thyssen workers. Politicians right up to Chancellor Helmut Kohl became involved, and pressure was put on Krupp's bankers (who also had seats on Thyssen's board) to persuade Krupp to be more conciliatory. While a consensus was eventually reached, and the two firms merged with both managements sharing power, the process was much more highly politically charged and protective of the status quo than would have been the case in the United States.

The relationship system differs from a market-based system on two important attributes: *transparency* and *access*.

Consider transparency first. When large, friendly firms and institutions oversee decisions made by a firm's managers, they are likely to feel little need to reveal the firm's actual state and its decision-making processes to the public. After all, what will the powerless individual investor do other than get upset if some inconvenient tidbit about managerial incompetence is revealed to him? Far better that the interested parties who own, or have lent to, the firm decide collectively the remedial action to be taken to protect their investment. Moreover, unlike the individual, who may have a fleeting relationship with the firm as he buys and sells its stock in the market, related firms and institutions will care about the long-term future of the firm being governed. Finally, too much transparency could bring large outside investors, determined to make changes. This could disrupt the whole system of relationship finance. At least, this is how a German (or Japanese or Swiss) banker might justify keeping investors in the dark.[4]

Because, whatever the merit in the above rationales, the end result in the German system is that the individual investor, employee, or outsider is left fairly ignorant of corporate affairs. In 1989, a study was undertaken to examine whether multinational firms' consolidated financial statements had fully implemented OECD (Organization for Economic Cooperation and Development) guidelines on disclosure. Sixty-four percent of U.S. firms studied had fully implemented the guidelines on disclosure, but *none* of the German firms had done so.[5] Similarly, a committee scoring the annual statements of the largest companies in each country for the extent of disclosure gave Germany a rating of 67 in 1995. To put this in perspective, an emerging market like South Korea received a rating of 68, while the United States and the United Kingdom had ratings of 76 and 85, respectively: Finally, a study comparing the transparency of financial statements from 34 countries over the period 1985–1998 places the United States at the top while Germany is ranked only in the middle of the group.[6]

Recent accounting scandals in the United States have revealed that a number of firms have deliberately sought to mislead shareholders. In Germany, misleading investors is not an aberration but a tenet of policy. The extent to which German accounting and disclosure have been uninformative is perhaps best brought home by the concept of hidden or secret reserves. In years of high profits, German firms were allowed to stash away some of the profits into a special fund without revealing them to the public investor. In bad years, these profits would be brought back into the bottom line. The logic behind such reserves was accounting conservatism—to set aside for a rainy day. But the true reasons were probably paternalism and self-interest: the public investor could not be entrusted with a true and fair picture, for she might panic unduly and take precipitous action (to the discomfort of incumbent management). So her pretty head had to be calmed with smooth earnings, allowing only those large institutions and firms that were close to management to know the true, awful state. And this could be quite different from what the public was presented.

When Daimler Benz, one of the most venerable of German corporations, wanted to list on the New York Stock Exchange in 1993, it had to restate its accounts according to the accounting rules followed by the exchange (rather than the permissive rules followed in Germany). This revealed a lot about the difference between German accounting and generally accepted accounting practices in the United States: a half-yearly profit of DM 168 million turned into a loss of DM 949 million, a difference of DM 1.1 billion of profit over the half year![7]

In sum, even though households are the ultimate owners of savings, systems such as Germany's give them little direct or indirect control over where or how their money is invested. Firms and institutional financiers make all their decisions without informing, or seeking the approval of, the ultimate owners, the individual investors. The German banker Carl Furstenberg probably misrepresented only slightly the views of his fellow managers when he said, "Shareholders are stupid and impertinent—stupid because they give their money to somebody else without any effective control over what this person is doing with it, and impertinent because they ask for a dividend as a reward for their stupidity."[8]

A second difference between the relationship system and the market-based system has to do with limited access. When information about firms is not made publicly available as a matter of course, borrowers already inside the "system" cannot go outside their narrow circle of financial institutions unless they have an impeccable reputation. These constraints can be compounded by legislation. In fact, till the early 1990s, industrial firms in Germany had to obtain approval from the Federal Ministry of Economics for permission to issue commercial paper and long-term bonds. Approval was granted only if the credit standing of the issuer was satisfactory *and* if the application was supported by a bank. Additionally, a variety of taxes made nonbank finance extremely costly for the average German corporation. So corporations had limited access to finance outside a narrow circle of financiers.

Even with limited transparency and access, however, incumbent firms may have plenty of finance in the normal course in relationship-based economies, with a far lower burden of disclosure and a longer effective maturity of repayment than in the more transparent, free-access, arm's-length system that exists in the United States. While it is entirely possible that an orgy of mutual back-scratching might lead the related firms that are inside the system to refuse to discipline the incompetent or dishonest managers in their midst, in practice, they seem to sense that it is in their longer-term interest to do so. So even though out-siders are not allowed to discipline inside managers via the device of hostile takeovers, top managers in Germany and Japan are fired about as quickly, and as often, in response to poor corporate performance as are managers in the United States.[9] If we also take into account the fact that households in financial systems like those in Germany and Japan, till recent changes, had few alternative avenues in which to invest, the inescapable conclusion is that insider firms in a relationship system may enjoy as easy access to finance as similarly sized firms in a market-based system. Consistent with this, studies typically fail to find a difference in the cost of capital that large, established firms face in the two kinds of systems.[10]

So do the differences between these two types of systems matter? We believe they do, and they matter most in times of great change.

The Relationship System and Change

Established firms can easily handle incremental change. Extraordinary change, however, typically requires extraordinary measures, both to change mind-sets and to foster actions. Relationship systems may be incapable of both.

To see why they may not have the mind-set to finance change, let us start with an analogy.[11] Suppose you just wrote your version of the Great American Novel and wanted to get it published. You could send it to Fusty House, where a couple of editors would look at it and make a joint decision on whether to publish the manuscript. The book would be published only if both agreed. Or you could send it to Chancy House, where editors decide independently. If an editor rejects the manuscript, you have the option of sending it to another editor within the house who will not know the book's previous history (Chancy's editors simply do not talk to one another). Clearly, you, as the author, would prefer to send the book to Chancy House, where the book has more chances of getting accepted and any one editor's biases against it do not doom it. But which house will make the better choice from a business perspective?

The books Fusty House will pick will invariably be of good quality because they will have been through a more rigorous screening process. But Fusty will also reject many more good books than will Chancy House. Chancy will accept more books and, in the process, reduce the likelihood of rejecting good ones. But it will also publish more rotten ones. Which house has the better system depends, as one might guess, on the relative proportion of good and bad manuscripts that are sent to a house and the relative cost of rejecting a good book versus the cost of accepting a rotten one.

If good books are best-sellers and earn millions, while rotten books just cost a few thousands each in returns, then Chancy's system is better. If good books sell only a moderate amount while rotten books not only cost in terms of returns but also cost the house its reputation, then Fusty's system is better. Now let us draw the analogy to the financing of innovation.

A system in which there is plenty of public information tends to be like Chancy: it gives new firms attempting new technologies a better chance of obtaining financing. The reason is that there are many investors from a variety of backgrounds, each of whom has the basic information to assess a new technology. While each investor may be biased, and each investor may receive only part of the information that is collectively known, each investor investigates the firm's prospects independently. Thus, the firm gets a number of chances to attempt to convince investors of the merits of its technology. If the technology is sufficiently new, it may need all those chances to obtain financing somewhere.

The relationship-based system works in a very different way, much indeed like Fusty. Given the paucity of public information and the limited access in a relationship-based system, the firm has, at best, one or two well-informed financiers who can make an assessment. Since information in such a system is generated through contacts rather than posted publicly, those financiers are likely to talk to one another. So while collectively they may have more information and make a better decision about whether to finance the new technology, the firm will not get much more than a single chance to make its case.

If the technology is a minor modification of tried and tested technologies, the payoffs from funding eventually successful technologies is likely to be small, at least relative to the costs of funding failures. A relationship-based system is likely to be better here because it has the ability to probe deeper and screen out most of the likely failures. The system's conservatism, as reflected in the extreme scrutiny to which innovations are subject, could lead to the rejection of some worthwhile innovations. But this is not very costly relative to the gains from not funding failures. In normal times, when change is incremental (and innovations are as likely from within the establishment as from outside), the relationship system works well.

If, however, we are in a period of extraordinary change, in which revolutionary innovations may enable firms to create entirely new profitable markets, the free-access, market-based, arm's-length system is better in making sure that most of these get financed, even though many failures will also be financed. The value from the successes far outweighs the costs of failures at such times, so Chancy's method—using independent but informed evaluations—works better in financing innovation.

One can even extend the parallel to venture capital, the latter being an institution that seems to emerge only in free-access financial systems with high disclosure. Venture capitalists invest only a little at a time. They continue only projects that look as if they will be great successes but quickly cut short those that look as if they will be dogs. Thus, they reap a bonanza from the successful projects while losing little from those that fail. This sort of return profile makes them willing to experiment, much like Chancy. As a result, entrepreneurs need not be dejected by a single rejection by a venture capitalist since there may always be some other venture capitalist who sees things more their way. Successful entrepreneurs in market-based financial systems often have tales, much as successful authors do, of how they peddled their project from door to door until they eventually found a venture capitalist willing to put pen to checkbook.

Venture capitalists themselves, let alone such tales, are rare in relationship-based economies. They are rare because venture capitalists need a reliable system of disclosure, not just because they fund young companies but also because they get their reward only when they grow these firms to the point that they can be sold on the public equity markets. And for public investors to pay an adequate price for the shares that are sold, they have to be confident of what is truly going on inside the firms. Reliable disclosure makes such confidence possible.[12]

In the last few years, the relationship-based financial systems of continental Europe have been changing and converging to the market-based, arm's-length models of the United States and the United Kingdom. Some of these countries have introduced new equity markets—such as the Neuer Markt in Germany or the Nouveau Marché in Paris.

While some of these markets may have been set up as a response to stock market euphoria rather than as a result of a fundamental change in approach (and did not survive the technology meltdown), what is particularly interesting for our purpose is how the advent of these markets affected the volume of venture capital financing. The volume of venture capital financing went up substantially in the countries that introduced markets with stricter disclosure rules than that previously prevailing in the country.[13] This is not just the effect of the creation of a new market, since countries that introduced new markets with disclosure rules equal to or lower than the established exchange did not experience such an increase. Thus, better public disclosure makes it easier to finance at arm's length and makes it easier to fund revolutionary new technologies.

Even if financing is available, however, it is not safe to assume, as we have done, that established firms will want to undertake projects that lead to extraordinary change. Technological change can render obsolete the expertise of those who run the firm: even though IBM's personal computer set the industry standard, it was Intel and Microsoft that constantly pushed the technology forward and reaped much of the gains. Part of the reason why IBM did not exploit the possibilities in the personal computer better is that IBM's agenda was set by top management, which had cut its teeth on mainframes. In an attempt to avoid cannibalizing mainframes, management placed constraints on the development of the personal computer, which undermined IBM's leadership position in the PC industry. For example:

> IBM crippled its own Displaywrite word-processing package [for PCs] by limiting its ability to handle electronic mail, which became a hugely popular application. This was back in the days when IBM still thought of typing as something to be done on a mainframe or minicomputer, and the mainframe people wanted to protect their mainframe-based email system, called PROFS, by keeping email off PCs. In addition, mainframe executives argued that the hundreds of thousands of secretaries who had gotten used to PROFS and the mainframe version of Displaywrite didn't really want any new features.[14]

Were it not for Intel, Microsoft, Compaq, Dell, and many others, it is not clear that the personal computer would have been the enormous success it was. Had the development of the industry been left to IBM and to DEC (Digital Equipment Corporation), perhaps we would be still using personal computers as glorified calculators and typewriters.

Young firms are therefore special when there is a potential for extraordinary change because they have no vested interests in the status quo. More disclosure and transparency, and the associated free access to finance, help the emergence of new firms. In stark contrast, the relationship system is particularly bad at giving newcomers a chance. Newcomers invariably have to become part of the system before they can get finance because no one can trust their accounts or will give them access before they pay their dues. No wonder the average age of corporations making initial public offerings on the Deutsche Bourse between 1960 and 1990 was fifty-seven years, an age that would be deemed ancient for American corporations.[15] Within the United States itself, the deregulation of banking to which we alluded earlier in the book led to a substantial increase in competition in the financial sector in states that deregulated. This was tantamount to a shift from an uncompetitive, relationship system before deregulation to more competitive, arm's-length financing afterward. Not surprisingly, the rate of creation of new enterprises jumped significantly after deregulation.[16]

Relationship finance therefore has at least two strikes against it at times of great change. First, the way the system scrutinizes new ventures makes it more likely that more out-of-the-ordinary new opportunities will be left without finance than in the arm's-length system: decision by consensus is inherently conservative. Second, the opaque nature of the system makes it discriminate against outsiders, especially newcomers. Thus, those who have the greatest incentive to force change have the least resources to do so. Since the players in the system lack both the mind-set and the incentive to innovate, relationship finance is a serious drag in times of great change.

But there is a third strike also. Relationship systems tend to protect mature incumbent firms that get into trouble. In normal times, this lends stability to the system. In times of extraordinary change, this can keep resources far too long in unproductive uses. There is no better example of the ambivalent nature of the protection afforded by financiers to firms—the fabled long-term view taken by financiers in the relationship system—than Sumitomo Bank's rescue of Mazda in the 1970s.

In 1974, Mazda Motors was in deep financial trouble.[17] Unlike other Japanese car manufacturers, it was ill prepared for the extraordinary rise in oil prices after the Arab-Israeli War of 1973. Its cars used gas-guzzling rotary Wankel engines, many of them giving at most ten miles per gallon, while competing Japanese car manufacturers produced cars with more conventional, fuel-efficient gasoline engines, giving twice the mileage. With the tripling in oil prices, the latter were far more attractive, and Mazda's sales plummeted.

Mazda's productive efficiency was also very low. In contrast to the average Japanese automobile manufacturer, which produced thirty cars per employee annually, Mazda produced only nineteen. Its suppliers were equally inefficient.

It was not clear that Mazda's management was capable of meeting the challenges posed by the crisis. Since its founding in 1920, Mazda had been run autocratically by members of the Matsuda family, and a third-generation family member, Kenji Matsuda, was now president. Unfortunately, he was much less capable than his predecessors, though no less powerful.

Mazda's managerial weakness came to the fore in its reaction to the crisis. The firm did not cut production and continued to ship to its dealers, with the consequence that very soon, dealers were stuck with a year's supply of inventory. The company tried to help dealers finance the inventory, but despite this, dealer morale fell, and salesmen quit in droves. The long-term viability of the firm was threatened since auto sales in Japan were highly dependent on personalized selling. Mazda also did not alert its workers to the crisis. Despite its already high costs and declining sales, it increased wages substantially in 1974, which further weakened Mazda's financial position.

By late 1974, however, the problems were too grave to ignore. Mazda's main bank, Sumitomo, decided to make its move. Even though Sumitomo had sent two officers to Mazda in early 1974 to familiarize themselves with Mazda's operations, it intervened massively only in late 1974. It installed its Tokyo office head as Mazda's executive vice president and put other executives in charge of Mazda's key operations. It also announced it would guarantee any financing Mazda might need. Finally, in 1978, Kenji Matsuda was ousted, and the manager who replaced him was essentially Sumitomo's choice.

New management implemented major organizational changes. Mazda's management control systems were streamlined, costs cut, and suppliers made more efficient. Labor was persuaded to defer some compensation, and some production-line workers were retrained as salesmen. Labor productivity improved dramatically, so much so that in

1981, production per employee was a remarkable forty-three vehicles per year. Sales also picked up, in part because the Sumitomo Keiretsu (the Japanese term for industrial combine) and numerous other interested parties stepped up their purchase of Mazda vehicles. For example, Mazda's share of taxis in Hiroshima (its home base) increased from 2 percent to 40 percent between 1975 and 1983.

The limited competition in the relationship system was an important reason why Sumitomo could afford to bail out Mazda. Since the market for loans in Japan was far from competitive, Sumitomo knew that if Mazda survived, it would continue borrowing from Sumitomo at a premium. The prospect of these future profits gave Sumitomo a stake in Mazda's survival. Thus Sumitomo was able to provide Mazda a kind of insurance against economic downturns that would not be available in a more competitive arm's-length system.

Sumitomo also had other reasons to save Mazda. Its privileged position in the uncompetitive banking system implied a responsibility to share the burden with the government of reducing economic instability. Other client firms also had come to expect that help would be provided if they were in need. A bank that did not play by the rules when it could well afford to do so would soon find business hard to come by.

Was the rescue worth it? Here the answer is more ambiguous. In the short run, Mazda recovered. It may, however, have been a mistake to ignore the signals obtained from Mazda's poor performance. A reinterpretation of the Mazda example is that perhaps Mazda deserved to be taken over by another automobile manufacturer: after all, it was in trouble again in the early 1990s, when it had to be rescued by Ford! Maybe it should have been shut down, thus reducing the overcapacity with which the automobile industry has been plagued in recent years. Who knows whether the net long-run benefits to Mazda from Sumitomo— the guarantees and the credit, less the interest payments, the tied deals, and the long-term submission to Sumitomo's direction—were positive? And even if positive, did this deal make sense for Sumitomo's depositors and equity holders, or for Japan as a whole?

Unfortunately, as we have argued, the relationship system makes it difficult to undertake such a cost-benefit analysis: after all, that is why the system is so attractive to politicians. How does one value the loss borne by other members of the Keiretsu for being "encouraged" to buy Mazda cars? How big are the profits forgone by Sumitomo for spending so much of its managers' time in rescuing Mazda? It is precisely the opacity of the relationship system that makes it so appealing from a political perspective: it is easier to hide the cost of the cross-subsidies. But it is precisely this opacity that condemns the system to make mistakes. And all the mistakes go in one direction—toward protecting unviable incumbents. The fabled long-term view of the relationship system may, in fact, be very short-term.

In sum, then, the relationship system allows neither dramatic innovation nor necessary destruction. And it has one additional deep flaw. One may not agree with the way the market allocates resources, but there is no denying its impartiality. The problem when the market is dispensed with is that there is no good rule to allocate rewards or punishment. While economic merit is the only criterion in a market system, less quantifiable motives such as solidarity and equity assume importance in its absence. Eventually, whatever the stated objectives, resources and rewards go to powerful incumbents rather than the truly needy or deserving.

Let us now see how relationship capitalism fared and why, despite its obvious appeal to incumbents, it was unsustainable in the long run.

The Decline and Fall of Relationship Capitalism

There is no denying that relationship capitalism seemed to work—at least, at first. Economies grew at tremendous rates in the immediately postwar years. In Western Europe, real per capita income grew 80 percent between 1950 and 1970; in Japan, it grew by 163 percent.[18] What is also remarkable is that this incredible growth was achieved with relatively few social tensions, thanks to the cushion provided by the relationship system.

The relationship system may indeed have been appropriate initially. Workers with stable jobs and safe futures were willing to spend, so consumer demand, which had plummeted during the depression and had been suppressed during the war, got a boost. And on the supply side, the absence of competition did not seem to hurt—at least, initially. In the first few postwar years, the primary task was reconstruction. The next step in much of the developed world was to modernize, to compensate for years of neglected investment, and to catch up with the innovative American corporations, which seemed to dominate the world. The nature of the investments to be made for recovery and catch-up was fairly clear. The innovation that was needed was incremental. As we have argued, relationship systems are fairly good at this kind of innovation. So initially, the market's role in guiding the allocation of resources could be dispensed with. But the costs of the relationship system eventually became clear as innovation and destruction became more important to the world economy.[19]

In the flurry of reconstruction, when economies were growing at a tremendous pace in the 1950s and 1960s, it was easy for incumbents to agree on splitting the pie. There was so much more of it every year that all differences could be papered over. But as growth slowed, disputes over the economic pie increased. Unionized workers demanded more, as did government employees, farmers, teachers, students, the elderly, the poor . . . Companies opened their coffers, and wage costs soared. Governments opened their purse, and the transfers and subsidies column in government budgets grew significantly in the 1960s. From 9.7 percent of GDP in 1960, it went up by over half to 15.1 percent of GDP in 1970 for developed countries.[20] The consequence of corporations' and governments' trying to reconcile the enhanced expectations of their workers or citizens with their now more limited budgets was rising inflation.[21]

The quadrupling of oil prices by OPEC countries in 1973 created a new problem for economies already struggling with stagnation and inflation ("stagflation"). Many industries had to be restructured. But in a system of relationship capitalism, there are few price signals to indicate which firms deserve to be shut down. Moreover, the system is geared toward bailing out rather than closing down the distressed, partly because firms are such an integral part of the social security system and partly because incumbents have so much political clout. Economies became weak because they could neither obtain the information to know which firms to close nor summon the political will to effect the necessary destruction.

Even though there were inner stresses within the system as relationship capitalism faced difficulty in allocating rewards in slowing economies, and even though the system became increasingly inefficient as it could not withdraw resources from declining industries, there was great stability built into the system. Because so many benefited from it, and those who did not had little organization or voice, it was unlikely that internal contradictions alone would cause it to break down in countries where it was deeply entrenched. But a new challenge was coming from outside, which ultimately forced change: the breakdown of the Bretton Woods system.

The Bretton Woods agreement did succeed in increasing the volume of trade, so domestic economies faced increasingly fierce foreign competition. But Bretton Woods also ultimately failed in its attempt to suppress cross-border capital flows, and this compounded the degree of competition. It is instructive to understand why Bretton Woods failed, for it was loopholes in the original Bretton Woods agreement that gave capital a chance. The small crack in the Bretton Woods architecture widened over time and ultimately brought down relationship capitalism.

At Bretton Woods, Keynes had proposed obligatory cooperative controls on capital. In other words, if somehow private French wealth could evade French capital controls and find its way to the United States, under a cooperative system, the United States would be obligated to return it to the French authorities. These draconian measures would have made the system of capital controls leakproof. Pressure from the U.S. delegation, especially the bankers, however, ensured that this proposal was watered down in the final draft and effectively rendered inoperative. This was the crack in the system.

In the late 1950s, a market started up in London whose primary virtue was that it was free of government interference and control. The market originated when the British government, in order to protect the value of the pound sterling, imposed restrictions on the ability of British banks to finance trade among countries outside the sterling area. The banks then met the demand for loans, and skirted the capital controls, by offering dollar loans against the dollar deposits they had from foreign depositors. Thus was born the Eurodollar market, initially a short-term market in which dollar deposits and loans were made.[22]

The market obtained further impetus during the Cuban missile crisis, when Russian banks, which were afraid of having their American accounts frozen, shifted their dollar reserves to London. For British financial authorities, beset with the weakness of the sterling and the need to maintain capital controls, the Eurodollar market provided an attractive way to restore London's position as a premier financial center. As a consequence, they regulated with a light hand, providing legal and supervisory support whenever needed.

But perhaps the greatest support to the market was given involuntarily by the United States. As the United States started running deficits during the 1960s to finance the war in Vietnam, dollar holdings outside the United States ballooned. To prevent dollars from leaving the country at an even greater pace, the U.S. government imposed an interest equalization tax on purchases by Americans of foreign securities. The tax essentially raised the effective annual cost to foreigners of borrowing in the United States by one percentage point.[23] As a result, foreign borrowers now turned to the Eurobond market.

As the United States became more desperate to staunch the outward flow of dollars, the measures to stop citizens lending to foreigners became ever harsher. In 1965, "voluntary" restraints on foreign lending by U.S. banks were introduced, extended to other financial institutions, and made compulsory in 1968. Initially, the U.S. banks met the foreign demand for dollar loans through their overseas dollar deposits, thus evading the new capital controls. But they soon discovered that the Euromarket also enabled them to evade domestic restrictions such as reserve requirements and the interest rate ceilings on deposits imposed by depression-era regulation. United States banks were not the only ones to be attracted to the Euromarket. For multinationals, the Euromarket provided a convenient location to maintain dollar balances earned abroad, without fear that their use would be restricted by future government action.

Despite being inconvenient at times to either the United States or the United Kingdom, the Eurodollar market thrived. It was on British soil, but eventually, many of its major players were American. So neither country could unilaterally close it down. And with both countries competing to make their financial centers dominant in the world and attract international finance, they could not make common cause to shut it down.

With the increase in cross-border trade, the volume of rootless capital also increased. Multinationals could delay or hasten the timing of payments and receipts, and trade could be overinvoiced or underinvoiced (an importing firm desiring to keep capital abroad could simply ask the supplier to bill it more than the true value of the goods and place the difference—the extent of overinvoicing—in its name in a foreign account). All these actions created pools of capital that could be deployed. The Euromarket provided a legal venue from which, and to which, capital could flow without being subject to national regulation. Even before the formal breakdown of the Bretton Woods agreement, and despite the existence of formal capital controls, these markets could supply large firms in a country with finance that had no national strings attached.

As capital became more mobile, governments started losing control over certain policies. In the fixed exchange rate regime mandated by Bretton Woods, a country's ability to maintain low interest rates and favor particular industries was threatened if savers could take their money to the Euromarket and if those who were denied credit by the government could borrow there. Similarly, macroeconomic management—squeezing inflation by maintaining high interest rates—was made more difficult if the high interest rates attracted a flood of capital from outside.

In 1971, the Bretton Woods agreement collapsed, as the U.S. government suspended its commitment to convert dollars to gold at the price of $35 an ounce. While the reasons for its demise are not relevant for our story, it is relevant that cross-border capital movements hastened its end. In response, countries clamored for a general tightening up of capital controls, as they saw their freedom of policy action becoming constrained. They also demanded action against the Euromarket, the base for what they saw as unwarranted speculation. But by this time, the United States, seeing an opportunity to reestablish itself as the world's premier financial center, had become a staunch supporter of fully open borders. The official U.S. view in the 1973 *U.S. Economic Report of the President to Congress* now was:

> [R]estrictions have a distorting influence whether they are focused on trade in commodities, in services, or in assets (the capital account), and this parallelism should be recognized in the rules governing the reformed international monetary system. In contrast, the provisions of the earlier [Bretton Woods] system made a sharp distinction between controls on trade and other current transactions and controls on capital transactions.[24]

Cross-border capital was no longer a pariah. The United States' enthusiasm was not entirely on principle. It clearly saw opportunity for its own financial sector in intermediating the potentially large flows of capital that were building up.[25] It became almost evangelical, preaching openness at international forums while holding up cooperative international attempts to control these flows. With the largest economy in the world not willing to control these flows, and with substantial activity already taking place across their borders with the Euromarket, countries had little choice but to open themselves up. By the late 1980s, much of the developed world was open to cross-border capital flows.

The point is that the halfway openness to trade but not capital mandated by Bretton Woods, which created space for government intervention and brought domestic financial markets under government direction, was possible only if there was cooperation among countries. But because of the desire of some countries to attract financial business to their shores, cooperation broke down, and the plan to promote trade at the expense of finance proved unviable in the long run.

As feared by Keynes, the emerging cross-border flows started imposing discipline on governments. It is useful to outline the nature of this discipline a little better. Foreign investors are not stupid enough to demand a blind uniformity of governments or countries. Contrary to the common allegation of critics, international investors do not demand that all countries should have the same social security system, the same securities laws, the same national brands, the same food, the same theater . . . They demand, however, that government decisions be transparent and advance the interest of the country's economy—after all, this is what would give investors the most confidence in the security of their investment.

Governments complain all the time about speculative short-term investors who sell their investments and depart the country without understanding government policy. These complaints sound much like those of firm managers who wail plaintively that the stock market undervalues them. In truth, investors are far savvier than they are given credit for. Their departure usually signals that government policy is both opaque and targeted at appeasing certain interest groups. Since foreign investors have little clout in domestic policy circles, their only weapon in opposing these policies, which are often against the national economic interest (and hence left opaque by the government), is to depart. It is not that they do not know or do not understand; it is that they understand too well.

Of course, fleeing foreign investors cause a rapid fall of the country's exchange rate. To retrieve the situation, the government must either explain why its policies are not detrimental or change them. This, then, is the source of discipline. For governments in relationship systems, it meant they could no longer continue to direct subsidized credit toward favored large firms or promote the cartelization of entire industries. Such actions hurt the economy at large and were possible only when capital controls protected and disguised such malfeasance.

With large firms no longer protected, competition heated up, and innovation became more important, as we have described in Chapter 3.

Advances in information and telecommunications technology, as well as in management, meant that corporate innovation could no longer afford to be incremental. The deficiencies of the relationship system in promoting disruptive innovation came to the fore, compounding the problems we have already noted—that the system did not offer a relatively objective way to allocate surplus in a slowing economy and it did not offer an easy way for resources to be withdrawn from dying industries and firms. Countries knew that they could not realistically contemplate the option of unilaterally withdrawing from the world economy, given its potential future growth. Therefore, they had to become more competitive or watch their national industries perish. With at least three strikes against it, countries knew they had to dismantle the extensive regulatory infrastructure that made the relationship system possible. Free markets were again in ascendance.

With competition becoming legitimate, the malign neglect of domestic financial markets became history. One fact to which we have already alluded in fragments summarizes well what could happen if the powers that be became interested in developing financial market infrastructure: the number of countries (in a sample of 103) adopting regulations against insider trading shot up from 34 to 87 in the 1990s. The growth rate in the number of countries enforcing these laws was even higher, going from just 9 to 38. And enforcement, more often than not, followed the opening of economies to capital flows, suggesting that openness was a factor in promoting regulatory change.[26] It is not just a coincidence that financial markets boomed all over the world during this period. All they needed was the dismantling of political barriers.

The Effects on Economic Security

Since the security provided by relationship capitalism relied intimately on the absence of competition, it is useful to see how the breakdown of the system changed economic security. We described how the Italian system was supported by subsidies from the government, which was paying for them through higher debt, higher taxes, and higher inflation. Increased international capital mobility, however, limited all these sources of government finance. When capital is free to move across borders, it naturally moves where it expects to be treated better. Since large budget deficits signal current and future taxes and/or inflation, capital shies away from countries that lack fiscal discipline.

Of course, the first reaction of a country faced with an exodus of capital is to contemplate reintroducing capital controls. But this is problematic in the new environment. First, capital controls can only force domestic capital to stay, but they cannot force foreign capital to come in. In fact, they will certainly scare away foreign investors who desire liquidity. Second, when international capital markets work, it is very difficult for a country that is open to trade to prevent capital flight. Underinvoicing of exports and overinvoicing of imports soon become a national sport. Any attempt to prevent these activities only increases the bureaucratic burden imposed on citizens, without stopping the exodus of capital. Italian students will well remember, as one of us does, all the different forms one had to complete in 1987 to get permission to obtain foreign exchange to pay the small application fees to U.S. universities!

Without cooperative controls on capital, it was impossible for a single country to restrict capital movements unilaterally. Hence, even Italy had to give up controls and set its budgetary situation in order. This process was made politically imperative in Europe because the Maastricht Treaty, signed in 1991, required countries joining the European Monetary Union to set their budgetary houses in order. Italy had to bring its fiscal deficit below 3 percent of the GDP. This gave Italian politicians an additional excuse to tighten their belts. But it would be wrong to attribute the change in Italy solely to the treaty. In a world where capital is mobile, Italy had no choice. Had it chosen not to join the Euro, Italy would have had a harder time convincing capital to stay, forcing even tighter fiscal discipline.

With the government's hitherto limitless pockets emptying, the system was forced to change. In 1991, the quantity of "temporary" unemployment insurance was reduced, and tighter limits were imposed on when it would be available and when it would be extended. In 1992, state agencies, such as the postal and railway systems, were transformed into corporations. This seems like a minor change, but a corporation, when insolvent, can be liquidated. And state-owned companies could no longer count on the government's bailing them out. Not only did the need for fiscal discipline limit government intervention, but also the European Union started to fine countries that subsidized firms. State-owned companies, faced for the first time with the prospect of default, lost any desire to act as "employer of last resort."

There were other changes. Reforms in 1995 and 1997 made the pension system less generous, and early retirement was no longer an option.

To minimize the pain imposed on workers by pension reform, the government allowed workers to choose where their new contributions to the corporate pension would go. This took away a cheap source of financing for companies.

With the state subsidy that papered over all problems vanishing, the inefficiencies of relationship capitalism became more obvious. Employers, having lost their cheap source of internal funds and their ability to dump excess workers on the state, lobbied for legislation that would rid them of the constraints they had tolerated for so long. Political support for right-wing parties that promised deregulation increased. And the government has attempted to meet these new demands, most recently by proposing legislation giving companies the flexibility to hire and fire workers.

Overall, Italy, like many other countries, has become more market-based, more flexible, and more efficient. This has certainly hurt the grand coalition that benefited from the relationship system, for it has lost the cozy certainties of yesteryear. But the large minority who were left outside the system and thus squeezed by it—the would-be entrepreneurs, the young, the foreigners—have come into their own. And society is better off in many ways, as we saw in Chapter 3, for it can freely harness the talents of all its citizens rather than only the talents of a privileged and shackled majority.

Ideas versus Economic Forces

In emphasizing the fundamental importance of economic and political forces in the rise and fall of the managed economy as well as the parallel fall and rise of finance, we have skirted the role of ideas. Others, by contrast, have seen the economic events of the twentieth century as a battle of ideas, Keynes versus Hayek, Friedman and Stigler versus Marx, and so on. Keynes himself suggested that he belonged to this camp when he wrote:

> The ideas of economists and political philosophers, both when they are right and when they are wrong, are more powerful than is commonly understood. Indeed, the world is ruled by little else. Practical men, who believe themselves to be quite exempt from any intellectual influences, are usually the slaves of some defunct economist. Madmen in authority, who hear voices in the air, are distilling their

frenzy from some academic scribbler of a few years back. . . . Sooner or later, it is ideas, not vested interests, which are dangerous for good or evil.[27]

We do not dispute the fact that ideas eventually matter. But in history as in stand-up comedy, timing is everything. Politicians espousing particular ideas do not come into a position of authority unless the circumstances are ripe for them and the vested interests are either supportive or overcome. Hayek wrote *The Road to Serfdom,* his searing critique of the managed economy, in 1944, but it was only with Margaret Thatcher's accession to power in 1979 that a major government was willing to espouse his ideas. Did it take so long for his ideas to be recognized, or were the circumstances just not right?

It is economic and political circumstances that open the way to leadership for charismatic politicians like Margaret Thatcher and Ronald Reagan. Deregulation and the taming of inflation are two economic successes with which Reagan is credited. Yet the deregulation of airlines and trucking took place under his Democratic predecessor, Jimmy Carter. And it was Carter who appointed the eventual hero of the fight against inflation, Paul Volcker, as chairman of the Federal Reserve. Our point is simply that the move toward markets preceded the leader who is seen as one of their saviors. As described in this chapter, the revival of markets had much to do with the weaknesses of the relationship system—its inability to allocate rewards, leading to growing inflation, and its inability to reallocate resources, especially in the face of an enormous adverse shock like the 1973 oil price hike. At the same time, the increasing flow of international capital because of competition between London and New York for supremacy as financial centers further highlighted inefficiencies in the old system. The breakdown of Bretton Woods was the beginning of the end for relationship or managed capitalism.

That said, ideas are not unimportant. Ideas offer a template when the circumstances are right. They also have other uses. They give a veneer of academic respectability to a predetermined agenda or an overlay of moral justification to what is otherwise indefensible. Even someone as rapacious as Philip IV had to undermine the Templars' reputation for moral integrity before stripping them of their assets. Not doing so would have allowed the population to easily overcome their rational ignorance and see his action as naked expropriation. Perhaps one benefit of reading this book is that our readers will be able to discern more easily the self-interest in antimarket actions that are cloaked with public-interest rhetoric.

And politicians are also not unimportant. Few would have had the determination of a Margaret Thatcher in standing up to the radical unions, or the golden voice of a Ronald Reagan, who managed to convert complex themes into simple and stirring ideas. But attributing too much to them and too little to economic forces is dangerous. For example, there are many who want to slow down the movement of global capital through some kind of new global architecture along the lines of Bretton Woods. What they do not realize is that the free flow of capital may be the key to preserving much of the liberalization they value and take for granted. To restrict capital flows may be to push us back toward the days of relationship capitalism. Those who trust in the current crop of politicians and their promarket leanings alone, without recognizing the economic forces that have made them relevant, would not recognize this danger.

There is one last point worth noting. For those inside the relationship system, the world was indeed safer. Some have expanded this into a full-blown critique of the market economy, arguing that it does not allow for the same level of safety.[28] In some ways, this is irrefutable. Insiders were safe because they were privileged. This is, in part, why so many of them are against the process of opening up that is broadly termed "globalization." It was the outsiders in society who bore the risk, not only of short-term economic volatility but also of inevitable long-term decline. But taken as a whole, therefore, from the perspective of both insiders and outsiders, and considering that without change, the long term was bleak, it is not immediately obvious that the move to the market economy has increased overall economic risk.

There is a more specious argument that is sometimes made. Critics of markets argue that competition requires that workers be left uninsured, increasing the risk they ultimately bear in the market economy.[29] The logic these critics offer—that competition demands that workers be constantly threatened with the prospect of starvation, else they will slacken off—takes a very dim view of workers. Since competition pushes everyone toward "best" practices, these critics suggest that the world will inexorably move toward the practices in the country with the least amount of social insurance. These ideas are reflected in the widespread fear that "unfair" competition from workers in developing countries will force developed countries to cut down on social security.

This fear is not realistic once one moves away from a medieval view of incentives. Fear is not the best motivator and is probably quite ineffective or even detrimental in a variety of situations. If a worker is less anxious about the future, she may invest more in building firm-specific human capital and work more enthusiastically and creatively. So a country can be more productive when it provides its citizens insurance. Since productivity determines who wins out in the long run, competition from countries that do not provide their citizens security need not drive the level of *social* insurance in other countries to zero. Though it is true that competition makes certain forms of informal insurance more difficult, by no means does it rule out all insurance.

Workers in developed countries do have to worry about the possibility that some social insurance they currently enjoy may in fact be excessive, consisting of entitlements they acquired in the grand bargain offered by the relationship system when markets were far less competitive. Certainly, these entitlements will come under competitive pressure from workers in developing countries, but the pressure is no different from the pressure on excessively high wages.

This does raise the point, however, that many of our systems of social security were structured for a different world—a world of managed competition. The market economy does introduce a variety of risks that were not a concern in the relationship system. How to prepare citizens better to meet these new sources of volatility in their lives is the subject of the next two chapters.

Summary

We have now come full circle. In the first part of the book, we described the changes that have taken place in finance in recent decades and how they have affected the lives of people. We then asked what circumstances helped a financial system overcome the political constraints that kept it underdeveloped. Having seen how financial development could take place, we then raised the possibility that financial development could be reversed and described the circumstances under which that had happened in the 1930s. In this chapter, we described the relationship system that emerged to provide the insurance that was demanded by citizens after the experience of the Great Depression. It was a system that was cobbled together to meet pressing demands, without thought for the long run. The system worked well initially, but it survived unchanged into the long run, when its deficiencies became apparent. Because it could not respond, either to the macroeconomic changes that took in the late 1960s and early 1970s or to the revival of finance and cross-border competition, it is now history in many countries.

The lesson we have learned is that markets are not all-conquering. Antimarket coalitions can build up and gain strength because markets do have their weaknesses. That markets have revived in recent years is, in no small part, due to the fortuitous set of macroeconomic disturbances that highlighted the weakness of the relationship system. Moreover, they have revived only after decades of being suppressed. The good news is that it takes the concerted actions of the most important nations to "ban" competition, so we can rely on national self-interest to break down such cooperation eventually. The bad news is that competition can disappear for a long time. We have to take more care to shore up the market's defenses. But we first have to understand where the threats to the market economy can come from today. And this is what we move to now.

PART FOUR

HOW CAN MARKETS BE MADE MORE VIABLE POLITICALLY?

CHAPTER TWELVE

The Challenges Ahead

FOR NEARLY TWO centuries, scholars and politicians have debated the future of capitalism. Its critics, most prominent among them Karl Marx, have seen capitalism as intrinsically unstable, full of contradictions that will lead eventually to its collapse. Its supporters see it as the best way to allocate resources and rewards. Some even hint that the democratic capitalistic society is not just a phase in the historical evolution of economic systems but its ultimate end.[1] In the middle are all those searching for a "third way," a kinder and gentler form of capitalism or a more market-driven form of socialism.

Our view in this book, which draws in many ways from a long tradition at the University of Chicago, has elements in common with all these positions, though it does not identify fully with any of them. We do think that capitalism—more precisely described today as the free enterprise system—in its ideal form is the best system to allocate resources and rewards. But the forms of capitalism that are experienced in most countries are very far from the ideal. They are a corrupted version of it, in which vested interests prevent competition from playing its natural, healthy role. Many of the accusations against capitalism—that it oppresses workers, that it creates private monopolies, that it is only an instrument for the rich to get richer—relate to the corrupted, uncompetitive systems that exist rather than a true free enterprise system.

Yet this cannot be a defense of capitalism, in the same way as the socialists cannot claim that the near inevitability with which socialist regimes turn repressive and kleptocratic is not intrinsic to the system of socialism but an aberration. If socialism is fundamentally flawed in its belief in the perfectibility of man, in its belief that man will overcome his narrow individualism and become an expansive social being, is capitalism also not fundamentally flawed in its belief in the perfectibility of markets, in its belief that markets will overcome the narrow interests of their participants and survive free?

We do not believe that capitalism is fundamentally flawed, because we believe that markets can be given the political support to remain free. Much of this book has been about why that support is necessary: markets cannot flourish without the very visible hand of the government, which is needed to set up and maintain the infrastructure that enables participants to trade freely and with confidence. But who has an interest in pushing the government to support the market? For even though everyone collectively benefits from the better goods, the services, and the equality of access that competitive markets make possible, no one in particular makes huge profits from keeping the system competitive and the playing field level. Thus, everyone has an incentive to take a free ride and let someone else defend the system. A competitive market is a form of public good (a good, like air, that is useful but hard to charge for), and somewhat paradoxically, collective action is needed for its maintenance.

Given its dependence on political goodwill, democratic capitalism's greatest problem is not that it will destroy itself economically, as Marx would have it, but that it may lose its political support. Capitalism's biggest political enemies are not the firebrand trade unionists spewing vitriol against the system but the executives in pin-striped suits extolling the virtues of competitive markets with every breath while attempting to extinguish them with every action. Adam Smith recognized the inexorable tendency toward suppressing competition when he wrote, "People of the same trade seldom meet together, even for merriment and diversion, but the conversation ends in a conspiracy against the public, or in some contrivance to raise prices."[2] Unfortunately, all too often and in all too many countries, the conspiracy enlists the help of the state in enforcing limitations on competition.

These limitations are best seen in the constraints placed on financial markets in country after country, over much of history. Free financial markets are not only problematic for incumbent financiers but also spawn competition for incumbent industrialists—hence, the need to suppress them directly by legislative fiat or keep the institutions they need underdeveloped.

Marx also understood that capitalists would enlist the power of the state in securing their position when he and Engels wrote in *The Com-*

munist Manifesto that the government is essentially "a committee for managing the common affairs of the whole bourgeoisie." But he thought that the problem was specific to bourgeois democracies and would disappear in a socialist state. Unfortunately, all the socialist revolution did was to change the identity of the elite and strengthen their hand by eliminating not just economic competition but all semblance of political competition.

Given all this, free enterprise capitalism is not the final stage of a deterministic process of evolution. It is better thought of as a delicate plant, which needs nurturing against constant attack by the weeds of vested interests. It is useful to consider where the weeds might spring from in the future, for that will help us build the appropriate defenses.

The market is threatened by two diverse groups: the incumbents, who want to retain their position and thus have a strong incentive to suppress any potential source of competition, and those who lost out, who would be happy if the rules of the game that caused their troubles were changed. The long-term feasibility of free markets rests on reducing the incentives of each of these groups to proceed against the market and limiting their chances of success if they do proceed.

The way to limit the chances of success of vested interests is not to expand the power of the state but to narrow its ability to take inefficient economic actions favoring the few at the expense of the majority of its citizens. In the same way as inefficient economic entities are forced to improve by competition, inefficient governments can be forced to improve, not so much by competition in the political arena, where the committed few can organize and thwart the will of the majority even in a democracy, but by forcing their subjects to compete in the economic arena. A powerful device to achieve this is to keep borders open to the flow of goods and especially to the flow of capital. The country's capitalists will then feel the impact of bad government policies, and they will become a force for good, market-liberating reform. The move by many countries in the last thirty years from a centrally managed, relationship-based economy with a heavily controlled financial sector to a free market economy with vibrant financial markets can be attributed to both the increasing trade and the increasing international financial flows across the world.

But open borders spawn political opposition themselves. Technological change and increasing international competition will create entirely new categories of the distressed. Can the political opposition be contained? And what are the biggest political challenges to markets in the years to come? That is what we turn to in this chapter.

Can the Interest Groups Be Contained?

Before we describe the looming challenges, it is useful to see an example of how economic institutions can adapt to defuse the incentives of interest groups to coalesce against market forces. Consider the evolution of the U.S. bankruptcy code in the nineteenth century. The economic role of bankruptcy law is not just to provide a mechanism for creditors to collect their money but also to offer a form of insurance to debtors, relieving them from some of their debt burden when it becomes overly oppressive. When a borrower owes so much that he has small hope of repaying it, he will have little incentive to exert effort to earn money, because any extra dollar earned, while requiring his blood and toil, will simply go to repay creditors. Both debtors and creditors may be better off in such situations if some of the debt is forgiven or renegotiated down in a bankruptcy proceeding. Debtors will have an incentive to work harder if they know there is some chance of repaying their debt and keeping their business, while creditors will get something back instead of nothing at all.

A modern bankruptcy code provides a mechanism by which debtors can get relief. In providing this flexibility, somewhat paradoxically, bankruptcy legislation enhances the security of property in two ways. First, it allows creditors to charge up front for the possibility that they will have to offer relief, thus protecting their property. At the same time, it heads off any need for debtors to organize politically, preventing them from arbitrarily wiping out their debts. This further enhances the security of property and the sanctity of contract.

But in early-nineteenth-century America, the contractual environment was not developed enough that a debtor could simply file for bankruptcy and escape his debts. Information about debtors was poor, few institutions existed to monitor them closely, the markets for repossessed assets in the nascent economy were limited, and the country was large enough that bankrupts could wash away their stigma by simply moving. If lenient bankruptcy laws had been perpetually in place, debtors would have had less resolve to pay, creditors would have pushed up interest rates to compensate, and fewer ventures would have been profitable enough to finance. Economic activity would have dwindled as credit dried up.

As a result, during much of the nineteenth century before the passage of the Bankruptcy Act of 1898, which forms the basis of the current law, there was no formal federal bankruptcy law in place in the United States. Instead, in periods of severe economic crisis, the sheer number of distressed debtors and their miserable conditions grew. As one contemporary described the 1837 crisis, "Society has played out its last stake; it is checkmated. Young men have no hope. Adults stand like day-laborers idle in the streets. None calleth us to labor. . . . The present generation is bankrupt of principles and hope, as of property."[3] The political pressure exerted by the distressed forced Congress to respond. Through much of the nineteenth century, federal bankruptcy laws were enacted in response to harsh business conditions, only to be repealed soon after. The passage of the Bankrupt Act of 1800 came soon after commercial losses in the 1799 war with France, and it was repealed in 1803.[4] The Bankrupt Act of 1841 followed the great banking panic of 1837 and the subsequent depression. The very Congress that enacted it repealed it in 1843.[5] The Act of 1867 followed the post–Civil War contraction, was much amended, and was finally repealed in 1878.

The number of people who took advantage of the bankruptcy acts was substantial. For example, 33,739 persons took advantage of the Bankrupt Act of 1841, and over 90 percent were discharged of their debts. The amount of debt involved was approximately $440 million at that time, an enormous sum in today's dollars.[6]

While creditors were often politically opposed to debt relief, politicians did recognize that if it did not take place, the consequences could be worse. As Senator Harrison Otis of Massachusetts wondered in a debate on debt relief in 1821,

> What may be expected when their numbers shall be increased and they seriously commence a system of measures for obtaining that relief by their active efforts, which is denied to their supplications. What could be more appalling and inauspicious to men of property, and the Government itself, than to see organized self-created corporations of debtors embodied in all the great commercial towns and formed into one vast combination, to influence elections! What state of things more dangerous than an universal alliance among all classes

of debtors, public and private, to effectuate their own freedom through the instrumentality of persons chosen into Congress with no other recommendation?[7]

Because private contracting could not provide the desired amount of leniency in harsh times, politics stepped in to provide relief if too many suffered. But if a debtor failed alone in more normal times, he was left to his own devices. More important, property rights, and the incentives provided by private contracting, were in place most of the time.

But periodically violating creditor rights was no panacea. What guarantee was there that organized debtors would stop at repudiating their current obligations? Could a debtors' revolt not spread to questioning other forms of property? To leave relief to concerted political action was tantamount to playing with fire.

A better solution eventually emerged. As financial markets and institutions developed, as information and communications technology like the telegraph knit the country together (so that, for example, debtors could not escape the stigma of bankruptcy by going west), as markets for assets improved in liquidity, creditors became more able to monitor their loans and obtain repayment. Some permanent leniency was possible. This is why there was a broad trend in the legislation that was contemplated over the nineteenth century. The bankruptcy laws that were enacted, albeit for short periods, became progressively friendlier to debtors, encompassing more of them and giving them more relief.[8]

The point is that there are solutions that help keep the sphere of markets and the sphere of politics separate while recognizing the imperatives of both. In considering some of the coming challenges that we will describe below, it is important to think of creative ways that the implicit tussle between free markets and politics can be managed, so that one does not destroy the other.

To think about solutions, however, we have to see the challenges more clearly. That is what we now turn to.

The Political Environment and the Coming Challenges

Recent corporate scandals and suggestions of extensive conflicts of interest among the guardians of trust in the market—such as the accountants, the investment bankers, and the analysts—are forcing people to ask the age-old question of whether there are in fact two tracks in the market economy, one for the very rich and one for everyone else. The $735 million earned by Gary Winnick, the CEO of Global Crossing, while his company was heading toward bankruptcy, the $112 million earned by Jeff Skilling, president and CEO of Enron, in the three years before his company collapsed after being accused of phony accounting practices, the $240 million earned by Tyco's Dennis Kozlowski before he was fired and accused of tax fraud undermine the faith people have in the fairness and justice of the market. It is not that people are concerned about disparities in wealth: very few Americans question the enormous amounts earned by superstar athletes like Michael Jordan and Tiger Woods. They can observe firsthand Michael Jordan's superior talent, and they are willing to accept that he deserves what he makes. In the boom years, this was also true for corporate America. But corporate disasters like Enron or Global Crossing have undermined the belief that corporate leaders deserve what they make or that financial analysts really understand the stocks they tout, creating room for envy and resentment. As we have seen, it is in these situations of public mistrust of market forces that antimarket forces find it easier to coordinate and act.

The public resentment in the current economic downturn feeds into a more long-standing distrust of markets that is embodied in the antiglobalization movement. While some of this movement is age-old protectionism in a new-age guise, there are also many groups involved in this movement that genuinely perceive global markets as unfair. Not all these groups understand what they are protesting against. Some long for the things the modern economy appears to crowd out (such as time, friendships, family, and conversation) and the things it appears to destroy (such as open spaces and a clean environment). It is change that they fear, and globalization is unfortunately the most visible and rapid form of recent change. The more discerning protesters see that the inadequate infrastructure that countries have for coping with some of globalization's adverse consequences, rather than globalization itself, is the problem. But it is easier to make common cause against globalization than focus on the more mundane task of fixing the infrastructure.

Already, politicians are responding in the natural way to the downturn by erecting tariff barriers and offering domestic subsidies, a way that is not only shortsighted but also completely oblivious of the lessons of history. The steel tariffs in the United States have been followed by a farm bill that increases the level of subsidies available to the agricultural sector substantially. This will inevitably enrage developing countries, which would willingly forgo all the foreign aid developed countries offer if only the developed world would reduce the extent to which it pampers its domestic agricultural sectors. Developing countries will respond by being more reluctant to lower their tariff barriers, for unfortunately, history suggests that protectionism is contagious.

We are in a dangerous period of hangover, the morning after the ecstasy of a boom. Many feel betrayed by the bust and are demanding action against the markets. And even when the economy picks up, as sooner or later it inevitably will, new challenges are coming that will cause severe dislocation in society. These could be exploited by the few to constrain the market, so it is important to understand what they are.

Technological Change

For centuries, technology has created new products and new ways of making them that render workers and their skills redundant. While the dislocation stemming from technological change is not new, its pace has increased tremendously. Moreover, it is now affecting the professions that have not much changed their way of doing business over the centuries. Because it will affect those who have not yet learned to fear for their jobs, its political impact will be all the more severe.

With the increasing sophistication of computers and software, it is not just trivial tasks that are being performed by the computer but also sophisticated tasks that hitherto required years of experience. Drafting, for example, used to be a significant component of an architect's job. Computer-aided design software has made this skill all but irrelevant. Older architects now find themselves at a serious disadvantage relative to younger colleagues who have been taught to use the software as an integral part of design. Even if older architects do not draft anymore, their ability to supervise and coach their younger colleagues is much diminished. In the race for career advancement, an entire generation has been handicapped.

Other jobs are vanishing because customers now have access to information and transactions technology to which only intermediaries had access earlier. Stockbrokers used their privileged access to research reports in order to entice customers into maintaining trading accounts with them—in the process, generating large brokerage fees. Now Internet brokers offer all the research customers need and charge minuscule trading commissions. Travel agents are also finding business increasingly difficult as customers not only have access to the same information they have but can sometimes get better rates directly from airlines and hotels. This does not mean that all stockbrokers and travel agents will vanish overnight, but that many will not survive, and the ones that do will work very differently from the way they work today.

Technology is also having a differential impact within professions. Take our own, teaching in universities. Using new communication techniques, one gifted professor can teach students in many locations around the country. While technology will increase the demand for such superstar teachers, it will reduce the demand for the merely good, and the demand for the mediocre may vanish completely. Teaching is a job that has been performed the same way for thousands of years, by people who have not feared becoming redundant even in the worst of economic depressions. This will change. While the new economy will increase the demand for education, it may not have room for all of us.

Not only is technology making certain human skills obsolete quickly, it is also creating entirely new sources of distress. As research into genetics progresses, scientists will more easily identify those who are likely to die of particular diseases at a young age. This knowledge has important benefits. It alerts individuals to warning signs and lets physicians diagnose and intervene more quickly. But those who are identified as highly prone to certain debilitating diseases will find it hard to keep jobs that involve substantial training by their employers, get insurance, or even maintain normal social relationships.

Imagine that you receive bad news from the medical lab: you have a genetic predisposition to a debilitating, irreversible disease. Though you may feel fine now, you anticipate a bleak economic future. You have everything to gain, and nothing to lose, by seeking redress through political action. If you organize with others in the same situation, together you will constitute a powerful political force because of your sheer numbers. You will be unlikely to settle for handouts if there is a possibility of also suppressing the disease-identifying technology (simply leaving it up to the individual to disclose if she chooses is tantamount to giving her no choice; those who test well will disclose their results, with the implication that anyone who does not disclose is predisposed to disease). If you achieve a ban on the technology, you restore the status quo ante—and your fears about getting health insurance and good jobs will evaporate. That society will be worse off today, and that pharmaceutical firms will not get the data to help future generations, will not particularly concern you—after all, for most sufferers, the gain will far exceed any sense of altruism they might have.

The fear that political constraints may be placed on the use of valuable new technologies is not unfounded. Twenty-one states in the United States already restrict the use of genetic records for employment purposes, even though this debate and genetics technology are still in their infancy.

Competition from Emerging Economies

Another challenge comes from hitherto distant lands. China and India, accounting together for over 2.5 billion people, are finally on the move. Never before in history have so many people become wealthier at such a pace. While the peoples of these and other developing countries add to the global economic pie in many ways, they will also compete for jobs that they can do more cheaply and more efficiently. This will engender enormous tensions, which will have to be defused.

The challenge from emerging economies is not unrelated to the challenge from technology, for technological advances will lead to competition in sectors that hitherto were immune to competition. Consider the following: a typical secretary in New York is about as well educated and productive as a typical secretary in Mumbai, India. They both use the same word-processing and presentation software, the same fax machines, the same E-mail programs to communicate over the Internet. The secretary in New York, however, makes about thirteen times the salary of her Indian counterpart.[9] In part, the salary differential reflects the difference in the cost of living in New York and in Mumbai. But even accounting for this, the Indian secretary makes only a fraction of the salary the American secretary makes. The reason for this difference is that secretarial work has, thus far, been immune from foreign competition. Immigration controls and perhaps an affinity for being in Mumbai keep the Indian secretary far from New York. Thus, her willingness to work at a lower wage has little effect on New York secretarial wages.

This is not to say that secretarial wages are determined arbitrarily. Like all prices, they are determined by demand and supply. One factor determining the supply of secretaries is their alternative employment possibilities. Suppose a secretary's alternative job is as a steelworker. There is a world market for steel (provided protectionism does not close it down), so no country can afford to pay its steelworkers much more than what they contribute at the margin to output. That U.S. steelworkers are paid much more than Indian steelworkers is because U.S. steelworkers are substantially more productive. Therefore, because U.S. steelworkers are more productive, the U.S. secretary is paid more, even though she herself is not more productive. Thus, in the United States, the secretary earns a hefty salary because she controls a scarce factor: labor. But what is scarce is secretarial labor in the United States, not secretarial labor in the world. And technology is increasingly making it possible for all kinds of labor to be supplied at a distance.

As the cost of communication falls, a Chicagoan complaining about his utility bill is just as likely to find a middle-aged woman in Manila, Philippines, on the other end of the line as an American. In the past, human-capital-intensive activities such as answering customer complaints had to be done on-site, so the displacement of American jobs could be moderated through immigration controls. These, obviously, no longer can be used to retain jobs answering telephones.

Not every job will be at risk. But competition will be intense for the most routine jobs, which typically tend to employ the most people. Over time, competition will move to more skilled activities as foreigners learn the local standards. While large firms may still employ partners in big accounting firms to advise them on arcane tax-minimization strategies, the small-business owner may well deal over the Internet with an Indian or a Chinese accountant who has familiarized herself with U.S. laws. A Russian physician may perform an operation over the Internet at a fraction of the cost that a Western European physician would charge. Of course, there will be barriers initially to such cross-border transactions, but once trust and confidence has built up, we see no natural limitations to such activities. In fact, one of us is a director of a company that offers real-time, personalized mathematics homework help out of Madras to students in Singapore and the United Kingdom. An important reason it was able to convince clients is that Cambridge University, through its mathematics outreach program, stood behind the venture, providing the necessary certification.

In short, while workers in "traded" industries like steel have faced up to foreign competition for decades and have adapted to it, for many in "nontraded" service sectors, this will be something they have never experienced before. They currently enjoy compensation in excess of what they would earn in a worldwide competitive market. An increase in competition will jeopardize this excess compensation. Hence, like the steelworkers, these new victims of competition will mobilize to try to block it. But unlike with physical goods, border controls will be ineffective. So if the distressed in the service industries organize, they will press for much more intrusive actions to keep out the foreign menace.

They will have strong incentives to do so since their very livelihoods will be at stake. When a worker loses her job as a result of a downturn in the business cycle, she has a fair expectation that she will regain her job when the cycle turns up. When she loses her job because her industry is technologically obsolete or because foreign competition closes it down, she is unlikely ever to regain it. These new risks create a new type of economic distress. In earlier times, the distressed could retain hope in the market as long as they were given enough to tide them over the cyclical downturns. A worker today who has lost her career cannot regain faith in the future with mere handouts. She needs a new lease on life, not a temporary subsidy.

The Fear of Developed Economies

Even while developed countries fear competition from cheap, skilled, educated labor from developing countries, the latter fear that their industries could be wiped out overnight by multinationals with global brands, with strategies honed in highly competitive markets, and with access to cheap power and capital. In the same way as workers in the developed world see cheap, low-cost labor in the developing world as an unfair threat (no matter how much this fear is disguised as concern for the working conditions and benefits of developing-country workers), owners and managers in the developing world see the better infrastructure in the developed world as unfair. In truth, each side has a source of comparative advantage, which will help it compete. And in a world of open borders, each side can benefit from the other's strengths, the developed world getting access to cheap labor and the developing world getting access to infrastructure. But all this will imply dislocation and distress in the short run. And the developing world is even less prepared than the developed world to handle it.

In some developing countries, the preconditions for respect for property or for creating market infrastructure have not yet been established. Property is highly concentrated in the form of large feudal landholdings or monopolies, especially in extractive industries. Not only can these countries not cope with volatile, competitive markets, but their dominant political groups have little interest in creating the infrastructure that would allow them to cope.

But even in developing countries that have a sizable and widely held manufacturing and service sector, there is no guarantee that there will be political support for a competitive market. The reason is simple. All too often, too many of the firms that populate these countries are uncompetitive. This matters: inefficient incumbents have more of an incentive to lobby for protection, not just because they cannot face competition but also because they have little prospect of gaining in an expanded market. This is not just theoretical speculation. The most active lobbyists for protection in the U.S. steel industry are indeed the larger, older, less innovative, and less profitable firms, in which top managers typically have had long tenures on the job.[10]

One reason many firms in developing countries are inefficient, despite their access to cheap labor, is that they have been protected for a long time against domestic and foreign competition and have consequently become slow and lazy. Equally important, however, is that these firms are not managed by the best talents available.

To see why, consider the following. As is well known, the largest firms in the United States are typically not managed by their owners but instead run by professional managers. With the increased pressures of competition and the quickening pace of technological change, more is required of top management. Professional managers are easier to fire when they do not perform. In recent years in the United States, many more CEOs have been found to be inadequate for their jobs, fired, and replaced with outsiders. While in the early 1970s, only 10 percent of CEO successions (a change of CEO) were forced departures, in the early 1990s, this percentage more than doubled. Similarly, while in the early 1970s, only 15 percent of the incoming CEOs came from outside the firm, in the early 1990s, twice as many were outsiders.[11]

In order to obtain the management they need in an increasingly competitive world, this evidence suggests that firms look farther and wider and dispense more quickly with managers who are not up to the mark. But such a change requires an outsider-dominated governance system: it is easier to fire top managers when they do not control a large fraction of a firm's voting rights and when they are actively monitored by outsiders on the board.[12] Unfortunately, these are not the conditions prevailing in most of the world. Many companies are controlled by insiders, who acquired that right at birth rather than in the market-place.[13] Heir-controlled firms, as we have seen, tend to be managed particularly poorly.[14] In a rapidly changing world with immense dislocation, such entrenched management is likely to have strong incentives to co-opt the distressed into demanding protection. A classic example of such an organization is what is loosely termed the Bombay Club in India, an amorphous organization led by the scions of the old, venerable business families, which strongly opposes opening up the economy.

Another serious concern in developing countries is the near complete absence of a formal safety net for those hurt by competition. In the quest for growth, many countries have neglected to build a reliable system of social security that will help citizens buffer the market's volatility. Transfers and subsidies still occupy a small part of the government budget: in a sample of newly industrialized countries, it is about one-quarter of what it is in developed countries.[15] As a case in point, until the Asian crisis in 1998, even South Korea had little in the way of unemployment compensation and had to institute such a scheme rapidly when faced with worker demonstrations.

Of course, the low level of government social spending is somewhat misleading because some spending that has found its way into the public sector in developed economies (such as old-age pensions) is still in the private sector in these newly industrialized countries. But in part, it reflects a belief that the role of the government is only to create market infrastructure, while social networks can provide insurance in case of adversity. This belief has served countries well during the period of rapid economic growth. But with the expansion of the market economy, social networks tend to break down: it is suggestive that Singapore passed legislation in the 1990s empowering parents to sue children who did not support them in their old age![16] Legislation, however, is unlikely to fully repair social bonds that have been sundered by the market, and the absence of a significant explicit safety net can leave a citizenry overexposed to short-term fluctuations.

The developed world has to care about these vulnerabilities in the developing world. As developed and developing economies become more intertwined, not just through trade in goods but through services, they are becoming more exposed to disturbances in each other. Moreover, as trade moves from manufacturing to services, the degree of mutual dependence and specialization is likely to increase: it is arguably harder to change your accountant or the firm that maintains your system software than to change the firm from which you purchase steel. It is also hard to build inventories of services to serve as buffers. Of course, businesses will attempt to diversify risk by sourcing from multiple countries. But diversification has its costs and its limits.

There is a silver lining to these interdependencies. When, in May of 2002, the governments of India and Pakistan started threatening each other about the possibility of a nuclear war, domestic businesses in those countries became alarmed at the possibility that foreign buyers would get scared off by increased perceptions of risk. As a result, businesses in India and Pakistan put pressure on their governments to tone down the rhetoric. Business is placing limits on politics. These benefits notwithstanding, growing global integration is exposing the world to new risks of disruption that have to be addressed.

Aging Populations

No analysis of the potential future threats to the political viability of free markets can ignore the dramatic effects that the rapidly aging population in developed countries will have on the distribution of resources.

With decreasing birthrates and increasing life expectancy, the population of developed countries is aging rapidly even while it has slowed to near zero growth. In 1970, there were 17.2 million children under age five and 3.7 million adults over eighty in the United States. By 1995, the figures were 19.6 million and 8.1 million, respectively, and by 2040, they will be 25 million and 26.2 million, respectively.[17] And the United States, with substantial immigration, is not even close to being the most rapidly aging country. According to projections, by 2010, Japan will have fewer than three working-age adults for each elderly citizen, and by 2050, it will have only 1.5 taxpaying workers per pensioner. At that time, Italy will have fewer taxpaying workers than pensioners.[18]

A smaller and smaller working population will have to support a larger and larger group of the nonworking. The size of transfers each worker has to make to give the elderly their promised retirement benefits will keep increasing. If no change occurs, future working generations will pay more and more to the elderly while expecting less and less for their own old age. This will set up a clash of interests between the incumbent old and the younger working generation, between those that democracy renders powerful because of their numbers and organizational power and those that economics renders powerful because of their control over human capital. Historically, a mismatch between political power and economic power has represented a threat to the security of property rights. Such a threat is possible again in the future.

Another source of tension arises from the international distribution of resources. If the productive capabilities of the economy fall as the population ages, then consumption goods will have to be imported. In anticipation of this, developed economies will have to invest abroad, not in other developed economies, as has been the trend in the past, but in younger, developing countries. Developing countries need to develop the capacity to absorb these investments in sensible ways.

Moreover, if developed countries are to hold significant quantities of financial claims on developing countries, they will demand safeguards to ensure that they will not be dispossessed at a later date when they need to cash in those investments. We have seen that, historically, respect for property rights emerged when owners were sufficiently represented politically to make expropriation politically difficult and when expropriation hurt the expropriator in the long run. Clearly, investors from developed countries have had little or no political representation in developing countries, at least since the days of gunboat diplomacy. So whether their rights will be respected hinges on whether, going forward, developing countries will find it costly to expropriate owners in developed countries. Population aging will force developed countries to be increasingly reliant on the climate of respect for property in developing countries. It is in our collective interest that market infrastructure expand worldwide.

International Governance

This then brings us to questions of international governance. We have argued that the cause of markets is helped within a country if its large industrial and financial firms are competitive, for they will then not have to rely on shackling the free market to survive. Internationally, the cause of free markets is helped if the dominant political power is also an efficient producer, for it then wants to press others to open up their borders. During the nineteenth century, England, which at the time was the most industrially advanced nation and politically very powerful, promoted free markets around the world. A similar role has been played by the United States in the post–World War II period. It is periods when the political leadership of the world changes hands or when the dominant political power loses its economic leadership that we are especially likely to face ambivalence about open markets.

The United States is still the dominant economy in the world as well as the sole superpower, but neither attribute is unchangeable. Certainly, with the steel tariffs and the farm subsidies, we see the consequences of U.S. economic weakness in some sectors impinging on its commitment to open borders. What if weakness spreads? Will the United States continue to champion free markets?

Of course, the United States is only one country. Competition among different political entities can still further the cause of the market even if a major player jumps ship. The danger we see here is the growing political integration among countries of the type occurring in Europe: it reduces political competition and makes coordinated anti-market moves more feasible.

In its early years, what is now the European Union was the European Economic Community (EEC)—a focused attempt to break down national barriers in Europe to promote trade and enlarge the market. When it was largely intent on a narrow, promarket goal, it was a force for the good, and coaxed many countries to liberalize. In ensuring equal access to foreigners, countries also were forced to level the playing field for their own citizens, thus fostering the development of competitive arm's-length markets.

As the aims of the European Union have broadened to go beyond market expansion and trade liberalization to a common program of governance, its directives could well have the potential of becoming more intrusive and illiberal (it should not be forgotten that even the EEC promoted protectionist agricultural policies).

Consider an extreme but illustrative case. Suppose after a severe stock market crash, the European Union decides that too many companies brought to market were little more than a dream and a prayer. It decides to tighten the rules under which companies can issue shares on the market, a move that incumbents across countries might well support because it starves entrants of financing. Given that these rules would apply immediately in all neighboring countries that a new European firm might conceivably think of tapping, that potential entrant might be hard-pressed to raise finance under the new rules, making the rules much more effective and making incumbents in each country more eager to press for them with the union. By contrast, if a single country tried to impose those rules, it would see the potential entrant go to a neighboring country to raise finance. Thus, the migration of business to friendlier political entities is a very strong disciplinary force for keeping policies market-friendly. This force is suppressed when neighboring political entities coalesce.

That policies are still market friendly is, in part, because member countries have veto power over serious economic change. As the union broadens its membership, there are pressures to reduce the areas over which member countries have a veto. This will make the union more of a political monopoly, with attendant dangers to markets.

Summary

After decades of uninterrupted expansion of markets, in which free markets, especially financial markets, have tamed, converted, or conquered those who opposed them, it is easy to get overly complacent. Borders are more open than ever before, reducing the ability of domestic politicians to play favorites. And the generous systems of social security set up by developed economies since World War II, while trimmed a little in recent years, still provide insurance to most in the developed world. Thus, buffers are in place to prevent an antimarket reaction from coalescing. Does all this not ensure the viability of free markets going forward?

Not necessarily. Technology is advancing rapidly. In addition to changing the skills that are valued and thus creating entirely new legions of the distressed, it is bringing competition from developing countries to the doorsteps of professionals in developed countries. Even though the uncertainties facing the average worker in the near term (whether she will have enough to tide her through the next downturn) have diminished, they have been replaced by profound anxiety about the long term (whether she will have the skills to earn a living for enough years to support a steadily lengthening span of retired life).

Developing countries are facing intense competition, but they do not have the stabilization or coping mechanisms that developed countries have put in place over the years. Both developed and developing countries are becoming mutually dependent, a dependency that will only grow as populations in the developed world age. How can the tensions these mutual dependencies create be managed without setting off political movements to close borders and suppress markets? All this is the subject of the next chapter.

CHAPTER THIRTEEN

Saving Capitalism
from the Capitalists

T HE MAIN POINT of this book is that free markets, perhaps the most beneficial economic institution known to humankind, rest on fragile political foundations. In a competitive free market economy, the decisions of myriad anonymous participants determine prices, which, in turn, determine what is produced and who is rewarded. The invisible hand of the market substitutes for bureaucrats and politicians in all these decisions. This has engendered the misperception that markets do not need governments. But markets cannot flourish without the very visible hand of the government, which is needed to set up and maintain the infrastructure that enables participants to trade freely and with confidence.

Here is where the political tension arises: The very same difficulties of organizing collective action that necessitate the intervention of the government also make it hard for the public to ensure that the government acts in the public interest. Organized private interests can thus have their way against the larger interests of the public. The nightmare scenario, which has played out before, is that under the cover of obtaining security for the distressed, the incumbents also obtain security for themselves by repressing the market. The victim is the free market and all those who look to it for opportunity.

In the last chapter, we outlined a number of scenarios that could cause a rapid rise in the number of distressed, both in developed and in developing countries. We also explained what type of incumbents might have the strongest incentive to feed on the fears and hopes of the distressed.

Having outlined the threats, we now move to proposing solutions.

Given the fundamental tension that is at the heart of the problem, there is no magic bullet. A call for forceful action by the government runs the risk that the action will be distorted by incumbents. A call to neuter the government runs the risk that the necessary infrastructure will remain underdeveloped and the market will be overexposed to political backlash during the inevitable process of destruction. The only way out is a set of proposals that can collectively check and balance each other so that the government supports, but does not intrude on, the functioning of the market. In isolation, each proposal may seem benign, or even counterproductive. But together, they become a force to foster free markets.

Our proposals rest on four pillars. First, incumbents who are not overwhelmingly powerful and who are capable of being competitive are less likely to attempt to constrain market forces. So an important pillar of policy should be to ensure that the control of productive assets is not concentrated in a few hands and that those who do have control also have the ability to use the assets well. Second, competition will create losers. A safety net is essential for the distressed, one that does not simply help the distressed cope with business cycle downturns but helps them bounce back from the complete loss of a career. Third, the scope for political maneuvering can be limited if borders are kept open. Of course, in extremis, borders will be forcibly closed down by antimarket forces, but that is why all four pillars should be seen as mutually reinforcing. Finally, the public should be made more aware of how much it benefits from the market and what the costs of seemingly innocuous anticompetitive policies are, so that the public is less willing to remain passively on the sidelines. Let us examine these proposals in detail.

Reduce Incumbents' Incentives to Oppose Markets

We cannot wish away the fact that economic power translates to political power. No matter what kinds of campaign finance reforms are proposed and enacted, some form of the "golden rule"—he who has the gold makes the rules—will always apply. But the nexus between economic and political power is of special concern in two situations. If a few incumbents have much of the economic power, they can rely on their own political clout to achieve business ends and may feel little need to establish transparent rules that make markets accessible to all. This is more likely to be a problem in a country that does not have an established market infrastructure because the pressure to create it will then be low. More dangerous still than this benign neglect of the market is if the incumbents are incompetent at business, for they may then actively attempt to suppress the competitive market so as to preserve their own positions.

The two concerns are not unrelated. An example may help fix ideas. The diamond trade in India is dominated by a small community of Palanpuri Jains from Gujarat. For nearly half a century, these traders have worked in secrecy, dealing largely with other members of extended families, to buy, cut, polish, and resell diamonds around the world. Working without legal contracts, they have been so effective that nine out of ten diamonds in the world now pass through India.[1] The reason this system has worked so far in a country with a creaky legal system is that it is based on trust. The community will ostracize anyone who violates the implicit understanding among traders. The problem, however, is that outsiders cannot participate in the system, and insiders have no incentive to create a more arm's-length, transparent system: it is easier to build trust when profits are large and trading is only among a few, well-known people.

The concentration of trading in a few hands can be harmful if the system stops working as well. And there are signs of this as trade expands and business has to be done with more and more outsiders: a courier recently absconded with $10 million worth of diamonds, and two Bombay traders lost their clients' money in stock speculation (they were so ashamed, they committed suicide).[2] But members of the community are not eager to accept modernization and professionalism, however necessary they are, because these changes will also bring competition. Change is therefore coming slowly, perhaps overly so. The point is, concentration of economic power, even if currently benign, need not always remain so, especially if the privileged few have their own ways of doing business.

This suggests two goals of policy: to keep economic power from getting overly concentrated—an aim that is especially pertinent to developing countries—and to ensure that those who control economic resources are capable of using them efficiently.

The two goals are often, but not always, compatible. For example, it is clear that a policy of subjecting firms to competition from the outside helps keep them efficient: there is little pressure on a protected industry to become competitive, and it will use the windfall profits earned while being protected to lobby for more protection instead of taking the steps necessary to restructure. The Indian Ambassador car (a version of the British Morris Oxford) was introduced in 1957 and sold virtually unchanged till March 2002, simply because it had little domestic, and no foreign, competition during much of its history. Even a purportedly temporary cessation of discipline, such as the recent steel tariffs in the United States, which are slated to disappear in a few years, risks creating incumbents who cannot compete and who will fight to make the barriers permanent.

But in order to compete at the right scale in a world market, a firm from a small country may end up accounting for a significant portion of that country's economic output. Firms like Nokia in Finland do have significant domestic clout. Whether such a firm uses its domestic clout responsibly, helping improve the access of others to the market, or whether it uses it to constrain their access and monopolize domestic resources will indicate whether more instruments of policy have to be brought to bear.

A POLITICAL ANTITRUST LAW

One such instrument is antitrust law. Antitrust law has been framed in the context of product markets: the questions regulators ask are, will a firm account for an excessive fraction of output, is there external or incipient competition that will help keep prices down . . . It has been used to prevent firms from monopolizing industries and squeezing supernormal profits out of customers. An additional salutary effect is that competition helps keep firms efficient by preventing them from enjoying the quiet and debilitating life of a monopoly.

But it is also useful for countries to consider a political version of antitrust law—one that prevents a firm from growing big enough to have the clout in domestic politics to eventually suppress market forces. There are obvious problems in framing such a law precisely, but it has been implicitly in place in the United States, especially in the financial sector. The attack on the Second Bank of the United States by Andrew Jackson in the 1830s, the breakup of John D. Rockefeller's Standard Oil in 1911, the creation of the Federal Reserve in 1913 to counter the power of the House of Morgan, the Glass-Steagall Act of 1933 to curb the power of the large national banks, and the ongoing case against Microsoft can all be seen as consequences of an implicit political antitrust law.3 There is a risk that such a law will be misused against those who are not favorites of the government. This is why this law makes sense only as part of our full set of proposals, which include other checks and balances on the government.

PROPERTY TAX

A change in the taxation system offers another way of creating pressure for efficiency. In the current system of income taxes, whoever produces more pays more. As a result, efficient managers who produce more have to share the gains from their efficiency with the government through higher taxes. The government also absorbs (through lower taxes) a fraction of the losses of the incompetent. But this favors the inefficient. Those who waste resources in lavish and extravagant expenses or who make unsound investments are subsidized by the taxation system, which absorbs part of these expenses or losses, while efficient managers are penalized because part of their superior returns goes to the government.

Not all taxation systems have this effect. A tax based on property (not income) tends to penalize the inefficient and reward the efficient. To see this, consider a tax of 1 percent levied on all productive assets that a person directly holds. The tax due on farmland worth $1 million would then be $10,000. Suppose a would-be author from the city who likes rustic surroundings but has little ability to farm can produce only $5,000 in net income from this land. All her farming income will be taken by the government, and she will have to find an equal amount elsewhere. If her books do not sell or she cannot lobby for farm assistance, she will have to sell her land to someone who can do a better job of farming it.

Contrast her with a son of the soil who knows his farming and earns $100,000 from a similar piece of land. Only one-tenth of his income will be paid in taxes. More important, if he improves the productivity of his fields and increases his income to $150,000, he retains all the gains rather than only a fraction of them as under an income tax system. Moreover, he can expand by buying the city dilettante's land. The son of the soil has less of an incentive to lobby for farm subsidies or for trade barriers against foreign products: subsidies will keep the dilettante in business, preventing him from expanding, and trade barriers will invite retaliatory barriers that will prevent him from selling his grain abroad. In this way, a property tax favors efficient producers and helps strengthen promarket forces.4

Some readers may wonder why a free market in land will not lead to the efficient allocation of resources. In other words, why does the efficient son of the soil not buy out the incompetent writer? The problem is that the writer gets psychic nonmonetary value from the land that makes up for her incompetence at farming. This psychic income is not taxed. As a result, even if her psychic income does not make up for the lost monetary income, the son of the soil will find it hard to buy her out. Under the current tax regime, psychic income is tax exempt while anyone who produces monetary income faces the full burden of taxes. So everything else being equal, the producer of monetary income is willing to pay less for a piece of property than one who enjoys psychic income from it. Similarly, the current tax regime subsidizes the survival of incompetent businessmen who get personal value from running their firms. A change from taxes on the income generated by property to a tax on the value of property itself will avoid these inefficiencies.

There are, of course, issues about how such a system would be administered. For example, how would the value of property be measured? It cannot be measured as the value of assets under the current inefficient producer's control, for that would artificially depress the value and hence the taxes she would pay. To avoid rewarding incompetence, the value should be measured as a notional market value under average alternative management. There are ways of making these values quite precise. We do not see the problems in administering a system based on property taxes as significantly greater than the complexities of administering one based on income taxes.

Traditionally, the argument against a property tax has been that it discourages investment. Under certain assumptions about the timing of the tax, this is true: for a given level of tax revenues, a property tax reduces the incentive to invest more than does an income tax. This should be set off, however, against the benefits of a property tax system in allocating ownership to more efficient hands, which contributes both to the general well-being of society and to the stability of the free market system. Thus, it makes sense to shift at least some of the tax burden from income to property.

BETTER CORPORATE GOVERNANCE

Some of the most important properties in advanced economies are not operated by their owners but by professional managers. We refer, of course, to corporations. On the one hand, the separation between owner-ship and control facilitates a better matching between firms and man-agers, leading to more efficient firms. On the other hand, it creates conflicts of interest between managers and shareholders, leading to potential inefficiencies. To facilitate a healthy separation between owner-ship and control, more legal protection should be guaranteed to those investors who entrust their savings to somebody else's hands. In addi-tion, appropriate mechanisms such as independent boards, effective auditors, and a vibrant market for corporate takeovers are essential to ensure that managers are coaxed into maximizing the value of the com-panies they run and are quickly replaced when they demonstrate their inability to do so. In other words, corporate governance is important not just to enhance value for investors but also to ensure that some of the largest and most powerful players in the economy, incumbent firms, wel-come rather than fear competition. Recent scandals suggest that much needs to be done on this front even in advanced market economies.

INHERITANCE TAX ON TRANSFER OF CONTROL

Finally, there is a form of transfer of control of assets, inheritance, that tends typically to be inefficient because the receiver has little qualifica-tion other than the accident of birth for obtaining control. To impose serious impediments on how the rich can dispose of their wealth would reduce their incentive to create that wealth in the first place. Inefficient and concentrated control of wealth does, however, impose all kinds of costs on society. That is why an inheritance tax, structured so that the rich are encouraged to transfer passive ownership of productive assets (for example, minority stakes in a portfolio of firms), rather than active control, to their children would make sense. To the extent that it also nudges society toward less concentration of economic power, it would help. But its primary aim should be to achieve the efficient distribution of control.

Inheritance taxes may be especially important in developing countries where there is immense concentration of landholdings. Another way to break down the excessive concentration of asset ownership is to make equal inheritance by all children, male and female, the default. Such pre-scriptions are not new. They can be traced back at least to the British philosopher James Harrington (see Chapter 6), who had tremendous influence on William Penn (and thence on the Constitution of Philadelphia), Thomas Jefferson (and thereby on the Constitution of Virginia), and Theodore Roosevelt (and thus on federal antitrust legislation).

A Safety Net for the Distressed

When interstate transportation was highly regulated, a lot of trucking firms had a very easy life, and very few were forced to exit. The situation changed dramatically in 1977, when the Interstate Commerce Commission (ICC) started to authorize all requests for entry. In the five years following deregulation, more than 50 percent of the prederegulation firms were forced out of the industry. While competition brought lower prices and more efficient services to customers, it also destroyed the economic viability of many firms.[5]

Competition triggers failures. These failures are essential to the creative destruction process but are extremely painful for the people affected. The bigger the cost of adjustment imposed on them, or the larger the numbers of the distressed, the stronger the political demand to intervene.

INSURE PEOPLE, NOT FIRMS

This demand, while perfectly understandable, is very dangerous, because it can be easily manipulated. As we have seen in the case of the steel industry, the demand from a group of *people* who are hit particularly hard gets immediately transformed into a subsidy to existing *firms*, with all the negative consequences we have described. To prevent the victims of the process of creative destruction from being transformed into human shields for special interests, we need to provide for them in other ways. One rule, therefore, to prevent the politicization of relief is to insure people directly, not through firms.

For example, economists generally agree that the best way to provide relief to workers who lose their job is to offer them a lump-sum payment, possibly dependent on the duration of their previous employment. Not only does this payment to individuals not interfere with the competitive process, but it also gives workers the right incentive to look for another job (they get to keep the payment regardless of how long it takes them to find a new job) while at the same time relieving them of the privations of unemployment. Unfortunately, such simple solutions are rarely implemented because they completely disassociate relief to the worker from politics.

DESIGN INSURANCE BEFORE THE FACT

A second rule to prevent the politicization of relief is to design the guidelines for future relief before the event that prompts relief rather than after it. There are a number of reasons why this makes sense. Governments, though, typically prefer to wait for the event to take place before responding instead of preparing for the uncertain eventuality: not only can the magnitude of the relief required be better gauged after the fact, but resources do not have to be held in reserve, crowding out other activities that the government deems essential.

One reason to design relief in advance is simply that a well-designed plan provides people a greater sense of security. Moreover, it eliminates the need for the distressed to organize to obtain relief. Since the actions of their political organizations are not likely to be friendly to the market, a plan for relief before the fact eliminates a significant threat to the markets. This, in fact, is suggested by our brief account of the history of the U.S. bankruptcy law. Once a flexible enough law was put in place, the need for debtors to organize to press for relief during each recession disappeared. Also, they could obtain relief based on individual circumstances rather than wait for collective misery to tip the political scales.

Relief provided after the fact is not insurance but pure redistribution. As such, it is driven solely by the political power of the parties involved, not by the needs of people. As an example, consider the Federal Emergency Relief Act, a large ($3.6 billion) New Deal program implemented between 1933 and 1935 to provide assistance to all persons whose income was inadequate to meet their needs. Since the United States entered the Great Depression with no unemployment insurance, the decision on whom this relief was distributed to was made after the fact. It turns out that the amount of aid received in each county was positively correlated with the number of radios owned in the area, even after accounting for the wealth of citizens in the county.[6] In the 1930s, people who owned a radio were better informed politically and more likely to vote, so this suggests that relief went to counties that were more able to press for it. In addition, counties with more illiterates received *less* aid, suggesting again that informed voters obtained more assistance. Even though all relief is determined by political power rather than economic need, relief after the fact tends to be particularly driven by political power.

Therefore, one of the most important benefits of putting in place a system of relief before a crisis is the veil of ignorance on who will be affected and how. Most people will not know whether they will be the beneficiaries of the scheme or will be the ones who will have to pay for it. As a result, they do not have strong incentives to distort the system one way or another. In fact, they would prefer the system that is most effective in terms of cost per unit of benefits. By contrast, after the fact, it is very clear who will receive the transfer and who will have to pay for it. Thus, the return to lobbying is extremely high. Relief provided on an ad hoc basis is thus much more a slave to vested interests than an insurance scheme designed before the fact.

One of the problems with the current system in developed countries is that it was designed during a time of crisis and targeted only certain groups. These systems are not universal in their coverage. It is a travesty that children in the United States, the future of the nation, do not have health insurance as a matter of course, while politicians are vying with one another to offer prescription drug benefits to the predominantly wealthy elderly.[7] It is equally worrisome that so many working families have no medical insurance. The system will no doubt provide in the wake of a severe crisis, but benefits will have to be extracted through political action, with all the attendant consequences. Moreover, in the United States, too much of worker health insurance and retirement benefits are closely tied to the survival of existing firms. In Italy, too, workers in the largest and most politically influential firms have a special deal and therefore strong incentives to press for their survival. The system of insurance needs a dramatic overhaul—a broadening of the base and a more direct relationship between the individual and the insurer without involving others like the employer.

INSURE AGAINST PERMANENT CHANGE

There is also a need to rethink the focus of these programs. The programs were designed to fight the last wars, the war against acute poverty and the war against the effect of temporary dislocation caused by business cycles. But today, workers have different concerns. In the jargon of economists, *structural* and not *cyclical* change is the concern now. Workers fear for the long-term future of their jobs and their lives, so even though their level of uncertainty increases during economic downturns, it is also more persistent. In earlier times, the distressed were tided over by aid that helped them weather the business cycle downturns. A worker today who has lost her career cannot regain faith in the future with such handouts. Her questions are: Will I have the flexibility to acquire the necessary skills to keep myself productive? Will I have the good health to make those changes, especially as I grow older? And as I grow older, will I have enough put away to live a happy and fulfilling retired life?

How might governments think about providing security so that there are fewer distressed as a result of long-term technological or competitive changes in the economy? The most valuable asset people have is typically their human capital. The greatest help the government could offer its citizens in this changeable world is to help them create and maintain the value of that capital, for flexible human capital will be the best form of insurance. And to those who simply cannot change, a secure minimum pension will be the safety net.

In order for a worker to develop flexible human capital, it is important that he have sound health into old age, a basic general education that gives him the ability to learn instead of filling him with facts that have a very short half-life, and an education system that can take him in whenever he needs retraining.

We have little new to say about sound health or basic education other than noting that studies increasingly show that the seeds of future illnesses (and learning disabilities) are sown in early youth. Poor nutrition in early years seems to be associated with the early onset of the degenerative diseases of old age, such as coronary heart disease and diabetes.[8] Poor habits of expectant mothers, such as drinking and smoking, also contribute to the long-term impairment of their progeny's health. Unfortunately, these problems are likely to be more severe among the children of the poor and the poorly educated, which then perpetuates the cycle of poverty and ill health. To break it, more resources have to be devoted to very young children, whether in the form of nutritional supplements, medical monitoring and treatment, or parental education. This will give the children a better chance of staying healthy and thus staying competitive going forward.

Consider next whether people will have the flexibility to acquire new skills. This question has become particularly important because, even as the pace of change increases, life expectancy has also increased: in the United States, it has increased by twenty-nine years since 1900, almost the span of an entire working career.[9] Yet the fundamental way most people prepare to be productive citizens has not changed much during that time. Despite their longer life spans, most people stop formal education early on in life, much as they did a hundred years ago. No doubt, more of them get advanced degrees—enrollment in higher education increased more than ten times between 1940 and 1997—and some get training on the job.[10] But education is still geared toward that first job, even though technological change, competition, and greater job mobility mean that for most people, that first job, or even that first career, will not be the last.

A system of formal education that terminates when one is twenty-five probably leaves one with too much information relative to what one needs for the first few years of one's career and too little knowledge for the half century that follows. Would it not make more sense to cut back a little early on and have more formal doses of reeducation later on so that individuals can cope with changes in environment and preferences?

Business schools have taken a lead here by offering open-enrollment refresher courses to senior executives who feel that the skills obtained during their M.B.A. studies need updating. But there may be reason to rethink the entire structure of higher education, a system designed at a time when students typically left the university for a career with one employer. We need more modular degrees and lifelong admission to a university (at least for the general programs)—so that the student can pick and choose what she wants and when she needs it.

There are reasons to believe that such flexible degrees will become more feasible in the near future, and educators should seize this opportunity. Advances in distance education using the Internet will help individuals keep up to date even while working full-time and help reduce the cost of higher education. A few universities already offer a full M.B.A. degree with only a few weeks of direct contact, with much of the necessary communication being done electronically through chat groups, E-mails, and lectures over the Internet. These kinds of programs will spread. One important tool, therefore, in helping citizens cope with the greater uncertainty in their lives will be a revolution in higher education. If it succeeds, students will spend less time on campuses, but they will look more like the people we find in a shopping mall today—young and old, rich and poor, reflecting a broad cross section of society. The G.I. Bill, which paid for veterans to go to college, reduced inequality tremendously in the United States and increased the level of security.[11] A revolution in higher education has the potential to do far more.

One of the advantages of providing insurance in the forms we have suggested is that it makes it harder for incumbents to capture the allocation of relief. In fact, instead of subsidizing inefficient incumbents like the traditional relationship system, which we described in past chapters, our design of insurance undermines their position by making individuals more independent. A worker with flexible human capital can avail much better of opportunities that come her way. Taken together, insurance provided in the right way can aid the market rather than stand in its way.

Finally, it should be possible for those who have neither the desire nor the ability to make career changes to take retirement and work in other ways in society. A viable pension scheme would allow this. Unfortunately, the generations coming of age today, when the risks of structural change are great, have little reason to feel secure about their pensions.

Since pension schemes or social security was started in many countries in the midst of an economic downturn, the old were initially granted benefits for which they had not paid. Those benefits were paid out of the social security contributions of younger generations, who, in turn, were promised a similar level of benefits in the future. This system, also known as pay-as-you-go, can be sustained as long as the growth in population and productivity outpaces the growth in benefits. The slowing of population growth and the progressive aging of populations means that the social security system currently in place in almost every developed country will prove inadequate for future generations.

We are skeptical of political claims that the current level of social security can be maintained without any dramatic changes in the fertility or productivity of the population or without changes in current government expenditure. In the absence of such miracles, the only alternative is to redistribute the burden and benefits of social security more equitably across generations. No politician wants to risk antagonizing the powerful elderly by suggesting that their benefits will have to be cut, and no one wants to break the news of the consequences to today's younger generations. Unless politicians find the courage, we will have to live with uncertainty about pensions, making it harder for us to deal with change.

Much of what we have written about systems of relief or insurance has been in the context of developed countries. In some ways, the current situation in developed countries is much better than the one in developing ones. There are few formal systems in place in developing countries, and extensive reliance is placed on the social networks like extended families and villages to serve as buffers for economic volatility.

Not only do these countries lack formal social security systems, but they also lack other important modern institutions like personal bankruptcy laws that would reduce the penalty suffered by those who lose out in the competition. These countries simply do not have formal insurance mechanisms to absorb the volatility of a market economy. They will have to build them.

The silver lining is that the level of government expenditure on social security in many of these countries is low. So they have the ability to create formal security systems without repeating the mistakes made by developed countries: they can broaden the base and reduce the coverage to the minimum adequate amount, leaving citizens to choose a greater level of coverage on their own if they so desire. They can also rely more on the private sector, thus avoiding the creation of a self-perpetuating bureaucracy.

Developing countries are better prepared on another dimension. In their quest for growth, many have emphasized good health care and a strong basic education for their children. Their health and education systems are better in some respects than what is available for children in developed countries. Going forward, this will help them deal better with the volatility inherent in the market economy.

Reduce the Ability of Incumbents to Affect Governance

Thus far, we have proposed ways of reducing the incentives of incumbents and the distressed to go against markets. We now turn to measures that would reduce their ability to affect governance.

OPEN GOODS AND CAPITAL MARKETS

The most effective way to reduce the power of incumbents to affect legislation is to keep domestic markets open to international competition. It is especially important to keep financial markets open. This is the main lesson we have drawn from our historical analysis, a lesson that cannot be overstressed today at a time of growing opposition to open borders. Countries have little incentive to close their borders to trade and capital flows unilaterally when the rest of the world is open. This is because goods and capital will leak through anyway unless the country goes the totalitarian route of a Cuba or a North Korea. But a mass movement against open borders, even if only in a few large countries, can make it attractive for politicians to close borders. This is the danger posed by the growing antiglobalization protests that have become louder, larger, and more violent in recent years.

To these growing protests, economists have responded by emphasizing the efficiency gains generated by international trade—through the law of comparative advantage—which allow countries to specialize in the product they produce best, enhancing worldwide production and making all countries better off.[12] On the other hand, economists have generally been lukewarm in their support for free international capital movement. While we certainly do not dismiss the importance of the efficiency gains generated by trade, we emphasize a different argument in favor of openness: its effect in reducing the power of domestic incumbents. Free movement of capital plays a central role here.

Why, according to us, is openness beneficial? The answer is blindingly simple. Openness creates competition from outsiders—outsiders that incumbents cannot control through political means. A commitment to openness forces incumbents to abandon politics and focus on the tougher task of defending their position in the marketplace the hard way: by becoming more efficient. Because the United States could not dictate British financial regulation, the Euromarket flourished and was able to threaten U.S. dominance in the financial world. Eventually, the competition and alternatives the Euromarket generated helped the development of financial markets in both the United States and the United Kingdom, as well as in many other countries around the world. Put another way, openness forces political authorities to compete in improving the general economic well-being of the entities they rule. To the extent that political authorities would otherwise tend to focus on the well-being of an influential few rather than the unimportant many, openness tends to benefit economies that open up.

While openness is clearly beneficial for developed economies with sound infrastructure underlying their goods and financial markets, we have seen that sudden liberalization can be risky for underdeveloped economies. Even if a liberal, market-oriented economy is more productive and fair, economies that have spent decades protected from competition need to create the institutions that will permit a functioning market economy. Subjecting these economies at short order to the full gale-force winds of international competition may be harmful, in part because it may wipe out those very constituencies—the professional classes, small and medium-sized entrepreneurs, commercial farmers—that can push for a market economy.

The right policy for the large developing economy, according to some, is to limit competition until the institutions necessary for a market economy are in place.[13] But there is a great risk in such a policy of gradualism: by slowing down the liberalization process, it might bring it to a standstill. If incumbents knew that opening up to competition hinges on infrastructure and skills being improved, they would simply block any movement on either front. In fact, while gradualism would predict that financial-sector reforms should precede the opening up of a country to capital flows, in practice they seem to follow it.[14] So the dilemma for a developing country that has a reforming government is how to create a commitment to increase the level of competition while allowing time for market institutions to be built.

PROVIDE INCENTIVES THROUGH TRADING ZONES

The best way the outside world can help is to provide incentives for reform. Richer countries, which have come together in large trading zones, have a very powerful instrument to encourage, rather than force, reforms.[15] If they offer membership in their trading zones conditional on certain market infrastructure's being built, they create the political incentive to undertake those reforms and not postpone them indefinitely. By using the carrot of the opportunity to trade with a large group of countries (like the European Union or NAFTA), they make reform politically appealing for the developing or transition economy and thus credible.[16] It is impressive how much Turkey is trying to change, not only its economic structure, but also its respect for human rights, as exemplified in its treatment of the Kurds, so as to qualify for membership in the European Union.

There are, of course, countries that do not fit naturally into any such zone. Nevertheless, the broad principle of providing incentives for reform again applies here. Developed countries could do a great deal for the cause of markets, both in their countries and around the world, by stopping subsidies to their domestic agricultural sector and reducing the degree of trade barriers in goods like textiles. Farmers and small entrepreneurs in developing countries, who have a better chance of growing rich if protectionism in developed countries is reduced, can be a great force for creating vibrant, open markets in their own countries, much as they have been in the developed world.

Public Awareness

Throughout the book, we have argued that organized vested interests drive government policies. We have also claimed that promarket forces, while in a majority, are weak, dispersed, and typically no match for antimarket interests. Then at whom is this book, especially this chapter, aimed? What hope do we have that any of our recommendations will be implemented, since they are not meant to favor any organized interests?

Our conviction of the power of narrow interests does not blind us into thinking that the public and its beliefs do not matter. The antimarket reaction during the Great Depression was made possible because the public was all too willing to believe that the market was fatally flawed. Similarly, the promarket wave in recent decades has thrived on stories about the wastefulness of the government. The wheel is turning again with stories of corporate scandals and greed. The truth, clearly, lies somewhere in between. Unfortunately, the truth is usually complicated. One reason politicians ignore the public interest with impunity is that they believe the public is often not aware of what that interest is and cannot be bothered to find out. If these politicians are right, then this book may have some educational value but little else.

If, however, the public is willing to listen provided economists are willing to make an effort to communicate their ideas, then books like ours have a chance of influencing our world in a small way. Our purpose has been to show that even though government intervention is necessary for the functioning of markets, the nature of the intervention has typically gone toward favoring the few, against the public interest. Our purpose is to make more people think like economists do, to make more people see the Japanese car registration fees, which are set to effectively prevent cars that are more than five years of age from running on the streets, as a disguised subsidy to car companies rather than simply sound environmental practice.[17]

If the wider public sees the benefits of free markets and understands their political fragility, it will be harder for narrow interest groups to push their own agenda. It will become easier for public-spirited politicians (we do not deny that there are some) to propose sound, politically feasible reforms. And the world will become a fairer and better place.

Summary

Given that there are political forces arrayed against the market, how can a promarket government put in place measures that might weaken those forces? We have offered some suggestions in this chapter. We called for an integrated approach, which addresses both the incentives of the parties involved and their ability to influence policy against free markets. Specifically, we propose measures that would result in efficient but not overly concentrated ownership of productive assets, instill flexibility in the labor force to adapt to change, provide a safety net in cases of extreme distress, and create the external competition that will prevent the regulatory apparatus from becoming overly oppressive.

None of the measures we have suggested is outside the realm of possibility. We propose them not because they are individually original but because they have some chance of being enacted, and as a package, they will bring greater structural stability to the market economy.

Conclusion

AFTER TWO DECADES of massive privatization, sweeping deregulation, and widespread liberalization, it may seem absurd for us to claim that free markets could be in danger. In fact, events such as the collapse of Enron are interpreted as evidence that markets have become too free. After all, in the "good old days" of regulated public utilities, such problems did not arise.

In this book, we argue otherwise. Not only are markets not too free, but they cannot possibly become too free: markets are always shackled and suppressed, because they rest on very fragile political foundations. While everyone benefits from competitive markets, no one in particular makes huge profits from keeping the system competitive and the playing field level. Even capitalists do not gain from defending it. Indeed, in their continuous quest for government protection from competition, they often turn out to be capitalism's worst enemies. Without a strong political constituency supporting them and under the continuous pressure of vested interests, markets are always too restricted, never too free.

This is not to say that the markets do not need rules. Our ideal of free markets is not the anarchy of the jungle or the Wild West but a transparent, level playing field where everybody has a fair chance of participating and those who provide the best value for the money prevail. In order to become a level playing field, markets need rules. Often, these rules emerge from the competitive process—as in the formation of self-regulating associations—but sometimes, they need to be imposed and enforced by a superior authority. Without properly enforced rules, the law of the jungle, not that of the playing field, prevails.

While the absence of rules makes the playing field uneven, too many rules of the wrong kind might make it uneven again, especially when these rules are introduced (as so often happens) under the pressure of incumbent firms. A truly free and competitive market occupies a very delicate middle ground between the absence of rules and the presence of suffocating rules. It is because this middle ground is so narrow that capitalism in its best form is very unstable. It easily degenerates into a system of the incumbents, by the incumbents, for the incumbents. Through much of history, this is the form of capitalism we have experienced, and unfortunately, this is still the form of capitalism prevailing in many parts of the world today.

But a truly competitive market is not just a utopian ideal; it is within our reach. With better financial markets, which give people a chance, and intense political competition, which keeps vested interests in check, in the last two decades, we have experienced the benefits of moving toward that ideal. The greater availability of capital is slowly redressing many of the evils of capitalism—the tyranny of capital over labor, the excessive concentration of industry, the unequal distribution of income in favor of the owners of capital, the lack of opportunity for the poor . . . People have more opportunities to strike on their own, and even when they work within a firm, they are treated better, since firms have become less authoritarian places in which to work.

But all these achievements are far from irreversible. The markets are not perfect, nor is the regulatory superstructure overseeing them. Aberrations like Enron do occur, and some revisions in the system of corporate governance are called for. But the anger of workers and investors who have lost everything should not become the excuse for massive intervention: historical experience suggests that intervention at such times is invariably misdirected. The current storm will blow over—hopefully, without much damage—but what is to prevent a serious crisis from setting back the development of markets for another fifty years?

It is only in recent years that economists have started paying attention again to the institutions underpinning markets. Hence, it is perhaps not surprising how little the public is aware of their political fragility. But too many economists play with elegant models of perfectly competitive markets without asking questions about how markets come about, how they prosper, and how they die. Maybe this bias is simply because most prominent academic economists live in countries where markets function. But it stops them from worrying about the future of their own market economies. And it prevents them from having more of an impact in countries that desperately need sound economics.

When, ten years ago, economists from the West were called to advise countries facing the difficult transition from socialism to the market, they saw their task as primarily that of creating basic institutions. For example, they thought that once state-owned assets were transformed into private property, many of the other institutions necessary for a market economy would follow. But economic institutions neither arise nor flourish unless there is political will to back them. And by political will, we do not mean support for the privatization process only, but also the creation of groups that will benefit from free markets and have the clout to support them politically. This is what Henry VII and Henry VIII did, probably unconsciously, when they "privatized" the land expropriated from the church and the nobles. This is what did not happen in many countries in Eastern Europe. We need to understand the political underpinnings of markets better so as to build greater support for them.

Unfortunately, the battle for markets does not have to be fought only in transition economies. It has to be fought every day even in the most developed countries. Markets need political support, yet their very functioning undermines the support. As a result, the market is a fragile institution, charting a narrow path between the Scylla of overweening government interference and the Charybdis of too little government support.

The greatest danger for the market democracy today is not that it will lapse into socialism, but that it will revert to the relationship system, suppressing competition under the excuse of reducing risk. But we cannot avoid this by preaching a hands-off attitude for the state. Not only will we risk leaving the necessary infrastructure underdeveloped so that the market works poorly and access is limited to the privileged few, but we will also leave the market overexposed to the political backlash from the inevitable market downturn. It is precisely because we need a balance of forces that no single mantra will work.

Instead, we offer a balanced set of proposals, which taken together will fortify the political foundations of the market. The proposals ensure that incumbents have little incentive to oppose markets; that even if incumbents want to hamper competition, they have little ability to do so; that the public does not fear or resent the market overly; and that the public at large sees the vested interests of those who oppose them.

But perhaps most important is the message of the overall book. Politicians disregard the public interest because the public is often unaware of what that interest is. If books like ours can raise public awareness, they reduce one important cost of collective action—the cost of understanding the issues—and force politicians to pay attention. If we have succeeded in convincing the reader—at least, in part—then this book has fulfilled its objective.

NOTES

INTRODUCTION

1 Muhammad Yunus, *Banker to the Poor: The Autobiography of Muhammad Yunus, Founder of the Grameen Bank* (London: Aurum Press, 1998), 46–48.

2 Ibid.

3 The description of the search fund relies on Professor Howard Stevenson, "Early Career LBOs Using the Search Fund Mode," HBS case note 9-897-092. We thank Kevin Taweel and Jim Ellis for consenting to be interviewed for this book.

4 Center for Entrepreneurial Studies at Stanford University, *Search Fund Study—2001*, www.gsb.stanford/ces/search_funds_study_2001.html.

5 This is from David Eltis's work, cited by Kenneth Sokoloff in "Institutions, Factor Endowments, and Paths of Development in the New World" (UCLA, working paper, 2000).

6 Adam Smith, *The Wealth of Nations*, Book 1, Chapter II, ed. Edwin Canan (1776; Chicago: University of Chicago Press, 1976), 278.

7 See Kathy He, Randall Morck, and Bernard Yeung, "Corporate Stability and Economic Growth" (New York University, working paper).

8 See Stanley Engerman and Kenneth Sokoloff, "Factor Endowments, Institutions, and Differential Paths of Growth among New World Economies: A View from Economic Historians of the United States," NBER historical working paper no. 66, 1994.

9 See D. Acemoglu, S. Johnson, and J. Robinson, "The Colonial Origins of Comparative Development: An Empirical Study," *American Economic Review* 91 (2001): 1369–1401, on the differences in the nature of European rule based on mortality rates.

10 For low education, see Kenneth Sokoloff and Stanley L. Engerman, "Institutions, Factors Endowment, and Paths of Development in the New World," *Journal of Economic Perspective* 14 (2000): 217–232; for poor finance, see Stephen Haber, "Financial Markets and Industrial Development: A Comparative Study of Governmental Regulation, Financial Innovation, and Industrial Structure in Brazil and Mexico, 1840–1930," in *How Latin America Fell Behind*, ed. Stephen Haber (Stanford, Calif.: Stanford University Press, 1997).

11 From Gabriel Kirkpatrick, "Rural Credit in North Carolina." CUNA, www.cuna.org/dats/cu/research/irc/archive4_1.html.

12 See R. Kroszner and P. Strahan, "What Drives Deregulation? Economics and Politics of the Relaxation of Bank Branching Restrictions," *Quarterly Journal of Economics*, November 1999: 1437–1467, and Jith Jayaratne and Philip Strahan, "Entry Restrictions, Industry Evolution, and Dynamic Efficiency: Evidence from Commercial Banking," *Journal of Law and Economics* 41 (1998): 239–274.

13 Address on April 3, 1913, of Mr. Bryce, president of the International Congress of Historical Studies, cited in E. Powell, *The Evolution of the Money Market (1385–1915): A Historical and Analytical Study of the Rise and Development of Finance as a Centralized Coordinated Force* (London: The Financial News, 1915), 704.

1. DOES FINANCE BENEFIT ONLY THE RICH?

1 Tom Wolfe, *The Bonfire of the Vanities* (New York: Farrar, Straus and Giroux, 1987), 229. This passage is also cited in Daniel Fischel, *Payback: The Conspiracy to Destroy Michael Milken and His Revolution* (New York: Harper Business, 1995).

2 Cited in Louis D. Brandeis, *Other People's Money* (Washington, DC: National Home Library Foundation, 1933), 1.

3 See J. Stiglitz and A. Weiss, "Credit Rationing in Markets with Imperfect Information," *American Economic Review* 71 (1981): 393–410.

4 For work on collateral, see Yuk Shee Chan and Ajan V. Thakor, "Collateral and Competitive Equilibria with Moral Hazard and Private Information," *Journal of Finance* 42 (1987): 345–364, and D. Besanko and A. Thakor, "Collateral and Rationing: Sorting Equilibria in Monopolistic and Competitive Credit Markets," *International Economic Review* 28 (1987): 671–689.

5 It is important that Shylock hate the merchant, else he would not want to collect on the pound of flesh, and the threat to collect it would not be credible.

6 T. Jappelli, M. Pagano, and M. Bianco, "Courts and Banks: Effects of Judicial Enforcement of Credit Markets," CEPR working paper no. 3347, April 2002. Similar studies include M. Chiuri and T. Jappelli, "Credit Market Imperfections and Home Ownership: A Comparative Study," CEPR discussion paper no. 2717, 2001; D. Fabbri and Mario Padula, "Judicial Costs and Household Debt," working paper, Center for Studies in Economics and Finance, University of Salerno, Italy, 2001; Lee Alston, "Farm Foreclosure Moratorium Legislation: A Lesson from the Past," *American Economic Review* 74, no. 3 (1984): 445–458; and R. Gropp, J. Scholz, and M. White, "Personal Bankruptcy and Credit Supply and Demand," *Quarterly Journal of Economics* 112 (1997): 217–251.

7 Gropp, Scholz, and White, "Personal Bankruptcy and Credit Supply and Demand," 217–251.

8 Hernando de Soto, *The Mystery of Capital: Why Capitalism Triumphs in the West and Fails Everywhere Else* (New York: Basic Books, 2000).

9 See, for example, M. Petersen and R. Rajan, "The Benefits of Lending Relationships: Evidence from Small Business Data," *Journal of Finance* 49 (1994): 3–37.

10 Luigi Guiso and Luigi Zingales, "The Rise of Bank Relationships," University of Chicago, working paper, 1999.

11 Naomi Lamoreaux, *Insider Lending: Banks, Personal Connections and Economic Development in Industrial New England* (Cambridge, U.K.: Cambridge University Press, 1994).

12 See R. G. Rajan, "Insiders and Outsiders: The Choice between Informed and Arm's Length Debt," *Journal of Finance* 47 (1992): 1367–1400.

13 Pujo Committee report, as cited in Brandeis, *Other People's Money*, 31.

14 E. J. Hobsbawm, *The Age of Capital, 1848–1885* (New York: New American Library, 1979), 242.

15 See Harris Corporation, *Business History Review*, "Founding Dates of the 1994 Fortune 500 U.S. Companies," spring 1996, 69–90.

16 See J. Fear, "German Capitalism," in *Creating Modern Capitalism: How Entrepreneurs, Companies, and Countries Triumphed in Three Industrial Revolutions*, ed. T. McCraw (Cambridge, Mass.: Harvard University Press, 1997), 181.

17 See R. W. Fogel, *The Fourth Great Awakening and the Future of Egalitarianism* (Chicago: University of Chicago Press, 2000), 112, and the references there.

18 T. McCraw, "American Capitalism," in *Creating Modern Capitalism*, 320.

19 A. Chandler, *Scale and Scope: The Dynamics of Industrial Capitalism* (Cambridge, Mass.: Belknap Press, 1990), 18.

20 R. Chernow, *Titan: The Life of John D. Rockefeller* (New York: Random House, 1998), 226.

21 Chandler, *Scale and Scope*, 25.

22 Chernow, *Titan*, 288.

23 Chandler, *Scale and Scope*, 25.

24 Chernow, *Titan*, 265.

25 David Blau, "A Time Series Analysis of Self-Employment in the United States," *Journal of Political Economy* 95, no. 3 (1987): 445–468.

26 For a model of this phenomenon, see R. Rajan and L. Zingales, "The Firm as a Dedicated Hierarchy: A Theory of the Origins and Growth of Firms," *Quarterly Journal of Economics* 116 (2001): 805–852.

27 Chandler, *Scale and Scope*, 598.

28 See L. Stole and J. Zwiebel, "Organizational Design and Technology Choice under Intra-Firm Bargaining," *American Economic Review* 86 (1996): 195–223, for a model of overstaffing by the owners to appropriate rents.

29 In short, the vertically integrated corporation used a number of sources of motivation. Internal competition and bureaucratization of routines kept workers from becoming too indispensable, while the possibility of promotion to more powerful positions kept them from becoming demotivated. See Rajan and Zingales, "The Firm as a Dedicated Hierarchy."

30 Claudia Goldin and Lawrence Katz, "The Returns to Skill in the United States across the Twentieth Century," NBER working paper 7126, 1999.

31 Dani Rodrik, "Democracies Pay Higher Wages," NBER working paper 6364, 1998.

2: SHYLOCK TRANSFORMED

1 For the effects of liberalization on premiums, see Anusha Chari and Peter Henry, "Does Diversification Drive Stock Price Revaluation?" Stanford research paper

no. 1677, 2001; for effects on investment, see Peter Henry, "Stock Market Liberalization, Economic Reform and Emerging Market Equity Price," *Journal of Finance* 55 (2000): 529–564.

2 Technically, derivatives are contracts whose payoff is a function of (or is derived from) the value of another underlying security. A call option on Microsoft shares, for instance, gives the buyer the right, but not the obligation, to purchase Microsoft shares at a predetermined price (say, $50) within a prespecified period (say, three months). If, in three months, the Microsoft stock price is less than $50, then it is not worthwhile for the buyer to exercise the option. The option expires unused with the buyer receiving nothing. If the price is above $50, the buyer will exercise the option and essentially pocket the difference between the actual stock price that day and $50.

3 This description is largely based on Peter Tufano's article "How Financial Engineering Can Advance Corporate Strategy," *Harvard Business Review* 79 (1996), and on Donald Collat and Peter Tufano, "The Privatization of Rhone-Poulenc," Harvard Business School Case 9-295-049.

4 Kenneth Froot, "The Market for Catastrophic Risk: A Clinical Examination," NBER working paper 8110.

5 Data from Dun and Bradstreet Web site.

6 M. Petersen and R. Rajan, "Does Distance Still Matter? The Information Revolution in Small Business Lending," *Journal of Finance*, forthcoming (2002).

7 Clayton Christensen, *The Innovators' Dilemma: When New Technologies Cause Great Firms to Fail* (Boston: Harvard Business School Press, 1997).

8 A recent study of financial statements across 34 countries for the period 1985–1998 finds that U.S. accounting statements are, overall, most transparent. See Utpal Bhattacharya, Hazem Daouk, Michael Welker, "The World Price of Earnings Opacity," Indiana University working paper, 2002.

9 M. Lang, K. Lins, and D. Miller, "ADRs, Analysts, and Accuracy: Does Cross Listing in the U.S. Improve a Firm's Information Environment and Increase Market Value?" University of Utah, working paper, 2002.

10 R. Morck, B. Yeung, and W. Yu, "The Information Content of Stock Markets: Why Do Emerging Markets Have Synchronous Stock Price Movements?" *Journal of Financial Economics* 58 (2000): 215–260.

11 Jeffrey Wurgler, "Financial Markets and the Allocation of Capital," *Journal of Financial Economics* 58 (2000): 187–214.

12 "Market Says No to UniCredito-Commerz. Alliance," abstracted from *Il Corriere della Sera,* in Italian, *Corriere della Sera,* September 4, 2001. "UniCredito Concerned over Share Price Fall," *Financial Times* (London), September 10, 2001, 24.

13 "Borsa: UniCredito (+5.9%) strappa dopo rottura trattative Commerzbank," AFX News Limited, September 11, 2001.

14 Mark L. Mitchell and Kenneth Lehn, "Do Bad Bidders Become Good Targets?" *Journal of Political Economy* 98 (1990): 372–398.

15 This is known as the Grossman-Stiglitz paradox. See Sanford Grossman and Joseph Stiglitz, "On the Impossibility of Informationally Efficient Markets," *American Economic Review* 70, no. 3 (1980): 393.

16 B. Black, "Does Corporate Governance Matter? A Crude Test Using Russian Data," Stanford Law School, working paper, 2000.

17 Ibid.
18 Alexander Dyck and Luigi Zingales, "Private Benefits of Control: An International Comparison," NBER working paper no. 8711, 2002.
19 R. La Porta, F. Lopez-de-Silanes, and A. Shleifer, "Corporate Ownership around the World," *Journal of Finance* 54, no. 2 (1999): 471–517, provide the first systematic cross-country evidence that institutional underdevelopment could lead to concentrated holdings.
20 The seminal work in this area is Rafael La Porta, Florencio Lopez de Silanes, Andrei Shleifer, and Robert W. Vishny, "Law and Finance," *Journal of Political Economy* 106 (1998): 1113. For a correlation between private benefits and legal protection, see Dyck and Zingales, "Private Benefits of Control."
21 Dyck and Zingales, "Private Benefits of Control."
22 Leora Klapper and Inessa Love, "Corporate Governance, Investor Protection, and Performance in Emerging Markets," World Bank, working paper, 2002.
23 Michael C. Jensen, "Agency Costs of Free Cash Flow, Corporate Finance and Takeovers," *American Economic Review* 76 (1986): 323–339.
24 G. Zachary, "His Way," *Wall Street Journal,* June 2, 1994.
25 The following draws heavily on G. Baker, "Beatrice: A Study in the Creation and Destruction of Value," *Journal of Finance* 47, no. 3 (1992): 1081–1120.
26 Ibid., 1096.
27 O. J. Blanchard, F. Lopez-de-Silanes, and A. Shleifer, "What Do Firms Do with Cash Windfalls?" *Journal of Financial Economics* 36 (1994): 337–360.
28 Ibid., 358.
29 Ibid.
30 Darin Clay, "The Role of Institutional Investors" (University of Chicago, Ph.D. diss., 2001).
31 Ibid.
32 We have work in progress with Stewart Myers of MIT on this.
33 Steven Kaplan and Per Stromberg, "How Do Venture Capitalists Choose and Monitor Investments?" University of Chicago, working paper, 2000.
34 Josh Lerner, "Venture Capitalists and the Oversight of Private Firms," *Journal of Finance* 50 (1995): 301–318.
35 Ibid.
36 Kaplan and Stromberg, "How Do Venture Capitalists Choose and Monitor Investments?"
37 M. Gorman and W. Sahlman, "What Do Venture Capitalists Do?" *Journal of Business Venturing* 4 (1989): 231–248.

3: THE FINANCIAL REVOLUTION AND INDIVIDUAL ECONOMIC FREEDOM

1 For year 1970, R. Rajan and L. Zingales, "The Great Reversals: The Politics of Financial Development in the 20th Century," *Journal of Financial Economics* (forthcoming); and for year 2000, data are from Federation Internationale pour Bourse Valeurs.
2 For year 1970, Rajan and Zingales, "The Great Reversals"; and for year 2000, data are from Federation Internationale pour Bourse Valeurs.

3 *Bank for International Settlements Quarterly Review,* March 2002.

4 Council of Economic Advisers, *Economic Report of the President* (Washington, DC: U.S. Government Printing Office, February 2002), 412.

5 Ibid., 261.

6 Louis D. Brandeis, letter to Robert W. Bruere, *Columbia Law Review* 31 (1922): 7.

7 Louis D. Brandeis, *Other People's Money* (Washington, DC: National Home Library Foundation, 1933), 62.

8 Joel Seligman, *The Transformation of Wall Street* (Boston: Northeastern University Press, 1995), 42.

9 For the evidence that it was politically, not economically, motivated, see George Benston, *The Separation of Commercial and Investment Banking* (Oxford: Oxford University Press, 1990), and Randall Kroszner and Raghuram G. Rajan, "Is the Glass Steagall Act Justified?: Evidence from the U.S. Experience with Universal Banking, 1921–1933," *American Economic Review* 84 (1994): 810–832.

10 The venture capital data are from J. Lerner, *Venture Capital and Private Equity: A Casebook* (New York: Wiley, 2000). According to the International Monetary Fund (International Financial Statistics), Italian gross fixed capital formation in 1997 was L 324.9 trillion, equal to $184 billion at the exchange rate at the time.

11 PricewaterhouseCoopers/Venture Economics/National Venture Capital Association MoneyTree Survey. Www.pwcglobal.com/cy/eng/about/press-rm/PressRel Current/Money_Tree.html.

12 See Fischel, *Payback: The Conspiracy to Destroy Michael Milken,* 24.

13 From 1977 to 1986, data are from B. Holmstrom and S. Kaplan, "Corporate Governance and Merger Activity in the U.S.: Making Sense of the 1980s and the 1990s," *Journal of Economic Literature* 15, no. 2 (2001), 121–144.

14 *Christian Science Monitor,* "Time Might Be Right for a Hunk of Junk," February 11, 2002.

15 Typically, a large order obtains unfavorable prices. Specialists have to hold it for a while before being able to unload it on others. They may also fear that the large trader knows something they do not. They demand compensation for the risk through a lower price.

16 For a detailed description of the effects of the elimination of fixed commissions, see M. Blume, J. Siegel, and D. Rottenberg, *The Revolution on Wall Street: The Rise and Decline of the New York Stock Exchange* (New York: Norton, 1993).

17 P. Gompers and A. Metrick, "Institutional Investors and Equity Prices," *Quarterly Journal of Economics* 116, no. 1 (2001): 229–260; J. Poterba and A. Samwick, "Stock Ownership Patterns, Stock Market Fluctuations, and Consumption," *Brookings Paper on Economic Activity* 2 (1985): 295–357; and *Statistical Abstract of the United States, 2001,* Washington, DC: U.S. Bureau of the Census (2001): 739.

18 *Statistical Abstract of the United States, 2001,* table 1214.

19 Holmstrom and Kaplan, "Corporate Governance and Merger Activity in the U.S."

20 James M. Poterba, "The Rate of Return to Corporate Capital and Factor Shares: New Estimates Using Revised National Income Accounts and Capital Stock Data," NBER working paper no. W6263, 1999.

21 William Shepherd, "Causes of Increased Competition in the U.S. Economy, 1939–1980," *Review of Economics and Statistics* 64, issue 4 (1982): 613–626, cited

in David Audretsch and A. Roy Thurik, "What's New about the New Economy? Sources of Growth in the Managed and Entrepreneurial Economies," discussion paper 44, ERIM, 2000.

22 *Economic Report of the President* (1998, 2001).

23 Audretsch and Thurik, "What's New about the New Economy?"

24 G. Dosi, "Sources, Procedures and Microeconomic Effects of Innovation," *Journal of Economic Literature* 26 (1988): 1120–1171; and Frederic Pryor, "Will Most of Us Be Working for Giant Enterprises by 2028?" *Journal of Economic Behavior and Organization* 44, no. 4 (2000): 363–382.

25 See, for example, B. Carlsson, *The Rise of Small Business: Causes and Consequences,* cited in W. J. Adams, ed., *Singular Europe: Economy and Policy of the European Community after 1992* (Ann Arbor: University of Michigan Press, 1992), 145–169.

26 Erik Bynjolfson, Thomas W. Malone, Vijay Gurbaxani, and Ajit Kambil, eds., *The Impact of the Modern Corporation* (New York: Columbia University Press, 1994); and Nicholas Komninos, *The Effect of Information Technology on Average Firm Size and the Degree of Vertical Integration in the Manufacturing Sector* (American University, Ph.D. diss., 1994).

27 The rest of this subsection relies heavily for quotes and facts on "The Record Industry Takes Fright," *Economist,* January 29, 2000, 69.

28 Ibid.

29 Ibid.

30 *Statistical Abstract of the United States, 2001,* 377. The data are the number of jobs held between the ages of eighteen and thirty-four, measured over the period 1978 to 1998.

31 David Jaeger and Ann Stevens, "Is Job Stability in the United States Falling? Reconciling Trends in the Current Population Survey and Panel Study of Income Dynamics," NBER working paper no. 6650, 1998. Some of this instability may be due to the removal of layers of middle management in the corporate restructurings that took place in the 1980s and 1990s.

32 For a model, see R. Rajan and L. Zingales, "The Firm as a Dedicated Hierarchy: A Theory of the Origins and Growth of Firms," *Quarterly Journal of Economics* 116 (2001): 805–852.

33 Tim Jackson, *Inside Intel: Andy Grove and the Rise of the World's Most Powerful Chip Company* (New York: Penguin Group, 1997).

34 Amar V. Bhide, *Origin and Evolution of New Business* (New York: Oxford University Press, 2000), 94.

35 Martin Caree, Andre van Stel, Roy Thurik, and Sander Wennekers, "Economic Development and Business Ownership: An Analysis Using Data of 23 OECD Countries in the Period 1976–1996," *Small Business Economics,* June 2000; David M. Blau, "A Time-Series Analysis of Self-Employment in the United States," *Journal of Political Economy* 95, no. 3 (1987): 445–467; and D. B. Audretsch, M. A. Carree, A. J. van Stel, and A. R. Thurik, "Impeded Industrial Restructuring: The Growth Penalty," Institute for Development Strategies, research paper, October 2000.

36 B. Carlsson, "The Evolution of Manufacturing Technology and Its Impact on Industrial Structure: An International Study," *Small Business Economics* 1 (1989):

21–37; and B. Carlsson, "Small Business, Entrepreneurship, and Industrial Dynamics," in *Are Small Firms Important? Their Role and Impact*, ed. Z. Acs (Dordrecht, Netherlands: Kluwer Academic Publishers, 1999), 99–110.

37 General Motors annual reports.

38 Rebecca Blumenstein and Fara Warner, "GM Seeks to Make Delphi Unit Independent," *Wall Street Journal*, August 4, 1998.

39 These facts are from S. Davis and J. Haltiwanger, "The Distribution of Employees by Establishment Size: Patterns of Change and Co-movement in the United States, 1962–85" (University of Chicago, 1989, mimeo). An establishment does not correspond to a firm, but it would be surprising if the trends were grossly different.

40 Pryor, "Will Most of Us Be Working for Giant Enterprises by 2028?"

41 This question was first posed by Armen Alchian and Harold Demsetz, "Production, Information Costs and Economic Organization," *American Economic Review* 62 (1972): 777–795.

42 Early antecedents of critical resource theory come from the focus of sociologists like Richard Emerson, "Power Dependence Relations," *American Sociological Review* 27 (1963): 31–41, on the sources of power. Management theorists like Birger Wernerfelt, "A Resource Based View of the Firm," *Strategic Management Journal* 5 (1984): 171–180, and G. Hamel and C. Pralahad, "The Core Competence of the Corporation," *Harvard Business Review* 68 (1990): 79–91, have developed on this theme focusing on the firm's competencies as being the critical resource. The seminal work in economics is S. Grossman and O. Hart, "The Costs and Benefits of Ownership: A Theory of Vertical and Lateral Integration," *Journal of Political Economy* 94 (1986): 691–719, who focus on property rights as a source of power but also address the fundamental question of why power can be noncontractual. Since then, the theory has moved away from Grossman and Hart's focus on property rights as the sole critical resource to other resources (see R. Rajan and L. Zingales, "Power in a Theory of the Firm," *Quarterly Journal of Economics* 112 [1998]: 387–432, or Bengt Holmstrom, "The Firm as a Subeconomy," *Journal of Law, Economics, and Organization* 15 [1999]: 74–102).

43 The data in this paragraph are from *Statistical Abstract of the United States, 2001*, table 593.

44 See Rebecca Demsetz, "Human Resources Needs in the Evolving Financial Sector," *Current Issues*, Federal Reserve Bank of New York, vol. 3, no. 13, November 1997.

45 See Larry Hunter, Annette Bernhardt, Katherine Hughes, Eva Skuratowicz, "It's Not Just the ATMs: Technology, Firm Strategies, Jobs, and Earnings in Retail Banking," Wharton Financial Institutions Center, working paper, 2000.

46 We thank Mark Knez for this example.

47 L. Katz and K. Murphy, "Changes in Relative Wages, 1963–1987: Supply and Demand Factors," *Quarterly Journal of Economics* 107 (February 1992): 33–78.

48 Paul Beaudry and David Green, "Changes in U.S. Wages 1976–2000: Ongoing Skill Bias or Major Technological Change?" NBER working paper no. 8787. One puzzle is that if human capital is becoming more important, why have the factor shares of capital and labor remained relatively constant through much of the century (Thomas Piketty and Emmanuel Saez, "Income Inequality in the

United States, 1913–1998," NBER working paper no. w8467, 2001). A possible explanation is that work is more capital-intensive, reflecting in part the greater availability of capital. Another possible piece of the explanation is that labor is now partly compensated through options.

49 For the organizational problems in dealing with soft information, see Jeremy Stein, "Information Production and Capital Allocation: Decentralized vs. Hierarchical Firms," *Journal of Finance*, October 2002; and A. Berger, N. Miller, M. Petersen, R. Rajan, and J. Stein, "Does Function Follow Organizational Form? Evidence from the Lending Practices of Large and Small Banks," NBER working paper w8752, 2002. For the elimination of middle management positions in banks, see Hunter et al., "It's Not Just the ATMs." For the elimination of such positions in industrial firms, the flattening of their organizational structure, and decentralization see R. Rajan and J. Wulf, "The Flattening Firm," University of Chicago, working paper, 2002.

50 See "John Meriwether by the Numbers," *Institutional Investor*, November 1996, 62.

51 "John Meriwether by the Numbers" reports a conversation between Derek Maughan, the CEO of Salomon, and Gerald Rosenfeld, from Lazard Freres. Maughan asked Rosenfeld what his worst nightmare for Salomon was. "That the arb people would all leave now that Meriwether wasn't coming back," Rosenfeld said. According to Rosenfeld, Maughan shot back: "No way. Those guys are all tied to Salomon."

52 John Gutfreund, Meriwether's boss at Salomon at the time of the crisis, used to walk the trading floors. But his successors were more distant.

53 *Economist*, April 8, 2000, 76.

54 See C. Prendergast, "The Provision of Incentives in Firms," *Journal of Economic Literature* 37, no. 1 (March 1999): 7–63.

55 Piketty and Saez, "Income Inequality in the United States, 1913–1998."

56 Robert Fogel, *The Fourth Great Awakening and the Future of Egalitarianism* (London: University of Chicago Press, 2000), 219.

4: THE DARK SIDE OF FINANCE

1 International Financial Risk Institute, "Not Just One Man—Barings," http://newrisk.ifci.ch/137550.htm.

2 For a model of this, see Douglas Diamond and Raghuram Rajan, "Liquidity Risk, Liquidity Creation and Financial Fragility: A Theory of Banking," *Journal of Political Economy* 109 (2001): 287–327.

3 For a model, see S. Myers and R. Rajan, "The Paradox of Liquidity," *Quarterly Journal of Economics* 113, no. 3 (August 1998).

4 One way to define market efficiency is that prices equal fundamental value. The second way is that it is very hard to earn excess risk-adjusted returns. For classic discussions, see Eugene Fama, "Risk, Return, and Equilibrium," *Journal of Political Economy* 78, no. 1 (February 1971): 289–298; and Eugene Fama, "Efficient Capital Markets II," *Journal of Finance* 46, no. 5 (December 1991): 1575–1617.

5 L. Roshental and C. Young, "The Seemingly Anomalous Price Behavior of Royal Dutch Shell and Unilever nv/plc," *Journal of Financial Economics* 26 (1990):

123–141. K. Froot and E. Debora, "How Are Stock Prices Affected by the Location of Trade?" *Journal of Financial Economics* 53 (1999): 189–216.

6 We base our account on O. Lamont and R. Thaler, "Can the Market Add and Subtract? Mispricing in Tech-Stock Carve-outs," working paper, University of Chicago, 2000. See also Brad Cornell and Qiao Liu, "The Parent Company Puzzle: When Is the Whole Worth Less Than One of the Parts?" *Journal of Corporate Finance* 7, no. 6 (2000): 341–366; Michael Schill and Chunsheng Zhou, "Pricing an Emerging Industry: Evidence from Internet Subsidiary Carve-guts," and Mark Mitchell, Todd Pulvino, and Erik Stafford, "Limited Arbitrage in Equity Markets," *Journal of Finance* 32, no. 2 (February 2002). For an accessible and prescient history of the Internet boom, see Michael J. Mandel, *The Coming Internet Depression: Why the High-Tech Boom Will Go Bust, Why the Crash Will Be Worse Than You Think, and How to Prosper Afterward* (New York: Basic Books, 2000).

7 Another pertinent question is "Why are you telling us?," a question that should be asked of all those who peddle books with titles like *How to Make a Million on the Stock Market in Your Sleep.*

8 Michael C. Jensen, "Some Anomalous Evidence Regarding Market Efficiency," *Journal of Financial Economics* 6 (1978): 95–101.

9 See L. Summers, "Does the Stock Market Rationally Reflect Fundamental Values?" *Journal of Finance* 41, issue 3 (1986): 591–600, for a criticism of tests of efficient markets. For a wonderful book on market irrationality, see Robert Shiller, *Irrational Exuberance* (New York: Broadway Books, 2001).

10 The seminal article here is A. Shleifer and R. Vishny, "The Limits to Arbitrage," *Journal of Finance* 52, no. 1 (1997), 35–56.

11 See Carol Loomis, "A House Built on Sand," *Fortune Magazine*, October 26, 1998, and David Shirreff, "Five Days That Shook the World," *Euromoney* (November 10, 1998), for the figures that are cited in the next few paragraphs.

12 Eli Ofek and Matthew Richardson, "DotCom Mania: A Survey of Market Efficiency in the Internet Sector," working paper, New York University, 2001.

13 Justin Baer, "Buyback, Palm Distribution Boost 3Com Shares," *Chicago Sun Times*, May 9, 2000.

14 Ofek and Richardson, "DotCom Mania."

15 The other reason why the arbitrage might not have been feasible is that to implement it, investors had to borrow Palm shares and sell them. Since 3Com floated only 5 percent of Palm shares, only a few shares were physically available, and most of them were held by individual investors, who generally do not lend them. Hence, borrowing Palm shares became extremely costly, if not outright impossible.

16 Lamont and Thaler, "Can the Market Add and Subtract?," 27.

17 See, for example, Merton Miller's presidential address to the American Finance Association (Merton Miller, "Debt and Taxes," *Journal of Finance* 32 (1977): 261–275).

18 Ofek and Richardson, "DotCom Mania."

19 In a study one of us did, we found that the extent of analysts' following an initial public offering increases the initial returns experienced by investors (Raghuram

Rajan and Henri Servaes, "Analyst Following of Initial Public Offerings," *Journal of Finance* 52 [1997]: 507–529).

20 Ofek and Richardson, "DotCom Mania."

21 See Barbara Donnelly and Michael Sesit, "U.S. Bears Bets May Roil Japan's Turmoil," *Wall Street Journal*, April 17, 1990. More generally, the introduction of options on a stock reduces the stock market price by 5 percent (see Sorin Sorescu, "The Effect of Options on Stock Prices: 1973 to 1995," *Journal of Finance* 55 (2000): 487–514).

22 Cited in R. Wermers, "Mutual Fund Herding and the Impact on Stock Prices," *Journal of Finance* 54, no. 2 (1999): 584.

23 See Judy Chevalier and Glenn Ellison, "Risk Taking by Mutual Funds as a Response to Incentives," *Journal of Political Economy* 105, no. 6 (December 1997): 1167–1200, for evidence.

24 Randall Morck, Andrei Shleifer, and Robert Vishny, "The Stock Market and Investment: Is the Market a Sideshow?" *Brookings Papers on Economic Activity* 2 (1990): 157–202.

25 Oliver Blanchard, Changyong Rhee, and Lawrence Summers, "The Stock Market, Profit, and Investments," *Quarterly Journal of Economics* 108 (1990): 115–137.

26 Ibid.

27 James Poterba, comments to "The Stock Market and Investment: Is the Market a Sideshow?" *Brookings Papers on Economic Activity* 2 (1990): 208–213.

28 From www.globalfindata.com.

29 Total nonresidential investments from the Council of Economic Advisers, *Economic Report of the President, 2002,* 342. The 2002 number is estimated on the basis of the first three quarters.

30 Nicholas George, "Sonera Abandons 3G Plans and Returns License," *Financial Times,* August 10, 2001.

31 Dan Roberts, "Glorious Hopes on a Trillion-Dollar Scrapheap," *Financial Times,* September 5, 2001.

32 $809 billion in syndicated loans, $415 billion in the bond market, and $500 billion in the private equity and stock market issues. See Roberts, "Glorious Hopes."

33 G. Kaminsky and C. Reinhart, "The Twin Crises: The Causes of Banking and Balance of Payments Problems," *American Economic Review* 89 (1999): 473–500.

5: THE BOTTOM LINE ON FINANCIAL DEVELOPMENT

1 Kenneth Sokoloff and Stanley L. Engerman, "Institutions, Factor Endowments and Paths of Development in the New World," *Journal of Economic Perspectives* 3 (2000): 217–232.

2 After studying data from thirty-five countries between 1860 and 1963, the economist Raymond Goldsmith concluded, using very careful language, that "a rough parallelism can be observed between economic and financial development if periods of several decades are considered" and "there are even indications in the few countries for which data are available that periods of more rapid economic growth have been accompanied, though not without exception, by an

above-average rate of financial development." Raymond Goldsmith, *Financial Structure and Development* (New Haven, Conn.: Yale University Press, 1969), 48.

3 Or as the Cambridge University economist Joan Robinson once put it, "Where enterprise leads, finance follows."

4 R. King and R. Levine, "Finance and Growth: Schumpeter Might Be Right," *Quarterly Journal of Economics* 108 (1993): 734.

5 Ibid.

6 R. Rajan and L. Zingales, "Financial Dependence and Growth," *American Economic Review* 88, no. 3 (1998): 559–586.

7 J. Jayaratne and P. Strahan, "Entry Restrictions, Industry Evolution and Dynamic Efficiency: Evidence from Commercial Banking," *Journal of Law and Economics* 41, no. 1 (1998): 239–273.

8 See S. Black and P. Strahan, "The Division of Spoils: Rent-Sharing and Discrimination in a Regulated Industry," *American Economic Review* 91, no. 4 (2001): 814–831.

9 J. Jayaratne and P. Strahan, "The Finance-Growth Nexus: Evidence from Bank Branch Deregulation," *Quarterly Journal of Economics* 111 (1996): 639–670.

10 However, there is still a concern. An assumption underlying our example is that the tracks are not changed in anticipation of the train's coming. States may have deregulated their banking systems anticipating greater economic growth and hence a greater need for financing. If so, deregulation may simply precede, but not actually cause, growth. Fortunately, we can exclude this possibility. If states deregulated anticipating growth in financing needs, the volume of bank lending should have exploded after deregulation. It did not! Instead, deregulation led to better credit evaluation and thus improved resource allocation by banks. It is the improvement in the quality of loans the banks made that led to fewer loan losses and more growth.

11 Campbell Harvey and Christian Lundblad, "Does Financial Liberalization Spur Growth?" NBER working paper no. 8245, 2001.

12 Sandra Black and Philip Strahan, "Entrepreneurship and Bank Credit Availability" (MIT, March 2001, mimeo).

13 Rajan and Zingales, "Financial Dependence and Growth."

14 See L. Guiso, Paola Sapienza, and Luigi Zingales, "Does Local Financial Development Matter?" NBER working paper no. 8923, 2002.

15 Much of what follows draws on the work of Stephen Haber, an economic historian at Stanford University.

16 Carlos Marichal in *How Latin America Fell Behind: Essays in the Economic Histories of Brazil and Mexico, 1800–1914*, ed. Stephen Haber (Stanford, Calif.: Stanford University Press, 1997), 122.

17 Ibid.

18 Ibid., 122–123.

19 Haber, *How Latin America Fell Behind*, 157.

20 Ibid.

21 Ibid., 159.

22 Stephen Haber, "Industrial Concentration and the Capital Markets: A Comparative Study of Brazil, Mexico, and the United States," *Journal of Economic History* 51, no. 3 (1991), 559–580.

23 Haber, *How Latin America Fell Behind,* 159.

24 Ibid.

25 Ibid., 151.

26 Ibid., 152.

27 Ibid., 153.

28 Ibid., 156.

29 Ibid., 153.

30 Ibid., 162–163.

31 Ibid.

32 Haber, "Industrial Concentration and the Capital Markets," 562.

33 Ibid., 574.

34 The next few paragraphs draw from Jim Levinsohn and Wendy Petropoulos, NBER working paper no. 8348, 2001.

35 This effect is present even controlling for other regional differences in the economic conditions. See L. Guiso, Paola Sapienza, and Luigi Zingales, "Does Local Financial Development Matter?" NBER working paper no. 8923, 2002.

36 The pattern persists after we account for the influence of a country's per capita GDP and its recent growth rate. One obvious explanation is that billionaires are more likely to own publicly traded firms, and their stock prices tend to be high when the country's equity markets are high. Those who inherit wealth, however, also tend to own stock—the heirs of Sam Walton, the Fords, and the Siemens come to mind—but the relation between frequency of inherited billionaires per million people and stock market capitalization is much weaker. More important, the relationship exists even if we measure financial development in a way that is not directly affected by the level of stock market valuations—such as the number of listed firms per million of population. Countries with better accounting standards also have more self-made billionaires.

37 Randall Morck, David Strangeland, and Bernard Yeung, "Inherited Wealth, Corporate Control, and Economic Growth: The Canadian Disease?" in *Concentrated Capital Ownership,* ed. R. K. Morck (Chicago: University of Chicago Press, 2000).

38 Ibid.

39 Francisco Perez-Gonzalez, "Does Inherited Control Hurt Performance?" Columbia University, working paper, 2002.

40 Joseph A. Schumpeter, *The Theory of Economic Development: An Inquiry into Profits, Capital, Credit, Interest, and the Business Cycle* (New Brunswick, London: Transaction Publishers, 1993), 96.

41 See Asli Demirguc-Kunt and Enrica Detragiache, "Financial Liberalization and Financial Fragility," *Proceedings of the Annual World Bank Conference on Development Economics, 1998.*

42 Ibid., Demirguc-Kunt and Detragiache show that countries that are financially restrained have higher growth even after suffering a banking crisis.

6: THE TAMING OF THE GOVERNMENT

1 This chapter has benefited tremendously from comments by Candice Prendergast. It is partly based on work with Abhijit Banerjee.

2 See D. North and B. Weingast, "Constitutions and Commitment: The Evolution of Institutions Governing Public Choice in Seventeenth-Century England," *Journal of Economic History* 49, no. 4 (1989): 803–832.

3 This is reminiscent of Gary Becker's argument (Gary Becker, "A Theory of Competition among Pressure Groups for Political Influence," *Quarterly Journal of Finance* 98, no. 3 [1983]: 371–400) that economically inefficient policies tend to lose out when in competition with more efficient policies. Our point is that economically efficient owners will be better able to command power than inefficient ones, provided they can come to the fore. Through much of the feudal period, they were not able to do so because of their lack of organization, the suppression of markets, and the primacy of coercive power. It is also related to the idea in S. Myers and R. Rajan, "The Paradox of Liquidity," that illiquid assets are particularly hard to expropriate.

4 Jack Weatherford, *The History of Money: From Sandstone to Cyberspace* (New York: Crown, 1997), 65.

5 Malcolm Barber, *The New Knighthood: A History of the Order of the Temple* (London: Cambridge University Press, 1994), 268.

6 Ibid., 266.

7 Ibid., 270.

8 See Barbara Tuchman, *A Distant Mirror: The Calamitous 14ᵗʰ Century* (New York: Ballantine Books, 1979), 42–44, and Weatherford, *History of Money*, 69.

9 Barber, *New Knighthood*, 298.

10 Richard Pipes, *Property and Freedom* (New York: Knopf, 1999), 17–18.

11 See North and Weingast, "Constitutions and Commitment."

12 Henry Hallam, *Constitutional History of England* (New York: Harper and Brothers, 1876), 26.

13 Bruce Carruthers, *City of Capital: Politics and Markets in the English Financial Revolution* (Princeton, N. J.: Princeton University Press, 1996), 122.

14 North and Weingast, "Constitutions and Commitment," 822–824.

15 See North and Weingast, "Constitutions and Commitment."

16 See Carruthers, *City of Capital*, 122, for a development of this argument.

17 S. E. Finer, *The History of Government*, vol. 3 (London: Oxford Press, 1997), 1271.

18 See H. Pirenne, *Economic and Social History of Mediaeval Europe* (New York: Harcourt, Brace and World, 1937), 63.

19 Lawrence Stone, *Crisis of the Aristocracy* (Oxford: Clarendon Press, 1956), 97.

20 C. G. A. Clay, *Economic Expansion and Social Change: England, 1500–1700* (Cambridge, U.K.: Cambridge University Press, 1984), 70.

21 Ibid., 83.

22 For the greater readiness to use new knowledge by the gentry, see, for example, H. J. Habakkuk, "The Market for Monastic Property, 1539–1603," *Economic History Review* 10, no. 3 (1987): 362–380, and Clay, *Economic Expansion and Social Change*. The passage is from R. H. Tawney, "The Rise of the Gentry, 1558–1640," *Economic History Review* 11 (1949): 16.

23 G. G. Coulton, *The Mediaeval Village* (Cambridge, U.K.: Cambridge University Press, 1925), 13.

24 Ibid., 39.

25 Stone, *Crisis of the Aristocracy,* 121.

26 Finer, *History of Government,* 1338.

27 Many of these historians drew from the investigations of Arthur Young. See the references in Robert Allen, *Enclosure and the Yeoman: The Agricultural Development of the South Midlands, 1450–1850* (Oxford: Clarendon Press, 1992), for a list of his works.

28 See Allen, *Enclosure and the Yeoman,* for a cogent analysis.

29 See Gregory Clark, "Yields per Acre in English Agriculture, 1250–1860: Evidence from Labor Inputs," *Economic History Review* 44 (1991): 445–460, for a time path of productivity increases, and Allen, *Enclosure and the Yeoman,* for the controversies surrounding it.

30 Tawney, "Rise of the Gentry," 75.

31 Hallam, *Constitutional History of England,* 55.

32 Ibid.

33 See, for example, Hallam, *Constitutional History of England,* 36–37.

34 Hallam, *Constitutional History of England,* 35, 38.

35 Ibid., 151.

36 Hallam, *Constitutional History of England.*

37 Pipes, *Property and Freedom,* 33.

38 We are being very imprecise about what part of the landed gentry opposed the monarchy. Certainly, the opposition to Charles I was concentrated among the lower gentry. But it also included elements of the nobility and the upper gentry.

39 G. Negley and J. Patrick, *The Quest for Utopia: An Anthology of Imaginary Societies* (New York: Henry Schuman, 1952), 383.

40 Allen, *Enclosure and the Yeoman,* 305–306.

41 Fredrick Dietz, *An Economic History of England* (New York: Henry Holt and Company, 1942), 263.

42 Ibid., 267.

43 See Allen, *Enclosure and the Yeoman.*

44 Finer, *History of Government,* 1325.

45 Robert Brenner, "Agrarian Class Structure and Economic Development," in *The Brenner Debate,* ed. T. H. Aston and C. H. E. Philipin (Cambridge, U.K.: Cambridge University Press, 1985).

46 Patrick Karl O'Brien, "Path Dependency, or Why Britain Became an Industrialized and Urbanized Economy Long before France," *Economic History Review* 49 (1996): 240.

47 Peter McPhee, "The French Revolution, Peasants, and Capitalism," *American Historical Review* 94 (1989): 1265–1280.

48 See R. Rajan and L. Zingales, "Which Capitalism? Lessons from the East Asian Crisis," *Journal of Applied Corporate Finance* 11 (1998): 40–48, for an early statement of this point in a different context.

49 Regressions available from the authors.

50 In an atmosphere in which property rights are not enforced, it is better for a skilled lord to let the wealth be "buried" in the ground and draw it out at regular intervals to pay his peasants than to convert it into cash and see them take it away.

51 See Kenneth Sokoloff and Stanley L. Engerman, "Institutions, Factor Endow-

ments, and Paths of Development in the New World," *Journal of Economic Perspective* 3 (2000): 217–232.

52 John P. Powelson, *The Story of Land: A World History of Land Tenure and Agrarian Reform* (Cambridge, Mass.: Lincoln Institute of Land Policy, 1988), 89.

53 See Abhijit Banerjee and Lakshmi Iyer, "History, Institutions, and Economic Performance: The Legacy of Colonial Land Tenure Systems in India," MIT, working paper, 2002.

54 See D. Acemoglu, S. Johnson, and J. Robinson, "The Colonial Origins of Comparative Development: An Empirical Study," *American Economic Review* 91 (2001): 1369–1401, for a theory of development based on the pattern of settlement.

55 See, for example, Maxim Boycko, Andrei Shleifer, and Robert Vishny, *Privatizing Russia* (Cambridge: Massachusetts Institute of Technology, 1995). Hindsight is always twenty-twenty. In all fairness, given that there was little in the way of an entrepreneurial class, those who reformed Russia had very little with which to work and not much guidance from past work. Many of the recent advances in institutional economics have come from those who learned from their Russian experiences.

56 Richard Ehrenberg, *Capital and Finance in the Age of the Renaissance: A Study of the Fuggers and Their Connections* (New York: Harcourt, 1928).

7: THE IMPEDIMENTS TO FINANCIAL DEVELOPMENT

1 This account is based on E. Glaeser, S. Johnson, and A. Shleifer, "Coase vs. the Coasians," *Quarterly Journal of Economics* 116, no. 3 (2001): 853–899.

2 Alexander Dyck and Luigi Zingales, "Private Benefits of Control: An International Comparison," NBER working paper no. 8711, 2002.

3 Glaeser, Johnson, and Shleifer, "Coase vs. the Coasians."

4 Dyck and Zingales, "Private Benefits of Control."

5 Glaeser, Johnson, and Shleifer, "Coase vs. the Coasians."

6 Carol J. Simon, "The Effect of the 1933 Securities Act on Investor Information and the Performance of New Issues," *American Economic Review* 79, no. 3 (1989): 295–318.

7 R. La Porta, F. Lopez-de-Silanes, A. Shleifer, and R. Vishny, "Investor Protection and Corporate Valuation," *Journal of Finance* 57, no. 3 (2002): 1147–1171.

8 U. Bhattacharya and H. Daouk, "The World Price of Insider Trading," *Journal of Finance* 57 (2002): 75–108.

9 As quoted in Paul Halpern, Michael Trebilcock, and Stuart Turnbull, "An Economic Analysis of Limited Liability in Corporate Law," *University of Toronto Law Review* 117 (1980): 30.

10 Mancur Olson, *The Logic of Collective Action: Public Goods and the Theory of Groups* (Cambridge, Mass.: Harvard University Press, 1971), and G. Stigler, "Theory of Economic Regulation," *Bell Journal of Economics* 2 (1971): 3–21.

11 Three eminent economists who contributed to the development of this work and who are still active are Sam Peltzman ("Toward a More General Theory of Regulation," *Journal of Law and Economics* 19, no. 2 [1976]: 211–240), Richard Pos-

ner ("Taxation by Regulation," *Bell Journal of Economics* 2 [1971]: 22–50), and Gary Becker ("A Theory of Competition among Pressure Groups for Political Influence," *Quarterly Journal of Finance* 98, no. 3 [1983]: 371–400).

12 These are 1997 data from the Taxi and Limousine Commission, reported in www.schallerconsult.com/taxi/intro.htm.

13 The term *rational ignorance* was coined by Anthony Downs, *An Economic Theory of Democracy* (New York: Harper & Brothers, 1957).

14 See R. Rajan and L. Zingales, "The Tyranny of Inequality: An Inquiry into the Adverse Consequences of Power Struggles," *Journal of Public Economics* 76 (2000): 521–558, for a development of these ideas.

15 Cited in Randall Morck, David Strangeland, and Bernard Yeung, "Inherited Wealth, Corporate Control, and Economic Growth: The Canadian Disease?" in *Concentrated Capital Ownership,* ed. R. K. Morck (Chicago: University of Chicago Press, 2000), 347.

16 Tarun Khanna and Krishna Palepu, "Is Group Affiliation Profitable in Emerging Markets?" *Journal of Finance* 55, no. 2 (2000): 867–891.

17 Simeon Djankov, Rafael La Porta, Florencio Lopez de Silanes, and Andrei Shleifer, "The Regulation of Entry," NBER working paper no. 7892, 2000.

18 This negative relationship is statistically significant, and regression estimates show that it persists after correcting for the level of GDP per capita and a constant term.

8: WHEN DOES FINANCE DEVELOP?

1 Rondo Cameron, *Banking in the Early Stages of Industrialization* (London: Oxford University Press, 1967), 102.

2 Ibid., 103.

3 Ibid., 104–106.

4 Rondo Cameron, *France and the Economic Development of Europe, 1800–1914* (Princeton, N.J.: Princeton University Press, 1961), 84. Also see David Landes, "French Entrepreneurship and Industrial Growth in the Nineteenth Century," *The Journal of Economic History* 9, no. 1 (May 1949), 45–61.

5 Cameron, *France,* 86, 98, 99.

6 Ibid., 100. Also see Niall Ferguson, *The House of Rothschild: The World's Banker 1849–1999* (New York: Viking, 1999), 61.

7 Ibid., 103.

8 Cameron, *Banking in the Early Stages of Industrialization,* 105. Ferguson, *The House of Rothschild,* 62–64.

9 Ibid., Cameron, *France,* 106.

10 Ferguson, *The House of Rothschild,* 82–87.

11 Cameron, *Banking in the Early Stages of Industrialization,* 104.

12 Ibid., 130.

13 Elizabeth Plautet, *The Role of Banks in Monitoring Firms: The Case of Crédit Mobilier* (New York: Routledge, 1999), 14.

14 Ferguson, *The House of Rothschild,* 86–87.

15 The more it changes, the more it is the same thing.

16 Alessandro Aleotti, *Borsa e Industria* (Milan: *Edizioni Comunità*, 1990), 99.

17 R. Kroszner and P. Strahan, "What Drives Deregulation? Economics and Politics of the Relaxation of Bank Branching Restrictions," *Quarterly Journal of Economics* 114, no. 4 (November 1999): 1437–1467.

18 Ibid.

19 M. Petersen and R. Rajan, "Does Distance Still Matter? The Information Revolution in Small Business Lending," *Journal of Finance* (forthcoming, 2002).

20 Kroszner and Strahan, "What Drives Deregulation?"

21 J. Jayaratne and P. Strahan, "The Finance-Growth Nexus: Evidence from Bank Branching Deregulation," *Quarterly Journal of Economics* 111, no. 3 (1996): 639–670.

22 Sofia A. Perez, "From Cheap Credit to the EC: The Politics of Financial Reform in Spain," in *Capital Ungoverned*, ed. Michael Loriaux et al. (Ithaca, N.Y.: Cornell University Press, 1997).

23 Ibid., 170, 190.

24 John Zysman, *Governments, Markets, and Growth: Finance and the Politics of Industrial Change* (Ithaca, N.Y.: Cornell University Press, 1983), 155–156.

25 Ibid., 157.

26 Ibid., 129.

27 Nigel Adama, "L'État c'est nous," *Euromoney*, October 1980, 110, cited in Zysman, *Governments, Markets, and Growth*, 114.

28 Ibid., 133.

29 For one thing, because of product market competition, these firms will now be much less profitable while needing much more investment. Moreover, competition in financial markets will make long-term relationships, through which the traditional financier could have hoped to recover investments, more difficult. Both factors would combine to make finance more difficult.

30 See Frances Rosenbluth, *Financial Politics in Contemporary Japan* (Ithaca, N.Y.: Cornell University Press, 1989).

31 For a detailed account of the Bond Committee, see Mark Ramseyer, "Explicit Reasons for Implicit Contracts: The Legal Logic to the Japanese Main Bank System," in *The Japanese Main Bank System*, ed. M. Aoki and H. Patrick (New York: Oxford University Press, 1994), 238–239, and Rosenbluth, *Financial Politics in Contemporary Japan*.

32 Rosenbluth, *Financial Politics in Contemporary Japan*, 146.

33 Ibid., 149.

34 Ibid., 56.

35 Ibid., 163.

36 Technically, it is the ratio of equity issues by publicly traded companies to gross fixed capital formation, which represents total investments, not just corporate investments.

37 See R. Rajan and L. Zingales, "The Great Reversals: The Politics of Financial Development in the 20th Century," *Journal of Financial Economics* (forthcoming, 2002), for details. Openness to trade is the sum of exports and imports divided by GDP. In drawing this graph, we have adjusted for the obvious relationship that more industrialized countries should have larger equity markets. So we plot

the residual (in a regression of the total equity market capitalization to GDP against a constant and an index of industrialization for the country in 1913) against the product of industrialization and openness. The product of industrialization and openness is meant to capture the fact that openness can only undermine incumbents' opposition to the development of finance, not create a demand for finance where that does not exist.

38 We instrument openness with exogenous drivers of trade such as a country's population to show that the exogenous and predetermined component of trade is correlated with financial development. H. Svalaeryd and J. Vlachos, "Market for Risk and Openness to Trade: How Are They Related?" *Journal of Public Economics* 57, no. 2 (2002), 364–395, find that openness causes financial development, but they do not find evidence of the opposite.

39 Randall K. Morck, David A. Strangeland, and Bernard Yeung, "Inherited Wealth, Corporate Control, and Economic Growth: The Canadian Disease?" in *Concentrated Capital Ownership*, ed. R. K. Morck (Chicago: University of Chicago Press, 2000).

40 Ibid.

9: THE GREAT REVERSAL BETWEEN WARS

1 See Barry J. Eichengreen, *Globalizing Capital: A History of the International Monetary System* (Princeton, N.J.: Princeton University Press, 1996), and Peter Temin, *Lessons from the Great Depression* (Cambridge, Mass.: MIT Press, 1989), for excellent accounts.

2 Eichengreen, *Globalizing Capital*, 31.

3 William H. McNeill, *The Pursuit of Power: Technology, Armed Force and Society since AD 1000* (Chicago: University of Chicago Press, 1982), 339.

4 Eichengreen, *Globalizing Capital*, 4.

5 Temin, *Lessons from the Great Depression*, 11. Charles Feinstein, Peter Temin, and Gianni Toniolo, *The European Economy between the Wars* (Oxford: Oxford University Press, 1997).

6 Charles S. Maier, *In Search of Stability: Explorations in Historical Political Economy* (Cambridge, U.K.: Cambridge University Press, 1987), 87.

7 Cited in Maier, *In Search of Stability*, 84.

8 Franklin D. Roosevelt, *Public Papers and Addresses*, vol. 2 (New York: Russel & Russel, 1933), 11–12.

9 Franklin D. Roosevelt, *Public Papers and Addresses*, vol. 3 (New York: Russel & Russel, 1934), 414.

10 Franklin D. Roosevelt, *Public Papers and Addresses*, vol. 5 (New York: Russel & Russel, 1936), 232–233.

11 Roosevelt, *Public Papers and Addresses*, vol. 2, 264–265.

12 See Kevin H. O'Rourke and Jeffrey G. Williamson, *Globalization and History: The Evolution of the Nineteenth-Century Atlantic Economy* (Cambridge, Mass.: MIT Press, 1999), for an excellent recent survey.

13 David M. Kennedy, *Freedom from Fear: The American People in Depression and War, 1929–45* (New York: Oxford University Press, 1999), 179.

14 Roosevelt, *Public Papers and Addresses*, vol. 2, 202.

15 Luigi Zingales, "The Survival of the Fittest or the Fattest: Exit and Financing in the Trucking Industry," *Journal of Finance* 53 (1998): 905–938.

16 Denis A. Breen, "The Monopoly Value of Household-Goods Carrier Certificates," *Journal of Law and Economics* 20 (1977): 153–185.

17 Sam Peltzman, "Toward a More General Theory of Regulation," *Journal of Law and Economics* 19 (1976): 211–240, and "The Economic Theory of Regulation after a Decade of De-regulation," *Brookings Papers on Economic Activity: Microeconomics* (1989): 1–41, offers a view of regulation in which not just the regulated firms but a variety of interest groups share the spoils in proportion to their political power.

18 Nancy L. Rose, "Labor Rent Sharing and Regulation: Evidence from the Trucking Industry," *Journal of Political Economy* 95 (1998): 1146–1178.

19 Kennedy, *Freedom from Fear*, 177.

20 McNeill, *The Pursuit of Power*, 346.

21 G. Borgatta, "La politica monetaria nel sistema corporativo," *Annali di Economica* 12 (Padova, 1937): 257.

22 Gianni Toniolo, "Crisi economica e smobilizzo pubblico delle banche miste (1930–1934)," in *Industria e banca nella grande crisi 1929–1934*, ed. G. Toniolo (Milano: Etas Libri, 1978).

23 Ibid., 330.

24 P. Mazzucchelli in *Rivista Bancaria* (1933), cited in Aleotti, *Borsa e Industria*, 117.

25 Toniolo, "Crisi economica e smobilizzo pubblico delle banche miste," 329.

26 The chairman of the Confederation of Industrialists stated in front of a parliamentary commission created in 1946 to decide the fate of the state holding company IRI: "From the economic point of view if we could think that the private sector was able to absorb IRI we could say: let's liquidate IRI and have it bought by the private sector. But today we could not think of a private company able to buy, let's say, Ansaldo." Ministero per la Costitiente, 1946, p. 89, cited in F. Barca and S. Trento, "La Parabola delle partecipazioni statali: Una missione tradita," in *Storia del capitalismo Italiano*, ed. F. Barca (Rome: Donzelli Editore, 1997).

27 Toniolo, "Crisi economica e smobilizzo pubblico delle banche miste," 331.

28 Marcello de Cecco and Giovanni Ferri, *Le banche d'affari in Italia* (Bologna: Il Mulino, 1996).

29 Barca and Trento, "La Parabola delle partecipazioni statali," 194.

30 Giancarlo Galli, *Il padrone dei padroni* (Milano: Garzanti, 1995).

31 G. Ferri and S. Trento, "La dirigenza delle grandi bancje e delle grandi imprese: Ricambio e legami," in *Storia del capitalismo Italiano*, ed. F. Barca (Rome: Donzelli Editore, 1997).

32 Galli, *Il padrone dei padroni*, 74.

33 Ibid., 83.

34 Napoleone Colajanni, *Il capitalismo senza capitale* (Milano: Sperling and Kupfer, 1991), 64, as cited in Galli, *Il padrone dei padroni*, 83.

35 Galli, *Il padrone dei padroni*, 9.

36 Barca and Trento, "La Parabola delle partecipazioni statali."

37 Marcello De Cecco, *Saggi di politica monetaria* (Milan: Giuffre, 1968), 40.

38 M. Pagano, F. Panetta, and L. Zingales, "Why Do Companies Go Public? An

Empirical Analysis," National Bureau of Economic Research, working paper, 1995.

39 M. Pagano, F. Panetta, and L. Zingales, "Why Do Companies Go Public? An Empirical Analysis," *Journal of Finance* 53 (February 1998): 27–67.

40 M. Aoki, H. Patrick, and P. Sheard, "The Japanese Main Bank System: An Overview," in *The Japanese Main Bank System*, ed. M. Aoki and H. Patrick (New York: Oxford University Press, 1994), and T. Hoshi and A. Kashyap, *Corporate Finance and Government in Japan* (Cambridge, Mass.: MIT Press, 2001), 59, table 3.2.

41 J. M. Ramseyer and F. M. Rosenbluth, *The Politics of Oligarchy* (New York: Cambridge University Press, 1995), 104.

42 This paragraph is drawn from Hoshi and Kashyap, *Corporate Finance and Government in Japan*, 29.

43 Ibid., 58.

44 Aoki, Patrick, and Sheard, "The Japanese Main Bank System," 44.

45 These figures are from J. Teranishi, "Loan Syndication in War-Time Japan," in *The Japanese Main Bank System*, ed. M. Aoki and H. Patrick (New York: Oxford University Press, 1994), 57, table 2.2.

46 That this was a cartel is further reinforced by Hoshi and Kashyap's observation that security houses that were not part of the 1931 agreement started competing fiercely for underwriting business and continued to underwrite unsecured bonds. Thus, the market itself did not appear to develop a distaste for unsecured bonds. Hoshi and Kashyap, *Corporate Finance and Government in Japan*, 31.

47 Tetsuji Okazaki (1991), 382, cited in Hoshi and Kashyap, *Corporate Finance and Government in Japan*, 61.

48 Hoshi and Kashyap, *Corporate Finance and Government in Japan*, 80.

49 Lucian Bebchuk and Mark J. Roe, "A Theory of Path Dependence in Corporate Ownership and Governance," *Stanford Law Review* 52 (1999): 127–170, develop a theory of path dependence of governance to account for phenomena such as these.

50 Mark J. Roe, *Strong Managers, Weak Owners: The Political Roots of American Corporate Finance* (Princeton, N. J.: Princeton University Press, 1994).

51 See G. Benston, "The Origins and Justification for the Glass-Steagall Act," in *Universal Banking in the United States: What Could We Gain? What Could We Lose?* ed. A Saunders and I. Walter (New York: Oxford University Press, 1994).

52 Paul G. Mahony, "The Political Economy of the Securities Act of 1933," working paper no. 00–11, Social Science Research Network, 2000, 8.

53 R. Kroszner and R. Rajan, "Organization Structure and Credibility: Evidence from the Commercial Bank Securities Activities before the Glass-Steagall Act," *Journal of Monetary Economics* 39 (1997): 475–516.

54 Mahony, "Political Economy of the Securities Act of 1933."

55 See George J. Benston, *The Separation of Commercial and Investment Banking: The Glass-Steagall Act Revisited and Reconsidered* (New York: Oxford University Press, 1990), for general evidence and R. Kroszner and R. Rajan, "Is the Glass-Steagall Act Justified? A Study of the U.S. Experience with Universal Banking before 1933," *American Economic Review* 84 (September 1994): 810–832, for systematic evidence.

56 See Kroszner and Rajan, "Organization Structure and Credibility."

57 See Roe, *Strong Managers, Weak Owners.*

58 See Benston, "Origins and Justification for the Glass Steagall Act," 38.

59 Mahony, "Political Economy of the Securities Act of 1933."

10: WHY WAS THE MARKET SUPPRESSED?

1 Standard and Poor's, "U.S. Steel Tariffs: Who Gains, Who Loses, and at What Price?," March 14, 2002.

2 AISI, "The New Steel Industry," www.steel.org/facts/newsindus.htm.

3 Employment numbers are from Bureau of Labor Statistics, *National Current Employment Statistics,* www.bls.gov/webapps/legacy/cesbtabl.htm. Production numbers from American Iron and Steel Industry, *1997 Annual Statistical Report.*

4 Alan Greenspan, chairman, Federal Reserve Board, before the Senate Banking Committee, July 28, 1999.

5 W. H. Barringer and K. J. Pierce, 256–257, cited in B. Linsey, D. Griswold, and A. Lucas, "The Steel "Crisis" and the Costs of Protectionism," Cato Institute, trade briefing paper, April 16, 1999, 6.

6 www.steelnet.org.

7 *Economist,* "Anger over Steel," March 11, 2002.

8 *Economist,* "Romancing Big Steel," February 14, 2002.

9 W. H. Barringer and K. J. Pierce, 112, cited in Dan Ikenson, "Steel Trap: How Subsidies and Protectionism Weaken the U.S. Steel Industry," Cato Institute, trade briefing paper, March 1, 2002, 5.

10 "Rep. Brown Joins Calls for Immediate Assistance to Steel Industry," press release of the office of Rep. Sherrod Brown, D-Ohio (13th district), December 19, 2001, cited in Ikenson, "Steel Trap," 3 (emphasis added).

11 See Dan Ikenson, "Steel Trap."

12 Gosnell (1937), 321–329, cited in Frances Fox Piven and Richard Cloward, *Regulating the Poor: The Functions of Public Welfare* (New York: Vintage, 1971), 62.

13 Piven and Cloward, *Regulating the Poor,* 63.

14 See an extensive compilation of material on Ponzi at www.mark-knutson.com.

15 See David McCullough, *The Path between Seas: The Creation of the Panama Canal, 1870–1914* (London: Simon and Schuster, 1977).

16 See Marco Pagano and Paolo Volpin, "The Political Economy of Finance," CEPR discussion paper no. 3231, 2002, for a model in which management and workers get together to bilk investors. The former get a quiet life, while the latter get employment security. This is an attractive model. Our point, however, is that the antimarket consensus is much broader and is catalyzed by bad times.

17 Vito Tanzi and Ludger Schuknecht, *Public Spending in the 20th Century: A Global Perspective* (Cambridge, U.K.: Cambridge University Press, 2000), 31.

18 Ibid.

19 Peter Gourevitch, *Politics in Hard Times: Comparative Responses to International Economic Crises* (Ithaca, N.Y.: Cornell University Press, 1986).

20 Harold Wilensky and Lowell Turner, *Democratic Corporatism and Policy Linkages: The Interdependence of Industrial, Labour-Market, Incomes, and Social Policies in*

Eight Countries (Berkeley: Institute of International Studies, University of California, Berkeley, 1987), 12.

21 Steven Nickell, "Unemployment and Labor Market Rigidities: Europe versus North America," *Journal of Economic Perspectives* 11, no. 3 (summer 1997): 55–74.

22 U. Bhattacharya and H. Daouk, "The World Price of Insider Trading," *Journal of Finance* 57, no. 1 (2002): 75–108.

23 Kristian Rydqvist and Kenneth Hogholm, "Going Public in the 1980s: Evidence from Sweden," *European Financial Management* 1 (1995): 287–315.

24 Paul Gompers, "Grandstanding in the Venture Capital Industry," *Journal of Financial Economics* 42 (1996): 133–156.

25 R. La Porta, F. Lopez-de-Silanes, and A. Shleifer, "Government Ownership of Banks," NBER working paper no. 7620, 2000.

26 Dimitri Vittas and Yoon Je Cho, "Credit Policies: Lessons from East Asia," The World Bank, 1994.

27 Ibid.

28 Michael Loriaux, "Socialist Monetarism and Financial Liberalization in France," in *Capital Ungoverned*, ed. Michael Loriaux et al. (Ithaca, N.Y.: Cornell University Press, 1997), 143.

29 Ibid.

30 For the difficulty for large bureaucracies in financing small firms, see A. Berger, N. Miller, M. Petersen, R. Rajan, and J. Stein, "Does Function Follow Organizational Form? Evidence from the Lending Practices of Large and Small Banks," NBER working paper w8752, 2002. For the effects of state ownership on the allocation of credit, see Paola Sapienza, "What Do State-Owned Firms Maximize? Evidence from Italian Banks," Northwestern University, working paper, 2002.

31 For excellent accounts, see E. Helleiner, *States and the Reemergence of Global Finance: From Bretton Woods to the 1990's* (Ithaca, N.Y.: Cornell University Press, 1994), and Robert Skidelsky's authoritative biography of Keynes, especially volume 3: Robert Skidelsky, *John Maynard Keynes: Fighting for Freedom 1937–1946* (New York: Viking, 2001).

32 Keynes (1980), 149, cited in Helleiner, *States and the Reemergence of Global Finance*, 34. The interest rate that really matters for investment is the long-term interest rate. There is much less consensus today that long-term interest rates can be easily manipulated by the government.

33 Helleiner, *States and the Reemergence of Global Finance*, 35.

34 Ibid., 39.

35 Pauly.

36 Peter G. Peterson, *Gray Dawn: How the Coming of Age Will Transform America and the World* (New York: Times Books, 1999), 77.

11: THE DECLINE AND FALL OF RELATIONSHIP CAPITALISM

1 These figures and the ones that follow in this section (unless stated otherwise) are from Stephen Prowse, "Alternative Models of Financial System Development," Federal Reserve Bank of Australia, 1996.

2 This is from Rafael La Porta, Florencio Lopez-de-Silanes, Andrei Shleifer, and Robert W. Vishny, "Legal Determinants of External Finance," *Journal of Finance* 52, no. 3 (1997): 1131–1150.

3 See Julian Franks and Colin Mayer, "Bank Control, Takeovers and Corporate Governance in Germany," *Journal of Banking & Finance* 22 (1998): 1231–1480.

4 See, for example, the discussion in Christoph von Greyerz, "Accounting in Swiss Company Law," *Der Schweizer Treuhander* (March 1984): 85–88.

5 Prowse, "Alternative Models of Financial System Development," 122, citing 1989 OECD study.

6 See Utpal Bhattacharya, Hazen Daouk, and Michael Welker, "The World Price of Earnings Opacity."

7 Graham Searjent, "Why Daimler Went Red over a Share Quote in New York," *Times* (London), October 7, 1993.

8 Cited by Martin Hellwig in "Economics and Politics of Corporate Finance and Control," in *Corporate Governance: Theoretical and Empirical Perspectives,* ed. Xavier Vives (Cambridge: Cambridge University Press, 2000), 109.

9 See Steven N. Kaplan, "Top Executive Rewards and Firm Performance: A Comparison of Japan and the United States," *Journal of Political Economy* 102, no. 3 (June 1994): 510–546.

10 See C. Kester and T. Lueherman, "The Myth of Japan's Low Cost of Capital," *Harvard Business Review* 70, no. 3 (May 1, 1992): 130–140.

11 This analogy is based on work by Raaj Sah and Joseph Stiglitz, "The Architecture of Economic Systems: Hierarchies and Polyarchies," *American Economic Review* 76, no. 4 (September 1986). Also see Franklin Allen, "Stock Markets and Resource Allocation," in *Capital Markets and Financial Intermediation,* ed. Colin Mayer and Xavier Vives (Cambridge, U.K.: Cambridge University Press, 1993), for a different application of the Sah and Stiglitz point.

12 B. Black and R. Gilson, "Venture Capital and the Structure of Capital Markets: Banks versus Stock Markets," *Journal of Financial Economics,* 47 (1998). Jörg Kukies, "Stock Markets for High-Technology Firms and Venture Capital Financing: Evidence from Europe" (University of Chicago, Ph.D. diss., 2001).

13 Kukies, "Stock Markets for High-Technology Firms and Venture Capital Financing."

14 See Paul Carroll, *Big Blues: The Unmaking of IBM* (New York: Crown, 1993), for example, p. 76.

15 Kristian Rydqvist and Kenneth Hogholm, "Going Public in the 1980s: Evidence from Sweden," *European Financial Management* 1, no. 3 (1995): 287–315.

16 Sandra Black and Philip Strahan, "Entrepreneurship and Bank Credit Availability" (MIT, March 2001, mimeo).

17 The description of this case relies heavily on Richard Pascale and Thomas P. Rohlen, "The Mazda Turnaround," *Journal of Japanese Studies* 9, no. 2 (1983): 219–263, and Hoshi and Kashyap (1994). Unless stated otherwise, all figures come from their work.

18 Authors' calculations using the Penn World Tables data.

19 For a discussion of the relative merits of relationship and market-based systems, see R. Rajan and L. Zingales, "Which Capitalism? Lessons from the East Asian Crisis," *Journal of Applied Corporate Finance* 11, no. 3 (fall 1998): 40–48.

20 Vito Tanzi and Ludger Schuknecht, *Public Spending in the 20ᵗʰ Century: A Global Perspective* (Cambridge, U.K.: Cambridge University Press, 2000).

21 There is a long and somewhat obscure history behind this point that inflation is a political phenomenon. See E. M. Bernstein and I. G. Patel, "Inflation and Economic Development," IMF Staff Papers, 1953, for an early version, and Lester Thurow, *The Zero-Sum Society: Distribution and the Possibilities for Economic Change* (New York: Basic Books, 1980).

22 Helleiner, *States and the Reemergence of Global Finance: From Bretton Woods to the 1990's*, 85.

23 Barry J. Eichengreen, *Globalizing Capital: A History of the International Monetary System* (Princeton, N. J.: Princeton University Press, 1996), 129.

24 U.S. government (1973), 128, cited in Helleiner, *States and the Reemergence of Global Finance*, 106.

25 Helleiner, *States and the Reemergence of Global Finance*, 114.

26 Graciela Kaminsky and Sergio Schmukler, "Short-Run Pain, Long-Run Gain: The Effects of Financial Liberalization," working paper, World Bank, 2002.

27 See, for example, Daniel Yergin and Joseph Stanislaw, *The Commanding Heights: The Battle between Government and the Marketplace That Is Remaking the Modern World* (New York: Touchstone, 1999).

28 Prominent among the older critics was Karl Polanyi, *The Great Transformation* (Boston: Beacon Hill, 1944). Among the newer ones is Dani Rodrik, *Has Globalization Gone Too Far?* (Washington, D.C.: Institute for International Economics, 1997).

29 For the classic statement, see Polanyi, *Great Transformation*.

12: THE CHALLENGES AHEAD

1 While Francis Fukuyama qualifies his message at the end of his book, this is what most readers would take away. Francis Fukuyama, *The End of History and the Last Man* (New York: Free Press, 1992).

2 *The Wealth of Nations*, book 1, chapter 10.

3 Ralph Waldo Emerson (May 1837), quoted in Charles Warren, *Bankruptcy in United States History* (Cambridge, Mass.: Harvard University Press, 1935), 56.

4 Ian Domowitz and Elie Tamer, "Two Hundred Years of Bankruptcy: A Tale of Legislation and Economic Fluctuations," Institute for Policy Research at Northwestern University, working paper, 1997.

5 Erik Berglof and Howard Rosenthal, "The Political Economy of American Bankruptcy: The Evidence for Roll-Call Voting, 1800–1978" (paper presented at UCLA, Political Economy of Contractual Obligations, 1999).

6 Noel F. Regis, *A History of the Bankruptcy Law* (Washington, D.C: C. H. Potter & Co., 1919), 143–144.

7 C. Warren, *Bankruptcy in United States History* (Cambridge, Mass.: Harvard University Press, 1935), 37.

8 Ibid., 8.

9 Authors' calculations from R. Freeman and R. Oostendorp, "Occupational Wages around the World Database," NBER (www.nber.org/oww).

10 See Stefanie Lenway, Randall Morck, and Bernard Yeung, "Rent Seeking, Pro-

tectionism, and Innovation in the American Steel Industry," *Economic Journal* 106 (1996): 410–421.

11 M. Huson, R. Parrino, and L. Starks, "Internal Monitoring Mechanisms and CEO Turnover: A Long-Term Perspective," *Journal of Finance* 56 (2001): 2265–2298.

12 Robert Parrino, "CEO Turnover and Outside Succession: A Cross-sectional Analysis," *Journal of Financial Economics* 46 (1997): 165–197, and Michael S. Weisbach, "Outside Directors and CEO Turnover," *Journal of Financial Economics* 20 (1988): 431–461.

13 Rafael La Porta et al., "Corporate Ownership around the World," *Journal of Finance* 54 (1999): 471–517.

14 Francisco Perez Gonzalez, "Does Inherited Control Hurt Firm Performance?" Columbia University, working paper, 2002.

15 Vito Tanzi and Ludger Schuknecht, *Public Spending in the 20th Century: A Global Perspective* (Cambridge, U.K.: Cambridge University Press), 123.

16 Nicholas Barr, *The Welfare State as Piggy Bank: Information, Risk, Uncertainty, and the Role of the State* (Oxford: Oxford University Press, 2001), 269.

17 U.S. Bureau, of the Census, *Population Projections of the United States by Age, Sex, Race, and Hispanic Origin: 1995 to 2050* (Washington, DC: U.S. Bureau of the Census, February 1996).

18 Peter G. Peterson, *Gray Dawn: How the Coming of Age Will Transform America and the World* (New York: Times Books, 1999), 72, taxpayer per pensioner on p. 36.

13: SAVING CAPITALISM FROM THE CAPITALISTS

1 Manjeet Kripalani, "Polishing India's Diamond Business," *Business Week*, September 11, 2000.

2 Ibid.

3 See Mark J. Roe, *Strong Managers, Weak Owners: The Political Roots of American Corporate Finance* (Princeton, N.J.: Princeton University Press, 1994), for a discussion of how the financial sector has been kept from getting too powerful in the United States.

4 Of course, it is possible to concoct an example in which the more efficient producer has a greater incentive to lobby for subsidies (for example, if subsidies are based on quantities produced). The general intuitions on which we rely are that the more efficient producer sees greater value in facing a larger, unrestricted market and also does not worry much about local competition's making a dent in that market, for there is plenty for everyone to share. Moreover, the efficient producer has a higher opportunity cost of spending time lobbying, and finally, if closure is immensely costly, the inefficient producer has a much stronger incentive to lobby for help to stave off otherwise certain closure.

5 Luigi Zingales, "The Survival of the Fittest or the Fattest: Exit and Financing in the Trucking Industry," *Journal of Finance* 53 (1998): 905–938.

6 David Stromberg, "Radio's Impact on Public Spending," Stockholm School of Economics, working paper, 2001.

7 R. W. Fogel, *The Fourth Great Awakening and the Future of Egalitarianism* (Chicago: University of Chicago Press, 2000), 209, suggests that the median

income of those households whose head is older than sixty-five is now equal to the income of those whose head is younger than sixty-five. Since they have fewer dependents, their per capita consumption power should be greater.

8 David Barker, "In Utero Programming of Chronic Disease," *Clinical Science* 95, no. 2 (1998): 115–128. David Barker, "Maternal and Fetal Origins of Coronary Heart Disease," *Journal of the Royal College of Physicians* 28, no. 6 (1994): 544–551. David Barker, "The Fetal Origins of Adult Hypertension," *Journal of Hypertension* Supplement 10, no. 7 (1992): S39–44.

9 U.S. Bureau of the Census, *Historical Statistics of the United States, Colonial Times to 1970* (Washington, DC: U.S. Bureau of the Census, 1975), 55.

10 *Statistical Abstract of the United States, 1999* (Washington, DC: U.S. Bureau of the Census, 1999), 194.

11 See K. Olson, *The G.I. Bill, the Veterans, and the Colleges* (Lexington: University of Kentucky Press, 1974), and T. Skocpol, "The G.I. Bill and U.S. Social Policy, Past and Future," in *The Welfare State*, ed. E. Paul, F. Miller, and J. Paul (New York: Cambridge University Press, 1997).

12 For two excellent books by economists on the virtues of free trade, see Douglas Irwin, *Free Trade under Fire* (Princeton, N.J.: Princeton University Press, 2002), and Jagdish Bhagwati, *Free Trade Today* (Princeton, N.J.: Princeton University Press, 2002). For a dissent, see Dani Rodrik, *Has Globalization Gone Too Far?* (Washington, D.C.: Institute for International Economics, 1997).

13 See Joseph E. Stiglitz, *Globalization and Its Discontents* (New York: Norton, 2002), for a detailed exposition of this view. We do not have the space here to mount a full defense of globalization. But others have. For two excellent nontechnical books, see Thomas Friedman, *The Lexus and the Olive Tree* (New York: Farrar, Straus and Giroux, 1999), and John Micklethwait and Adrian Wooldridge, *A Future Perfect: The Challenge and the Hidden Promise of Globalization* (New York: Crown Business, 2000).

14 Graciela Kaminsky and Sergio Schmukler, "Short-Run Pain, Long-Run Gain: The Effects of Financial Liberalization," World Bank, working paper, 2002.

15 Of course, these trading zones are themselves aberrations. In the long run, we would hope they would give way to free trade.

16 These trading blocks do have adverse effects on overall trade. In the long run, it would clearly be better if they disappeared. In the short run, however, it makes sense to use them while they exist.

17 The fees are described by Phil Spender in "Second Hand Vehicle Imports Equals Doom?" *Economic Times* (Mumbai), January 18, 2000.

BIBLIOGRAPHY

Acemoglu, D., Johnson, S., and Robinson, J. 2001. The colonial origins of comparative development: An empirical study. *American Economic Review* 91, 1369–1401.

Adama, N. 1980. L'État c'est nous. *Euromoney* (October), 110.

Alchian, A., and Demsetz, H. 1972. Production, information costs and economic organization. *American Economic Review* 62, 777–795.

Aleotti, A. 1990. *Borsa e industria, 1861–1989: Gnto omni de rapporti difficuli*. Milan: Edizioni Comunita.

Allen, F. 1993. Stock markets and resource allocation. In Mayer, C., and Vives, X. (Eds.), *Capital markets and financial intermediation*. Cambridge: Cambridge University Press.

Allen, R. 1992. *Enclosure and the yeoman: The agricultural development of the south midlands, 1450–1850*. Oxford: Clarendon Press.

Alston, L. 1984. Farm foreclosure moratorium legislation: A lesson from the past. *American Economic Review* 74, 445–458.

American Iron and Steel Industry, "The New Steel Industry," *www.steel.org/facts/power/newsteel.htm*.

American Iron and Steel Industry: 1997. *Annual Statistical Report*.

Anonymous. 1996. Founding dates of the 1994 Fortune 500 U.S. companies. *Business History Review* 70, no. 1, 69–90.

Anonymous. 2000. "The Knowledge of Monopolies: Patent Wars." *Economist*, 8 April, 76.

Anonymous. 2001. Market says no to UniCredito-Commerz Alliance. *Il Corriere della Sera* (Italian), 4 September.

Anonymous. 2001. Borsa: UniCredito (+5.9%) strappa dopo rottura trattative Commerzbank. *AFX News Limited*, 11 September.

Anonymous. 2002. Anger over steel. *The Economist Global Agenda*, 11 March.

Anonymous. 2002. "Romancing big steel." *Economist* 362 (16 February), 52.

Aoki, M., Patrick, H., and Sheard, P. 1994. The Japanese main bank system: An overview. In Aoki, M., Patrick, H. (Eds.), *The Japanese main bank system*. New York: Oxford University Press.

Audretsch, D. B., Caree, M. A., van Stel, A. J., and Thurik, A. R. 2001. Impeded industrial restructuring: the growth penalty. Unpublished research paper. Bloomington, Ind.: Institute for Development Strategies.

Audretsch, D. B., and Thurik, A. R. 2000. What's new about the new economy? Sources of growth in the managed and entrepreneurial economies. Discussion paper 44. Rotterdam: Erasmus Research Institute of Management.

Baer, J. 2000. Plans for Palm, buyback help boost 3Com shares. *Chicago Sun-Times,* 10 May, 27.

Baker, G. 1992. Beatrice: A study in the creation and destruction of value. *The Journal of Finance* 47, 1081–1120.

Banerjee, A., and Iyer, L. 2002. History, Institutions and Economic Performance: The Legacy of Colonial Land Tenure Systems in India. Unpublished working paper, Cambridge, Mass.: MIT.

Barber, M., 1994. *The new knighthood: A history of the order of the temple.* London: Cambridge University Press.

Barber, T. 2001. UniCredito concerned over share price fall. *Financial Times* (London) 10 September, 27.

Barca, F., and Trento, S. 1997. La parabola delle partecipazioni statali: Una missione tradita. In Barca, F. (Ed.), *Storia del Capitalismo Italiano.* Rome: Donzelli.

Barker, D. 1992. The fetal origins of adult hypertension. *Journal of Hypertension Supplement* 10, S39–44.

Barker, D. 1994. Maternal and fetal origins of coronary heart disease. *Journal of the Royal College of Physicians* 28, 544–551.

Barker, D. 1998. In utero programming of chronic disease. *Clinical Science* 95, 115–128.

Barr, N. 2001. *The welfare state as piggy bank: Information, risk, uncertainty, and the role of the state.* Oxford: Oxford University Press.

Beaudry, P., and Green, D. 2002. Changes in U.S. wages 1976–2000: Ongoing skill bias or major technological change? Working paper 8787. Cambridge, Mass.: National Bureau of Economic Research.

Bebchuk, L., and Roe, M. J. 1999. A theory of path dependence in corporate ownership and governance. *Stanford Law Review* 52, 127–170.

Becker, G. 1983. A theory of competition among pressure groups for political influence. *Quarterly Journal of Economics* 98, 371–400.

Bell, D. 1999. The coming of post-industrial society. New York: Basic Books.

Benston, G. 1990. *The separation of commercial and investment banking: The Glass-Steagall Act revisited and reconsidered.* Oxford: Oxford University Press.

Benston, G. 1994. The origins and justification for the Glass-Steagall Act. In Saunders, A., and Walter, I. (Eds.), *Universal banking in the United States: What could we gain?* (pp. 31–69). New York: Oxford University Press.

Berger, A., Miller, N., Petersen, M., Rajan, R., and Stein, J. 2002. Does function follow organizational form? Evidence from the lending practices of large and small banks. Working paper 8752. Cambridge, Mass.: NBER.

Berglof, E., and Rosenthal, H. 1999. The political economy of American bankruptcy: The evidence for roll-call voting, 1800–1978. Working paper on political economy. Cambridge, Mass.: MIT.

Bernstein, E. M., and Patel, I. G. 1953. Inflation and economic development. Unpublished staff paper. Washington, DC: International Monetary Fund.

343

Besanko, D., and Thakor, A. V. 1987. Collateral and rationing: Sorting equilibria in monopolistic and competitive credit markets. *International Economic Review* 28, 671–689.

Bhagwati, J. 2002. *Free trade today*. Princeton, N.J.: Princeton University Press.

Bhattacharya, U., and Daouk, H. 2002. The world price of insider trading. *Journal of Finance* 57, 75–108.

Bhattacharya, U., Daouk, H., and Welker, M. 2002. The world price of earnings opacity. Working paper. Bloomington, Ind.: Indiana University.

Bhide, A. V. 2000. *Origin and evolution of new business*. New York: Oxford University Press.

Black, B. 2000. Does corporate governance matter? A crude test using Russian data. *University of Pennsylvania Law Review* 149, 2131–2150.

Black, B. and Gilson, R. 1998. Venture capital and the structure of capital markets: Banks versus stock markets. *Journal of Financial Economics* 47, 243–277.

Black, S., and Strahan, P. 2001. The division of spoils: Rent-sharing and discrimination in a regulated industry. *American Economic Review* 91, 814–831.

Black, S., and Strahan, P. 2002. Entrepreneurship and bank credit availability. *Journal of Finance* (forthcoming).

Blanchard, O. J., Lopez-de-Silanes, F., and Shleifer, A. 1994. What do firms do with cash windfalls? *Journal of Financial Economics* 36, 337–360.

Blanchard, O., Rhee, C., and Summers, L. 1990. The stock market, profit, and investments. *Quarterly Journal of Economics* 108, 115–137.

Blau, D. 1987. A time series analysis of self-employment in the United States. *Journal of Political Economy* 95, 445–468.

Blume, M., Siegel, J., and Rottenberg, D. 1993. *For the revolution on Wall Street: The rise and decline of the New York Stock Exchange*. New York: Norton.

Blumenstein, R., and Warner, F. 1998. GM to make Delphi unit independent. *Wall Street Journal*, 4 August, A3.

Borgatta, G. 1937. La politica monetaria nel sistema corporativo. *Annali di Economica* 12, 257.

Boycko, M., Shleifer, A., and Vishny, R. 1995. *Privatizing Russia*. Cambridge, Mass.: MIT.

Brandeis, L. D. 1922. Letter to Robert W. Bruere. *Columbia Law Review* 31, 7.

Brandeis, L. D. 1933. *Other people's money*. Washington, DC: National Home Library Foundation.

Breen, D. A. 1977. The monopoly value of households-goods carrier certificates. *Journal of Law and Economics* 20, 153–185.

Brenner, R. 1985. Agrarian class structure and economic development. In Aston, T. H., and Philipin, C. H. E. (Eds.), *The Brenner debate*. Cambridge: Cambridge University Press.

Bureau of Labor Statistics. *National Current Employment Statistics*, www.bls.gov/webapps/legacy/cesbtabl.htm.

Bynjolfson, E., Malone, T. W., Gurbaxani, V., and Kambil, A. 1994. *The impact of the modern corporation*. New York: Columbia University Press.

Cameron, R. 1961. *France and the economic development of Europe, 1800–1914*. Princeton, N.J.: Princeton University Press.

Cameron, R. 1967. *Banking in the early stages of industrialization.* London: Oxford University Press.

Canan, E. 1976. *The wealth of nations* (Book 1, Chapters 10 and 11). Chicago: University of Chicago Press.

Caree, M., van Stel, A., Thurik, R., and Wennekers, S. 2000. Economic development and business ownership: an analysis using data of 23 OECD countries in the period 1976–1996. *Small Business Economics* 19, no. 3 (November), 271–290.

Carlsson, B. 1989. The evolution of manufacturing technology and its impact on industrial structure: An international study. *Small Business Economics* 1, 21–37.

Carlsson, B. 1992. The rise of small business: Causes and consequences. In Adams, W. J. (Ed.), *Singular Europe, economy and policy of the European community after 1992.* Ann Arbor, Mich.: University of Michigan Press, 145–169.

Carlsson, B. 1999. Small business, entrepreneurship, and industrial dynamics. In Acs, Z. (Ed.), *Are small firms important? Their role and impact.* Dordrecht: Kluwer Academic Publishers, 99–110.

Carroll, P. 1993. *Big blues: The unmaking of IBM.* New York: Crown Publishing.

Carruthers, B. 1996. *City of capital: Politics and markets in the English financial revolution.* Princeton, N.J.: Princeton University Press.

Chan, Y. S., and Thakor, A. V. 1987. Collateral and competitive equilibria with moral hazard and private information. *Journal of Finance* 42, 345–364.

Chandler, A. 1990. *Scale and scope: The dynamics of industrial capitalism.* Cambridge, Mass.: Belknap Press.

Chari, A., and Henry, P. 2001. Does diversification drive stock price revaluation? Research paper 1677. Stanford, Calif.: Stanford University.

Chernow, R. 1998. *Titan: The life of John D. Rockefeller.* New York: Random House.

Chevalier, J., and Ellison, G. 1997. Risk-taking by mutual funds as a response to incentives. *Journal of Political Economy* 105, no. 6, 1167–1200.

Chew, L. "Not just one man—Barings." Case study. International Financial Risk Institute. http://risk.ifci.ch/137550.htm.

Chiuri, M., and Jappelli, T. 2001. Credit market imperfections and home ownership: A comparative study. Discussion paper 2717. London: CEPR.

Christensen, C. 1997. *The innovators' dilemma: When new technologies cause great firms to fail.* Boston: Harvard Business School Press.

Clark, G. 1991. Yields per acre in English agriculture, 1250–1860: Evidence from labor inputs. *Economic History Review* 44, 445–460.

Clay, C. G. A. 1984. *Economic Expansion and Social Change: England 1500–1700.* Cambridge: Cambridge University Press, p. 70.

Clay, D. 2001. The role of institutional investors. Ph.D. dissertation. Chicago: University of Chicago Graduate School of Business.

Colajanni, N. 1991. *Il Capitalismo Senza Capitale.* Milan: Sperling and Kupfer, 64.

Collat, D., and Tufano, P. 1994. The privatization of Rhone-Poulenc. Case 9–295–049. Boston: Harvard Business School.

Cornell, B., and Liu, Q. 2001. The parent company puzzle? When is the whole worth less than one of the parts? *Journal of Corporate Finance* 7, no. 4, 341–366.

Coulton, G. G. 1925. *The mediaeval village.* Cambridge: Cambridge University Press.

Council of Economic Advisers. 1998. *Economic Report of the President.* Washington, DC: United States Government Printing Office.

Council of Economic Advisers. 2001. *Economic Report of the President.* Washington, DC: United States Government Printing Office.

Council of Economic Advisers. 2002. *Economic Report of the President.* Washington, DC: United States Government Printing Office, Table B-77, 412.

Council of Economic Advisers. 2002. The United States in the international economy. *Economic Report of the President.* Washington, DC: United States Government Printing Office, 261.

Davis, S., and Haltiwanger, J. 1989. The distribution of employees by establishment size: Patterns of change and co-movement in the United States, 1962–85. Unpublished working paper. Chicago: University of Chicago.

De Cecco, M. 1968. *Saggi di Politica Monetaria.* Milan: Giuffrre.

De Cecco, M., and Ferri, G. 1996. *Le Banche D'Affari in Italia.* Bologna: Il Mulino.

Demirguc-Kunt, A., and Detragiache, E. 1998. Financial liberalization and financial fragility. Working paper #1917. Washington, DC: World Bank Group.

Demsetz, R. 1997. Human resources needs in the evolving financial sector. *Current Issues in Economics and Finance* (Federal Reserve Bank of New York) 3 no. 13, 1–6.

De Soto, H. 2000. *The mystery of capital: Why capitalism triumphs in the West and fails everywhere else.* New York: Basic Books.

Diamond, D., and Rajan, R. 2001. Liquidity risk, liquidity creation and financial fragility: A theory of banking. *Journal of Political Economy* 109, 287–327.

Dietz, F. 1942. *An economic history of England.* New York: Henry Holt and Company.

Djankov, S., La Porta, R., Lopez-de-Silanes, F., and Shleifer, A. 2000. The regulation of entry. Working paper 7892. Cambridge, Mass.: NBER.

Domowitz, I., and Tamer, E. 1997. Two hundred years of bankruptcy: A tale of legislation and economic fluctuations. Unpublished working paper. Evanston, Ill.: Northwestern University Institute for Policy Research.

Donnelly, B., and Sesit, M. 1990. U.S. bears bets may roil Japan's turmoil. *Wall Street Journal,* 17 April, C1.

Dosi, G. 1988. Sources, procedures and microeconomic effects of innovation. *Journal of Economic Literature* 26, 1120–1171.

Downs, A. 1957. *An economic theory of democracy.* New York: Harper & Brothers.

Dyck, A., and Zingales, L. Cambridge, Mass.: 2002. Private benefits of control: An international comparison. Working paper 8711. Cambridge, Mass.: NBER.

Ehrenberg, R. 1928. *Capital and finance in the age of the renaissance: A study of the fuggers and their connections.* New York: Harcourt.

Eichengreen, B. J. 1996. *Globalizing capital: A history of the international monetary system.* Princeton, N.J.: Princeton University Press.

Emerson, R. 1963. Power dependence relations. *American Sociological Review* 27, 31–41.

Fabbri, D., Padula, M. 2001. Judicial costs and household debt. Unpublished working paper. Salerno: Center for Studies in Economics and Finance, University of Salerno.

Fama, E. 1971. Risk, return, and equilibrium. *Journal of Political Economy* 79, no. 1, 30–57.

Fama, E. 1991. Efficient capital markets II. *Journal of Finance* 46 no. 5, 1575–1617.

Fear, J. 1997. German capitalism. In McCraw, T. (Ed.), *Creating modern capitalism: How entrepreneurs, companies, and countries triumphed in three industrial revolutions* (p. 181). Cambridge, Mass.: Harvard University Press.

Feinstein, C. H., Temin, P., and Toniolo, G. 1997. *The European economy between the wars*. New York: Oxford University Press.

Ferguson, N. 1999. *The house of Rothschild: The world's banker 1849–1999*. New York: Viking.

Ferri, G., and Trento, S. 1997. La dirigenza delle grandi bancje e delle grandi imprese: Ricambio e legami. In Barca, F. (Ed.), *Storia del Capitalismo Italiano*. Rome: Donzelli.

Finer, S. E. 1997. *The history of government III*. London: Oxford University Press. 1271, 1325, and 1338.

Fischel, D. 1995. *Payback: The conspiracy to destroy Michael Milken and his financial revolution*. New York: HarperCollins.

Flanagan, C. S. 2001. *Search fund study—2001*. Stanford, Calif.: Stanford Business School Center for Entrepreneurial Studies.

Fogel, R. W. 2000. *The fourth great awakening and the future of egalitarianism*. Chicago: University of Chicago Press.

Franks, J., and Mayer, C. 1998. Bank control, takeovers and corporate governance in Germany. *Journal of Banking and Finance* 22, 1231–1480.

Freeman, R., and Oostendorp, R. 2000. Occupational wages around the world database. Cambridge, Mass.: NBER (www.nber.org/oww).

Friedman, T. 1999. *The Lexus and the olive tree*. New York: Farrar, Straus, and Giroux.

Froot, K. 2001. The market for catastrophic risk: A clinical examination. Working paper 8110. Cambridge, Mass.: NBER.

Froot, K., and Daboora, E. 1999. How are stock prices affected by the location of trade. *Journal of Financial Economics* 53, 189–216.

Fukuyama, F. 1992. *The end of history and the last man*. New York: Free Press.

Galli, G. 1995. *Il Padrone Dei Padroni*. Milan: Garzanti, Milano.

George, N. 2001. Sonera abandons 3G plans and returns license. *Financial Times*, 10 August.

Glaeser, E., Johnson, S., and Shleifer, A. 2001. Coase vs. the Coasians. *Quarterly Journal of Economics* 116, 853–899.

Goldin, C., and Katz, L. 1999. The returns to skill in the United States across the twentieth century. Working paper 7126. Cambridge, Mass.: NBER.

Goldsmith, R. 1969. *Financial structure and development*. New Haven, Conn.: Yale University Press.

Gompers, P. 1995. Optimal investment, monitoring, and the staging of venture capital. *Journal of Finance* 50, 1461–1490.

Gompers, P. 1996. Grandstanding in the venture capital industry. *Journal of Financial Economics* 42, 133–156.

Gompers, P., and Metrick, A. 2001. Institutional investors and equity prices. *Quarterly Journal of Economics* 116, 229–260.

Gorman, M., and Sahlman, W. 1989. What do venture capitalists do? *Journal of Business Venturing* 4, 231–248.

Gourevitch, P. 1986. *Politics in hard times: Comparative responses to international economic crises.* Ithaca N. Y.: Cornell University Press.

Gropp, R., Scholz, J., and White, M. 1997. Personal bankruptcy and credit supply and demand. *Quarterly Journal of Economics* 112, 217–251.

Grossman, S., and Hart, O. 1986. The costs and benefits of ownership: A theory of vertical and lateral integration. *Journal of Political Economy* 94, 691–719.

Grossman, S., and Stiglitz, J. 1980. On the impossibility of informationally efficient markets. *American Economic Review* 70, 393–408.

Guiso, L., Sapienza, P., and Zingales, L. 2002. Does local financial development matter? Working paper 8923. Cambridge, Mass.: NBER.

Guiso, L., and Zingales, L. 1999. The rise of bank relationships. Unpublished working paper. Chicago: The University of Chicago Graduate School of Business.

Habakkuk, H. J. 1987. The market for monastic property, 1539–1603. *Economic History Review* 10, 362–380.

Haber, S. 1991. Industrial concentration and the capital markets: A comparative study of Brazil, Mexico, and the United States. *Journal of Economic History* 51, 559–580.

Haber, S. 1997. *How Latin America fell behind: Essays on the economic histories of Brazil and Mexico, 1800–1914.* Stanford, Calif.: Stanford University Press.

Hallam, H. 1876. *Constitutional history of England.* New York: Harper and Brothers.

Halpern, P., Trebilcock, M., and Turnbull, S. 1980. An economic analysis of limited liability in corporate law. *University of Toronto Law Review* 117, 30.

Halverson, G. 2002. Time might be right for a hunk of junk. *Christian Science Monitor*, 11 February, 20.

Hamel, G., and Pralahad, C. 1990. The core competence of the corporation. *Harvard Business Review* 68, 79–91.

Harvey, C., Lundblad, C., and Bekaert G. 2001. Does financial liberalization spur growth? Working paper 8245, Cambridge, Mass.: NBER.

He, K., Morck, R., and Yeung, B. 2002. Corporate stability and economic growth. Unpublished working paper. New York: New York University.

Helleiner, E. 1994. *States and the reemergence of global finance: From Bretton Woods to the 1990's.* Ithaca, N.Y.: Cornell University Press.

Hellwig, M. 2000. Economics and politics of corporate finance and control. In Vives, X. (Ed.), *Corporate governance: Theoretical and empirical perspectives* (Cambridge: Cambridge University Press. 109).

Henry, P. 2000. Stock market liberalization, economic reform and emerging market equity prices. *Journal of Finance* 55, 529–564.

Hobsbawm, E. J. 1979. *The age of capital 1848–1885.* New York: New American Library.

Holmstrom, B. 1999. The firm as a subeconomy. *Journal of Law Economics and Organization* 15, 74–102.

Holmstrom, B., and Kaplan, S. 2001. Corporate governance and merger activity in the U.S.: Making sense of the 1980s and the 1990s. *Journal of Economic Perspectives* 15 Cambridge, Mass.: 121–144.

Hoshi, T., and Kashyap, A. 2001. Corporate Finance and Government in Japan. No. 2, MIT Press.

Hunter, L., Bernhardt, A., Hughes, K., and Skuratowicz, E. 2000. It's not just the ATMs: Technology, firm strategies, jobs, and earnings in retail banking. Working paper. Philadelphia: Wharton Financial Institutions Center.

Huson, M., Parrino, R., and Starks, L. 2001. Internal monitoring mechanisms and CEO turnover: A long-term perspective. *Journal of Finance* 56 no. 6, 2265–2298.

Ikenson, D. 2002. Steel trap: How subsidies and protectionism weaken the U.S. steel industry. Trade Briefing Paper No. 14. March 1, Washington, DC: Cato Institute, 3, 5.

Irwin, D. 2002. *Free trade under fire*. Princeton, N.J.: Princeton University Press.

Jackson, T. 1997. *Inside Intel: Andy Grove and the rise of the world's most powerful chip company*. New York: Penguin Group.

Jaeger, D., and Stevens, A. 1998. Is job stability in the United States falling? Reconciling trends in the current population survey and panel study of income dynamics. Working paper 6650. Cambridge, Mass.: NBER.

Jeanneau, S. 2002. Derivatives. *Bank for International Settlements Quarterly Review*, March, 32.

Jappelli, T., Pagano, M., and Bianco, M. 2002. Courts and banks: Effects of judicial enforcement of credit markets. Working paper 3347. London: CEPR.

Jayaratne, J., and Strahan, P. 1996. The finance-growth nexus: Evidence from bank branching deregulation. *Quarterly Journal of Economics* 111, 639–670.

Jayaratne, J., and Strahan, P. 1998. Entry restrictions, industry evolution, and dynamic efficiency: Evidence from commercial banking. *Journal of Law and Economics* 41, 239–274.

Jensen, M. C. 1978. Some anomalous evidence regarding market efficiency. *Journal of Financial Economics* 6, 95–101.

Jensen, M. C. 1986. Agency costs of free cash flow, corporate finance and takeovers. *American Economic Review* 76, 323–339.

Kaminsky, G., and Reinhart, C. 1999. The twin crises: the causes of banking and balance of payments problems. *American Economic Review* 89, 473–500.

Kaminsky, G., and Schmukler, S. 2002. Short-run pain, long-run gain: The effects of financial liberalization. Working paper. Washington, DC: The World Bank.

Kaplan, S. N. 1994. Top executive rewards and firm performance: A comparison of Japan and the United States. *The Journal of Political Economy* 102, 510–546.

Kaplan, S., and Stromberg, P. 2000. How do venture capitalists choose and monitor investments? Unpublished working paper. Chicago: The University of Chicago.

Katz, L., and Murphy, K. 1992. Changes in relative wages, 1963–1987: Supply and demand factors. *Quarterly Journal of Economics* 107, 33–78.

Kennedy, D. M. 1999. *Freedom from fear: The American people in depression and war 1929–45*. New York: Oxford University Press.

Kester, C., Lueherman, T. 1992. The myth of Japan's low cost of capital. *Harvard Business Review* 70, no. 3, 130–140.

Khanna, T., and Palepu, K. 2000. Is group affiliation profitable in emerging markets? *Journal of Finance* 55, 867–891.

King, R., and Levine, R. 1993. Finance and growth: Schumpeter might be right. *Quarterly Journal of Economics* 108, 734.

Kirkpatrick, G. Rural credit in North Carolina. Credit Union National Association (CUNA) Archivist. http://www.cuna.org/data/cu/research/irc/archive4_1.html.

Klapper, L., and Love, I. 2002. Corporate governance, investor protection, and performance in emerging markets. Unpublished working paper. Washington, DC: The World Bank.

Komninos, N. 1994. The effect of information technology on average firm size and the degree of vertical integration in the manufacturing sector. Ph.D. dissertation. Washington, DC: The American University.

Kripalani, M. 2000. Polishing the diamond business. *Business Week* (international ed.), 11 September, 26.

Kroszner, R., and Rajan, R. G. 1994. Is the Glass-Steagall Act justified? Evidence from the U.S. experience with universal banking, 1921–1933. *American Economic Review* 84, 810–832.

Kroszner, R., and Rajan, R. G. 1997. Organization structure and credibility: Evidence from the commercial bank securities activities before the Glass-Steagall Act. *Journal of Monetary Economics* 39, 475–516.

Kroszner, R., and Strahan, P. 1999. What drives deregulation? Economics and politics of the relaxation of bank branching restrictions. *Quarterly Journal of Economics* 114 no. 4, 1437–1467.

Kukies, J. 2001. Stock markets for high technology firms and venture capital financing: Evidence from Europe. Ph.D. dissertation. Chicago: The University of Chicago Graduate School of Business.

Lamont, O., and Thaler, R. 2000. Can the market add and subtract? Mispricing in tech-stock carve-outs. Unpublished working paper. Chicago: The University of Chicago.

Lamoreaux, N. 1994. Insider lending: Banks, personal connections and economic development in industrial New England. Cambridge: Cambridge University Press.

Landes, D. 1963. A chapter in the financial revolution of the nineteenth century: The rise of French deposit banking. *Journal of Economic History* 23, 224–231.

Lang, M., Lins, K., and Miller, D. 2002. ADRSs, analysts, and accuracy: Does cross listing in the U.S. improve a firm's information environment and increase market value? Unpublished working paper. Salt Lake City: University of Utah.

La Porta, R., Lopez-de-Silanes, F., and Shleifer, A. 2000. Government ownership of banks. Working paper 762. Cambridge, Mass.: NBER.

La Porta, R., Lopez-de-Silanes, F., and Shleifer, A. 1999. Corporate ownership around the world. *Journal of Finance* 54, 471–517.

La Porta, R., Lopez-de-Silanes, F., Shleifer, A., and Vishny, R. W. 1997. Legal determinants of external finance. *Journal of Finance* 52, 1131–1150.

La Porta, R., Lopez-de-Silanes, F., Shleifer, A., and Vishny, R. W. 1998. Law and finance. *Journal of Political Economy* 106, 1113–1155.

La Porta, R., Lopez-de-Silanes, F., Shleifer, A., and Vishny, R. W. 2002. Investor protection and corporate valuation. *Journal of Finance* 57, 1147–1171.

Lenway, S., Morck, R., and Yeung, B. 1996. Rent seeking, protectionism, and innovation in the American steel industry. *The Economic Journal* 106, 410–421.

Lerner, J. 1995. Venture capitalists and the oversight of private firms. *Journal of Finance* 50, 301–318.

Lerner, J. 2000. *Venture capital and private equity: A casebook.* New York: Wiley.

Levinsohn, J., and Petropoulos, W. 2001. Creative destruction or just plain destruction?: The U.S. textile and apparel industry since 1972. Working paper 8348. Cambridge, Mass.: NBER.

Linsey, B., Griswold, D., and Lucas, A. 1999. The steel "crisis" and the costs of protectionism. Trade briefing paper no. 4, April 16. Washington, DC: Cato Institute. 6.

Loomis, C. 1998. A house built on sand. *Fortune Magazine* 138, no. 8, 110–116.

Loriaux, M. 1997. Socialist monetarism and financial liberalization in France. In Loriaux M. (Ed.), *Capital ungoverned: Liberalizing finance in interventionist states* Ithaca, N.Y.: Cornell University Press, 143.

Mahony, P. G. 2000. The political economy of the Securities Act of 1933. Working paper #00–11. Social Science Research Network (www.ssrn.com).

Maier, C. S. 1987. *In search of stability: Explorations in historical political economy.* Cambridge: Cambridge University Press.

Mandel, M. J. 2000. *The coming Internet depression: Why the high-tech boom will go bust, why the crash will be worse than you think, and how to prosper afterward.* New York: Basic Books.

McCarthy, F. T. 2000. The record industry takes fright. *The Economist*, 29 January, 69.

McCraw, T. 1997. American capitalism. In McCraw, T. (Ed.), *Creating modern capitalism: How entrepreneurs, companies, and countries triumphed in three industrial revolutions.* Cambridge: Harvard University Press, 320.

McCullough, D. 1977. *The path between seas: The creation of the Panama Canal, 1870–1914.* London: Simon and Schuster.

McNeill, W. H. 1982. *The pursuit of power: Technology, armed force and society since AD 1000.* Chicago: University of Chicago Press.

McPhee, P. 1989. The French revolution, peasants, and capitalism. *American Historical Review* 94, 1265–1280.

Meriwether, J. 1996. By the numbers. *Institutional Investor*, November, 62.

Micklethwait, J., and Wooldridge, A. 2000. *A future perfect: The challenge and the hidden promise of globalization.* New York: Crown Business.

Miller, M. 1977. Debt and taxes. *Journal of Finance* 32, no. 2, 261–275.

Mitchell, M. L., and Lehn, K. 1990. Do bad bidders become good targets? *Journal of Political Economy* 98, 372–398.

Mitchell, M., Pulvino, T., and Stafford, E. 2002. Limited arbitrage in equity markets. *Journal of Finance* 57, no. 2, 551–584.

Morck, R., Shleifer, A., and Vishny, R. 1990. The stock market and investment: Is the market a sideshow? *Brookings Papers on Economic Activity* 2, 157–202.

Morck, R., Strangeland, D., and Yeung, B. 2000. Inherited wealth, corporate control, and economic growth: The Canadian disease? In Morck, R. K. (Ed.), *Concentrated Capital Ownership.* Chicago: University of Chicago Press.

Morck, R., Yeung, B., and Yu, W. 2000. The information content of stock markets: Why do emerging markets have synchronous stock price movements? *Journal of Financial Economics* 58, 215–260.

Myers, S., and Rajan, R. 1998. The paradox of liquidity. *Quarterly Journal of Economics* 113, no. 3, 733–773.

Negley, G., and Patrick, J. 1952. *The quest for utopia: An anthology of imaginary societies.* New York: Henry Schuman.

Nickell, S. 1997. Unemployment and labor market rigidities: Europe versus North America. *Journal of Economic Perspectives* 11, 55–74.

North, D., and Weingast, B. 1989. Constitutions and commitment: The evolution of institutions governing public choice in seventeenth-century England. *The Journal of Economic History* 49, 803–832.

O'Brien, P. K. 1996. Path dependency, or why Britain became an industrialized and urbanized economy long before France. *Economic History Review* 49, 213–249.

Ofek, E., and Richardson, M. 2001. DotCom mania: a survey of market efficiency in the Internet sector. Unpublished working paper. New York: New York University.

Olson, K. 1974. The G.I. Bill, the veterans, and the colleges. Lexington, Ken. University of Kentucky Press.

Olson, M. 1971. *The logic of collective action: Public goods and the theory of groups.* Cambridge, Mass.: Harvard University Press.

O'Rourke, K. H., and Williamson, J. G. 1999. *Globalization and history: The evolution of nineteenth-century Atlantic economy.* Cambridge, Mass.: MIT Press.

Pagano, M., Panetta, F., and Zingales, L. 1998. Why do companies go public? An empirical analysis. *Journal of Finance* 53, 27–67.

Pagano, M., and Volpin, P., 2002. The political economy of finance. Discussion paper 3231. London: CEPR.

Parrino, R. 1997. CEO turnover and outside succession: A cross-sectional analysis. *Journal of Financial Economics* 46, 165–197.

Pascale, R., and Rohlen, T. P. 1983. The Mazda turnaround. *Journal of Japanese Studies* 9, 219–263.

Peltzman, S. 1976. Toward a more general theory of regulation. *Journal of Law and Economics* 19, 211–240.

Peltzman, S. 1989. The economic theory of regulation after a decade of deregulation. *Brookings Papers on Economic Activity*, Microeconomics 1989, 1–41.

Perez, S. A. 1997. From cheap credit to the EC: The politics of financial reform in Spain. In Loriaux, M. (Eds.), *Capital ungoverned: Liberalizing finance in interventionist states.* Ithaca, N.Y.: Cornell University Press.

Perez-Gonzalez, F. 2002. Does inherited control hurt performance? Unpublished working paper. New York: Columbia University.

Petersen, M., and Rajan, R. 1994. The benefits of lending relationships: Evidence from small business data. *Journal of Finance* 49, 3–37.

Petersen, M., and Rajan, R., 2002. Does distance still matter? The information revolution in small business lending. *Journal of Finance*, December, 57.

Peterson, G. P. 1999. *Gray dawn: How the coming of age will transform America and the world.* New York: Times Books.

Piketty, T., and Saez, E., 2001. Income inequality in the United States, 1913–1998. Working paper 8467. Cambridge, Mass.: NBER.

Pipes, R. 1999. *Property and freedom.* New York: Alfred A. Knopf.

Bibliography

Pirenne, H. 1937. *Economic and social history of mediaeval Europe.* New York: Harcourt, Brace and World, Inc.

Piven, F. F., and Cloward, R. 1971. *Regulating the poor: The functions of public welfare.* New York: Vintage.

Plautet, E. 1999. *The role of banks in monitoring firms: The case of Crédit Mobilier.* New York: Routledge.

Polanyi, K. 1944. *The great transformation.* Boston: Beacon Hill.

Posner, R. 1971. Taxation by regulation. *Bell Journal of Economics* 2, 22–50.

Poterba, J. 1990. The stock market and investment: Is the market a sideshow? *Brookings Papers on Economic Activity* 2, 208–213.

Poterba, J. 1999. The rate of return to corporate capital and factor shares: New estimates using revised national income accounts and capital stock data. Working paper 6263. Cambridge, Mass.: NBER.

Poterba, J., and Samwick, A. 1995. Stock ownership patterns, stock market fluctuations, and consumption. *Brookings Papers on Economic Activity* 2, 295–357.

Powell, E. 1915. *The evolution of the money market (1385–1915): A historical and analytical study of the rise and development of finance as a centralized coordinated force.* (London) *The Financial News.*

Powelson, J. P. 1988. *The story of land: A world history of land tenure and agrarian reform.* Cambridge: The Lincoln Institute of Land Policy.

Prendergast, C. 1999. The provision of incentives in firms. *Journal of Economic Literature* 37, 7–63.

Prowse, S. 1996. Alternative models of financial system development. Sydney: RBA Annual Conference Volume 1996–06, Federal Reserve Bank of Australia.

Pryor, F. 2000. Will most of us be working for giant enterprises by 2028? *Journal of Economic Behavior and Organization* 44, 363–382.

Rajan, R. G. 1992. Insiders and outsiders: The choice between informed and arm's length debt. *Journal of Finance* 47, 1367–1400.

Rajan, R., and Servaes, H. 1997. Analyst following of initial public offerings. *Journal of Finance* 52, 507–529.

Rajan, R., and Wulf, J. 2002. The flattening firm: Evidence from panel data on the changing nature of corporate hierarchies. Unpublished working paper. Chicago: University of Chicago Graduate School of Business.

Rajan, R., and Zingales, L. 1998. Financial dependence and growth. *American Economic Review* 88, 559–586.

Rajan, R., and Zingales, L. 1998. Power in a theory of the firm. *Quarterly Journal of Economics* 112, 387–432.

Rajan, R., and Zingales, L. 1998. Which capitalism? Lessons from the East Asian crisis. *Journal of Applied Corporate Finance* 11, 40–48.

Rajan, R., and Zingales, L. 2000. The tyranny of inequality: An inquiry into the adverse consequences of power struggles. *Journal of Public Economics* 76, 521–558.

Rajan, R., and Zingales, L. 2001. The firm as a dedicated hierarchy: A theory of the origins and growth of firms. *Quarterly Journal of Economics* 116, 805–852.

Rajan, R., and Zingales, L. 2002. The great reversals: the politics of financial development in the 20th century. *Journal of Financial Economics* (forthcoming).

Ramseyer, M. 1994. Explicit reasons for implicit contracts: The legal logic to the Japanese main bank system. In Aoki, M., Patrick, H. (Eds.), *The Japanese main bank system*. New York: Oxford University Press, 231–257.

Ramseyer, J. M., and Rosenbluth, F. M. 1995. *The politics of oligarchy*. New York: Cambridge University Press.

Regis, N. F. 1919. *A history of the bankruptcy law*. Washington, DC: Potter & Co.

Roberts, D. 2001. Glorious hopes on a trillion-dollar scrapheap. *Financial Times* (London), 5 September, 12.

Rodrik, D. 1997. Has globalization gone too far? Unpublished working paper. Washington, DC: Institute for International Economics.

Rodrik, D. 1998. Democracies pay higher wages. Working paper 6364. Cambridge, Mass.: NBER.

Roe, M. J. 1994. *Strong managers, weak owners: The political roots of American corporate finance*. Princeton, N.J.: Princeton University Press.

Roosevelt, F. D. 1933. Public Papers and Addresses. New York: Russel & Russel.

Roosevelt, F. D. 1934. Public Papers and Addresses. New York: Russel & Russel.

Roosevelt, F. D. 1936. Public Papers and Addresses. New York: Russel & Russel.

Rose, N. L. 1998. Labor rent sharing and regulation: Evidence from the trucking industry 95, 1146–1178.

Rosenbluth, Frances. 1989. *Financial politics in contemporary Japan*. Ithaca, N.Y.: Cornell University Press.

Roshental, L., and Young, C. 1990. The seemingly anomalous price behavior of Royal Dutch Shell and Unilever nv/plc. *Journal of Financial Economics* 26, 123–141.

Rydqvist, K., and Hogholm, K. 1995. Going public in the 1980s: Evidence from Sweden. *European Financial Management* 1, 287–315.

Sah, R., and Stiglitz, J. 1986. The architecture of economic systems: Hierarchies and polyarchies. *The American Economic Review* 76 no. 4, 716–727.

Sapienza, P. 2002. What do state-owned firms maximize? Evidence from Italian banks. Unpublished working paper. Evanston, Ill.: Northwestern University.

Schill, M., and Zhou, C., 2001. Pricing an emerging industry: Evidence from Internet subsidary carve-outs. *Financial Management*, 30, no. 3, 5–35.

Schumpeter, J. A. 1993. *The theory of economic development: An inquiry into profits, capital, credit, interest, and the business cycle*. New Brunswick; London: Transaction Publishers.

Searjent, G. 1993. Why Daimler went red over a share quote in New York. *The Times* (London), 7 October.

Seligman, J. 1995. *The transformation of Wall Street*. Boston: Northeastern University Press.

Sen, A. 1999. *Development as freedom*. New York: Knopf.

Sharkey III, A. G. The Power of the New Steel Industry. American Iron and Steel Industry, http://www.steel.org/facts/power/newsteel.htm.

Shepherd, W. 1982. Causes of increased competition in the U.S. economy, 1939–1980. *Review of Economics and Statistics* 64, 613–626.

Shiller, R. 2001. *Irrational exuberance*. New York: Broadway Books.

Shirreff, D. 1998. The Eve of Destruction. *EuroMoney* 355, 34.

Shleifer, A., and Vishny, R. W. 1997. The limits to arbitrage. *Journal of Finance* 52, no. 1, 35–56.

Simon, C. J. 1989. The effect of the 1933 Securities Act on investor information and the performance of new issues. *American Economic Review* 79, 295–318.

Skidelsky, Robert. 2001. *John Maynard Keynes: Fighting for freedom 1937–1946.* New York: Viking.

Skocpol, T. 1997. The G.I. bill and U.S. social policy, past and future. In Paul, E., Miller, F., Paul, J. (Eds.), *The welfare state.* New York: Cambridge University Press.

Sokoloff, K. 2000. Institutions, factor endowments, and paths of development in the new world. Unpublished working paper. Los Angeles: UCLA.

Sokoloff, K., and Engerman, S. L. 2000. History Lessons. Institutions, factors endowment, and path of development in the new world. *Journal of Economic Perspective* 3, 217–232.

Sokoloff, K., and Engerman, S. L. 1994. Factor endowments, institutions, and differential paths of growth among new world economies: A view from economic historians of the United States. Historical working paper 66. Cambridge, Mass.: NBER.

Sorescu, S. 2000. The effect of options on stock prices: 1973 to 1995. *Journal of Finance* 55, 487–514.

Spender, P. 2000. Second-hand vehicle imports equal doom? *The Economic Times* (Mumbai), 18 January.

Stein, J. 2002. Information production and capital allocation: Decentralized vs. hierarchical firms. *Journal of Finance* 57.

Stevenson, H. 1996. Early career LBOs using the search fund model. Case Note 9–897–092. Boston: Harvard Business School.

Stigler, G. 1971. Theory of economic regulation. *Bell Journal of Economics* 2, 3–21.

Stiglitz, J. E. 2002. *Globalization and its discontents.* New York: W. W. Norton.

Stiglitz, J., and Weiss, A. 1981. Credit rationing in markets with imperfect information. *American Economic Review* 71, no. 3, 393–410.

Stole, L. A., and Zwiebel, J., 1996. Organizational design and technology choice under intra-firm bargaining. *American Economic Review* 86, 195–223.

Stone, L. 1965. *Crisis of the aristocracy.* Oxford: Clarendon Press.

Stromberg, D. 2001. Radio's impact on public spending. Unpublished working paper. Stockholm: Stockholm School of Economics.

Summers, L. 1986. Does the stock market rationally reflect fundamental values? *Journal of Finance* 41, 591–600.

Svalaeryd, H., and Vlachos, J. 2002. Market for risk and openness and to trade: How are they related? *Journal of International Economics* 57, no. 2, 369–395.

Tanzi, V., and Schuknecht, L. 2000. *Public spending in the 20th century: A global perspective.* Cambridge: Cambridge University Press.

Tawney, R. H. 1941. The rise of the gentry, 1558–1640. *The Economic History Review* 11, no. 1, 1–38.

Temin, P. 1989. *Lessons from the Great Depression.* Cambridge, Mass.: MIT Press.

Teranishi, J. 1994. Loan syndication in war-time Japan. In Aoki, M., Patrick, H. (Eds.), *The Japanese main bank system.* New York: Oxford University Press, 57 table 2.2.

Thurow, L, 1980. *The zero-sum society: Distribution and the possibilities for economic change.* New York: Basic Books.

Toniolo, G. 1978. Crisi economica e smobilizzo pubblico delle banche miste (1930–1934). In Toniolo, G. (Ed.), *Industria e Banca Nella Grande Crisi 1929–1934.* Milan: Etas Libri.

Tuchman, B. 1979. *A distant mirror: The calamitous 14th century.* New York: Ballantine Books.

Tufano, P. 1996. How financial engineering can advance corporate strategy. *Harvard Business Review* 74, no. 1, 136–146.

U.S. Bureau of the Census. 1975. *Historical Statistics of the United States, Colonial Times to 1970.* Washington, DC: U.S. Bureau of the Census.

U.S. Bureau of the Census. 1996. *Population of the United States by Age, Sex, Race, and Hispanic Origin: 1995 to 2050.* Washington, DC: U.S. Bureau of the Census, Current Population Reports, Series P-25, No. 1130.

U.S. Bureau of the Census. 1999. *Statistical Abstracts of the United States.* Washington, DC: U.S. Bureau of the Census.

U.S. Census Bureau. 2001. *Statistical Abstract of the United States.* Washington, DC: US Census Bureau, table 1214.

Vittas, D., and Cho, Y. J. 1994. *Credit policies: Lessons from East Asia.* Washington, DC: The World Bank.

Von Greyerz, C. 1984. Accounting in Swiss company law. *Der Schweizer Treuhander,* 85–88.

Watters, T., Vastola, P., Beroud, O., Anankina, E., Yoshimura, M., Saimen, T., Qu, H., Takara, R., Parker, C., and Sprinzen, S., 2002. U.S. steel tariffs: who gains, who loses, and at what price? *Standard and Poor's.* 14 March, www.standardandpoors.com/nordic/pdfs/ussteeltariffs.pdf

Warren, C. 1935. *Bankruptcy in United States history.* Cambridge, Mass.: Harvard University Press.

Weatherford, J., 1997. *The history of money: From sandstone to cyberspace.* New York: Crown Publishers.

Weisbach, M. S. 1988. Outside directors and CEO turnover. *Journal of Financial Economics* 20, 431–461.

Wermers, R. 1999. Mutual fund herding and the impact on stock prices. *Journal of Finance* 54, 584.

Wernerfelt, B. 1984. A resource-based view of the firm. *Strategic Management Journal* 5, 171–180.

Wilensky, H., and Turner, L. 1987. Democractic corporatism and policy linkages: The interdependence of industrial, labor-market, incomes, and social policies in eight countries. Working paper. Berkeley, Calif.: University of California Institute of International Studies.

Wolfe, T. 1987. *The bonfire of the vanities.* New York: Farrar, Straus and Giroux.

Wurgler, J. 2000. Financial markets and the allocation of capital. *Journal of Financial Economics* 58, 187–214.

Yergin, D., Stanislaw, J. 1999. *The commanding heights: The battle between government and the marketplace that is remaking the modern world.* New York: Touchstone.

Bibliography

Yunus, M. 1998. *Banker to the poor: The autobiography of Muhammad Yunus, Founder of the Grameen Bank*. London: Aurum Press.

Zachary, G. 1994. His way—How "barbarian" style of Philippe Kahn led Borland into jeopardy. *The Wall Street Journal*, 2 June, A1.

Zingales, L. 1998. The survival of the fittest or the fattest: Exit and financing in the trucking industry. *Journal of Finance* 53, 905–938.

Zysman, J. 1983. *Governments, markets, and growth: Finance and the politics of industrial change*. Ithaca, N.Y.: Cornell University Press.

INDEX

access to finance, 28–29, 155, 156, 240, 246; and benefits of market system, 25–43, 44–67; and bottom line on development, 114, 115, 118, 119, 120, 121; and collateral, 30–33, 43, 66; and connections, 33–34, 42, 43, 66; and development of financial markets, 3, 4–6, 8, 12–13, 14, 15; and financial revolution, 71, 75–76, 79, 80–81, 87, 90–91; and future of capitalism, 276, 286; and impediments to development, 28, 167–68, 169; and information, 30, 33, 34, 51–56, 66; and infrastructure, 30, 34, 43, 66; and misappropriation, 56–66; overview about, 42–43, 44–45, 66–67; and relationship capitalism, 249, 251–52, 256; and reversal, 18, 211, 215, 216, 218, 223, 224; and risk, 28, 45–51, 58, 59, 66; and vertical integration, 36–42, 76, 79, 80–81; and when finance develops, 177, 184, 186, 187, 189, 194–95, 196, 197. *See also* banking; financiers

accounting, 7, 70, 106; and financial development, 111, 120, 161, 169; and market suppression, 234, 235, 245; and relationship capitalism, 250, 251; standards, 27, 54, 111, 161, 169. *See also* disclosure; transparency

adverse selection, 29, 30

aging populations, 289–90

antiglobalization, 3, 16, 19–22, 281, 307

antimarket sentiment, 206, 294, 309; and future of capitalism, 281, 291, 292; and market suppression, 226–27 232, 235, 236, 237, 245; and relationship capitalism, 269, 271

antitrust laws, 76, 209, 296–97

arbitrage, 96–99, 102

authority, 158–61, 205

Bangladesh, 4, 7–8, 15

banking, 35–36, 59–60, 296; branch, 14, 112–13, 180–82; and dark side of finance, 94, 95, 106; deregulation of, 112–13, 114, 180–82, 256; and financial development, 13–14, 110, 112–13, 116, 117, 118, 120, 124, 167; and financial revolution, 85–86, 87–88; and market suppression, 240, 243; nationalization of, 240; and relationship capitalism, 248–49, 256, 258, 261, 262; and reversal, 18, 203, 205, 206, 211, 213, 214–15, 216–19, 220–24; and taming government, 133–34, 136; and when finance develops, 173–78, 180–82, 184, 187, 189, 192. *See also* financial institutions; *specific bank*

bankruptcy, 2, 31, 71, 163, 177, 231, 278–80, 301, 306

Barings, 94, 235